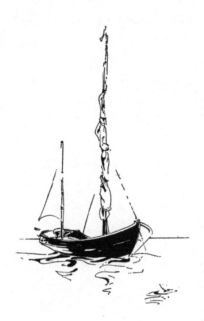

THE
LUGWORM
CHRONICLES

by
KEN DUXBURY

With an Introduction by ROGER BARNES

Lodestar Books

Lugworm on the Loose
First published 1973 by Pelham Books, London
Lugworm Homeward Bound
First published 1975 by Pelham Books, London
Lugworm Island Hopping
First published 1976 by Pelham Books, London

This combined edition published 2014 by
Lodestar Books
71 Boveney Road, London, SE23 3NL, United Kingdom

www.lodestarbooks.com

A CIP catalogue record for this book
is available from the British Library

ISBN 978-1-907206-28-3

Typeset by Lodestar Books in Equity

Printed in Spain by Graphy Cems, Navarra

All papers used by Lodestar Books
are sourced responsibly

CONTENTS

INTRODUCTION

EVERY MARINER ENJOYS READING SAILING STORIES, but sometimes the events described are so arduous and perilous that we finish the book hoping we may never experience anything similar—such as Shackleton's small boat passage from Antarctica to South Georgia. But to my mind, the very best sailing books recount adventures we could easily imagine having ourselves. This volume is one of those.

Ken Duxbury and his wife took a standard Drascombe Lugger to the Mediterranean by road and spent the rest of the summer exploring the Greek Islands. The following year they sailed *Lugworm* back to England—across the Adriatic, along the Italian coast, through the French canals and finally across the Channel. It is an exciting story, but not an adventure hopelessly unattainable by the rest of us. No extremes of fortitude nor absurdly large amounts of money were required. The Duxburys took their time, making the voyage in short legs, rarely covering more than twelve miles a day. They wanted to explore the coastline, not to cover the mileage in the shortest possible time.

They made a point of seeking out the simple, ordinary and workaday. This is not a book about glamorous yachting. Apart from a brief foray to Monaco, where he failed to win on the gambling tables, Ken shunned the fashionable yachting scene. "If mankind had conspired to kill stone dead any last vestige of sea fever in his soul, he could not have devised a more effective means than his invention of the marina," he writes. Instead *Lugworm* cruised between lonely rivers, isolated beaches and forgotten fishing ports.

Some readers may wonder if they would have been more comfortable in a small cabin yacht, instead of camping in the bottom of a centreboard dinghy. But that misses the point. Even the smallest cabin yacht would have restricted the places they could visit. The Duxburys could beach their boat almost anywhere, and then haul her out of the water with a block and tackle. They hugged the coastline, exploring virtually every bay and inlet, making many friends amongst the locals. A small open boat becomes part of the life of the coastline. Fishermen shared their catch, and gave them advice about what rivers were navigable; a Neapolitan chef sang as he cooked them pizzas.

I am writing this introduction while cruising my own dinghy around southern Brittany, meandering between the delightful havens and offshore islands of the Baie de Quiberon with a group of other small dinghies, rowing and sailing, camping ashore and afloat, and visiting a different restaurant in a different port every night: days of utter uncomplicated contentment. Only those who have experienced it know the true delight of cruising in a small dinghy. A certain austerity is enforced by the small space, but the blissful simplicity and freedom of the lifestyle rapidly becomes addictive. There is something almost monastic about escaping from the clutter of contemporary life. Ken Duxbury certainly valued this aspect of dinghy cruising. The final part of his trilogy of books, included in this volume, recounts his adventures around the British coast. Using his dinghy to live close to the seashore, he rediscovered an older and more authentic way of life, that of the longshore boatman and beachcomber. He fished for his food, collected firewood and even made a tender for his Lugger out of driftwood.

Ken is unfailingly plucky and resourceful. One of the generation who fought in the Second World War, he retains the laconic language of his Navy days—a rough sea is for him a "wetting sea." His writing is humorous and vivacious, and illustrated with his own drawings and photographs. The drawings are a sheer delight: well-observed and economical. No one will reach the last page of his three books included in this volume without wanting to buy a small seaworthy dinghy and sail in the author's wake—and why not?

Roger Barnes
June 2014

LUGWORM ON THE LOOSE

To Shirley and Brian,
who not only dried out the powder,
but tamped it down—and fired the gun!

ONE MAN'S HELL

IT WAS RAINING at eight o'clock that winter morning as I drove to the factory, and the clinical light of the neon tube over my desk did little to relieve the desolate view through the plate glass window. I suppose that rather depressing start to a new day helped to trigger off once more the—by now familiar—pattern of my thoughts.

On my desk were the audited accounts for the past twelve months' trading, together with the computation of tax which would be due on the profit, nearly all of which was already absorbed in stock and premises for our small business. Beneath the accounts was a thick sheaf of red tape; statistical returns, analyses, questionnaires and forms of one sort and another. I thumbed disconsolately through the depressing sheaf of papers, and I knew that in the outer office was a thick backlog of customers' letters, the actual flesh and blood of our business, to which I no longer had the time to give my personal attention as in the early days.

Through those doors, out in the workshops, they were building boats. Lucky chaps who were paid a straight wage for a straight day's work at something worth doing. I just wished I could get out there and help build a boat again. That, and summers teaching sailing in the craft we built, had been how it all started many years ago. But inexorably it had, for me, deteriorated into this—and I looked down at the arid desert of mind-twisting bureaucracy compressed into those pallid sheets of paper.

There are some, I reflected, who can find their challenge in battling with this sort of thing; I wasn't one of them. How much of yet another week, I thought, will be left when I've ploughed my way through that lot, to give attention to whether we're still actually making a living? More important still: how much enthusiasm will be left in me to press on making that living!

Outside, the first red tinge of dawn was glowing to the east, and the rain had stopped. I switched off the neon light and stood looking over the Cornish landscape. Far away on the crest of a small hill the silhouette of a derelict windmill jutted stark against the horizon. To me it looked like a tombstone. Once more I began to rebel inside. Was this—and I cast a loathing glance at the trough of red tape on my desk—was THIS what umpteen million years of evolution had developed the human brain to waste its precious days on? Six years of it had driven B., my wife, to the verge of a nervous breakdown; was this, then, success? Could I really face up to grinding away the remainder of my days at this barren nonsense?

Out there, the first gold tinges of the rising sun had caught the edge of a cloud beyond the windmill. As I watched, it grew steadily in brightness and with it, on that cold winter morning four years ago, my spirit seemed to burn with a challenging new certainty. I'D HAD ENOUGH!

It took two years before I managed to extricate myself from that seat with advantage to the firm and everybody else concerned, and it took another year—and two books—before my wife and I could really call ourselves free to start on a madcap adventure that had been forming in my mind.

*   *   *

Dinner was over and B. was curled up on the settee with a Georgette Heyer novel. Millar's delightful book *Isabel and the Sea* slid off my knee as I reached beneath the coffee table for the atlas.

'More wine, darling,' I murmured. I have no conscience whatever when trying to exercise low cunning with my wife; she sees through me like a window.

'MMmmm…' Her head turned and there was a quick grin of acceptance but her eyes stayed rooted to the page as I poured the last of the Sancerre into her glass. That makes the third, I thought; by now the furrow ought to be well watered to take the idea I was about to plant. The atlas fell open easily at the page covering the Eastern Mediterranean. Once more my finger and thumb roughly spanned the distance—about one thousand nine hundred miles. Allowing for the twiddly bits hugging the shore it would probably be more like two thousand five hundred miles. I knew that in an eighteen foot Drascombe Lugger such as *Lugworm* an average of ten miles a day was realistic. At that rate, I reflected, it would take more than eight months. Well; it wasn't good enough! There was something wrong with the realism; we'd just have to do better. I glanced to where B. was still reading, though now with a dreamier look in her eyes; it was time to take a sounding.

'Let's go and have a look at Greece,' I said.

There was a pause. I watched her mind disengage from the romantic fantasy to consider this abrupt intrusion of a romantic reality. Her brow creased as she looked at me.

'Greece?'

'Greece.'

'Yes, well... it would be marvellous but,' and she yawned and stretched before continuing, 'you know we can't afford it. Even with the package rates it would cost a small fortune.' There was another pause and I knew she was thinking. Seeds should be allowed to take root a little before being blown by the wind, so I put *Isabel and the Sea* back on the shelf and took down Robert Payne's *The Isles of Greece*, opening it at the exquisite colour photograph of Santorini.

'How serious are you?' she asked after a while, as I knew she would. The moment had come: if the climate wasn't propitious now, when would it be?

'It isn't a package deal I had in mind. Now we have the time, why don't we sail out there in *Lugworm* and spend a summer at it?' Her mouth opened, then closed. 'You're sozzled, darling,' she said, simply.

I thought about that. But the important thing I noticed, as I glanced back from the door, was that the picture of Santorini and the atlas were lying open on the coffee table, and Georgette Heyer was on the floor. Nine years of marriage to B. teach one when to retire.

I'm not one to ignore brain power superior to my own. It was Brian, his silver-white Captain Kettle beard a-quiver with enthusiasm, who three days later began to knock the slightly ridiculous idea into shape and with it changed the whole approach of B. 'Why not!' he crowed, 'But aren't you putting the barge before the tug? Far more sensible would be to tow *Lugworm* out there in the spring and spend the summer cruising round the islands, then sail gently back again to England over the following summer.

'Wintering in Greece!' B. chipped in.

That took a bit of digesting. It's one thing to leave home for a summer but quite another to spend two summers and a winter abroad. 'It makes a lot more sense,' Brian was ruminating. 'If you sail out there, you'll arrive in Greece just in time to lay the boat up for the winter gales. Tow her out in the spring and you'll be fresh for the cruise and then have the winter to re-coup ready for the mammoth trip back the following summer.'

'And you could write a book on it, darling.'

'Just like that!'

I had an odd feeling that the footwear was being changed over and the shoes now on my feet felt cold. But I didn't say anything; I just sat back and thought—imagine it! Summer in the Aegean—the challenge of a tow overland through France, Germany, Austria and Yugoslavia. Winter in a warmer climate and all this followed by a summer beach-hopping up the south and west coasts of Italy, across southern France and up through the canals to Bordeaux—what a rich experience it would be! Something—was it the first gentle flutter of that long dormant joie de vivre!—was stirring in my mature and mellow soul. Pushing the half century as I was, wouldn't it be a marvellous adventure before I actually fell to bits?

With a madcap idea of this kind there is not, I find, any point in time when a firm decision to go or not to go is made. Once the plan is voiced abroad an intoxicating flame of interest fans out like the blue transparency of burning alcohol, igniting the envy of one's friends. Things began to move quickly. It wasn't long before Brian, who is Managing Director of an engineering firm, proposed that he make a trailer which could be dismantled and stowed in a car boot. Next day he phoned again to make the proposition that he and his wife Shirley take three weeks holiday and do the towing job themselves. He's that sort of chap. Hurdles were tumbling like stacked cards. People started giving us presents and outstanding bills came in like rain.

In a moment of cold sanity B. and I talked it over with the bank manager. We left with arrangements in hand to make cash withdrawals at six selected towns in Greece and Italy; the manager nearly came with us! As it turned out, things hove-up to stop us leaving until mid-June. It was of no consequence because we didn't get our visas for the prolonged stay in Greece until the fourteenth of that month.

The mileometer read 54,054 as the Ford Corsair with the four of us aboard and *Lugworm* in tow pulled out into the narrow gravelled Cornish lane headed for Mount Olympus.

'Thus easily,' I reflected, 'can a chap be hoist by his own petard!'

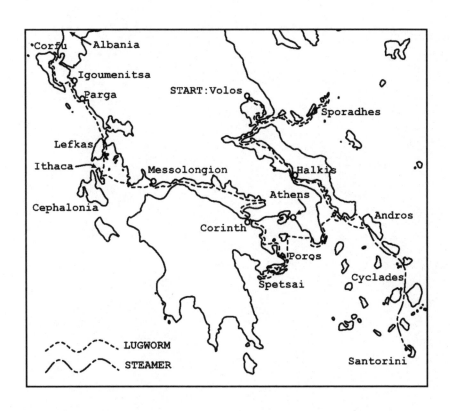

Corfu • Albania

Igoumenitsa

Parga   START:Volos

                                            Sporadhes

Lefkas

Ithaca   Messolongion   Halkis

Cephalonia   Athens

                    Corinth   Andros

                        Poros

                    Spetsai   Cyclades

~~~~ LUGWORM

~~~~ STEAMER   Santorini

CHAPTER I

INTRODUCTION TO GREECE

'TURN LEFT FOR VOLOS.'

'No! Keep right on this motorway,' came an instant duet from the back seat. Brian's blood vessels swelled, his foot poised between brake and accelerator. 'For mother's sake!' he exploded, two thousand nerve ends juddering. 'Give me a chance. I know I'm only driving this thing but...'

'TURN LEFT FOR VOLOS!' I roared in the sort of voice Hannibal undoubtedly used to deflect his elephants—dammit, the sign was big enough. We turned left. There was a pregnant silence as once again we flinched to the rhythmic hammer of chassis on axle. Brian dropped into third with a sigh of resignation. We had clocked up two thousand and twenty-six miles, and were back on one of those roads again. After Yugoslavia the motorway south of Katerini had been so sweet. The mudguard fell off the trailer with a metallic shriek and we stopped. Brian was looking out of his driving window, sweat pouring down his face, his fingers tapping expressively on the hot ledge. Across a heat-wavy field a donkey thrust its head in the air and guffawed brazenly. I left them looking at each other.

It was so hot my fingers burned when I picked up the mudguard. This was the third time since Belgrade it had tried to leave us and I felt unwanted as I put it inside the boat. With only fifty miles still to go we were close enough to the finishing line not to worry about it any more.

The road ahead, full of magnificent potholes, ran straight as a meridian, dancing a heat jig between fields of yellow stubble. You could hear the soil cracking and my feet kneaded treacly tarmac as I walked back to the car. Two hours later we rejoined the motorway. The silence was deafening and I still hadn't regained my pedestal when we entered the outskirts of Volos and then there was no time to brood for we'd evidently arrived in the middle of an event. The streets were fairly hopping with life as we headed hopefully southward to where the Gulf must lie. A crossroads loomed up. 'Right!' I said frantically, with a quick look up at the sun. 'I'm leaving it to you,' came a subdued voice from the back.

The road narrowed between what might have been a bus station and a sort of cattle pen, then broadened into a wide area. Throngs of pedestrians drifted with apparently no thought for traffic. We slowed to a crawl and a horsedrawn dray loaded with green pumpkins sidled gently across our bows and stopped. Brian looked at me. 'Now Skipper,' he asked, 'where exactly in Volos are we headed for?' I didn't know. I'd never been to Volos before; come to that none of us had, but back home it had seemed a good place to stick a pin in the map! I was telling him so when a wave of inspiration broke, and sticking my head out of the window I called to a dapper little man in a brown suit who was carrying two live hens and an umbrella.

'Can you direct us to the harbour please?'

He placed the umbrella on top of the car and the chickens on the bonnet where they burst into life, then stuck his head inside.

'Ἀπαγορεύεται ἡ διέλευσις ὀχημάτων σήμερον.'

'?'

'Θά πρέπει νά γυρίσετε πίσω.'

'!'

Brian had a go. 'Porto!' he hissed with what he thought was a smile, leaning across me and flinching as a chicken tried to attack him through the windscreen.

'Θά πρέπει νά γυρίσετε πίσω.'

Seeing our blank faces the little man, whom we felt was falling over himself in an effort to help, appealed to his fellow jay-walkers and before we knew it the car was surrounded by well-wishers taking a keen interest. Three urchins were playing at fixing limpet mines on to the belly of the boat and the horse was being unharnessed. More and more unintelligible advice was offered in rising tempo and suddenly B. had a brain wave. Making a blast like a siren, she bellowed:

'SHIPS!'

There was a shocked silence. Taking advantage of the calm she hammered the point home and, with an action meant to indicate the pulling of a siren cord she repeated 'Ships!' 'SHIPS!'

A clipped voice spoke from the back of the crowd … 'Eh! Anglica I spek … you go first lefts then straight but,' and he waved his hands in the air, 'mens only.'

We got out, but it was a tactical error. Eager hands grasped us, faces pressed against ours uttering stacatto but volubly meaningless sounds, so we piled back in again, Brian first tactfully removing the chickens, then giving a friendly roar with the throttle. We had one thought between us: to find a peaceful lane running by the edge of the sea where we might launch the boat and expire gracefully. We started backing gingerly to avoid the urchins and the pumpkins. Somebody screamed. We all got out again feeling like an International Situation but there were no corpses. Brian and I looked under the car, B. disappeared and Shirley stood trying to strike a cigarette. Nobody was taking a blind bit of notice now. 'Somehow,' Brian said as we all got back into the car, B. now clutching one of the pumpkin things, 'we've got to find the sea, and the sooner we get clear of this Piccadilly Circus the better, or there's going to be an accident.' Nobody disagreed.

So we worked our way slowly through the labyrinth of streets orbiting the main town and struck south again since the Gulf, if not the actual harbour, had to lie somewhere in that direction. The road began to deteriorate, tarmacadam giving way to loose gravel, and eventually the gravel succumbed to dusty earth. Ahead, between a derelict building and a clump of tamarisk bushes, we saw the glint of water and our hearts leapt. The track grew narrower and finally, after shouldering its way along the edge of the sea it turned a right angle and plunged in. A breath of cool air fanned through the car as we opened all four doors and took stock. To one side was the sea, calm as a millpond, while on the other was a low white stucco wall hemming in a grove of lemon trees. Ahead, across a large dusty open space, was a picture we were in the months ahead, to recognise as an integral part of the Greek scene. We had arrived at a beach taverna.

On the landward side of the space an old building stood foursquare, two storeys high. Its outer walls had once been whitewashed but the weather had played its game and the overall impression now was of pockmarked grey. An upstairs window sagged a little from the horizontal which gave the place an appearance of having suffered a stroke. A clothes line ran from its sill out to a telegraph pole and I was wondering idly how the laundry was recovered from such a height when a pipe end, jutting from the wall nearby, gurgled and spat a jet of water. It splashed on to a parked car below and a dog shot from between the wheels with a frenzied bark. To the front of the house had been added a new one-storey building with a glass frontage, and extending out from this to cover part of the dusty space was a huge canvas awning, held erect at its outer edge by a gantry of rusty iron tubes. Round the edge of the shadowed area a row of kerosene tins, somewhat rusty but painted bright reds, greens and blues, held a riot of scarlet geraniums. A derelict building with no roof formed the boundary at the far side of the space. Two goats, tethered by a leg, chewed dispiritedly at a patch of brown grass under an orange tree, and the rusty metal cabin from a lorry did service as a chicken house. Hard wooden upright chairs with wicker seats, and crude wooden tables were scattered beneath the awning. A litter of empty 'Coke' bottles, a few plates and dirty cutlery remained uncleared. There wasn't a soul in sight and even the goats were wilting in the heat.

On the seaward side of the space another covered area ranged alongside the water, its concrete floor forming a small quay. Here, however, the roof was of bamboo laths giving a tiger stripe of shade beneath.

We wandered up to the glass doors and entered the cavernous outer building whose walls throbbed with imaginative murals. At the back was a monumental piece of equipment looking somewhat like a bank counter but with an elaborately embellished surround at the front, framing what appeared at first to be frosted

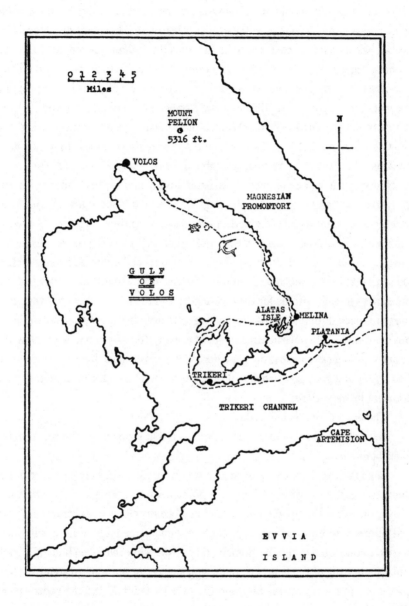

0 1 2 3 4 5
Miles

MOUNT
PELION
5316 ft.

N

● VOLOS

MAGNESIAN
PROMONTORY

G U L F
O F
V O L O S

ALATAS
ISLE
●MELINA

PLATANIA

TRIKERI

TRIKERI CHANNEL

CAPE
ARTEMISION

E V V I A

I S L A N D

glass. Through it we could make out the bottom of bottles, a huge round of white
flaky cheese, and various plastic cartons. It was an ice-box cum display cabinet
and we were to see its counterpart in tavernas throughout the whole of Greece.
Nobody appeared, and we were in two minds whether to turn round and chance
our luck with the launching elsewhere, but it was an ideal place to get the boat into
the water, so we got on with the job—and *Lugworm* was lashed to that trailer like a
trussed chicken! The 130 lb metal centre-plate had to be eased into its casing, and
the two masts rigged. After two thousand and seventy-six miles of crosscountry
hazards there was but one small thumbnail score where a rope had worked off
its chafe pad. It spoke volumes for Brian's driving and for the trailer. So it was
early evening before the boat, fully rigged, rode to an anchor just off the quay,
and the trailer components formed a neat pile beneath the orange tree. Presently
a stalwart on a scooter roared in with a cloud of dust and disappeared inside the
taverna. While B. sliced into the pumpkin which turned out to be a water melon,
we settled at one of the tables and talked things over. Brian and Shirley had but
one day to remain with us for they were keen to return via Italy rather than face
the roads back through Yugoslavia, and we were deep in the pros and cons of various alternatives when we became aware of a large, thick-set and powerful looking
figure standing over against the glass doors. He surveyed us, the car, the dismantled trailer and the boat at anchor off the frontage. The moment seemed to have
come for introductions.

'The proprietor?' I enquired.

'German?' came the query in a deep voice that seemed to roll around in his
chest before escaping.

'English,' I replied, and a huge arm was wrapped round my shoulder. I was
drawing breath to begin explaining our problems when 'Poppa' as we affectionately came to call this good natured giant grabbed my elbow in a vice-like grip. He
had summed up the situation completely and taking me forcibly along with him,
started a conducted tour of his domain, talking the while in broken Italian, French
and a smattering of English. 'Of course you stay. Why you want to go now? Here
good …' and I was propelled beyond the derelict building and the goats. 'Here
all mine,' he said with a sweep of his other arm which took in an apple orchard, a
waste field with an iron bedstead and about twelve rusty oil drums in the middle

... 'All this mine. You stay where you like, put car where you want, sleep where you want ...' Then, with a conspiratorial whisper: 'You got womans—they need washing. You use my showers, toilets ... better you stay here, eat here too ... much better ... sleep under tree,' and he indicated the patch of grass newly vacated by the goats.

We had another conference. There was much in what he said; if we were to have the services of this taverna and a free car park, then it would be churlish not to eat there too. We thanked him and started planning the night, drawing the car into the entrance of a narrow thistly track which separated the taverna from the lemon grove. It gave a modicum of privacy and when the boat cover was stretched over the parched earth, well away from the water pipe, it flattened the thistles. By the time all was ready it was getting dark and the taverna had woken up. Cars flowed in, and strings of coloured electric light bulbs were glowing under the bamboo lattice over the way. Somebody had started a jukebox inside and the plaintive, somewhat Arabic, wail of a popular Greek song reverberated at full blast in the quivering night air. In the garden of the bungalow alongside, a row of huge illuminated plastic mushrooms, red topped and white spotted, glowed through the foliage. Above it all, throwing into silhouette the leaves of the lemon trees, the great orange face of the full moon rose and shone like a benign visage on the whole palpitating scene.

While the other three retired to clean up prior to a meal I wandered back along the track, savouring the warm subtropical night. Across the water of the Gulf a dancing gold highway pointed to the moon, its finger stopping short of a darker line on the horizon which was the hills to westward of the Gulf. With a tingle of excitement I sniffed the air. 'Now,' I ruminated, 'we've spent six days in a car and burned over eighty gallons of petrol to cross the border of ... how many countries? England, France, Germany, Austria, a bit at the top of Italy, Yugoslavia and Greece. Seven countries! And is it, after all, so very different? If I close my eyes and breathe can I be certain that I'm not back in old England on a summer eve?' I closed my eyes and breathed. There was a continuous high pitched chirruping, a rhythmic wave of sound that came from everywhere in the night. I knew it well, from some thirty years previously in Bermuda: it was the cicadas—small winged cricket-like insects with a decibel output quite out of proportion to their size. Sticking my fingers in my ears to exclude the sound I tilted my head back and breathed deeply again. There was a strong smell of thyme and something else, very faint … what was it … something that took me back more years than I cared to remember … something to do with being a child in bed with a runny nose.

'Eucalyptus!'

'Eucalyptus?' said a quiet voice behind me. I nearly leapt over the wall. A figure, visible only as a darker shadow among the foliage, was standing in the garden.

'My apologies. I startled you. But you have a good nose, it's true there is a eucalyptus tree there behind my house though you can't see it. But,' he added, 'surely you don't expect to hear it also?' He laughed at my explanation. 'So that is your boat out there; have you brought her from England too?'

'Over two thousand miles.'

A long way to tow a boat. You must be a very keen sailor. How long will you be in Greece?'

'All summer.'

'Ah, I see. Now it makes more sense. And are you staying here at Volos?'

"We shall be exploring a lot of Greece in her,' I informed him, and he opened the gate and walked to the water's edge to examine *Lugworm* more closely.

'But there is no cabin; where do you sleep?'

'We have an airbed each. One goes down either side of the centreplate casing; it's very comfortable really.'

'We?'

'My wife and I.'

'So you and your wife are going to live aboard this dinghy all summer. How far did you say you hope to sail?'

'We're thinking of heading for the Northern Sporadhes first to look at Skiathos and Skopelos before going south into the Cyclades islands. After that we'll probably work westward into the Ionian and take a house for the winter. Next spring we're going to sail back to England.' I tried to make it sound casual.

'In … THAT!'

'She's a very splendid boat.'

'But where do you cook?'

He was genuinely interested so I pulled *Lugworm* on to the beach and proudly explained our portable stainless steel two-burner alcohol stove, the chartboard that also served for a table and writing desk, the steering and hand-bearing compasses, and how the clock and barometer slotted into special brackets on the forward bulkhead. I explained how our bedding and change of clothes stowed in the large forward locker while the food and cooking gear went into one of the after lockers. 'And when it rains,' I enthused, warming to the subject, 'both masts quickly unship. The mainmast then rests on two light crutches to form a ridgepole and a waterproof tent fits over the whole boat lapping over the rubbing strake so that we have eighteen feet of space.'

'I see,' he said, and seemed to be thinking. 'Tell me,' he continued after a while, 'and forgive me for asking, but are you an experienced sailor?'

'Very,' I replied emphatically.

'And your wife?'

'... she loves me.'

His eyebrows went up slightly and he gave a small bow. 'I too have spent many years at sea, mostly in the Mediterranean, before retiring and building this small bungalow. I, too, have a boat,' and then, almost as an afterthought, 'so what will you do about the *meltemi*?'

There was something in the way he looked at me as he asked that question that turned on a little red light in the bilges of my soul.

I'd read about this meltemi. It is a northerly wind that blows in the Aegean during the months of July and August. It can continue through the first half of September and is caused by a low pressure system over Cyprus and the Middle East. According to the books it starts around midday, freshens during the afternoon, and dies away with sunset. All very predictable, and I was counting on it to run southward right down to the Cyclades.

'I shall use it to run south,' I answered. He was standing back, sighting *Lugworm* from this angle, then that, eyeing the line of her bow and the graceful sheer of her top-sides.

'Well ... you may be able to use this wind while in the north of the Aegean, but to the south of Evvia ...' He stroked his chin and took another significant look at the shrinking eighteen feet of *Lugworm*, 'I have seen well-found forty foot caiques running to shelter from the meltemi at Mykonos. On occasions the inter-island steamers postpone their sailings because of its fury. I would not like to feel its anger in this little boat. What will you do when it becomes too rough for her—as it will!' I looked him straight in the eye.

'I shall not be there.'

He was a little taken aback, but smiled with his parting words "Then I wish you exceptional fortune with your forecasting!'

B. was changed and waiting when I got back to the taverna. 'You've been a long time,' she said. 'What have you been doing?' I told her of my talk with the Greek next door who spoke excellent English. She thought for a while before asking, 'And what does he think of the venture?' I rummaged about for a towel, my head down in the sail bag to give myself time to think. He'd seemed a level-headed fellow with obvious experience who knew what he was talking about. But dammit, two thousand miles is just too far to turn round and go home again!

'He's fascinated,' I replied, and dived for the shower.

*   *   *

The menu, yellow and creased, was tacked up in a glass case at the taverna door. It was, of course, quite incomprehensible. We eyed the groups at the other tables under 'Poppa's' awning, trying to see what was on offer but nobody appeared to be eating anything. There were glasses of red and white wine and smaller glasses of clear ouzo—a strong aniseed brew made from grape pips—and here and there the odd bottle of beer. Nearly all the tables had little dishes like ashtrays containing olives and a few chips of white cheese stuck through with cocktail sticks. It was about nine o'clock and the stalwart youth of the scooter was briskly sweeping up the lunchtime clutter. He eyed us as we drifted uncertainly around, then grabbed two chairs in each hand, swung them high and banged them down at an unoccupied table uttering one stacatto word:

'Ορίστε!'

We looked at each other and it was evident that the sum of our understanding didn't even amount to the exclamation mark.

'Mangare,' I said hopefully in what I think is Italian for 'Eat'.

'Θέλεις νά φᾶς.'

Deliberately I pointed to the other three, then myself. 'English,' I said. He bolted.

'Really,' Brian murmured, 'we ought to have mastered a few basic words of this language before arriving; we don't even know how to say "No", never mind "Yes". Do you think that youth is the waiter?'

But from inside a strange sound could be heard above the general hubbub, a sort of 'Blum', 'Blluum', 'BLUUUM!' getting nearer and louder. Poppa emerged, stood for a moment eyeing the motley throng under the awning, then homed in on us. 'BLUUUUM!' he exclaimed in crescendo, banging his fist down on the table and pulling up another chair. We wilted. It was like watching the last act of a Wagnerian opera. 'Mangiare? Buono Psari ... vaary good ... fresco.' Once more we looked at each other but there were no flies on Poppa. Without more words he rose, swept his hand towards the taverna and issued the order 'COME!' He led us behind the bank counter which was now illuminated from within with green and pink lights, and went through an archway into the kitchen.

A vast bench stretched the length of one wall and at the far end a small middle-aged woman in black was fighting with a huge fish clamped firmly between a sort of crude wire toaster. She held it above a glowing bed of charcoal. The fish sizzled and dripped and smoke spat up to fill the room. At the near end of the bench a co-lossal tray held a pond of hot water in which were standing large aluminium pans with lids. He raised one of the lids. 'Psari ... very good!' Inside was what looked like potato soup with chunks of fish floating in it and it smelt delicious. Another pan contained highly seasoned meat balls in a rich red gravy. 'Keftethes,' Poppa roared, banging down the lid and raising others to expose great chunks of beef, courgettes, broad beans, string beans, stuffed tomatoes and aubergines and, inevitably, chips. It was tantalising and we were hungry. When we had chosen he swept us towards the woman with the fish. 'Momma, 'he exploded. She eyed us with a pair of twinkling black eyes set in a sallow but happy face. I liked her. A fat little girl, all of two years old, rolled from under the table and beamed at us holding up a huge beach ball. Poppa crowed. 'Six I have ... three sons—Costa here, him sailor too,' and he pointed to the stalwart youth who issued an ear splitting whistle and threw a pan lid at a cat. 'This Elli,' he added, picking up the cherub and in the same breath, 'you want krassi? Vino?' So now we understood that the Greek word for wine is krassi and, yes, we did want it. 'Retsina?' he queried. This was new. He poured us a small glass from a flagon and it was obviously rough white wine but it had a strange unpalatable taste of turpentine. None of us liked it, but since the first taste B. and I have, oddly, come to look for this admixture of bitterness; for us now, it is a part of the very essence of Greece.

Outside, more cars had pulled up and the place was fairly humming as we moved back to our chairs. Costa had spread a large sheet of greaseproof paper over the table, tucking the edges beneath a taut elastic band just under the lip to prevent the wind taking charge. A plastic basket contained four thick hunks of bread with hard crust, paper napkins and metal knives and forks. He returned with a frosted carafe of ice cold water, and glasses, banging the latter down on the table as though he'd just conjured them out of thin air. Other tables were filling up and the juke box blared even louder. Three men started to dance in a space between the tables, holding their arms outstretched, their fingers clicking to the broken tantalising rhythm and their feet performing a formal, highly stylised ritual step. Nobody watched them, and they continued, wrapped in a satisfying cloak of self-content as the tune wailed on. Elli's beach ball rolled out of the door, followed by Elli who came face to face with two other cherubs from a large group talking animatedly at a table alongside. A motor bike roared up, weaving through the tables, and parked by the glass doors in a cloud of dust. Nobody blinked an eyelid. It was a fascinating scene, vital with life, colourful, noisy, yet strangely relaxing. Everybody was simply being themselves. Two policemen in immaculate grey-green uniforms, military style flat caps and white shoulder straps were engrossed in conversation with a city-suited gent who could well have been a millionaire. An elderly man in a felt hat and dark glasses was fiercely playing cards with a youth, banging each card down as though in a paroxysm of anger. A woman started to sing, and the motor bike fell over causing pandemonium while the wide-eyed cherubs were searched for. The canvas awning above us rattled gently.

Looking back on those early days it is evident that my concern for the safety of the boat was beyond normal bounds. After all, we hoped she was to take us through a couple of thousand miles of adventure, and would certainly be our home for at least ten of the fifteen months ahead. The conversation with our friend next door was also fresh in mind, and when I noticed that the sky had become a canopy of ragged edged clouds, that flapping awning worried me. Seeking Costa's advice I pointed to the sky, making a noise I hoped he would interpret as high wind. 'Storm?' I asked hopefully. He made signs which could be taken as 'maybe yes … maybe no'—enough to decide me to put out a second anchor before the meal arrived.

I was flaking down the second warp aboard when a surge of voices surprised me, and looking back to the taverna I wondered if, already, I'd taken more wine than I ought. A trickle of patrons was spilling out into the gloom headed by Costa who was volubly issuing orders. Some of the men were rolling up their trousers and most of them had already removed their shoes and socks. Momma, carrying a short ladder, brought up the rear. While I watched, perplexed, *Lugworm* was surrounded. Then with me still aboard, she was half dragged, and half carried up the beach, over the ladder which was placed across some rougher boulders, and on to the end of the concrete quay close by the covered sea. It was all over in minutes. The helpers calmly put on their shoes and socks and returned to their ouzos and soup. The clouds disappeared and the sea returned to a flat calm!

So it was that we had our first practical example of this predominant characteristic of the Greek people: a willing kindness and hospitality which on occasions could be carried to an embarrassing stage. It was certainly the shortest period afloat that *Lugworm* ever experienced.

Since she was once more on shore high and dry, I gave her another coat of antifouling, which was completed by noon on the following day and then, sadly, came the time to bid adieu to Brian and Shirley. As their car disappeared slowly behind the tamarisk clump and the dust settled again on the suddenly very empty track, B. and I looked at each other. We both knew that there had gone, with those two stalwarts, our last link with home—and much besides.

There was no option now; we were here with *Lugworm*, and it was in her that we must return! We walked under the shade of the bamboo roof, and Costa, bless him, appeared with two stiff cognacs on the house. It was a small thing, but just at that time it made a hell of a difference. We were far from home maybe—but here in Greece we felt we were already among friends.

*   *   *

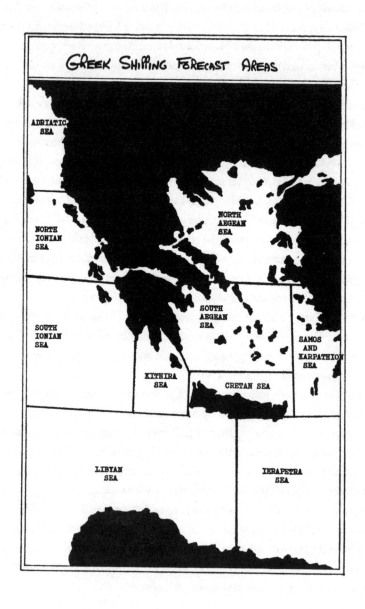

Greek Shipping Forecast Areas

We sat listening with fierce concentration to the weather forecast in English at quarter to eight the following morning. Our minute transistor just managed to pick this up on Athens Radio, 412 metres, and we knew there was another forecast at five past seven daily in the evening. It came in this sequence: state of weather, force of wind in the Beaufort scale, state of the sea, and the visibility in nautical miles. The areas referred to are shown on the map opposite and were given in the following order: South Adriatic and Ionian Sea, North Aegean Sea, South Aegean and Kithira Sea, Cretan Sea, Samos and Karpathion Sea, Libyan Sea and Ierapetra Sea, Saronic Gulf, Corinthian Gulf and South Evvian Gulf.

The last three are frequently grouped together, and in those first days it wasn't easy to understand clearly what the announcer said due to the quality of our reception and the fact that the forecast was read rather quickly and with odd emphasis which tended to throw us completely off track. But as our ears became attuned to the idiom of a Greek speaking English—together with an occasional Greek word being interposed—we came to use this excellent service as the basis for our plans for the next twelve hours.

In such a small craft, of course, we couldn't afford to take unnecessary risks; sufficient of those would come unasked in the months ahead. So far as provisions were concerned we could remain independent of shore contacts for four days in comfort, and a week at a pinch. We carried four gallons of fresh water in two plastic containers which were kept stowed beneath the side decks for coolth against the hull, and to get the weight as low as possible. For the outboard motor the three gallon metal fuel tank, plus a couple of spare two-gallon plastic containers gave us a reserve of more than seventeen hours under power, since from experience we knew that the four horsepower Mercury would run happily from two and a half to three hours on one gallon of fuel. At an average of, say, three knots (for remember that headwinds and sea will reduce a potential of five knots considerably) that meant we could cruise some fifty miles under power. It is a useful reserve to have up one's sleeve. The screw caps of the plastic containers proved inadequate, however, for the simple reason that once the heat of the day got under way the small amount of vapour left above the full container—or the large amount left in the empty container—expanded with a force enough to split the caps open. It was necessary to stow the containers upright therefore otherwise petrol seeped into the bilges. At night we would listen to the quiet whisper of the air hissing back in as the vapour within contracted again!

As mentioned before, the weather situation throughout Greece is very much governed in summer by a predictable low pressure area over Cyprus and the Middle East. For forecasting the country is divided into two well-defined areas: the Aegean Sea to the east and the Ionian Sea to the west. In summer the Aegean is roughly further divided into three zones running north and south. To the east, in the coastal areas of Turkey and the Dodecanese, one may expect winds from a northerly quarter, and while generally they are of less strength than those blowing in the zone of the central Aegean they can nevertheless in the area of the Dodecanese become strong on occasions.

In the central zone covering the Cyclades group of islands and similar longitudes further north, one has the Etesian wind or, to give its better known Turkish name, the meltemi. This wind can blow with great strength from anywhere between north-east and north-west and tends to reach a brisk climax around mid-afternoon daily, dying away with the sunset. The pattern of this meltemi is to first prevail over the North Aegean, blowing from a north-easterly direction. It progressively increases in strength as it spreads down towards the central and Eastern Aegean changing as it does so to blow from a north-westerly direction and simultaneously weakening over the North Aegean. During July and August, once the above pattern has established itself, it may be expected to last from five to seven days before subsiding. This wind can cause a steep wetting sea which soon becomes too much for a dinghy. I viewed it, since my talk with the sailor, with extreme caution.

The westerly zone of the Aegean, sheltered as it is by Attica and the Peloponnese, more rarely becomes rough and often has a good northerly sailing breeze and, in early summer, frequent light sea breezes from the south-east. All the books and other authorities seem to agree that during the summer months it is most unusual for a strong southerly wind to develop anywhere in the Aegean, and they add that in this sea the west wind is always a soft, kindly Zephyr.

Now, in a yacht of say twenty feet and over, fully decked and capable of keeping the sea, it is wise when faced with bad weather on a lee shore to stand off into deep water so as to gain plenty of sea-room to ride it out. In an open dinghy of course this is impossible. Safety depends on either clinging close to a weather shore, or making certain one is tucked up in harbour if the wind freshens from seaward. Everything, therefore, was to depend on our assessment of the forthcoming winds, and bearing this in mind we decided that if we were ever to run the risk of being caught on a lee shore it would be prudent to ensure that it was a kindly west wind which had to be dealt with. On this first leg of the trip therefore it was wise to hug the eastern shore of the Gulf. South of the excellent port of Volos there was no harbour until a natural lagoon down at the southern end called Port Vathudi. We saw from the chart that the northern side of this lagoon is formed by an island called Alatas and, since the forecast that morning was favourable, it was with this lagoon—and particularly Alatas Island—in mind that we stowed everything, hoisted all three of our tan sails, and with the outboard hopefully locked up clear of the water, ghosted away from the taverna, waving a last farewell to Poppa, Momma, Costa and little Elli who was held aloft to flourish her floppy hat vaguely seawards before flinging it defiantly into the water.

That was a momentous hour. It was from Volos that Jason, with his Argonauts, set off on their legendary adventures and for us in our cockleshell the departure was not one whit less charged with romance and portent. The superstition of placing a silver coin in the tabernacle prior to stepping a ship's mast has come down to us from olden times and in readiness for this voyage two silver sixpenny pieces—lucky coins from a Christmas pudding—were already in position under the foot of our mizzen mast; one face up and one tail up for good measure. To mark the event we also secured our ship's mascot 'Foogoo' to the base of the mast. He is a hideous African hand-carved idol given us by a friend and we placed the responsibility for a successful voyage wholly in his hands.

A light and fitful westerly played with the sails as the sun got into gear for the day's roasting; the water turned from silver green to bottle green as the seabed fell away, and finally the shadow of the boat radiated into a bottomless void of deep blue. We were floating in a warm, silent world of colour, free as the wind, full of excited anticipation, and happy as Zephyrs. More and more garments were shed as the sun got higher until, clad in our sweet nothings, we dropped the limp sails, threw out the sea-anchor and plunged for our first deep-water cooler down into the mauve void.

*   *   *

It is quiet down here. But what is the hollow pulsing? Of course! My own heart beat as I lock back my breath, weightless in a silent world of pressure. Below, a void of blue-black nothingness; up above, B.'s form, gold-green beneath, silver grey on top, kicks a wake of crystal bubbles in the bright green liquid sky. *Lugworm* is a dark whale beyond, her keel sharp-jutting like a fin. I ease a quarter breath and watch the tiny dancing bubbles of light expand, quiver and rock upwards; does time stand still down here?

Something catches my eye … another form down there, where there should be no other form; in panic I twist—RELIEF! It is the vague blur of the canvas drogue hanging limp and vertically below the boat. I see the rope now, fingering its way down, white, green, blue, then black against the dark of the sea-anchor. Can I pull myself down there? How long does time last in this alien world, time for but one breath! I pull myself hand-over-hand down into the darkness and suddenly the pressure squeezes my ears; my head is bursting; I turn and pull hard at the cord, exhaling heavily—TOO SOON!—there's no more breath to draw in. Madly I fight my way up through the blue into the green, the everlasting green where my lungs are screaming for air; slowly into the crystal, and through, THROUGH into the explosion of light and air gulping, gasping and inhaling.

*   *   *

We lazed about in the water, watching the reflections shimmer and dance on the shining black hull, then made sail again and by noon had drifted about six miles down the coast and were both lulled into an hypnotic trance by the heat, the colour, and the breathtaking view of the shore. Mount Pelion towered over five thousand feet into a brazen cloudless sky to the north. Southward of this, hills of around one thousand feet formed the ragged spine of the Magnesian Promontory which made a dark backcloth to the low-lying coastal belt. Tall pampas grass fringed the beaches, backed by shimmering groves of silver-green olives and here and there like green bunsen jets the statuesque flames of the cypresses gave a dignity to the landscape.

B. was stretched on the side deck, her head resting on the half-inflated lifejacket making lazy notes for the log and I propped sweating against the base of the mizzen mast. Now and then the main would fill sufficiently to give a welcome shadow from the heat, and I remember I had just remarked that we were both much the same colour as the varnished teak of the gunwales when my eye caught a disturbance in the water ahead. Something fairly large was just beneath the surface.

'WHALE!'

B. shot bolt upright and modestly put on her straw hat. I quickly lowered the outboard and jerked the cord, nosing the boat towards where the water continued to undulate gently.

'Grab the fish prong.'

'Is it really a whale?'

'Colossal'

'Don't you think ...' but by this time there was no need for either of us to think, for we could see quite clearly, suspended a few inches under the surface, the squared and horny back of a huge turtle. It seemed oblivious of the boat, its flappers gently waving, head swinging from side to side.

'Soup!' squeaked B., poised with the fish slice in one hand and our trident harpoon in the other, her economist mind already reducing the weekly budget by about one third, 'Get up alongside the thing, can't you!'

'Steady, we must approach it from the back. I don't think they can see more than twenty degrees abaft the beam. STAND BY!' and I swung *Lugworm* in a tight arc towards the lump of swimming soup. A shriek made me turn just in time to get the full blast of the splash. I cut the engine. There was complete silence; B.'s straw hat was floating peacefully alongside in a fringe of bubbles. The centreplate wobbled as though being wrestled with from below, and there was no sign of B. or the turtle.

She always maintains that as a last desperate effort to save the situation she grappled with the thing under the boat: I know full well that she was fighting with the centreplate but it's not a subject we broach often.

It was not more than ten minutes later that we both got a severe shock. In a blast of silver spray a whacking swordfish—its spike all of three feet in length—burst clear of the water, took a quick look at us, and disappeared with a crack like a pistol shot. It was so sudden that only gradually did the full possibilities sink into our minds. For a full hour B. sat in our thick galvanised washbowl as a precaution. Meanwhile, we drifted.

But pleasant though it may be, one cannot just go on drifting 'till bluebell time, and by five o'clock, since we were some two miles offshore and still over eight miles from the lagoon, there was nothing for it but to burn some valuable fuel. We closed the coast again to within a few yards of the sandy beaches and puttered idly along, the wind of our own making coming as a soft relief to the burning heat. Later there was a new slant of air and with relief we cut the engine and unfurled the sails. Immediately a new world made itself felt in the silence. Close inshore as we were, every little sound came out to us across the water together with a heady scent of herbs; hot and musky. As our ears became receptive after the blanketing drone of the engine, there came a continuous shimmering wave of sound as though the earth itself were sighing. It was the cicadas again, giving voice to the olives and the lemon trees; an audible expression of the quivering heat of the evening. The sea to the west was a burnished plate of pewter and a mother-of-pearl sky hung above the mountains to the south. The tiny fishing village of Melina appeared, its beach dotted with gaily coloured boats each with twin ungainly pressure lamps clamped to the stern, some piled high with yellow nets, and we ghosted on silently into the lagoon, both of us so wrapped in a hypnotic symphony of sound, colour and scent that the gentle crunch of our keel on the shingly beach of Alatas Isle seemed a noisy intrusion. Here, then, was our first Greek island. We hooked the anchor in a bush of spiny broom and set off to explore, while daylight remained.

Though it was little more than a mile in length and at most five hundred yards in width it was thickly covered with olives, the twisted, knotted trunks declaring their great age. At first, in the late evening, the din of the cicadas was overpowering but as the night cooled it diminished until only one or two stalwarts continued to call across the grove. When viewing the island from seaward we had seen a crumbling ruin crowning its highest point, the yellow stone of its walls poking above the billowing grey-green of the olives, and we made towards this along a goat track which led up from the beach, clambering over outcrops of contorted rock, unwarily grasping the spiky shrubs and marvelling at the profusion of grasshoppers. After the idleness in the boat it was good to feel brittle dry grass and the sharp warm rock on our bare feet, to stretch muscles again, and smell the scorched earth.

We worked our way slowly upward until, through the forest of trunks, we saw again the stones of a wall. It turned out to be the remains of a monastery, part of which was in a sad state of decay, but the remainder evidently still habitable, for as we walked round the perimeter of the building, passing high square towers at the corners, we came to the main entrance gateway. Two huge iron-studded doors hung aslant, held shut by a chain and padlock. To one of them was pinned a parched brown sheet of paper and on this, crudely painted in red, was the notice: 'ROOMS FOR RENT AT MONESTRY'. Through a vast keyhole we could see a cobbled courtyard surrounded by crumbling whitewashed walls. A well with a stone seat surround lay at one side and above this a massive fig tree spread a welcoming shade over the yard. There was an air of peaceful dereliction about the place and we pondered on the type of life which must have been lived by the monks, and wondered who, today, would seek out such a lonely retreat.

It was while idling down through an overgrown garden in front of the monastery, examining the laid paving stones and terraced walls which dropped in layered steps to the sea, that we became aware of a muted drumming sound as of many feet stamping the earth. We backed against a massive olive trunk feeling particularly defenceless without so much as a stick to ward off whatever might appear. The sound grew louder, approaching fast and—to our heightened awareness—ominously. It drummed and thundered hollowly until, round one corner of the monastery, came a herd of some twenty nannygoats, fleeing as though all the Devils in Hades were on their tails. Across the terraces, over the shrubs, weaving between the trees in a cloud of spurting dust they came, and behind them in close pursuit the largest and finest billy I've ever seen. He must have stood all of three feet high at the shoulders, his powerful legs hurling the sinewy body after the fleeing harem, his magnificent beard and mane flying. Down the hillside he clattered, hell-bent on rape, and as the dust settled we stood like Adam and Eve-and wondered anew at life in the wild.

As we retraced our steps back to the boat a snake, black, thick and sinuous slid noiselessly off the path into a sheltering bush. After that we kept strictly to the more open spaces, flinging stones ahead of us where the scrub was thicker to warn of our approach. There lay *Lugworm* at the water's edge, and for the first time in many we had an endearing feeling towards her. In that small black hull with the carved teak quarter badges was everything we possessed: our home, our mode of transport to a hundred such enchanted places as this, our safety and, if so the fates willed — our peril.

Dusty and hot from the walk, by common impulse we broke from the cover of trees and plunged together into the welcoming cool water. *Lugworm* rocked gently in our wake and a rustle of wind sighed down through the olives as we floated on our backs in a sea of content, watching the first crystal stars break through the darkening sky. We gathered driftwood and lit a fire at the water's edge and after a meal sat long into the night watching the red embers die and listening to the myriad small voices and movements in the grove behind, each of us deep in our own thoughts.

The adventure had begun.

CHAPTER II

THE NORTHERN SPORADHES

THAT FIRST MORNING after sleeping on the beach it was strange awakening to the brilliance of the white sandy bay, the un-believably blue cloudless sky, and behind us the shimmering green waves of the olives climbing the hill, their leaves chattering in the early wind. We spread our charts to dry on the white pebbles at the top of the beach, for they had become limp in the night air, and then renewed the fire. While the crackling wood died to a glowing bed of heat for the toast we discussed the days ahead. Our initial hunting ground was to be the Sporadhes, a group of large islands stretching some forty miles eastward of the Gulf. We decided to stick to the original plan of making good somewhere around ten to fifteen miles each day, which would allow a detailed exploration of the coast, and time to get to know the locality of our night berth before darkness fell. We intended to keep so far as possible off the tourist track, seeking the unpublicised and therefore unspoilt islands and bays; indeed our equipment was geared for such a cruise for we carried no clothes suitable for sophisticated shore-going. Our diet, we hoped, would be local produce augmented by our own catch of fish and we had plenty of hooks and lines.

Before breakfast was over that first promise of wind had petered out, leaving a sweltering unprotected world under the blinding sun, and it was good to feel the cool water as I waded out to check the lines we had laid from the boat the previous evening. Both hooks were fouled in a tangle of reddish weed a fathom down and as I plunged in to free them, B. joined me for a swim. We were both idly circling round the boat when a rustle on shore like a distant sigh caught our attention. A ripple of wind ran over the tops of the olives, and bent a solitary cypress to a sickle shape high on the hill. We watched as the ripple of movement fanned out, for all the world as though giant invisible fingers were stroking the tops of the trees. It died, then swirled with renewed vigour round a single point. A sprig of leaves, ripped from a tree, danced madly in a tight circle, leaping upwards as a pillar of invisible power swept in a line down the hillside. As it advanced, it was as though a huge vacuum cleaner were sucking at the earth, pulling every loose object to join the swirling dance upward. Fascinated, we saw the miniature whirlwind sweep towards us, happy that all *Lugworm*'s sails were secured. The column of dust and leaves was gathering momentum now, sweeping across the beach towards the sea. We both remembered at the same moment: too late! Our charts of the Aegean whirled skywards, twizzling madly in a column of rotating air, carried relentlessly over our heads seawards!

Relief mingled with dismay as the vortex abruptly disintegrated, leaving the bay to swelter again in the motionless heat. Motionless that is, save for our charts which languidly descended like falling leaves to settle soundlessly on the water. We rescued them, dragging the limp and delicate paper into shallow water, lifting them carefully by the corners to drip for a while before laying them again, under strict supervision, on the hot white stones. Within minutes they were dry but they had become brittle with it, and never since then have the mountains and sea lost an intriguing three dimensional impression. The parallel ruler never has run smoothly on those charts again, and to this day, when the atmosphere gets damp, they go as limp as rolled pastry.

But a light easterly had now settled in, and we broke camp, hoping that there would be a northerly slant out in the Trikeri Channel to get the sails filling, but it remained light and from the east, which was disappointing because we wanted to make the eastern extremity of the Trikeri Channel before nightfall, ready to strike across to Skiathos the following day.

Out in the channel, free of the protection of the Gulf, the coast had a quite different look. Rounded hillsides fell into the sea and fewer trees climbed their slopes. The shoreline was a pitted sharp escarpment of bleached white rock for a height of ten feet or so, from there up becoming deeply thicketed with bushes of spiny broom and hawthorn which lay densely in the protected cuttings of the small valleys, and thinning on the headlands. Here and there a solitary carob tree spread a ring of shade, its fleshy leaves making a darker patch against the silver-grey of the rock, but compared to the verdant cultivated shores inside the Gulf, this was sparse stunted maquis. We motored gently on within a few feet of the rocks, our time divided between peering into the crystal clear water to where their footings disappeared under the silvery sand, and watching the hillsides above for any sign of life.

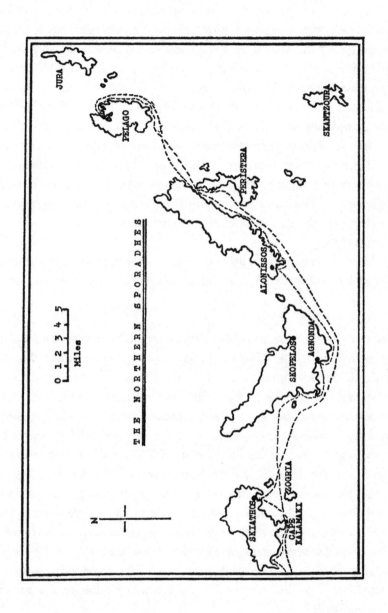

THE NORTHERN SPORADHES

Miles
0 1 2 3 4 5

JURA

PELAGO

SKANTZOURA

PERISTERA

ALONISSOS

AGNONDA

SKOPELOS

ZOOGRIA

SKIATHOS

CAPE
KLAMATI

N

There was none. Apart from the occasional low stone building roofed with bamboo laths interwoven with dried leaves and high enough only for goats to shelter against the heat, there was no sign of habitation until we passed the fishing village of Trikeri nestling in a tiny bay at the foot of a hill on whose crown the village of old Trikeri still stands. Throughout these rocky coasts and islands we often found that the main village or 'chora' to give it the Greek name, stood atop some almost impregnable hill, and we learned that this was generally for defence purposes against the pirates of olden times. Once these human predators had been wiped out, the need to build on the difficult—but easily defended—hilltops was gone, so newer and more accessible hamlets of the same name now nestle on the shoreline. Life still goes on in the majority of the choras but there are signs there of desertion, some of the buildings having fallen into decay.

After a frustrating day of light headwinds, it was late evening by the time we anchored in the bay of Platania just off the village, and prepared for a night afloat.

*   *   *

The trouble with those first nights sleeping aboard the boat was, quite simply, that we didn't sleep. As a first act of what became a nocturnal ritual, the airbeds would be inflated—three hundred hypnotic stabs of the footpump each—and the stove placed carefully on the flat after deck. We rarely bothered to erect the tent unless the weather was doubtful. Billycans, teabags, sugar, dried milk and the water canister would be placed secure against any rolling but ready to hand for making the morning cup while we were still warm in the sleeping bags. We would then snug down, listening to the quiet chuckle of water along *Lugworm*'s wooden sides, watching the stars gently circling as she swung to any wind which might blow. Gradually, as the sounds on shore died with the deepening night, another sound, so slight, so gentle yet so disturbing, would creep into the consciousness. It was the faintest crackling, akin to the noise of static electricity when one pulls off a nylon garment, but continuous, insidious, under, in and throughout the whole fabric of the hull. We would lie silent, listening to this peculiar and unaccountable noise.

'Ken.'

'Uh?'

'Do you think we've got Toledo Beetles?'

'Unlikely—and it's not Toledo, it's Teredo. Just keep quiet for a moment and listen.'

We would hold our breaths, trying to locate some source of the sound. Was it a wood borer? The inexorable crackling would continue, to my worried ears sounding more and more like the tearing of minute fibres in the wooden hull. Was it, after all, just small fish nibbling her underparts? That first night, I decided I just had to know. Cautiously, so as to make no noise I raised my hand, bringing it down with a resounding crash on the side deck. The result was electrifying.

'What the Devil!' from out of the violent eruption alongside.

'All right, dear; it's me.'

'YOU ...?'

'I wanted to frighten the fish.'

'My God ...!' It was minutes before the thumping of B.'s heart subsided sufficiently for me to concentrate again on the persistent, disturbing crackle. We were both wide awake.

'It's the shrimps,' I said, more to give B. confidence than from conviction. 'I think every time they jump under there they set up a minute shock wave that drums on the hull—thousands of them."

'Oh, DO go to sleep.'

'If it IS borers, we can't afford to just ignore it. You know what they do? They get into the keel and eat their way along, drilling a tunnel. When they get to the end do they call it a day? Not they! They simply turn around and drill another tunnel beside the first. Looking at the wood doesn't give you a clue. I remember a tale where a sailing ship was attacked by them. A gale sprang up off the Horn and there they were swimming around in a mass of sawdust; the ship just disintegrated.' I was keen that B. should appreciate my concern and I believe she did, but we never, during the whole trip, found the cause of that crackling. All we knew was that when anchored in deep water it was more echoing and hollow, while in shallow water it became sharp and stacatto. A Mediterranean mystery.

But there were other disturbing events. I made the mistake that first night of anchoring *Lugworm* close inshore in about two feet of water with a bow anchor out deep and a stern anchor up the beach. In a sea where there is no appreciable tide it seemed the logical thing to do for it's much easier to be able to wade ashore rather than have to pull the boat into the beach every time. At some unprintable hour of the night I was roused to full consciousness by the distant roar of breakers on rocks farther out in the bay. *Lugworm* gently lifted her bow, levelled off, then dipped. At the same time there was a disturbing tug on the headrope, then the sternrope. I sat up and hoped.

Next time the bow lifted it was too violent to be disregarded. When it came down she hit bottom gently, then lifted again. By the third time I was out and over the side, watching with horror a long line of black looming towards me. It reared: *Lugworm* despite my feeble efforts practically stood on end. As she levelled I felt the crest of the wave lick my armpits and then hurl me shorewards, playfully rolling me up the shingle. Above it all I heard a startled cry.

No, we didn't sleep much those first nights, but one learns quickly. Ships—vast floating citadels ablaze with light—doing their magnificent fifteen knots, make a wake which long after one has forgotten their passing, can turn a quiet beach into a maelstrom. I felt B. ought to understand this phenomenon in detail.

'The fact is,' I explained to her while wringing out my sodden jersey, 'that a large ship tends to make two distinctly separate wakes. This can be tricky because it is just when the first series of waves has died down that the second series catches you off balance. It's logical enough,' I continued, trying to locate a billycan that was clattering up and down the pebbles. 'If you watch a large ship moving through the water you'll see that the bow wave is augmented by the displacement of the sea as her fat belly forges along. But as this displaced water rushes back to fill in the space behind the ship it meets its counterpart on the other side doing the same thing. The resultant collision sets up another series of waves emanating from her stern.'

'Interesting,' came her voice from the darkness. 'But what are we going to do about it?'

'It's obvious: we will anchor out in deep water. She'll rise and fall out there but with nothing like the violence here in the shallows where the wave is about to break.'

'If you knew that,' said the voice, 'why didn't we anchor out there last night?'
It was a good question.

*   *   *

Nothing lifts the heart like sun and blue sea. Add a velvety warm wind flowing round your skin, a sky as blue as a kingfisher's tail, the sibilant chuckle of water gurgling away from your transom and ...

'Thou, beside me in the wilderness,' I quoted aloud.

'Some wilderness,' said the straw hat from down on the lee deck. Poking out of the sea ahead was the green crowned isle of Skiathos, the brilliant green of the pines forming a bright contrast to the marble slash of rock at the waterline. A heaven-sent northerly, funnelling between the mainland and the island, was flecking the blue with lines of white laughter.

'I'm going to sing,' I said.

'Don't. Not yet. Last time you tried that we got in irons and I'm comfortably wedged down here. Have a nut instead.' I had a nut.

'Would you agree that we're islomaniacs?' I asked the hat. B. and I met on the Scillies, spent our honeymoon in Malta, and had been marooned three times since on other islands. Here, just for a change, we were coming up to an island.

The hat bobbed and a long golden leg flopped over the side to trail toes in the cooling water.

'Not exactly. More escapomaniacs.'

'Tell me more.'

'Well, you and I suffer from the malaise that dogs twentieth century man. We've become depressingly aware of the prison we've spent our lives building around ourselves. But now we've taken steps to break out.'

That was fairly profound for a lyrically beautiful morning. I switched hands on the pivoting tiller and took another almond from the bag beside me. Placing it carefully beneath the hinge I brought the tiller down with a satisfying crack. *Lugworm* wiggled.

'Prisons?'

'The stresses and strains of everyday life that hedge us in. Crossing water does something ... it's like a moat that keeps them at bay. Small islands particularly;

they're an entity in themselves, a compact whole. Maybe unconsciously that helps to heal the cracks ... in the smallness of an island we more easily become again a whole individual away from the fracturing herd.'

I had another nut.

'Never really thought about it,' the voice from the other side of the hat went on musingly, 'but I think I feel safer on an island. And then, of course, there's the romance. Islands. Treasure. Pirates. Palm trees and grottoes; kid's stuff, but it's there. Deep down we're all kids at heart.'

The cap, I thought, certainly fits here. Who but an overgrown child would buy an open boat, lovingly carve teak decorations on her transom, then sail off on a wild voyage of discovery like this?

'Do you think we're less mature than most?' I asked, trying to count the gnat bites round my navel.

'No; more.'

'Because we're more like kids?' I teased provocatively.

'Because we admit being more like kids.'

'Ah! Now there's a thought.'

To port we could now see the long golden strand of Koukounaries beach, mentioned in the brochures as being the finest in the North Aegean. There was a plush looking hotel at the western end and another, but far larger, skeleton of grey concrete going up at the eastern end. A new road scarred the lovely hillside like a raw wound. We sailed on until the first white and red-roofed houses of Skiathos harbour came clear of Cape Kalamaki. It looked enchanting, the sugar-lump houses climbing atop one another up the steep hillsides round the bay. The wind, which had swung north-west as we first came under the lee of the island, now began to head us and we had to beat up inside Zogria Island, a lump of craggy rock to the east. On the water front gaily coloured awnings flapped in the wind and the cafes and tavernas were crammed with people. Yachts of all sizes jogged each other for room inside the basin. It was a scene of colour and animation and we watched fascinated as an inter-island steamer, towering immaculately white above the quay, detached herself and began to froth towards us, the white bone in her teeth lifting and widening as she gathered speed and swung smartly round to pass between us and the shore. *Lugworm* lifted gently to her wake, and the wind

grew fickle and died as we came close under the lee of the harbour. With B. securing the main, I rolled the mizzen round its mast and started the outboard.

We closed the basin, dodging the heads in the water near the rocks off the
entrance. Inside, the headropes of the larger yachts swept out to mooring buoys, others lay to a bow anchor; all had their sterns to the jetty and fenders were
squeaking complaint as the elegant bellies of the hulls jostled each other. There
didn't seem to be any room at the quay, even for a chip of a thing like *Lugworm*.
We circled round.

'Do I detect,' enquired B. who was studying the tavernas through the glasses,
'that you don't intend to make fast here in the basin?'

'Well, it isn't going to be very private is it. All right if we had a stateroom and
doors we could shut like those elegant ladies over there, but ...'

I nosed the bow seaward. Over at the far side of a larger bay beyond the
harbour was a small sandy beach under a low cliff. It had a lee from the north
wind and though it would mean a walk of about a mile round the top of the
bay into the town it appealed because of its privacy. In a few minutes we gently crunched on to the sand, B. springing ashore with the wine flagon in one
hand and a sardine tin in the other. 'No point in going shopping until after five
o'clock because they shut for the afternoon siesta at one-thirty. You bring the
opener and the tomatoes.'

Under the cliff the cool wind made the blazing sun just tolerable. We drank
and slept, and later that evening with the shopping done, had our first taste of
moussaka, the popular Greek dish of baked aubergines with mincemeat and be-
chamel sauce, eaten beneath an awning of a taverna on the water front watching
the harbour life. Here was Norman Wisdom's yacht *Conquest* alongside another
called *Richmond*. An ocean-going ketch *Rainbird* bobbed near the ferry mole unable to find a berth on the quay itself. A couple of German yachts and a magnificent large ketch called *Zara II* made a gorgeous picture in the fading light. I took
another sip of Plaka Spumante, savouring the surprisingly pleasant cool white
wine with the champagne style bubbles. 'We're supposed to be staying off the
tourist track,' I remarked, 'and here we are basking in the fleshpots! Indeed, Mrs
Duxbury, over there,' and I pointed to the far side of the bay, 'in splendid and
aloof isolation, lies our yacht awaiting our return. The steward will have turned

down our bedcovers, switched on the reading lamps and put the champagne in the ice bucket; what's it feel like to be a millionairess?'

'Tell you something,' came the voice alongside. 'I wouldn't enjoy it one half as much if it were like that! I'm happy with *Lugworm;* you can't beach a millionaire's yacht on a pocket handkerchief of sand at the back of a deserted little spit and go native with your hair down in the sun, can you? No, I'm happy with *Lugworm*, thanks.'

I had a nice warm feeling, and it wasn't only the wine, as we strolled idly back round the head of the bay, past the fishing caiques pulled up on the foreshore and the derelict windmill that had lost its arms, up through the olives softening the rocky hillside and down the twisty path through the myrtle bushes where the cicadas still chirrupped in the warm night. There again, a dark shadow against the moonlit water, lay our home. We laced a line taut between the two masts and threw the tent over it to keep the dew off the bedding, and turned in.

It was four o'clock in the morning when a small voice said, 'I think we ought to wake up!' The tent, carelessly lashed down from the corners, had come loose and was flapping madly above us. There was a patter of rain.

'Rain! It can't rain in the Aegean in late June.'

'No, it can't. But it is.'

It was not only raining, but one look at the ragged torn edges of cloud scudding across the tops of the hills to the north was enough. The meltemi had arrived. It was a bit ahead of the daily schedule but one thing was obvious: this small bay had not sufficient lee from a really good blow, and we were getting wet.

'No time to stow all the bedding now. Resecure that tent lashing and I'll motor across to the lee of that high cliff just south of the town. We'll sort ourselves out there, in the calm.' It was a mistake: we ought to have stowed the bedding there and then and removed the tent, but all the sleeping gear was strewn about the boat, not to mention the cooking utensils ready for breakfast, and I wanted to get into that lee as quickly as possible.

By now there was a faint lifting of the darkness, and I could see the cliff under the town, about half a mile across the mouth of the bay at most. The sea was already running steep and wetting with white horses galore for we had a fetch of about three-quarters of a mile to weather. The rain was setting in hard, driving almost horizontally with the force four to five wind. I could see that it was only a matter of time before the wildly flapping tent broke adrift altogether, and anyway I was far from happy with the windage it was offering. Four horse-power isn't enough to combat that pressure on the beam; we were making more leeway than headway. 'Get the bedding stowed, quickly as possible, and take that tent off her; we've got to get the jib and mizzen set.' Too late. The weather lashings parted together and that half of the tent swept across the boat carrying everything loose with it: billycans, water containers, stove and all the clutter on the side deck from the night before ended in the lee bilges. B.'s struggling outline bulged white and shiny through the p.v.c. She was doing a marvellous job in what might have been called difficult conditions. I cast off the ridge line and brought the boat more into the wind to reduce the spray which was sheet-ing over the weather bow. We were about halfway across the bay. With jib and mizzen set we frothed along, wet, but at least under control which was more than I had felt motoring with the tent frolicking. As we approached the cliff the wind died, but I still had the outboard running so we nosed up close to a small shingly beach and WHAM! A fistful of hard air slammed us almost on our beam ends—from the south!

'Do be careful, darling,' came B.'s justifiable complaint. 'I've just got every-thing propped for the starboard tack; I can't cope with both tacks at once!' It was ferocious, that back-eddy of wind under the cliff. We dropped all sail and watched the hammerblows of wind hitting the water from all directions. Certainly up there on top of the hills the force must have now reached a good six, and it seemed to be even more violent down here at sea level. It was against all my experience of wind behaviour, and I didn't like it. There was something about islands in the Aegean that played havoc with the rules of the game.

We sorted the mess out, and got the boat shipshape on the beach, but it had taught me a lesson.

'From now on,' I pontificated, 'we'll be in all respects ready for sea at a mo-ment's notice when we turn in at night, no matter what the weather may be like.'

'Can one be ready for sea with the tent up?' B. asked candidly. She had a point there. We compromised and agreed that at least all the gear should be properly stowed away so that the tent could be dropped immediately if need be. On occasions need did be.

That sudden rising of the wind, with virtually no warning, made me think. We had often discussed our action on being caught on a lee shore with a rising wind and sea, and always, as a last resort, I had casually assumed that when the worst came to the worst, we could haul *Lugworm* up a beach clear of the breakers.

Though the rain had now stopped and there was intermittent sun, the wind was still roaring over the island so, since coastal cruising was obviously out of the question this day, I thought it a good move to exercise getting *Lugworm* up the beach unaided. 'The thing is, to make a proper evolution of it,' I instructed B. 'Take it in slow time and get the hang of it at first, then, when we know what we're about, it can be speeded up.'

'You're wonderful darling,' she said. 'Give me my orders.' I never feel quite at ease when B. adopts this attitude, but in truth I had very often run through the whole procedure in my own mind, and thought I had it weighed up.

'Most important, of course, select an area of beach where you're not going to be stove in on a rock before you get ashore: that's common sense. Over there will do fine,' and I pointed to a wide sweep of fine shingle beyond. Oddly enough, since we had landed I had noted that the beach over there, despite the low land to weather, had apparently less wind on the water than where we shuddered under the cliff. We motored across and while approaching, B. made the comment that there appeared to be a long ground swell surging up and down the shore.

'All to our advantage,' I assured her. A lift up the beach from the sea will help no end. Now listen carefully: First, I'll remove the rudder and steer with the outboard. About ten yards off the beach I shall swing the boat bows to seaward and give her a pull full throttle astern before cutting the motor and tilting it clear of the water. As she beaches stern-first we must both leap out and use the top of the surge up the beach to get her as high as possible, holding her there and keeping the bow to seaward while the surge slides back down the beach. The important thing is to prevent the boat broaching across the swell in line with the beach, otherwise we'll have trouble. Ready?'

I swung the boat in a tight circle at the same time engaging reverse gear at full throttle, then lifted the engine. She swept gracefully stern first on to the shingle at the very peak of a surge. By the time we had leapt out she was almost high and dry as the water receded down the beach. At this point I must explain that I have an aversion to drilling any holes in a boat's hull, even to the point of not screwing fittings into the skin, and for this reason, when rigging our tent, rather than screw eyes into the planking, we rigged a stout girdle of terylene rope right round the hull and it was to this that the tent lashings were secured. Now two people—one man and a woman—could not expect to haul over nine hundred pounds dead-weight of boat quickly up a sloping beach, so prior to leaving the cliff I had rigged this girdle round *Lugworm* since it was to this I proposed securing a block and tackle for doing the heavy work.

'Very well managed,' I commented, giving myself a backhanded compliment. 'So far so good. Now all you have to do is stand at the bow and see she doesn't swing sideways while I rig the tackle and haul her clear of the water.' I carried the anchor and its ninety feet of one-and-a-half inch warp up the beach, hooking it round a tree before rigging the tackle. B. valiantly held the bow, her enthusiasm wilting with each successive surge.

While making these preparations a group of young men had idled along the beach towards us. They now stood close at hand engrossed in our activities. As I have mentioned before, one of the endearing characteristics of the Greeks is their willingness to help. At times it is almost compulsive, and they will carry it to any length in normal circumstances but, faced with a situation where an attractive blonde in a bikini is struggling valiantly to obey the commands of an idiot who's trying to do the impossible, they one and all fell to, gathering round *Lugworm* with gusto, dead set on carrying her bodily up the beach.

'Ohi ... efharisto poli!' I cried, squandering my total Greek vocabulary in what I hoped was, 'No ... thank you very much!' They looked astonished. 'Solo,' I tried to explain. 'Important ... she and I, SOLO.' Ah! They had the message. Delightedly they moved from *Lugworm* and ranged themselves behind me on the tackle. If this nut of a foreigner wanted to drag the boat up rather than carry it, who were they to argue?

'Ohi, ohi.' I started all over again. 'Ego, I ...' pointing to myself and B. who was, by this time both moist and embarrassed. I grasped the rope, dug in my heels and strained. *Lugworm* lifted on the rise of a surge up the beach and shot about three feet shorewards under the strain of the tackle. B., who had been putting all her weight on the bow, fell flat on her face in the shallows. Six bodies moved as one to render help and the boat slid gently back down the beach as the surge withdrew.

A crowd attracts a crowd. By this time our comic opera had been joined by a drift of other curious holidaymakers. A donkey hovered in the background. A large lady in peasant dress sat side-saddle balancing a box of small fish.

'Don't you think we'd better let them help?' queried B. 'I mean, it might be the easiest course in the long run.'

'There's no point B. The whole object of the exercise is to see whether we can do this by ourselves; you're forgetting that we don't want the boat up the beach anyway.'

No: by now I was truly on my mettle. We were going to get that gravelly boat up that shingly beach unaided or bust. We'd show them. I disentangled the tackle from among the feet of the bystanders, told B. to again take station at the bow and started once more to take the weight. Instantly a new group hastened forward to help. The original onlookers, puzzled but obedient, rushed to stop them. Violent arguments broke out. I stopped pulling, trying patiently again to explain the whole concept. More people joined the crowd. Through their sheer weight of numbers I was beginning to feel a little embarrassed myself. It was all rather like a solo circus act and there was no difficulty in imagining the conversations round about.

'What's going on?'

'I don't know, but it's worth watching. This idiot's going to rupture himself trying to get the boat up the beach but he won't let anyone help. Stick around: it's hilarious.'

Once more I grasped the rope. The crowd pressed forward. Somebody clapped expectantly. The tackle snapped taut and, just at that critical moment the donkey decided to move across it. Now donkeys are sure footed animals, we all know, but three taut bars of steel-like terylene snapping up under its fetlocks was too much: down it went as though poleaxed, its rider somersaulting volubly into the crowd. The hullabaloo cannot be described. Undamaged but resonant the large lady sat, quivering in the wet sand surrounded by hundreds of whitebait from the upturned box. The donkey got up and trod on someone. Out of the me-lee a larger, louder man clove a path towards me positively roaring with invective.

It may have been her husband or brother, I don't know, but he seemed to be in no doubt as to who was responsible. *Lugworm* swung sideways down the beach and listed dangerously seaward as a swell receded.

'I think he's going to hit you,' came B.'s warning shout from somewhere among the crowd and I saw her run and grab an oar from the boat. Things were getting out of hand. I lunged after her, snapping the tackle free from the girdle and saw, to my astonishment that the large man was haranguing the woman. She gave as good as she got, both hands bristling with sandy fish: for a moment the focus of attention seemed to have shifted as the crowd joined in the argument with relish.

'Come on,' I roared to B. and leapt to *Lugworm*, shoving her off as the surge lifted her weight. Immediately a united roar arose from the crowd: somebody at the back was brandishing something in the air. It was my anchor and warp.

We abandoned the idea for the moment, and retired to another quiet beach just outside the harbour at the north of the wider bay. For the rest of that day the rain held off but the wind continued with undiminished force so we unstepped the masts and rigged the tent properly as we should have done in the first place. That evening, after a meal on board, we settled into our bags early, with the battery reading lamp augmented by a couple of candles we became lost in the world of ancient Greece which comes wonderfully to life through the pages of Joseph Alsop's *From the Silent Earth*. The wind continued to sigh through the olive grove beyond the foreshore road, and we lay listening to this evocative sound planning the next day's leg up the string of islands, and were well on the way to sleep when, with an audible 'click' the air became resonant with the background crackle of a powerful amplifying system. To our horror, bludgeoning over the natural whispers of water and shore, came a blast of American 'Pop'. 'YEAH, YEAH ... KISS ME HONEY, KISS ME ... YEAH, YEAH, YEAH.' The moronic beat, the endlessly repeated hysteria of a decadent section of the teenage world, so discordantly out of tune with the atmosphere engendered by these islands, blazed across the bay.

I crawled from my sleeping bag and peered through the flap of the tent. A discotheque, its white stucco walls illuminated by garish coloured bulbs, pulsed among the olives not a hundred yards away. There was no movement nor gaiety; no voices nor dancing, only the overpowering sonic expression of this American sub-culture blasting its alien path across the fractured night. The record broke off halfway through a note to be immediately followed by an equally strident choral piece in different key and different tempo but of the same underlying hysteria. I listened for a minute or two, trying desperately to click into some sort of sympathy with the mood of the turmoil, but it was hopeless.

'I don't pretend to fully appreciate the popular Greek records I have heard,' I said to B, as I crawled back into the sleeping bag, 'but give it me anytime rather than this affront to the senses!'

"We agreed,' she replied, 'to keep off the tourist track. We can't grumble if we indulge the culinary delights of the flesh-pots when we have to take a bit of the other side of the culture too. It's a part of what we're escaping from: we shall appreciate tomorrow all the more for it.' But the mind-numbing decibels encroached two sonic hours into the morrow before, with a terminating 'click' we were plunged into peace again. Maybe we are just growing old.

*   *   *

If you look up the narrow channel between Alonissos and Peristera, you can see at the farthest end of Alonissos a golden buttress of cliff. On the opposite side of the channel the low-lying tip of Peristera is backed by the thousand foot peaks of Pelago Island beyond. It is an exciting prospect, that narrowing blue water between the two green islands, and beyond, the fainter backcloth of misty heights which is Pelago.

A few days after our enforced stay in Skiathos we were beating across the Khelidromi Channel, having skirted south of Skopelos Isle, the expected and predictable northerly giving us a vigorous sail in the open water, and while I was loath to sail past the entrancing bays and inlets of Alonissos, that distant outline of Pelago seemed to cast a spell: I wanted to get there. From the chart I knew there to be a deep protected lagoon on its northern side—safety against any inclement weather that might come—and so far as we had been able to ascertain the island was uninhabited. Fresh from our experience in Skiathos we were both keen to return to the open, wild and carefree life of the lesser known islands.

'If we don't loiter we can be at Pelago before night,' I said to B. 'Are you game?'

'O.K. by me, but I want to explore a lot of Alonissos on the way back including that hill on the point back there with the chora on top.'

I too had noted that chora, and it was certainly impressive. Like a fairy-tale illustration the white village perched on the crown of a rounded hill whose lower levels were thickly covered with maquis. Immediately below the walls of the village a grove of olives flourished and between this and the maquis was an area of waste land, the baked grey rock showing through patches of dry grass.

'Then that's a promise on the way back. Pelago it is.'

With the fickle wind, which swung dead ahead down the narrows and fell light before we were abeam of Gregali Point, it was five in the evening when we were off the southern tip of Pelago. It was densely covered with maquis, the stunted trees and thick leaved shrubs painting the whole island dark green. There was what appeared to be a low-roofed building halfway up the southern side but we could make out no track to it, nor was there any sign of life. By now the wind had died completely, so we closed the shore under power and skirted up the eastern side. At first the hills fell in a fairly steep incline straight beneath the water, but as we worked north the shore became an almost continuous line of medium height cliffs, contorted strata of rocks forming vivid patterns and grotesque figures. The sun was low now to the west, and beneath us, in the shadow of the overhanging rock faces the water was a deep blue-black, suggesting unfathomable depths full of mystery. The intrusive throb of the engine echoed and re-echoed off the cliffs. Suddenly it was cold.

I suppose it was the combination of fading light, bailing warmth, and the eerie hollow echo of our engine coming back from the dark cliffs that gradually turned the atmosphere of that island into a brooding alien place. Before we were halfway up its eastern shore we were wishing that we had stayed in the hospitable sunny bays of Alonissos, where fishing boats plied and life flourished. Ahead, the incredibly barren outline of Jura Island rose stark from the black water, a vast primaeval crag of mountain top. We felt we had arrived at the end of the earth, much as the early explorers must have done with their ever-present dread of the unknown.

It was close on six before we came abeam of the northeastern promontory, a jagged outcrop of rock that fell to the sea leaving a trace of treacherous black shapes beneath the water. The aspect to the west was appalling in the failing light. Deeply indented bays were fringed by great fingers of sharp rock stabbing above the surface, indicating very real hazards beneath. Pitted and hollowed by the restless swell which worked unimpeded here from the open sea, born of the north wind, it was a grim prospect to any sailor, and the silence was oppressive. Heaven help the ship that gets embayed here, I thought. We nosed across a deep bay to a second promontory no less awesome than the first, then skirted a second bay, watching all the while for the entrance to the lagoon. A long narrow outcrop of rock stood black against the shoreline to the west, and I knew from the chart that the entrance lay due south of this small island but such was the light effect and the merging of the foreground rocks into the far shore that we were actually on the narrow cutting before its presence was known.

By now the sun was well below the land, and as we turned southward into the lagoon it seemed that we were moving into a brooding bowl of gloom. The entrance, narrow, deep, and some half a mile long widened slowly into a dark lake which to our senses appeared to be holding its breath in silent scrutiny of our intrusion. We turned east, hugging the northern shore, while peering down into the water alert for any pinnacles which might tear out our bottom.

No sound, or movement, save our own unavoidable clamour, broke the silence of this mountain-ringed lagoon. Through the glasses I scanned the grey waterline of razor-sharp rocks that fringed the lake, looking for some inlet with perhaps sand or shingle where we could beach the boat and pitch camp for the night. None appeared, and we continued to creep along the rocky shoreline until ahead in the gloom I could make out a low stone wall built on the rocks close to the water. It appeared to be a pound of some sort—the type of enclosure used to herd animals. Such was our sense of loneliness in this desolate place that even the derelict outline of this work of man's hands gave some slight comfort. We nosed carefully into shallowing water close beneath the wall and threw an anchor ashore. I vividly remember the echo of the metal hitting the rocks, reverberating off the thousand hard faces of stone surrounding us, ghosting across the water into the dark abyss of the hills behind. Not a living thing stirred, where one might have expected a bird to rise with a startled flurry of wings; only the oppressive silence. Unwittingly we hushed our voices to a whisper feeling our way up the knife-ridged rocks until we stood inside the enclosure. It was a wholly dismal place. On the inside of the lower wall a trough had been constructed to catch rainwater which ran down the smooth sloping face of the rock above. The trough was green and stagnant with mould and animal droppings, for it was evidently a goat pen. The stale but overpowering stink of these animals pervaded the place, augmenting the alien atmosphere. Somewhere in the back of my mind, relic no doubt of childhood teaching, I still associate the devil with the cloven hoof and goat's form. In this dark outpost of brooding loneliness, I could easily have fallen prey had I allowed myself to wild imaginings of witchcraft and other dark happenings beyond the ken of warm human experience.

'I couldn't stand this smell all night,' I whispered to B. to sound her reactions.

'No: I'd rather anchor off than try to make camp anywhere in here,' she assented. 'Oddly enough I would feel safer on the water, dismal though it is, than on shore; there's something uncanny about this place.' Looking down into the shallow water we could see dimly on the bed the form of countless grotesque sea slugs, their obese corrugated skins black against the grey silt.

I am very susceptible to atmosphere. The fashion in which an environ affects me undoubtedly depends on my mood at the moment, but atmosphere is self-generating, and once the overall impression has been established the mind tends to feed only on data which will corroborate rather than contradict such an impression. Under guise of not wishing to risk damaging the propeller on unseen rocks, I told B. that I proposed rowing farther round the perimeter of the lagoon. If truth be told I was loath to violate the silence with the noise of the engine feeling that such advertisement would in some indefinable way focus the brooding attention of the place on we two unwanted visitors.

It was while quietly ghosting along the southern shore of the lake, sliding silently through black water, with the sky above already showing a full panoply of stars that we first noted the sound. I stopped rowing, and together we listened. Faint, almost imperceptible, distant, yet at the same time all about us, came a 'clop! ... clop! ... clop!' It could have been the distant beat of an unshod hoof on stone, but there was too long an interval between the sounds, and it was too regular. Whoever imagined a horse that hopped very slowly on one leg? We held our breath and waited. Continuous, insistent, the regular, soft yet strangely violent sound came across the water—from where?

'It must be some sort of animal.'

'Maybe. Sounds exactly like the drip of moisture off a cave roof plopping into water far below. I've heard it before now in deep underground caverns but never out in the open like this. I don't like this island a bit,' came B.'s hushed comment. 'What do you think it is?'

'I don't have the first idea, but I'm certain we can't turn in tonight without finding out.'

Of course there would be some quite ordinary explanation, I argued to myself as I pulled the boat silently along, following the contours of the black shore as close as I dared. After a while I rested on the oars. Did the sound seem nearer? Dull, continuous, regular with a frightening slowness the hollow 'clop, clop' filled the night. I found myself counting 'clop' one, two, three, 'clop' one, two, three. Regular as clockwork. And then it stopped.

If the sound itself was disturbing, its sudden cessation leaving utter silence was far more so. We had already, I suppose, in our minds, explained it by a vague idea of water dripping from a height. But dripping water doesn't stop suddenly like that. This, undoubtedly, meant that the noise came from a living thing. Then it started again.

I continued quietly easing the boat along—in fact I was skirting the perimeter of a rounded hill which formed a projection from the southern shore of the lake— and as we nosed round a small promontory on its western side we could make out a deeper gully leading into the blackness. Beyond, faintly visible in the light of the stars, was a deep valley. For the first time the sound began to emanate from one direction. Whatever it was, it was at the head of this bay, maybe somewhere up the valley itself.

'Take a sounding with the lead,' I whispered to B., for I was pulling away from the promontory into the centre of the bay now. I heard the splash as the weight went down. 'Thirty feet,' came the reply after a moment. 'Keep sounding, and let me know as it shallows up.' I pulled *Lugworm* out into the darkness, the shore still undetectable ahead. The oars were soft in the rowlocks, silent in the water—and then I caught a crab. Maybe I was concentrating on the sound too much, or just being very careless, but the oar came out of the port rowlock and thumped hollowly on the gunwale. It was like a single drum beat echoing across the lake. The sound stopped instantly.

'This is just ridiculous,' I said, and cupping my hands I bellowed into the darkness, 'Ahoy ... anybody there!' I felt highly theatrical and was half ashamed of the clamour I'd made, echoing and re-echoing back from the hills. On our starboard side a light flickered and there came an answering hail.

'So much for our ghosts,' I said to B. trying to keep the relief out of my voice, and pulling strongly for the light. As we closed the glow we could make out a man standing on shore, peering into the darkness towards us. Alongside him was a small fishing caique. On board, a woman and a small child peeped from behind a shelter rigged at the stern. As we watched the man bent and picked up a mass of what looked like slimy weed. He raised it above his head and brought it down with a hollow thwack on to a flat rock. It was an octopus. Again he raised it, and repeated the violent action. He stopped and straightened up as we drifted into the fringe of light. 'Kali spera,' he called to us—a greeting we had come to recognise as meaning 'Good evening'.

We pulled alongside the caique, grounding *Lugworm* on the shingly beach and, at the invitation of the fisherman, jumped aboard his boat, but I was more interested in the octopus which he had once more started to flay on the rock. It must have been going on for over fifteen minutes now; surely, I reasoned, the thing was dead before this.

We could not communicate of course, but from sign language we gathered that this treatment of what, after all, is a fairly harmless sea creature, was somehow connected with making it more edible. We learned later that the tough muscles of the tentacles need tenderising, rather in the same way that one would beat a thick steak to break up the fibres.

But that night, as I looked down at the pathetically small and defenceless creature ripped from the only environ where it might defend itself, two eyes—dreadfully human in size and shape—stared up at me beseechingly. As a brown hand once more lifted the trailing form into the air, an odd thought entered my head: 'I know,' a voice seemed to be saying, 'that to you I'm a repellent evil thing that preys on other life down there. But I'm made that way: I can't help it, can I?' I looked at the man bending again to close his fingers round the trembling muscles. I looked at the woman up there in the light, and the soft face of the child beside her. We too had to eat, and we too were made that way: we couldn't help it either, could we?

But that of course is the four billion dollar question.

We fled from that lagoon as the first green light of dawn filtered over the mountain tops, but the fishing boat was already gone. As we motored in the early calm out of the narrow neck it was as though we were spewing from some dolorous cavern out into the light where warmth and clean wind would once more reign. I am sorry, Pelago, to paint you in such sombre colours for I have no doubt that you are as beautiful as many other islands in the Aegean, more beautiful perhaps than some, but that was the mood of our meeting. Some day we may return, in the warm light of high noon, and be surprised.

The sun rose, a blood-red disk behind the silhouettes of Papu, Kubi and Prasso islands, with Jura a dark shape beyond—I have the photograph taken at five in the morning beside me as I write—and our spirits rose with it as the warm rays began to dry out the boat and gear. With it came the expected north-west wind, and by the time we cleared the southern end of Pelago white caps were forming. Under full sail we had a vigorous beat across Pelago Channel, just able to fetch Gregali Point, the wind freshening as the sun got higher.

Maybe there was something symbolic, something in the way of a ritual need, but once in the lee of the warm ochre cliffs of Alonissos we grounded *Lugworm* on a sparkling white pebble beach and stripped everything from the boat, airing the bedding and the clothes from the lockers, sponging out the bilges and stretching the spare halyards and warps from under the bottom boards to dry in the hot sun. Then we stripped, swam, and finally washed ourselves and our hair in fresh water before restowing the gear. By ten o'clock we were running before a force four following wind which swirled through the narrows. It was noon, and blistering hot, when we rounded up into Murtia Bay at the southern tip of the island, grounding on a white shingly beach for a snack of wine, olives, tomatoes and cheese before stretching out for a nap, our feet caressed by the cool wavelets.

*   *   *

On the hilltop above us was that white village we had noted on the way to Pelago, and after the effects of the wine had worn off we began to get restless as usual. B. was keen to see this chora, and I was game: why not? If the pirates could do it, we could.

To be honest, we knew from Denham's book *The Aegean, a Sea Guide to its Coasts and Islands*—which book, incidentally, was our Bible throughout this part of the cruise—that there was a donkey path from the next bay leading up to the chora. But behind our tiny beach there was a dried-up watercourse, and innocently we assumed that sooner or later the two would converge, or at least we would be able to strike across and join the path halfway up. It didn't work out like that. In fact that was the start of an experience we hope never to repeat on Earth, and most certainly we shall not do so in Heaven.

Of course, oven-hot air is not the best medium in which to attack a sixty degree incline, nor are bare feet and bikinis the best rig for tackling prickly spurge and holly, thistles and brambles. Only maniacs would set off that way, so off we went. The watercourse soon deteriorated into a deep boulder-strewn gully and finally ended, for us, at a vertical outcrop of bare rock. We struck sideways, picking our painful way between incredibly spiny broom, glad to see a patch of open baking space only to find that the dried thistles and a really lethal seed with needle-sharp spines made it untenable. This day I learned why all the wild shrubs left on Greek hillsides are either poisonous or armed with rapiers: it's defence against the goats. If the tough mouth of a mountain goat cannot tackle a green growth, you may be sure it's wise for humans to give that growth a wide berth. On this hillside it was difficult—in bare feet rather like walking on red-hot pin cushions. The trouble was that the rock, when there was enough of it to leap from chunk to chunk was too hot to stand on. You may ask why I was not wearing any shoes. The answer is not complicated: I don't like wearing shoes.

On the lee side of the hill there was not a breath of air, and the high pitched throb of the cicadas seemed to nail the blistering heat to the ground. We began to feel peculiar. Things appeared to quiver and slide about.

'Put your shorts over the nape of your neck, as I have done,' I counselled B. who was following glassy-eyed behind. I looked at her carefully. She hadn't heard me. 'B.,' I called, 'are you all right?' No answer: she was walking like an automaton, slowly, round in a small circle; it was appalling. Great Phoebus, I thought, she's got sunstroke! I dragged her beneath a huge bush of broom which gave little enough shade but it was better than nothing, and fanned her face with my shorts. We were both running with sweat. After a while her eyes began to focus and she made the understatement of the year: 'I think I'm just too hot!' There is no doubt in my mind that we were both suffering from heat exhaustion and very near to collapse, but the olive grove was there above us, and beyond that the chora.

We staggered on, trying to imagine that icicles hung from every bush, and the grove above was a green waterfall of cool lime juice. It helped. But it needed concentration. Finally we dragged ourselves on to the donkey track just where it led through the village walls—whitewashed walls that reflected the excruciating heat even more than the baked earth.

'I can't stand any more of this,' B. said, 'I'm going to faint.'

'Well, don't faint here darling, wait 'till we get to a taverna,' I encouraged her, and after more interminable steps upward there, blissful sight, was a flat square with a huge mulberry tree spreading coolth, and a wooden bench, and a sign: 'TABEPNA'. Which, in Greek, means TAVERNA, and Heaven!

'B.,' I said. 'I'm glad I'm not a pirate!'

After the fourth lemonade with ice-cream in it—the best substitute available for waterfalls of lime juice—my feet began to come to agonised life. I spent half an hour trying to remove the thorns while the landlord told us how many English soldiers he had hidden in the room above when the Germans were on the island, and great ripe mulberries kept falling from the tree with a squelch and gradually the world began to take proper proportion and things stopped quivering.

In between lemonades and thorns I had a haircut—the landlord was also a barber and the postmaster—and it lasted me four months. He did a good job.

Return to the shore was made by the cobbled mule track which Denham wisely recommends, but of course it took us to another bay. The delight of that luxurious swim back round the headland to where *Lugworm* danced in the clear water will remain with me for ever. Without more ado we hoisted all sail and with a light northerly coming through the straits, reached out towards Skopelos.

Looking back in the mellowing afternoon light at the small white village crowning the hilltop there, it was as though we were being magically dissolved from the reality of everyday life into a world of fantasy. This picture our eyes photographed could not possibly be reality; it was a world of pure imagination such as we had not experienced since living the enchanted pages of fairy tale books more years ago than we cared to remember.

One's hand, unthinking, rested on the tiller. A soft recurring pressure on the fingers was matched to the easy, rhythmic roll of the boat, and the sighing water beneath her hull chuckled into a small swirling wake astern. The occasional relief of shadow from the main denied the brazen heat and through it all the voice of the soft wind coaxed the following crests into playful leaps and pressed the russet faded canvas above with that effortless strength which is the mystery of sail. One breathed, thought and felt in complete harmony with the magical world around. Greece, I realised then, was for me a half conscious hope that new dimensions of experience might be tapped. I little thought that those forgotten worlds of colour and scent and feeling that were a part of my earliest being would here be unlocked again to marry fantasy with reality.

The shoreline of Skopelos drifted by to the north. Swards of translucent pines dropped, a green transparency, in a cicada throbbing volume of quivering heat down to the dividing line of white rocks which barred the deep mauve of the Aegean from further access. Astern, and misty now with a blue wash that softened the harsh edge of contours, Alonissos was fluid in the mirage. The blinding white chora up there had withdrawn from our awareness, folding its wings around it to pass back into the realms of fantasy. The green-brown maquis on the hillsides merged into distance, tinted by the first orange glow of late afternoon.

Something happens to the summer sky in Greece after four o'clock. The brazen blue of noon dissolves in an ever diminishing circle vertically above, relinquishing its kingdom to a softer, kinder, misty blue that gently draws a chameleon curtain of mauve, orange, then green up from the hazy horizon. Suddenly evening is with you.

So we ghosted on to Agnonda, a tiny fishing village, on the south shore of Skopelos, where we found a delightful taverna nestling under a riot of yellow mimosa and, despite painful feet and aching leg muscles, we slept better that night than we had done so far on the trip.

*   *   *

Just at the dying of the day as one sits on the terrace before some beach taverna with the carafe of wine perhaps only half empty, there may be seen out on
the water a sight which is so characteristic of Greece that it is worth describing
in detail.

A fishing caique has drawn out of the nearby harbour, and floats now, a black
silhouette on the glassy water as the sun disappears below the horizon. Astern
of her is a smaller boat with three or four men aboard and piled high with a

large fishing net. Out in the bay, waiting to be taken in tow, are four or five
small rowing boats each with one man aboard, and slung in a special bracket
over the stern of each are two—sometimes more—huge, ungainly paraffin pressure lamps, their glass bowls hanging down with a reflector above to direct all
the light down into the water. When the caique with the net boat in tow moves
from the harbour you will see these rowing boats gather together and pass a line
to one another until they are strung like beads on a necklace. As the large power
craft draws nearer, the man in the leading boat will throw his line to the net boat
and then, just like a mother duck and her brood, the caique with the whole fleet
behind her will chug off to sea.

Grigria assembling for a night's fishing. Later, when the night is quite
dark—and this type of fishing only takes place at around new moon or last of

the old—you will see, out in the blackness, the string of four or five brilliant lights. They will stay quite still, winking now and then as the long swell dips a lamp below the horizon perhaps, but if you were out there with them you would watch a fascinating scene of tense activity.

Arrived at the selected fishing ground, the small rowing boats, known locally as 'Grigria' cast off and separate, then drift. The lamps are lit and the single crew begins a long, long—often all night—vigil. Beneath the boat a pool of light illuminates a small area in the black depths, and the fisherman sits, chewing at his hunk of bread, looking down there into the void. After a while, if you were watching with him, you might see a quick silver flash deep below the boat, and he will lean over the gunwale and shield his eyes against the reflection of the lamps. Shortly, if it is a successful night, he will see more and more of these quick silver flashes, and something about the way they come and go tells this fisherman that deeper down, where they cannot be seen, is a shoal of small 'marides', what we know as whitebait. The fact is, that in common with the proverbial cat, fish are curious, and that curiosity proves disastrous. They cannot help investigating that light on the water above them, and collect in their hordes, fascinated by the glare. Once he is certain that the shoal is there, the watcher will hail the caique and net boat which are lying some distance off, and they will quietly approach. While they have been waiting, half of the net has been transferred from the net boat into the caique which is equipped with winches and reels, and when they are close to the watcher the net boat will cast off her tow. Then, from both caique and net boat, the net is fed over the side. The bottom of the net is weighted, the top buoyed with small cork floats, so that when it settles it hangs like a deep curtain. Caique and net boat gradually encircle the watcher paying out the net, and when his boat is completely surrounded, and the caique and net boat are alongside one another again, he will row across the top of the net out of the way.

Rings are attached at intervals along the bottom of the net, and a footrope is already rove through these, being brought up into both caique and net boat. As soon as the encircling by the net is complete this footrope is hauled taut which draws the base of the net together thus forming a huge bag—with the shoal of whitebait inside it. Then comes the mammoth task of drawing the net into both caique and net boat—about half into each.

It is wonderfully satisfying to watch the net coming aboard, bright now in the deck lights of the caique, and shimmering with the living silver harvest. Often the fleet remain out all night with a disappointing tale to tell when they return at dawn to harbour, but occasionally as much as several thousand kilos of marides are brought back in one night—and that takes some hauling aboard. The village will know before they land, for in that case there will be a telltale flock of gulls circling in their wake.

*   *   *

We left Agnonda at dawn, with heavy thunder clouds gathering to the north and a brisk north-easterly which showed every sign of freshening, but we had the island to weather and made good way to a magnificently protected bay at Panormos on the west coast where we anchored for a swim and breakfast, keeping a cautious eye on the wind in view of the open water ahead between Skopelos and Skiathos. It has a tendency to funnel with greatly increased force through these breaks in the island chain. Indeed, the Sporadhes are known locally as the 'Gates of the Wind'. By nine o'clock it showed no sign of any hazardous increase in strength so under full sail we worked our way well north of Dasa Islet before freeing off for Skiathos. It is a habit of mine always to work well to weather of a destination in case of a wind shift which might result in a heading. In the event we spanked along on a beam reach across the six miles of open water, and were clear of the rocks north of Zogria Isle by ten thirty.

The thunder clouds were breaking up, and now the wind—as we fully expected—fanned out round the south of Skiathos to give us a run until noon, when it freshened considerably and began to head us, sweeping round the western end of the island. We closed the beach at Koukounaries and had lunch aboard beneath the hideous skeleton of that new hotel, sun bathing in the boat away from the hordes on shore. By early afternoon the wind had eased a little so we reached across Skiathos Channel to the mainland where we picked up a splendid east-north-east airstream straight into the Trikeri Channel. By four o'clock it had swung due east so we boomed out the large jib and the main with the two oars and rolled along, hour after hour watching the green hills and the white shoreline slide by.

'Do you realise,' I asked B. after one long silence, 'that we're floating through a veritable Irish Stew of History! A stockpot of legend, romance and blood curdling drama? It was on that very headland,' and I pointed to where Cape Artemision was flushed red-gold to the south, 'that Themistocles undoubtedly sat to view the Persian invasion fleet in 482BC. He had a hundred triremes, each with a captain, twenty marines and four archers at the ready, pulling up and down in this very water, waiting for the signal fires to give warning of the Persian arrival off Skiathos. A hundred more ships were stationed off Piraeus and along the Attic coast to guard the mainland: all part of a strategic plan to harass the Persian fleet prior to the battle of Salamis.'

'You've been reading Denham.'

'Yes, I have, and it's exciting. I'll bet the sea bed right beneath us now is littered with Persian skeletons and bronze helmets and halberds and triremes. Just think of it: across the vast canvas of Greek mythology and history ships carrying immortals have sailed into these straits and looked at these same shores, and now, US!'

There was another long silence.

'Which bit did he sit on?'

'Who? On what?' I was far away in a bygone age of Homeric chivalry.

'Themocrates and the Persians.'

'Themistocles!' I surveyed the headland again. 'I don't know, but I suppose it must have been at the highest peak if he was keen to see the signal fires at Skiathos.'

'He must have been very fit!'

It's hard to be romantic with B. in the boat. The baking heat of early evening eased as the sky once more turned from deep blue through those lighter misty shades of pink to a full orange-red as Helios once more sank beneath the horizon. Then the greens set in, and still we ghosted silently along before a velvet warm wind, eating the miles effortlessly, listening only to the soft creak of the gaff on the mainmast and the whisper of water along the hull. It was gloaming as we slipped softly into Trikeri Bay, and our anchor plunged—a comet-tail of phosphorescence—into the black water. We swung stern to the beach and stowed the boat for the night before wading ashore for a meal in a taverna.

At first it seemed that we had entered a deserted village. None of the small whitewashed houses beside the dusty harbour frontage showed any signs of life. Windows were black hollows in the grey walls, no lights welcomed from within. Even the animals seemed to have disappeared. But faintly, along to the west of the village, we could hear a murmur and the occasional voice raised in a call. As we picked our way in the darkness towards the sound, the first strains of music reached us. Shortly we struck the cobbled alley way which served as the main thoroughfare of this quaint fishing village, and headed away from the bay to where, in the distance, we could see the glow of lights and hear the throb of the music. We stopped at some distance from the throng who were gathered in front of a taverna. But this was no ordinary night; a fiesta was in progress. The grape vines above the tavern front were strung with lights. Beneath this canopy of living green were seated two women and three men with string and percussion instruments. We both had the same thought: that they must be wandering gipsies, for this music they made bore no relation to our westernised concept of Greek music, conditioned as it was by Nana Mouskouri and the melodious bousouki and guitar. This was almost Moroccan, with a wailing hint of Indian discordance behind. We stood, a little back in the darkness, to watch without being seen, for it was evident that the whole population of the village had gathered at this spot to join in the fun.

Standing there, we became once more aware of the power which sound has to mould the mood of men, kneading them into pliant things responding to the hypnotic influence of the drum and strings. Not one of those present, could you have asked them, would have been aware that they were enslaved by that pulsing hypnotic rhythm, but watching the faces and the movements from without, it was plain to see that the rising and falling of the music, the subtle power which first suggests, then dictates a mood, had them in thrall. Here for the first time we were hearing our first real folk music, and though the sounds were strangely alien to our ears, it did nevertheless corroborate an impression I have always held that through the music of a people one has the most reliable and direct window on their soul.

Around the perimeter of the square vendors had set up their stalls, the orange flames of their oil lamps a soft contrast to the yellow-green brilliance of the pressure lamps. They were doing a brisk trade with cheap toys for the children, fruits and confections. The violinist, a man, commenced to sing in a high harsh key, the broken rhythm taken up by occasional hand clapping from the crowd. Another man stepped forward, holding in his right hand a white handkerchief, rolled into a short rope. He held this at arm's length, hanging down as his feet started the ritualised steps, the fingers of the left hand clicking as we had seen the dancers at Volos. Another man came from the crowd, took hold of the handkerchief and joined the steps, in perfect time. More followed, then a woman. All the time the line of dancers was moving slowly, winding as a snake, each figure's arms resting on the shoulders of his fellow. The watchers increased the clapping and it sighed like a breaking wave out across the square to be taken up by the crowds there. We moved closer, to where a low wall enabled us to see over the heads of the crowd. The woman violinist was singing now, big boned and strong, with a rich voice that went well with the black hair and eyes, set off by her brilliant green dress trailing to the ground, swinging to the beat of her feet.

A group of children spotted us and cautiously approached. Finding us friendly we were soon surrounded with a twittering aviary of small girls and boys, all pressing questions, one or two trying out their school English with the expected 'Halloee!' and 'Good-Byee!' wide eyes aflame with temerity, egged on by their friends. Their attention was soon conveyed to the crowd, and momentarily we felt a shift of the focus from the musicians and dancers to ourselves. Where had we come from and what were we doing here? This was no tourist attraction, how had we got here? You could see the questions being asked as they summed us up. The end man of the line of dancers caught my eye and held out his free arm, an invitation to join them. I felt B. pulling me and soon we too were under those bright lights hilariously trying to imitate the intricate footwork.

Groups outside the canopy of light were now forming up and dancing among themselves. The big woman singer moved away from the musicians and stood brazenly before a rheumy old man who was evidently well on in his cups. She held out a hand, inviting him to join her. Startled from his reverie, he looked up at her. Instantly a roar of laughter burst above the din. The old man straightened, looking round in disdain, then, to everyone's surprise he rose unsteadily to his feet and stood challengingly in front of her. Kindly she broke the step and commenced slowly, guiding, coaxing and finally flagrantly challenging him to respond. Unspoken, the sensual sexual contest flowed with the spirit of the dance. He set his feet wide, straightened and looked her full in the face. Slowly he started the difficult steps, giving then following, unsteady at first but gaining strength and confidence with the beat of the music. A roar of encouragement broke out from behind him. The woman played up to him and his watery old eyes took on a new life as he summoned up energy he had forgotten he possessed to give everything to the hypnotic compelling beat.

As suddenly as it had begun the music stopped. The dance was over, and the old man, feeble now with the effort, was escorted back to his seat. Head erect, eyes proud, those unexpected moments had come to him like a wild wind of youth and he was proud of his ability to accept the challenge. There were tears in his eyes as his glass was filled and hands pressed in warm regard on his shoulders. He was evidently popular.

Another, slower tune was struck, commencing with a regular beat of the drum and cymbals. Behind us I could hear a single cicada still strident, competing with the musicians. Above us and to the north I could see a yellow flicker up in the hills. It was Old Trikeri, balanced up there at the end of a cobbled mule track, deserted by its population, doubtless for this night's festivities. Certainly we were not going to get a meal at this taverna, for the landlord and staff were frantic serving wine and beer; any thought of cooking here was out of the question. Since the two other tavernas appeared to have stopped business for the night also, we joined the throng among the stalls, seeking something to appease vigorous appetites. Above a tin tray holding a glowing bed of charcoal, small juicy pieces of meat skewered six and eight together dripped temptingly, the smoke from the burning fat making our mouths water. 'Pos ta lete,' (What are they called?) I asked the vendor. 'Souvlakia,' he replied as we bought two each. 'They're a sort of shishkebab,' I heard B. mutter, 'Aren't they delicious!' Another meat vendor with a similar stand had longer skewers with what looked like brown elastic wound round them until they were about two inches thick. The smell here, too, was appetising, and we bought about six inches each of this tantalising cylinder of unidentifiable meat which was removed from the skewer, chopped into half-inch lengths, and given to us in greaseproof paper. It was delicious, the outer skin being browned to a rich crackling, the centre slightly tough but extremely tasty. Had we known it to be sheep's intestines we might have enjoyed it less, but we eat stranger things in England, so what matter!

There were stalls doing a brisk trade in Turkish Delight and another jelly-like brown sweet which was sold in large slabs cut to one's requirement. We were soon satisfied, having returned to the souvlaki stall for another round which we washed down with a glass each of resinated white local wine. Back aboard *Lugworm* we lay listening to the distant beat of the music and the murmur of the crowd. It was still pulsing when we fell asleep. *Lugworm*, her stern anchor back aboard and the bow anchor shortened in to clear the beach, swung gently in a flat calm. The stars were our night lights.

So far, I reflected, there has been little to fear in the meltemi. Will she favour us with a fair wind down the narrow but deep channel between Evvia and Thessaly, bowling us on towards the Cyclades?

CHAPTER III

THE EVVIA CHANNEL AND HAPPINESS

I T WAS ABOUT THIS TIME that we began to live again. This may sound odd, coming from two people so enviably placed as to be able to set off on a fifteen month cruise as we had. But the conditioned compulsive haste, the hysteria in the soul resulting from twelve years' business pressures, cannot be shaken off in a matter of weeks. We found ourselves, hardly aware that we did it, or why, planning in detail the next day's sail as though it were imperative that we reach our destination by some predetermined time. The mood was constantly one of pressure; to get on, plan our actions and cram each day with activity as though it were likely to be our last.

I remember early that morning after the fiesta at Trikeri studying the chart by torchlight and wondering if we could make the Likhada Islands about twenty miles down the coast before nightfall. Eastward out of the Strait the sky had taken on that luminous green which comes before the dawn while behind us to the north the brighter stars still shone above the silhouette of the trees. Southward, Cape Stavros stood black against a dark range of mountains beyond. It was while I watched a single puff of cloud, trying to assess the wind direction, that I heard a dog bark somewhere up the hill behind. A man's voice called, then broke into song, and I listened as the echoes volleyed back and forth giving resonance to the voice. He was singing, that man, because he was happy and for no other reason, and suddenly I found myself wondering when I had last burst into song for the sheer joy of being alive. It was a sobering thought. Certainly as a child I sang a great deal. . . and whistled a great deal more, but for many years now ... when exactly had the death-knell rung for un-inhibited self expression?

Meanwhile he was still singing up there; even the dog had joined in. 'Tra, la, la,' I blurted, and felt an absolute idiot. Courage, Duxbury, a little voice prompted from within.

'There's a hole in my bucket, dear Liza, dear Liza,' I bellowed, then looked round as if the hills would bite me. '... dear Liza, dear Liza.' The echoes faded. Nothing happened except that B. opened her eyes wide.

So I let rip. Why not? Joy wasn't the sole prerogative of the man and the dog up there. I sang 'Maria' from West Side Story, and 'Santa Lucia' in what I think is Italian because it's the only song I think I know in Italian. I have a respectable voice: never been quite sure whether it's tenor or baritone but the hills asked no questions. B. was laughing, and there to the south I saw the topmost peak of Cape Stavros flush to a rose pink. It was a wonderful beginning to another wonderful day and most certainly we were HAPPY!

So we sat and watched the misty gold glow creep down the hillsides. The sea, a dull primaeval green, turned silver and salmon pink fleck for a moment, then deep deep blue. The earth yawned and woke up.

'Cuckoo,' I said to B. in between crunches of toast and peach jam—you can't get marmalade easily in Greece—'What would you like to do today? We've got all summer to enjoy living again, and all winter to write a book about it. What shall we do today?'

'Ummm ...' Her face became dreadfully serious. This is splendid, I thought. Pleasure: pure uninhibited pleasure for its own sake is a serious matter and a very necessary part of life!

'Do you know what I'd like most of all? It's nothing special—simply to find a secluded beach somewhere with a little wind for coolth, and laze there the whole day. I want to go completely native and look at a tree and the sky and listen to the cicadas and the birds, drink a little wine and sleep and ...'

I topped up the mugs of coffee from the billycan. 'Keep it up,' I said. 'We are learning; we are learning fast!'

So we drifted down to Stavros in a peace you could caress while the world warmed up, and to Hell with pressing on to the Likhada Islands; we would get there in time enough. Meanwhile let's enjoy a sea as calm as a mirror, and rust sails that can't really bother to fill because it's too much effort, though if you look there's still a small whirlpool or two under the transom, but beware! That translucent blue-mauve void down there and the gentle warming sun on your bare back can lull you gently out of this world of reality.

We slid silently between Argyronesos Island and the Cape, and a mile away a rower in a small fishing boat swayed rhythmically as he stood at the oars, the thin creak of loom against thole-pin coming clear across the water, and a bee, urgent and curious, loomed up, busily inspected us, then droned off to leave us again to our own silent world. We drifted quietly past the tiny white houses of Glypha, but we had no taste that day for civilisation no matter how remote, and just kept idling across the mouth of the bay until the entrance to a deep landlocked lagoon opened up and, since we cannot resist enclosed lagoons, we rowed quietly in with the rising crescendo of the cicadas to herald our approach. It was a superb bowl of water surrounded by gently sloping hills shady with olives. We beached close to the ruin of an old olive-press, its wooden axle still jutting stiffly from the vast granite wheel that had crushed the fruit, and while B. settled down on the fine white shingle to drift off into a world of her own, I drifted out and anchored in water so clear that I could count the long leaves of weed carpeting the bottom, full fathom five below.

Carefully I baited the hook, rolling bread into paste pellets and watching them gently disintegrate as the hooks sank down. The fish enjoyed it immensely, but after a while I got wiser, stabbing the barb through a tough piece of crust. A group of sizeable chaps had collected down there—well worth grilling—and three soporific hours slipped by as I watched them taking a nibble, but their table manners were too refined for even the smallest to take a good gulp. In fact, from the vantage point of the future I will tell you that we caught but one fish during the whole of this Greek idyll. It was unbelievably exciting; all of four inches long, three of which were head and tail. We threw it back to make ourselves feel good.

So after a while I rowed to where B. was a slim brown shape on the beach, and lay down to savour the scents of rosemary and wild thyme drifting through the olive grove. At moments like that, there is a rare feeling which comes stealing over me. I don't know whether it is shared by my fellow men but for me, when the sun is warm, and the musky scent of earth suspires, and the sky is a chameleon of changing hues as afternoon transcends towards evening, then, within the limited enclave of my mind, a window seems to open. I see and feel myself an integral part of the whole vast macrocosm. No longer separate, observing, but participating through every fibre of my heightened senses; becoming an actual part of the earth and sky with a totality which leaves no space for 'otherness'. To the depths of my being I become 'at one' with the universe.

I suppose something of the sort is felt by the drug addict: perhaps mescalin will bring the effect, but I'm told that the depression when the effect wears off is almost intolerable. For me, though I have never taken a drug, it is quite the reverse. I feel immeasurably enriched by the experience. Ready to face again the stupidities of this separate life. Undoubtedly the mystics, locked in their solitary cells knew this transcendence. But for me, it is only when lost in the broad expanse of earth and sky that the alchemy can work: for an alchemy it certainly is—of a rare Happiness!

So I sank down through depths of warmth and well-being into sleep. We were awoken hours later by the distant throb of an engine. It came from outside the lagoon, and had an expensive note unlike the full blooded thump of the caiques. Both of us sat up, slightly apprehensive at this intrusion. It was a pleasant surprise; above the green shrub covered point at the entrance to the lagoon two slender masts fingered the sky. Round the end of the rocks nosed a superb black ketch, a real ocean-going racing craft, her sails trimly stowed, a woman at the helm and a bronze thickset figure at the bow. Her engine cut and she drifted gently to the centre of the lagoon before dropping anchor. Sailors the world over are imbued with the same sense of curiosity—I had to get the glasses and examine her lines. She was flying the American flag and across her transom I could see letters in gold 'XAPA' pronounced 'Hara' which is the Greek for happiness: as good a name for a boat as I can think of. I watched the man cast a glance our way then walk back to join the woman in the cockpit, and shortly after a pleasant American voice hailed us across the water bidding us join them for a drink. We pulled over to the ketch, *Lugworm* lying alongside, with her black hull looking for all the world as though the elegant lady had given birth to a beamy little offspring. It was a pleasant evening: these two had taken a year off to cruise the Eastern Mediterranean—two-and-a-half years ago. Like so many more the enchantment of the free life had been too much for them; they were still talking of the need to go back.

'It can be fairly violent under those hills,' he said, when we told them of our plans: how we proposed gently making our way down to the Cyclades hugging the Evvia shore for a lee. I pointed out our need at all cost to hug a weather shore, for he evidently shared the feeling I was finding common to all who knew these waters—a deep distrust of conditions close under a mountain. Here was a deep water man whose instinct was to stand off where the wind blew with uniform strength knowing that his craft was capable of taking anything the sea cared to bring. I explained to him that in a boat as small as ours we suffered one big advantage and one big disadvantage: the former being that we could literally float in inches of water and cruise within feet of the shore line so if disaster loomed we could literally get out and push. The latter was our inability to cope with anything like the sea I had found to be whipped up within a matter of minutes back there in the Sporadhes. We talked late into the evening for we had a strong feeling of affinity with these two nomads so similar in temperament to ourselves. As we pulled for the shore again he repeated his earlier warning: 'Don't forget now, it can be pretty violent under those hills!'

A small pebbly beach overhung by a bank with olives gave us a good lee from the north, and it was as B. started preparing the evening meal, our fire having died to a red glow, that we heard the first portentous rustle of leaves. Over the top of the hill came a first hard edge of black cloud. I hastily stowed all the loose gear as a buffet of wind hit us, then it roared down into that lagoon like an express train, bending the trees, lifting the dried leaves and blowing a cloud of dust out over the water. At the same time came the first flash and outrageous crack of thunder. We grabbed the canvas boat cover to make a wind break for the fire which was doing a Catherine wheel into the sea and we both huddled there in a cocoon eating the meal which B. had managed somehow to cook while torrents of rain thundered like shot on the canvas roof. Across the darkening lagoon a driving sheet of grey water lighter in colour than the pitch black cloud above obliterated everything. I watched the thin beam of an aldis lamp probe out from the ketch trying to pick out objects on shore and then above the fury of the wind I heard a far more perturbing noise—the clink of metal on stone. I leapt from the cover of the improvised tent and grabbed our shore anchor as its flukes disappeared under the water. *Lugworm* was slicing back and forth like a tethered wildcat and throwing the anchor into the roots of a bush I brought another line ashore making it fast to the bole of an olive tree above us. We slept that night—when we could sleep—on the airbeds wrapped in the thick green boat cover without the sleeping bags for everything was so wet we thought it best to keep those valuable items dry in the forward

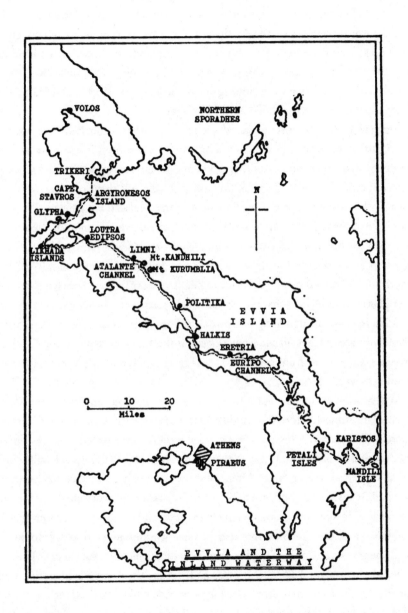

VOLOS

NORTHERN
SPORADHES

N

TRIKERI

CAPE
STAVROS

ARGYRONESOS
ISLAND

GLYPHA

LOUTRA
EDIPSOS

LIKHADA
ISLANDS

LIMNI   Mt.KANDHILI

ATALANTE
CHANNEL

Mt.KURUMBLIA

POLITIKA

EVVIA
ISLAND

HALKIS

ERETRIA

EURIPO
CHANNELS

0   10   20
     Miles

ATHENS

PIRAEUS

KARISTOS

PETALI
ISLES

MANDILI
ISLE

EVVIA AND THE
INLAND WATERWAY

locker. By four-thirty next morning we were up and brewing tea over a splendid fire in a world as still as an angel's siesta and by seven the sun was hot enough to be lifting steam from the wet beach and us. It is wonderful to feel that spreading dry warmth—one of the relative joys we forgo when, night after night, we lie in a cosy dry bed. While we were stowing aboard all the gear which had dried on the beach the ketch quietly slipped out of the lagoon with only her large Genoa set, running before a light north easter. We followed under all sail half an hour later.

The first week in July was now at an end: we had been in the boat a mere thirteen days, yet already that other world of care and routine we had left seemed immeasurably far away. Clear of the entrance, the full thrill of what we were tackling hit us once again. Ahead of us was the Atalante Channel and that in turn spilled through the narrows at Halkis into the Euripo Channel at the end of which, some hundred miles to the south, lay the threshold to the Cyclades. That morning as we cleared the lagoon with all sail drawing the range of hills on the south shore towered gaunt and black, while to the north the lower lying coastal belt glowed in brilliant sunshine. Small white crests were forming and the wind steadily freshened, funnelling down the confines of the channel. We could see the lighthouse at Cape Vasilinas just north of the Likhada Islands—a tiny white needle—and astern, from over the Trikeri range, ominous thunder clouds were bearing down on us.

I have always been puzzled at the speed with which a sea builds up in the Mediterranean. Almost before the wind has got into stride the short steep waves are there, white crested and very wetting when a small boat is on the beat. But here we creamed before them, lifting as they passed beneath us and occasionally surfing down the advancing faces. After a while we dropped the mizzen for the wind was still freshening and it's not wise to have too much pressure abaft one's plate and rudder in such conditions. It made no appreciable difference to our speed, and looking astern I realised that had we been working to windward I would already have been searching for a likely point behind which to take shelter. The sea to weather was a mass of broken white and still the wind increased, getting well into its midday meltemi routine. But *Lugworm* rode it like a bird, taking not a drop of water even up through the outboard well which is her most vulnerable spot when running. By eleven o'clock the wind was to my reckoning touching force six and I had the main reefed and had swopped our Genoa for the small jib, trailing a couple of ropes astern to reduce our speed for we were tending to surf continuously as the waves steepened up just to weather of Cape Vasilinas. In a small boat one notices the marked change in the water on the weather side of a headland. There is a rapid build-up of the sea and sometimes a nasty contra-running wave formation which is caused by a rebound off the shore. Soon we rounded the cape and the instant easing of conditions enabled us to set the mizzen again for the reach down to the low rocky Likhada Isles. The ketch, still under Genoa alone, had stood out to clear the islands but we sneaked close to the sandy spit, helped along by a two-knot tidal stream which boiled over the shallows and left a wake behind the ragged off-lying rocks just to seaward. Then we had the whole mountain range of the Likhada promontory to weather of us as we sat her out and beat eastward into the Atalante Channel.

*   *   *

'Concrete,' I said with conviction, 'is the ruination of the Greek countryside—and tourism will be the ruination of the Greek people!' About six miles beyond the Likhada Isles the sight of another really colossal hotel under construction triggered off a discourse on one of my pet aversions: mass tourism. The coastline was magnificent; pine woods falling down to an ever changing rocky shoreline which had gradually given way to shingly beaches and then, as we rounded a low projecting spit, a wonderful stretch of virgin white sand led straight back into the dark green depths of the woods. Now rearing over the pine tops like something out of a futuristic nightmare came another of those horrendous complexes of square concrete pigeonholes which pass for architecture in this ageing twentieth century. It was not until we had rounded the spit and could see across a shallow bay beyond that the real proportions of the monstrosity came into view. Stretched in a geometrical affront along the ruin of what had been a magnificent beach was this cadaver of grey cement, clambering skywards, sprawling over the land in a squalor of shuttering boards and rusty girders. The woods around were decimated by bulldozers, stacks of cement bags, compressors and mechanical diggers, while all the litter of a vast building project with its shanty annexes strewed the beach.

'It isn't as though the spoliation would cease when the job's completed,' I frothed to B. 'This squalor we see now will only be exchanged for the litter of the hordes which flow through the hotel in their thousands every month. It's true,' I continued, 'I've never loved my fellow man in bulk and these results of mass tourism that are springing up just make my blood boil. I'm damned if I can see what right hordes of us have to pack ourselves into containers and squirt all over the world, then burst like an avalanche and destroy every bit of natural beauty and character. We bring our own suburban fish and chip culture with us, battering underfoot everything that's worth preserving in the delicate and subtly different culture of peasant communities.' I paused for breath.

'Wish I had a tape recorder: you sound like Billy Graham—or do I mean Mussolini? Go on.'

'It'll sour them, just as pollution sours the sea.'

'What will sour whom?'

'Tourists will sour the hospitable Greeks.'

'Of course they will—but what's the alternative?'

I thought about that.

'There isn't one, I know. For this country there isn't one: it's just got to sell the one thing it has in bulk—the coastline and climate and scenic beauty, but it's sad, sad …'

'O.K.' B. took up the discussion, pensively. 'But is there really anything wrong with developing a country which has this scenic beauty and lots of sunshine so as to offer the hordes deprived of such commodities a chance, for one brief fortnight at least each year, to escape to luxury in the sun—and in the process bring prosperity and raise the standard of living of the countries they visit? Anyway, aren't you being rather hypocritical about all this—what are we but tourists? Granted we're in a lucky position of being able to make a full meal of it, but we're still tourists, and why shouldn't everybody else have their chance?'

'No,' I countered, 'I can't accept that. I'm not playing with words, but I would call myself a traveller not a tourist, and to my mind there's a wealth of difference.'

'I think you *are* playing with words.' I glared at her: she had one of those bulldog looks I associate with handcuffs and suffragettes, Germaine Greer and 'Women's Lib'. I would have to put my case lucidly.

'Let me explain,' I continued. 'A "tourist" as I see it is one who avails himself of the services offered to holiday in a foreign country but—and here is the essential difference—in doing so he takes his own brand of "culture" with him. To be more accurate the travel firms and tourist organisations see that it's there waiting for him when he arrives, and I'm thinking of all the so-called necessary luxuries of his own background, the fleet of taxis and hire cars, the modern hotel with running hot water, television, the bacon and egg for breakfast if he happens to be English, and the cups of tea and service with a smile for which he's paying. All the "tourist" wants to do is transpose everything that he's used to when on holiday at home into a new environ where there is sunshine. He expects it to be ready and waiting at the far end of his charter flight, and if it isn't he'll soon want to know why. And the alert businessman very soon makes certain that he gets these things because the law of wealth is the law of giving a supply where there is a demand, and that's what he's in business for: wealth.

'On the other hand,' I continued, warming to the subject, 'the traveller is to my way of thinking, one who visits a country and does his best to adjust to the different culture and not try to change it by imposing his own. In that sense I believe you and I are travellers. We enjoy the differences between our two cultures. O.K. Here in Greece some of the tavernas are primitive and unhygienic by our standards—not that English restaurants are a model to the world by any view. It has also come as rather a shock to us to realise the Greeks' lack of desire for creature comforts in the home; their joy in garish colours which to our eyes scream at each other, and the appalling untidiness of the areas around their houses. So what? That's all a part of being Greek. What right in Hell have we got to come and try to change it? They've got a damned sight more of one thing we lost a long time ago: contentment! Can't they realise that by modifying their way of life to suit the God Almighty "tourist" they're chucking overboard all that's of real value and moulding themselves into what the escaping "tourist" has become, a keyed-up neurotic apology for what ought to be a glorious end-product of millions of years of evolution.'

'You're impassioned, darling.'

'Yes, I am impassioned. It makes my blood boil. I suppose the truth of the matter is I'm not very proud of our Western values any more. And that leads me on to another aspect of the visiting hordes—the hippies. Did you know that in southern Crete the hippies so imposed on the natural hospitality of the country folk that an Edict had to be issued ordering them not to give away everything they had to the leeches? It's a fact. True to their natural character the peasants of southern Crete welcomed the hippies and took them into their houses. The hippies saw a good thing and took whatever was offered them. Those hospitable folk, unable to have any concept at all, never mind understand, the degenerate depths to which their new visitors were sunk, gave more when asked. It was their nature to do so. It was only when the priests realised that they were almost bled to death by a kindness that was being mercilessly exploited that they issued an episcopal edict which persuaded the locals to withhold their hospitality. You bet the hippies soon oozed away when there was nothing more to exploit.'

'But you can't bracket the hippies and "drop-outs" with tourists!'

'I'm not bracketing them with tourists. I'm merely quoting them as an example of the way a good in a people's character can be destroyed by contact with other cultures. Think of the harm that has been done by that one example: for the first time in their lives those Cretans have been taught that it is wrong to extend hospitality! What a splendid introduction to the encroaching world without! And in a minor way the hordes of tourists are doing the same thing. They're making the peasants—I wish there were some other word than peasant with its overtones of inferiority—the country people of Greece think that the rest of the world, which for them means the tourists, are immensely wealthy and live a perpetual life of indolence. It's the only side of the visitors they ever see: what else can you expect? They just cannot realise that the man in the luxury hotel down the road has saved and scraped for a year in order to afford that holiday, and has to keep his nose to a soul-destroying grindstone of routine that is beyond the concept of your olive-picker here. So they become dissatisfied, and with dissatisfaction they learn to exploit in their turn. It's here already in the shops: there's a price for the tourist and a price for the locals, although I must say the present government, with all its faults, is doing its best to stamp that out. But it comes in other ways: look at the shrewd fisherman back there who took care to lay his broken disused nets right round the yachts so as to ensure that they have to accidentally cut them when they move, and then holds up the tattered remnants with a dismal story of his livelihood gone. He knows the rich owners will, out of conscience, pay for new nets. It's a wonderful racket, but the point is it has come into being because contact with the rest of the world has developed the natural venality that's rooted in all of us.'

'So what are you advocating? Do you want to put an electrified fence right round Greece and big notices "Keep Out", "All Contact Forbidden". How long do you think a country like Greece would last if it didn't open every door to the tourist trade? To survive they've got to remain commercially viable in the world. What would you do if the problem were yours? Stop all the tourists? You've got to be a realist; Greece today is putting up a strong fight for survival as an independent people. This sort of thing,' and she scanned the block of concrete ashore, and the new road searing like a raw and still bleeding wound up the beautiful valley, 'is their only weapon, and it's a pretty powerful weapon at the moment.'

'True, but there are signs that the appeal of the "package deal with charter flight" holiday is waning. Look in any national paper today and you will see that the tourist organisations are breaking their necks to offer something other than the box in the sun with your next door neighbour from back home right there alongside you on the beach. There's a swing away from it. Hence the organised safari with its Land-Rover treks into the interior. Reindeer round-ups in Lapland. Here in Greece they're organising charter flights with accommodation in small out-of-the-way selected tavernas instead of the multibox like this one. If there is any significance in this—and I think there is—there are going to be an awful lot of empty concrete boxes in the sun in the next decade!'

I was a bit breathless by now. It isn't often I get hot under the collar about anything, but I warned you—tourism is my pet aversion. But I hadn't quite finished yet.

'What happens,' I continued, 'when this "different" style of holiday becomes over exploited? Who the devil will want to go on an "organised" boar hunt when the boar have been imported—and probably hobbled—so that the great white hunter tourist can get full value from the service he's paying for? What happens after that?'

'You tell me. I can't see any solution.'

'Well, there is a solution, though it may seem a far cry from this subject of tourism. And I think it may come far too late to preserve something well worth having in the world: individuality. The solution, my dearly beloved spouse, is to start acting like intelligent animals and control our population level. We've got to sweep aside pretty quickly and pretty thoroughly the idea of there being a virtue in prolific breeding. There's no virtue in it whatever in the present day. It's the greatest danger to the future survival of mankind there is. We've just got to get together and voluntarily adjust our population to the productivity of our environ. There ought to be a heavy fine imposed for every child born into a family above the first two, and it ought to be in direct proportion to the family's income otherwise it would be grossly unfair.'

There was a long pause.

'We've got a long way off concrete boxes,' said B.

'It's all part of the same problem. In 1966 there were about one million visitors to Greece. After the "coup" the number dropped sharply, of course, but by 1970 there were one and a half million and this year there are expected to be two million if not more, and three million in 1972. In fact the Government is working on a figure of eight million by 1980. What do you think that will do to Greece? Most of what you and I come for will founder on the advancing waves of mediocrity from the warrens of our human zoos. You and I have seen it happen in Spain, in Portugal, in North Africa, Sicily, Italy and Malta. It's such a shame it has to happen here in Greece as well. This country is just too beautiful to ruin.'

'Personally I think you're seeing the Greek people through rose-tinted spectacles. Greeks, just like the rest of the world, are human beings. And like all human beings they've got their share of venality, corruption, greed and self-centredness. It's nothing to do with being a member of a country: it's through being a member of the Human Race, and the Human Race has developed like this because the sort of world in which they happen to find themselves is a world of survival of the fittest. That's the law of nature and there's nothing you can do about it except to alter the law. In fact,' she warmed up, 'in fact any moral concept—and ironically enough some of the deepest moral concepts are cradled in man's many religions—is in direct opposition to the natural order of things. Dammit, "morality" is nature's greatest stumbling block! It's only so far as Man goes against his natural evolution-imposed instincts that he can become a "moral" creature!'

'You're impassioned, darling,' I said.

It was at that moment we hit the rock. You can't ghost along these shores within a few feet of the beach and discuss the nature of man at the same time. The boat jolted violently, staggered a bit, and slid forward. The outboard struck, tilted up with a roar, and plopped down again. We stopped the engine and held our breaths while I carefully withdrew the rudder assembly. It came—thank Heaven—out of its slot housing without trouble, but there was a splendid bend in the metal rudderpost!

'Never mind,' I said, looking at the bent tube—it was almost worth it to get that off our chests. So much for philosophy.

We anchored just as the light faded at Loutra Edipsos in the lee of a low cliff smelling peculiarly of sulphur and slept profoundly through a still night.

*   *   *

In my opinion, the finest time to reach a new harbour is late evening after a good day's sailing. Is there any pleasure greater than dropping anchor with the gathering darkness and watching the lights ashore, listening to the distant sounds of a port as you prepare to turn in: observing, but not observed, from one's vantage point of isolation? Then, with the dawn, comes the surprise spread out for your inspection, to be explored or left as you please. That next morning was no exception.

I awoke bright and early, but some change in the gentle lapping of the sea had alerted me. I listened. 'B.,' I whispered, 'there's something in the water alongside!' From our prone position in the bottom of the boat we could see nothing but sky. Gingerly I raised myself and peered over the gunwale. A few feet away a vast lady clad in voluminous black stood up to her shoulders in water, gently rising and falling like a hippopotamus. She wore dark glasses and a wide-brimmed straw hat. We glared at each other. 'Kali Mera,' I said, in an effort to relieve the tension. She pivoted slowly about a vertical axis and undulated away from me without a word. Behind me there were three more matrons similarly undulating, all vertical, and on shore a few elderly gentlemen were undressing under the sulphur cliffs. It was all rather unnerving.

Then I saw, to seaward of us, the tops of submarine fence-posts enclosing an area in which we were anchored. We had come right through them late the evening before and were evidently floating in the middle of a sulphur bath. I felt the water and it was warm. 'B.,' I pronounced, '*Lugworm*'s getting the benefit of the local thermal springs. Do you think we ought to have paid to come in?' Above us, lining the top of the low cliffs, was a row of onlookers, fascinated at the sight of this intrusion into what was evidently a private beach area belonging to a local restaurant where the ailing came to ease away their aches. Very politely they one

and all turned their backs as we dressed. 'Truly,' one could imagine them saying, 'one never knows quite what these foreigners are going to do next. What would they think if we went boating in the hot springs at Bath!'

In an embarrassing silence we negotiated the obstacles and motored in an ee-rie calm down a coastline of magnificent pineclad mountains, deeply gullied with dried-up watercourses. Here and there a tiny level area would be cultivated, a ceramic-tiled stone hut standing lonely guard over the small field. We wondered how any humans or animals managed to gain access to them, never mind cart away the produce.

So we pottered on to Limni where there is no harbour, just a waterfront with quay, and as usual for privacy we anchored clear of the populous area, walking back into this delightful little town which creeps up the steep hillsides in terraces of houses. We shall remember the place with pleasure, for that night, on the waterfront, a group of youngsters with guitars and an accordion made the night beautiful with exquisite Italian and Greek songs.

*   *   *

There is something about the look of deep black water in the shadow of high mountains that strikes awe into the heart. Next morning, buffeted by a fitful northerly, the Atalante Channel wore a brooding air, the lofty pinnacles of its eastern shore stretching on as far as the eye could see under a sky which was becoming blocked with fast moving ragged clouds. All the signs were for wind, and had it not been that we were hugging a weather shore, we would have remained on the beach at Limni. Already the sea to leeward was white-flecked, and we both looked forward to the moment when the sun would clear the Kandhili Range and bring perhaps some occasional warmth and comfort into what was a dark and glowering scene.

The 3,000 foot crest of Kandhili itself was hidden in cloud just ahead, and beyond that we knew that the peaks of Kalybgi, Strungitza, Drakoturla and Oxyngathos led up to the 4,000 foot high Mount Kurumblia—all within a stretch of about five miles. All these were names which we had bandied between us when studying the chart, but now the moment had come to feel our microscopic way along their bases. No beaches were evident and I was keen to make the bay of Politika some fifteen miles down the coast where I knew this mountain range swung inland to leave a fertile plain along the shore.

We were coasting about a quarter of a mile out, catching the occasional gust of wind that swirled off the land, when a fishing boat nosed from behind a bluff and waved us urgently toward the shore. It was impossible to make sense of their calls, but thinking that it must be a warning of nets laid ahead we closed the rocks to within some fifty yards and immediately lost the wind altogether. Any sailor will know the frustration of trying to make way close under a weather shore, the wind at one moment free, then heading; the next moment gone altogether. If time is important better far to hand all sail and use the engine, but for us this was not the case, and we managed to make the foot of Kandhili without lowering the outboard. It was here, beneath the towering heights of sheer rock that we began to understand exactly what the owner of the ketch had meant when he said, 'It can be pretty fierce under those hills!'

Looking down the ironbound coast ahead we could see across a small bay partly hidden by a bluff of grey cliff. It was calm, black and rather ominous looking and I was just about to start the engine and cut straight across the bay, when we heard what can best be described as a long deep sigh from up above. As we watched, the glossy surface of the bay turned to broken black, then frenzied grey, and finally creamy white as solid sheets of spray lifted off the surface to race in demented fashion out to sea. Then the spray did a horrifying thing. It swirled in a circle and turned back in a howling whirlwind to disappear again behind the bluff! And that was that! The bay returned to its oily black calm and the mountain settled into silence, leaving a horrible feeling of doubt in our minds. To be caught in that microhurricane aboard a decked yacht would probably end in a dismasting: in a dinghy it would be a certain capsize, sails or no sails. I have seen dinghies rolling across the surface of the sea in less wind than I had just witnessed. What made the mouth feel dry was the fact that it had ended up by sweeping back toward the shore.

It was a difficult decision at that moment whether to carry on or return to the comparative safety of the beaches at Limni, but I was not altogether happy anywhere under the lee of these vast hillsides, so we dropped the mizzen and main, keeping the small jib hoisted and the engine running just for good measure in case of difficulties. With both jib halyard and sheet in hand we nosed our way within feet of the cliff base round the bay; and we were not let off lightly! It came again like a herd of elephants that wind, charging down the mountainside with a terrifying roar, bending the pines and hitting the water like a hammer close to leeward. We watched appalled as once more sheets of spray lifted, swept up and commenced to swirl, then rushed back at us with a ferocity that was frightening. The jib flung the bow toward the shore, and before it could be brought down on deck a section of the leach was ragged and torn. The boat was drenched in a driving mist of spray, heeling violently under bare poles, and then it was all over and we were dripping in a flat calm wondering where it had gone. Seaward the surface was a line of white crests, angry and hissing; here under the very chin of the cliffs was an uneasy silence.

That was an eerie coastline. A peculiarity of the rocks in this almost tideless sea is the way they become undercut at water level, eroding over the ages into knobs with thin necks where the constant lapping at the same level has worn the stone away. From a distance, and particularly in the dawn or evening light, this can play tricks with the imagination. Grotesque forms surge toward one, faces peer from dark grottoes and the slap and chatter of the wavelets lends them ghostly whispering voices.

They make a hazardous shore for some of the ridges and crags are razor sharp and hollowed into fantastic shapes which would pulverise any craft trying to make a landing. So it was trying work for the next mile or so, rock-hopping to clear the violent squalls, knowingly risking the underwater spikes. But it was Hobson's choice if we were to carry on.

Once clear of Kurumblia however, we felt the worst was over. What wind did hit us now came mostly from off the shore so we got the main on her and soon emerged from under that cloud-crowned range into the midday sun, arriving off the village of Politika by early afternoon. Here we stretched the soaking gear from the boat on a sandy beach to dry before basking in the welcome heat ourselves.

One of the joys of this nomadic existence is the constant variety of atmosphere each hour brings. After the Wagnerian overtones of Kandhili it was rather like floating through a soothing Beethoven Symphony to let one's eyes range over that verdant hinterland. From our point on the secluded beach we could see, rising above the tops of the olive trees about half a mile inland, the red stone of a square tower. Sounds from the village in that area came lazily floating down on the warm northerly breeze: the bleat of a goat and the occasional goat bell, the call of a shepherd now and again the strident note of a radio. We decided to call it a day and remain there for the night so, with the approach of evening, we wandered inland. Here was a marked contrast to the rocky scrub and pine covered hillsides of the Sporadhes and the northern areas of this inland channel. We walked through fields of wheat, which had been cut by hand, the stubble standing in irregular patches of varying height, and we soon came across a well from which water had evidently been channelled for irrigation in the past. It was no longer in use, but the mechanism was still in working order. A chain of buckets passed over a wheel which was turned by a simple gearing from a centre windlass. This in turn was rotated by a crude beam just like a windlass bar. The outer end was worn thin from years of chafing by the donkey. Down this coast we saw many of these wells, and indeed washed often in their brackish water, but never saw the original mechanism being used. Instead a petrol operated portable pump would be brought discharging into the ditch or concrete runnels constructed for the irrigation. The gaudy plastic pipes, when of no further use, lay like alien snakes in the ditches.

A dusty road led through the olive groves toward the sounds of the village, and in the evening light we walked to find a taverna. There is always one taverna at least in a village in Greece, frequently two or three, and we often wondered how such small communities could support them all. Politika was no exception. The covered roofing above the tables—woven from pampas grass fronds overlaid with long grass—came into view with its wooden straight backed chairs and square tables, some of them bare wood, others covered in oilcloth. Just beside the door of the taverna stood a metal cabin with a large open front rather like an ice-cream kiosk but black with smoke from countless fires. Inside this was a large tray of charcoal with an iron griddle above. Chickens clucked and ferreted between the table legs and there was a profusion of cats. No fence or boundary stood between the road and the table area, and indeed throughout Greece we had noticed that fences appeared to be used solely to protect crops from the goats and not from any desire for personal privacy. In fact, in the villages, to erect a barrier around one's house would be considered unneighbourly.

'May we eat,' we asked the rather dishevelled proprietor in what we hoped was passable Greek. He made signs for us to go within, and from a metal meat-box hanging on the wall removed some atrocious looking sections of bloody flesh from which the flies rose in a cloud. It did not appeal and I asked if there was any fish on the menu. There was not. We could have omelettes and, of course, the eternal tomato salad—chopped tomatoes with a liberal soaking of olive oil—but we were hungry and despite the flies settled for the meat. It was an experience to watch it being cooked, sitting at a table adjacent to the griddle cabin in which the proprietor's wife was already lighting the charcoal fire. With a pair of bellows she coaxed the black sticks into a red glow, then placed the meat on the grid above. We drank an ouzo while it toasted and dripped, the gorgeous smell wafting to us with the smoke. Chips were frying on a bottled gas stove inside the taverna. The meal was delicious; we had no idea what cut or section of the goat or sheep it was, but despite the flies it appealed wonderfully to our palates, and the carafe of lightly resinated local wine made a good accompaniment.

It was moonlight when we strolled back down the shadowed road and struck across to the boat again, taking our bearings from a solitary cypress tree that stood guard over the irrigation well.

At noon next day we were passing under the bridge joining Evvia to the mainland at Halkis, spewed through the narrows by a six-knot tidal stream. We didn't even need to lower the mast in our cockleshell.

*   *   *

It was on the evening of the 13th July, having spent our first day coasting down the north shore of the Euripo Channel just south of Halkis, that we anchored off what we always now refer to as the 'haunted beach'. It was an unnerving experience. *Lugworm* was anchored as usual just off shore with a stern line made fast to the roots of a bush, and we had settled comfortably into our sleeping bags on the beach, the supper fire having died to a feeble glow. There was no moon, but the stars gave a very faint light, just enough to distinguish water from land, with the boat a black shadow about fifteen yards out.

The first splash came from some distance along the shore, and I remember thinking it must have been a large fish to make that amount of noise in the water. The next splash was much closer, alongside *Lugworm* in fact, and it did not sound at all like the disturbance a fish makes when jumping clear of the surface to flop back again. I sat up and listened. There was no sound; the night was as silent as the grave and there was not a breath of wind. The third splash was in the water right in front of us, a few feet off the beach, and was obviously caused by a fairly large stone pitching in. B. sat up in alarm. I was already out of my sleeping bag and drawing on some woollens for it was quite chill. 'Somebody's having fun and games with stones,' I said to B., 'and I don't like it at all. They must be up on the bank behind us—I'm going to see. You get under that thick bush and keep quiet because this is a stupid prank. If one of those stones hits you in the eye it could blind you, and whoever it is they can't possibly see exactly where we are, so they're throwing with pot luck anyway.'

I grabbed the heavy brass diver's torch, moved away from the sleeping bags and B., then switched it on and scanned the bank behind us. There was no sign of anyone and no sound. 'Ahoy there!' I shouted. A stone landed on the beach a few feet away. By now I was angry and not a little alarmed. I switched off the torch, since whoever was responsible would be able to aim at the light if he really was trying to hit us—and it was difficult to conceive any other purpose in this ridiculous game—and ran swiftly up the beach so as to put him off the track, shouting to B. to keep quite still and not to worry: I was going after this nutcase whoever it was. I ran up the grassy bank behind the beach on to a stubble field beyond, then stood quite still with the torch switched off, listening for any slight sound that would reveal the idiot's position, but there was none. Then came a thud farther into the field a little to my right. It was a nasty feeling, standing there not knowing whether at any moment a lump of rock would knock one's brains in. What puzzled me was the fact that I had heard no sound of the act of throwing. The night was so quiet that any movement such as the effort required to pitch a heavy stone would surely have resulted in a slight shuffling of the feet, the noise of a jacket flapping, or even the actual swish of the stone travelling through the air might have been discernible in the total silence. Only the heavy thud of the thing landing. And then a peculiarity struck me: if a stone is thrown, when it lands it generally rolls a short distance. If you happen to catch sight of it you will have a good indication of the direction from which it's come. That stone that had just landed to my right had not rolled at all. That meant it had fallen almost vertically, which indicated that the thrower was a good distance away, having to pitch it high. This was even more alarming, for it meant that any accuracy of aim could be discounted. Like pattern bombing, the stone might land anywhere: he was evidently throwing quite blind, for visibility was no more than a few feet.

It was a perplexing situation. If I moved, my own position would become apparent by the sound. If I switched on the torch the same applied. My only hope was to stay completely still, hope that B. would do the same down on the beach, and listen alertly for him to reveal his position by some slight movement. Minutes passed, long minutes of complete silence in which I tried to even muffle my breathing. Then another dull thud came from a few feet away in the stubble. Again the stone did not roll.

Before turning in that night B. and I had taken a short walk through the stubble field back into the hinterland to try and locate what the chart marked as an 'ancient road enclosed by long rails'. We had failed to find any such thing, but had been able to get a fair idea of the terrain. We always liked to do this before turning in, just so as to have an idea of the type of country we were in. At one side of this stubble field we had walked through scrub grass alongside a shallow irrigation ditch, and as far as I could remember there was the odd shrub and a small tree on that side. On the other side of the field I remembered seeing uncultivated land of barren rock and scrub hawthorn bushes—not the place to venture into on a pitch black night. I decided that if anyone had quietly approached our camp it was more than likely to have been via the irrigation ditch, which was dry, rather than through the difficult terrain on the other side, and certainly not along the beach itself for anyone walking on the pebbles would have given themselves away some distance off. The last stone to fall had landed between me and the ditch, so very quietly and with the torch still switched off I picked my way over the uneven surface of the stubble, careful not to twist an ankle on the stones and rubble which is typical of most tilled soil in this country. Another thud hammered to the right of me, toward the centre of the field. I switched on the torch, sending the beam toward the sound in the hope of seeing some hint of the type of stone, or even a thistle stalk still vibrating. Nothing. A stone landed with another thud a few feet to my left.

By now I was in that peculiar state where fright leaves one no alternative but to be very angry. I ran full pelt for the ditch, scanning the stubble with the powerful beam, picking out shrubs and tussocks, blundering across the difficult ground and roaring as I did so, in the hope that whoever was hiding there would be persuaded to run, or move—anything to give himself away. I reached the ditch and turned inland, following our tracks of the evening, and eventually ended up at the boundary field. Beyond that was uncultivated land with patches of bare rock and the odd shrub. I had seen no one. It was pointless to go further. Again I stood quite still, feeling a prize fool at the noise I had been making, feeling also particularly vulnerable since whoever was out there in the blackness would again without doubt be well aware of my exact position.

There were two more thuds, one close after the other, about twenty feet away. Then a far more alarming thought came to me. I was now at least three hundred yards from the beach, and considerably farther away from the point at which the first stone had splashed into the sea. How far can a man throw a stone? The blessed things were following me around, and I was quite certain that nothing had moved in the area for I have acute hearing, especially in a situation like this!

It was all so eerie that I had to keep a tight hold on my reasoning. Stones just don't fall out of the sky ... or do they? The whole situation reminded me alarmingly of another event which took place in broad daylight many years before when giving sailing instruction to two girls in a dinghy in North Cornwall. We were beating into a brisk wind slap in the centre of a wide estuary far from shore when there was a terrific 'thwack' on the foredeck of the boat, immediately followed by a metallic clang as a stone, which had dropped with enough force to deeply indent the thick marine ply ricocheted off the metal mast and hit one of the pupils over the right eye, cutting deeply. It was so unaccountable that it was ridiculous. We were far enough off shore to preclude any thought of the stone being thrown, but there, lying on the bottom-boards of the boat, was the stone itself—a grey beach pebble about four inches long and a couple of inches wide, flattish and with rounded edges. Too big for any normal catapult to manage. We made for the shore to get the wound dealt with, and came to the conclusion that some high-flying bird must have been carrying it in its beak and let it drop: unlikely enough, but what other explanation?

This occurrence came to mind as I walked back across that black field, expecting at any moment to be brained as I went. Back at the beach, B. was waiting anxiously, and it didn't help matters to have to report absolutely nothing tangible except that stones were falling from the sky. Further sleep on the beach was out of the question: imagine lying there in the blackness knowing that at any moment a rock may land on you! We packed up the sleeping bags, bundled everything aboard and anchored about two hundred yards off shore.

It seemed the safest thing to do, but there was a quite idiotic feeling in my mind that those stones, whatever they were, were just as likely to come from vertically above the sea as the land!

We heard no more, and it remains one of the mysteries of my life. But it was gone two o'clock on the following morning before we were quietly turned in again, and neither of us was sorry, with the first light of dawn, to get under way by engine for there was not a breath of wind, and push on to Eretria.

CHAPTER IV

The Cyclades, the Meltemi and Tourism

WE HAD NOTED THAT THE COAST OF EVVIA became progressively more barren as we moved southward, olives giving way to patches of wheat and then more and more bare rock and areas of parched brown earth with scrub. So it was a pleasant change to reach the little group of Petali Islands from which the gulf at the south end of the Euripo Channel gets its name and find them thickly wooded. They were in strong contrast to the Evvia coast around Karistos which lies at the head of a wide bay. We coasted down before a fickle northerly, sweltering in the July heat, and spent a night anchored off Karistos, then ran on before a freshening north-wester which was becoming too much to handle by the time we reached Mandili Island at the extreme south-east tip of Evvia. Hugging the coast for as much lee as was obtainable we beat up to a tiny deep bay where a splendid white shingle beach beckoned us in. There was no road, and little sign of human life in what was evidently, at a cooler time of the year, a well cultivated valley, and we spent three days there walking the wild and untamed hills on either side, waiting for a period of thundery squalls and fresh wind to abate.

By now you may be sure we had developed a healthy regard for the meltemi, for we had often watched it turn the sea close off shore to a cauldron of foaming white around midday. The time to move was from dawn until about noon, but it was wise to have a safe refuge in hand from ten-thirty onward. So it was not from choice, but of necessity that we set off at four in the morning to reach across to Andros Island, seven miles to the south-east. The channel between this island and Evvia is noted for its violent winds and treacherous seas, being subject to strong currents also, and though for us the crossing might be expected to take a mere two hours at most it was lucky we started so early. By five-thirty, with the island a black silhouette against the luminous eastern sky, the wind was already well in its stride and freshening by the minute. We freed off to the run just west of a prominent point, glad to find a slight lee from the rapidly mounting swell and breaking seas. Under full sail *Lugworm* winged along, surfing down the advancing faces, and by six-thirty we found a perfect lee on rounding up into a deep little cove.

After three days so far from civilisation, human contact becomes welcome even to such semi-recluses as us. Roused from our noon siesta on the hot beach by the sound of splashing, I saw a schnorkel tube approaching, the usual flippered assistance behind, and watched as it ploughed its way round the sweep of the bay. I took a keener interest when a shapely brown form in a bikini reared up and removed the pair of underwater goggles.

Dark eyes in an impish face crowned with long glossy hair blinked at us. White teeth flashed. 'Herete,' I saluted her with the lovely noonday greeting 'Be Happy', to be met with a short and unintelligible reply in Greek. 'English,' B. indicated with the usual sign language. But I didn't want the contact to end there, so holding aloft the wine flask I offered a drink. There was some reticence, but at that moment a short and portly black figure hove in sight at the far end of the beach, and Adorable—for such I shall call her—beckoned for it to approach. We were introduced to Grandma, a small apple faced old woman with leathery skin, sparkling brown eyes and dressed in the traditional peasant outfit of black shoes, loose black skirt and bodice, with a white scarf over her head and tied under her chin.

A characteristic of all the country folk we came across—and a very endearing one to us with our almost complete lack of privacy in the small open boat—was a well mannered and courteous reticence when it came to assuaging their lively curiosity. None of the boorish standing, staring and talking over we have experienced in other countries, our own included. A very real curiosity there always was, but it was never until we had made signs that conversation was welcome that the questions would flow fast and free. It wasn't long before Adorable and her Grandma knew exactly where we had come from and how, our respective ages, whether we were married, whether we had any children and where we were going to, and why, and what we proposed doing in this bay. We got along famously, for it's astonishing how much can be communicated by sign language and an obvious goodwill on either side. We collected wood together for a fire, and Grandma gathered dry grass from the top of the beach to make a mattress against the hard pebbles. Coffee—thick, black and very sweet Greek fashion—was soon brewing, and during this time there was much chuckling and chiding in progress between the old woman and the girl. I couldn't tell you how it came about, with our pathetic efforts at their language, and their total ignorance of ours, but somehow the girl made us aware that Grandma had that afternoon, after great resistance, been persuaded to join her in a swim. In fact, ready for the event she had already donned a brand new swim-suit, presented by Adorable that very morning. Over this she had put the copious and modest peasant regalia for the walk down to the water. Our unexpected presence there in this out-of-the-way bay had proved a surprise, for she had forthwith coyly withdrawn despite all arguments from her granddaughter. The girl, however, had not yet given up hope, and seeking to enlist our help in bringing her plan to fruition, lifted the corner of Grannie's skirt to reveal—before that worthy's protesting squawk ended the matter—the white frilled edge of a splendid pink swimsuit.

It was obvious that inhibitions had to be loosened. I waded aboard for the bottle of three star cognac. Grannie's eyebrows went up, and Adorable chuckled with glee. B. was getting on splendidly with the sweet old dear, and out of courtesy we gave them the toast 'stin iyia sas': your health. After that, communication—I can hardly call it conversation—loosened considerably. Adorable stretched out her delicious sun-tanned form and sighed contentedly; Grannie untied the head shawl displaying a crop of snow-white hair. B. filled up the coffee cups again and I replenished the cognac. We learned, drowsily there looking up at the incredibly blue sky, that Adorable had been married the previous year and her husband built houses.

They owned two donkeys and a black goat, and came down to the beach daily to tend their small field behind the bay where they had a stone croft. We were in that happy state where sleep lies just round the corner, enjoying the warmth, the soporific sigh of the waves on the shingle at our feet, and the company when a splutter caused B. to raise herself on one elbow. The old lady was lying with her feet up the beach, her head awash, smiling and spluttering happily as the little waves licked at her hair. Grannie had succumbed!

With a shriek of infectious laughter Adorable clutched the old woman by the feet and pulled. We managed between us to swing her head back up the beach, and she was rolling about with delight at what was evidently to the two of them a hilarious joke.

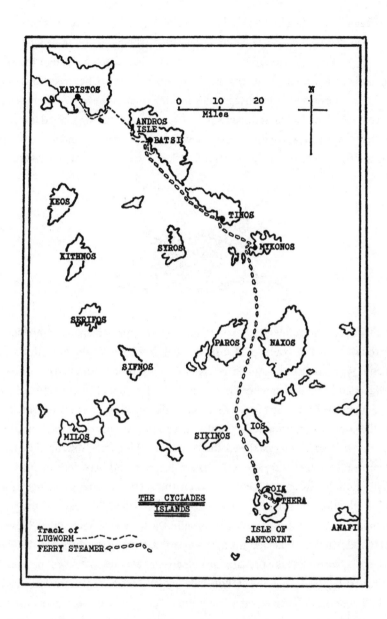

KARISTOS

0   10   20
Miles

N

ANDROS
ISLE

BATSI

KEOS

TINOS

SYROS

MYKONOS

KITHNOS

SERIFOS

PAROS   NAXOS

SIFNOS

MILOS

SIKINOS

IOS

THE CYCLADES
ISLANDS

OIA
THERA

ANAFI

ISLE OF
SANTORINI

Track of
LUGWORM
FERRY STEAMER

'We must get the old dear safely back to her field,' I said to B. I wish you could have seen that comic cavalcade progressing along the beach. Grannie was just capable of walking, but certainly not in a straight line. Adorable found the whole situation so unbearably funny that B. and I were drowned in her infectious mirth.

Back at the field Grannie disappeared inside a small stone hut. Adorable chased the goat which had a line trailing from its front leg, and having pinned the animal down, promptly milked it into a rusty tin which she then presented to us. We hastily made signs that we would take it back to the boat, and it was while thanking the

girl that B. choked suddenly, then spat out a grasshopper which had jumped inside her mouth! That of course had Adorable helpless with laughter again, but now Grannie was calling us inside the hut. It had a single room with a bed on which was a blanket and a donkey saddle. There was one rickety chair, and bunches of sweet smelling herbs lay in the corner. Grannie, still chuckling, was trying to take the lid off a coffee tin, not to prepare coffee, but to present us with some small green fruits which had been crystallised and stored in a thick treacly syrup. The colour of unripe olives, they were about the size of cherries, and were delicious.

Adorable's husband now appeared on the scene, leading a donkey, and after introductions all round we were escorted back along the beach by the family, Grannie having by this time sobered up sufficiently to walk unattended, bless her, and B. rode on the donkey. At the boat we parted, they up the track into the village in the hills, we back to the preparations for an evening meal. At dawn the next day, in the first light, we weighed and reached out of the bay, but as we cast our eyes back, there on the beach stood a small round figure in black, her arms raised and her dress blowing in the wind like some character out of a Greek chorus. Grannie was wishing us 'bon voyage'.

It was a wet sail that morning from the small off-lying islands outside Gavrion harbour along to Batsi. Already the wind had reached force four to five, rising as usual as the sun got higher. We put into Batsi, shopped and filled the water cans, then stowed the boat for sea. It was evident from the chart that the coastline south of Batsi was more inhospitable. It showed only rocky indentations with low cliffs and few beaches, but there was one long beach at Paleopolis where an ancient submerged mole was marked. Because of our usual abhorrence of sleeping in the open boat bang in the middle of a harbour, as soon as the wind began to ease as expected around five o'clock, we decided to carry on into a more secluded anchorage behind Cape Thiakon two and a half miles down the coast. It was the worst decision I made during the whole trip.

We cleared the entrance of the harbour to run southward under full sail. Half an hour later, just north of the cape, the wind unaccountably freshened from the northwest and we dropped the mizzen, reefed the main and sped on in style with small jib, happy that the bay behind the cape would provide an excellent lee for the night. But I was worried about that wind. Before we were under the cliffs at the foot of the cape it was all of force five to six and rising fast—an ominous state of affairs! Being in no mood for heroics we handed all sail and started the Mercury, nosing close in under the cliff so as to round the headland as soon as possible. It was then the drama began.

Obviously the meltemi had thrown the book of rules overboard. To the northwest—back towards Batsi Harbour—two and a half miles of seething white breakers were bearing down on us. To the north-east—up into the bay behind the cape—was a maelstrom of black and white fury. To weather of this, towering three thousand two hundred odd feet sheer into the sky, the top of Mount Kouvarion disappeared into ragged fronds of fast-moving black cloud, while southeastward across the span of the bay the wind and sea had begun to scream in a demented fashion. It was one of those situations you laugh about. Afterwards.

Nothing quickens the blood like good honest fear. Short of spending a stormy night on nodding terms with a hundred foot cliff which gave an unhappy lee under the cape, it was obvious that all stops had to be pulled out to make the shore up there at the foot of the mountain. We unshipped the mizzen mast and raised the centreplate to lessen windage and reduce drag, opening the throttle full and keeping the lugger dead into the eye of the wind. It took us three-quarters of an hour to make the shore under Kouvarion and the world had grown dark and ominous with that hideous racing cloud boiling over the peaks above.

We had spotted the long shingly beach at Paleopolis toward the eastern end of the bay, and I hoped the submerged mole might give some protection from a nasty ground swell which was developing. Inching along within feet of the shoreline we nursed the thin ribbon of comparatively calm water in the lee. Alas, that mole is one of those romantic archaeological remains, but there was nothing romantic about my language when I realised that it wasn't submerged at all but just breaking surface in the troughs of the swell. To my reckoning the wind was now touching force eight: sucked in a vast natural venturi action down the side of that towering lump of hate above us, Kouvarion.

To make the beach, we just had to go off shore round the southern end of that mole. Gingerly we eased down to leeward, keeping bow to wind and making sternway with the throttle eased. It was tricky, for the sea a few yards out was now thrashed into sheets of driven spray, and for fear of engine failure I dare not lower the mainmast to further reduce windage. I dread to think what might have befallen had the engine failed at that moment, for I firmly believe that the boat would have foundered within minutes had we drifted back into that maelstrom. When clear of the breaking end of the mole I opened the engine full again and slowly made up once more to the shore, B. lying flat along the foredeck with the twelve pound anchor ready to fling.

Then came the cruellest stroke of all. The beach—that of it which had been visible from a distance—was indeed shingle. But from a position a few feet to leeward I could see below the waterline, and there like a row of broken teeth, jagged tops of rocks were just touching surface with each drawback of the swell. Any attempt to beach was out of the question.

It is in moments like this that one wonders why the hell anyone puts to sea in small boats. I cursed myself for the fool I was to have left Batsi Harbour with its lights and tavernas and comfortable security, a sentiment I had no reason to doubt that B. endorsed. She let go the anchor and veered about forty feet of warp but it didn't hold. I hardly expected it to with that fury of wind but it gave us a chance to take stock of the situation. While working our way along the shore we had earlier

seen a tiny beach at the western end of the bay. Any thought of going eastward of
that mole was out of the question for it was an impossible coast. I knew that small
beach was our only hope before dark—and it meant going back round that mole! I
looked seaward with a sick feeling to where the fury waited for us, and signed for
B. to start weighing the anchor again; speech was impossible above that din.

It was then, clear above the roar, that I heard the clarion call of a horn. It
came echoing down from somewhere up the mountain, and for both of us its
warning note commanded immediate attention. It seemed, in that chaos of the
elements, that the Gods themselves were sending a warning against the action
I was about to take! And for me it had a special significance, for I had heard
that very note once in my life before. Up in the silent heights of the Himalayas,
that identical hollow trumpeting had saved not my life, but that of a friend
with whom I was out riding. I balanced there in the boat with an odd tingling
in my spine, and cocked my head sideways trying to locate the source of the
sound. My unseeing eyes ranged along the shore westward. It was not repeated, but it was not necessary: as my mind concentrated once more on what
my two eyes were seeing I realised that I was looking directly at the foot of
the mole where it joined the beach. And there, for a distance of about twenty
feet from the beach, the swell was not breaking. I watched trough after trough
surge back frothing over the mole but not once at that point did it show any
broken water. It was evident that there was a breach in the man-made wall—a
breach through which, with luck, we could pass without the need to skirt back
round the southern end.

We made it. The tumbled boulders of the mole were visible a foot or so down
in the dark angry water but we got the propeller across without contact and the
boat with it to continue working desperately back along the shore.

Our relief at getting the boat safely on to that beach cannot be described but
there was no time for rest. A dangerous ground swell was developing and we had
to get the boat ashore fast. Nine hundred pounds dead weight isn't easy to drag,
but with nobody to hinder us on this occasion, we hooked an anchor behind a
crag, rigged a threefold tackle, and with the aid of a long surge up the beach got
her high if not dry, with bow to seaward. Then we looked around. The beach was
only a few yards long with great crags of rock at either end and backed by a fifty-

foot cliff. This was our saving, for the wind was searing over the top to hammer down on the sea a few yards out. Apart from the odd unexpected backlash it left us in comparative peace. What cheered us was the sight of two small caves at the foot of the cliff, and driftwood galore. We made a kitchen of one cave and a bedroom of the other with equipment from the boat, lighting a brushwood fire to keep out the cold and raise our spirits.

I wish I could convey the sheer power of the wind that night. It thundered like a sonorous organ note down the mountainside, hammering vertically on to the tormented sea. About three in the morning it was augmented by a thunderstorm and torrents of rain. Dawn of the first day ashore brought a hideous grey light that made our world look as if it had been whipped, and with it came a sight I have never seen before nor since. About a quarter of a mile off shore the sea was rising up in a level sheet of white spray. For a height of some ten to fifteen feet above the surface this blanket of driven spume raced out into those empty wastes of wind-torn water, and it screamed as it went.

This maelstrom of fury is known locally as the 'white tempest' and it blew without break for four days. Later we learned that the excessive fury of wind probably extended only a mile or so off shore before easing to a normal near gale in the open sea. For us it was an awe-inspiring time. We clambered up one side of the low cliff and broke through on to the waste scrub land. A goat track led upwards, and we fought against the wind like a solid wall of force, to make our way some thousand feet up the hillside to where the road from Gavrion to the capital of Andros on the other side of the island passed above us. There was a cistern with pure sweet water from a spring about half way up and we filled the water canisters from this, and thankfully washed ourselves and our dirty clothes.

During that moment of chaos while trying to beach by the ancient mole farther along the bay I had caught sight of a large white rock just on the waterline half buried, or more correctly half exposed. Even at that hectic moment I had made a mental note that it might be worth investigating for there was something about that rock that looked remarkably like marble. The next morning, we battled our way over the bluffs and scrubland round the bay back to the mole. There, protruding out of the beach larger than life size, was the headless trunk of a marble statue. I scratched away the shingle from beneath it and using two stout chunks of timber that had been washed ashore levered it up. It ended at the knees: a robed figure of a man, the lines of the carving softened by the ceaseless erosion of the beach. It must have weighed close on a ton, and nearby was the square pedestal base. It was an exciting moment—one of the more romantic things I'd always wanted to do was to dig up a genuine Greek statue, and here it was—a reality! We photographed it, and nearly killed ourselves when the crude shoring timbers broke, letting the great headless thing fall back in its hole. I couldn't tear myself away from it—but what can one do with a ton of marble in a dinghy?

Finally we left it forlorn on the beach, and though we reported its presence to everyone who might conceivably be interested nobody cared a toot; I suppose it was like enthusing about coal in Newcastle. We learned that Paleopolis was the site of the ancient capital of the island, and indeed up the valley path were ruins of the old houses. Heaven knows why the ancients chose such an inhospitable spot to make their capital with its small harbour.

During our rambling round Andros we were fascinated by the method used on the island of building the stone walls which form dividing boundaries to the land. The walls were built by piling the large uncut rocks on top of one another in the normal rough way seen everywhere in the islands, but every four feet or so a large flat stone would be placed on edge like a tombstone, held in position by the adjacent thick wall. This gave a very odd appearance, and of course is done so as to economise in stone, for that one large slab so placed did the work of many smaller rocks. Another peculiarity of these dry stone walls throughout Greece is the habit of placing a thick layer of dry twigs, thorn and broom along the top so that they project either side. They are weighted down with heavy stones against the wind and form an effective barrier against sheep and goats jumping over.

Our enforced stay here made us realise that if caught between the islands in a small boat in this sort of wind the end would be a foregone conclusion. If we were to continue among the Cyclades in *Lugworm* we would have to be prepared to tackle open water spanning some thirty miles and more at a time. The speed with which the recent gale had come up—just when the normal behaviour of the wind persuaded me to put to sea—and the fact that the barometer had given no clue to the approaching change in the weather reluctantly decided me against continuing southward into the teeth of the meltemi playground. I could still hear the words of our friend at Volos: 'I have seen forty-foot fishing craft running for shelter at Mykonos!' Now I believed him!

When the wind abated we put back into Batsi and left *Lugworm* in the charge of a hoary old fisherman. Next day we caught the inter-island steamer bound for Santorini which lies just north of Crete. A friend of a friend had a cave dwelling there which she had offered us. We were ready for a change from the dinghy!

*   *   *

So, on the 29th July, we became tourists in the accepted sense of the word, dependent on normal transport systems and with our belongings suspended between us in the sail bag. After over a month living with the freedom of the boat, it was a new experience having to check into hotels again and study time-tables.

One of the peculiarities of the Aegean inter-island shipping lines is their complete non-cooperation with one another. This extends, in direct contradiction of the natural Greek hospitality, to a refusal on the part of a booking agent to divulge times or even the existence of a competitive line which may well be running a ship to the same island and frequently at the same time. Enquiries will elicit the simple answer: 'I don't know.'

Tourist—do your own sleuthing! We checked that no ship calling at Santorini (which is the Italian name for the Greek island of Thera) operated from Batsi. Gavrion, the larger port just to the north was, however the calling point for the motor vessel Μεγαλόχαρη which could take us to Tinos. The voyage took two and a half hours down the incredibly rocky southern shores of Andros and Tinos islands, and watching it from the deck of this ship we were happy not to have attempted this part of the cruise in *Lugworm* during the period of the meltemi. No small beaches appeared—just craggy points and coves, with the wind funnelling down the mountainsides as it had under Paleopolis, though with somewhat less force. Indeed these Cyclades islands are nothing more than the sun parched peaks of hills burnt like the top of a bald head poking out of the water.

By the time we had reached the narrow channel between the two islands the wind had fallen light, and our entry into the port of Tinos was effected in a baking heat such as we had not so far experienced. The cathedral—a square cream building of huge dimensions, looking rather like a yellow wedding cake—dominated the town, but alas, our connecting boat to Mykonos left within half an hour of our landing, so we had no time to investigate this Lourdes of Greece.

The motor vessel ΑΠΟΛΛΩΝ (Apollo) sped us to Mykonos, a voyage of less than one hour. Here the ships cannot berth in the shallow harbour but lie off, discharging the passengers and cargo into fishing boats. I do not propose to dwell on our two days in this centre of the tourist route. The beaches were scrofulous with humanity living rough and sleeping on the sand and rocks making large sections of the island disreputable. The more private grottoes when sought out stank with sewage. Tempers were frayed and the buses were a constant opportunity for a free fight with no holds barred. Many of the visitors looked dirty and the shops were crammed with tourist knick-knacks. The only redeeming impression I hold of this place was the equable temper of the tourist police who under a continuous onslaught of queries somehow managed to organise the hordes of perplexed tourists into their appropriate niches. It was a relief to board the motor vessel ΜΙΑΟΥΛΗΣ bound for Santorini, and as we headed south, straight through the channel between Naxos and Paros, Sikinos and Ios, we pondered again the value of independent travel.

I have long held the opinion that the only civilised way to move about is either by small boat or on foot, or perhaps by horse drawn caravan. This is because I know that the true flavour of arrival can only be gained after a slow savouring of the journey. It is just here, I am sure, that twentieth century man denies himself one of the greatest joys of living. The vacuum of transition spent in the fuselage of a supersonic jet merely destroys, not enhances, the adventure of travel. How can the soul possibly adjust itself to the psychic leucotomy occasioned by embarking on a plane in London fog, to disgorge a quick perplexity later into the baking heat of the tropics? This is not travel—it is brain washing. No wonder we take to narcotics!

So I mused, leaning on the warm and gently vibrating gun-wale of *Miaoulis*, lulled by her purring engines and a soothing knowledge that for a brief period anyway responsibility for the voyage was out of my hands. I looked back along the bleached deck where the white lifeboats were cradled in their davits, past the ensign staff with its striped blue and white Greek flag, over the taffrail and out down the path of the dissolving wake to where, smoke blue in a world of blue light the floating outlines of Naxos and Paros trembled on the brink of oblivion. We strolled to the bows. Somewhere there ahead, across this flat wavery mirage of light, was Santorini. Legendary, sleeping uneasily with its history of unparalleled disaster, she would in a few hours conjure herself out of the haze, tremble on the brink of perception and then materialise into ... what?

A written introduction to a caretaker provided by the friend who owned a 'hole in the cliff six hundred feet above the sea' to quote her own words, was our sole reason for nosing down to this forgotten dot in the blue wastes of the Mediterranean. A hole in a cliff fascinated us particularly since, to quote the friend's words again, 'you may have to saw your way in through the door: we haven't been near the place for two years! When you reach the village of Oia,' the letter continued, 'ask for the Americano—he is the only person in the village who speaks any English, and he will take you to Mr P. the caretaker.' Imagination had begun to play, but I can truly say that no imagination can begin to conjure up the actuality. To approach Santorini on the deck of a small ship in the baking heat of an August afternoon and watch as the island appears, is to float from reality straight into the realms of fantasy. Many accounts have been written about this unique place which is the remains of a volcano believed to have exploded with frightful carnage about 1500 BC. We had read some of them and I recalled that photograph I had so provocatively left with B. on the lounge floor some months ago in that other life back home. But no photograph can convey its grandeur as you enter the crater.

Two sections of the colossal circular rim have subsided, leaving an entrance to the crater at the north and south-west sides. The outer edge of the island slopes more or less gently down to the shoreline, but as the ship nosed her way through the northern channel we saw for the first time the towering volcanic cliffs of clinker and pumice dropping almost vertically into the deep blue of the flooded bowl: in places a sheer thousand feet or more. We began to have a terrifying idea of the power of this explosion in the earth's crust which had blown to heaven some eighty square kilometres of the island's centre and sunk beneath the sea vast areas of its outer plains. Black, brown, russet, grey and cream, the layers pile on top of one another in a huge cross section of the earth's crust, capped here and there with a dazzling line of white like icing on a chocolate cake. These are the villages, all of them bearing the scars of continuing earth tremors.

First view of Oia – Isle of Santorini

As we rounded the northern tip of the main island with the smaller isle of Thirassia to the west, *Miaoulis* sounded her siren three times. The echoes reverberated back and forth and from somewhere ashore we heard a faint answering blast. Atop the cliffs we could make out tiny figures standing on rooftops. They were waving white sheets, and as we watched, a brilliant light was reflected from a mirror being used as a heliograph by some relative perhaps of one of the crew. There was a sense of great occasion. Indeed, the arrival of these ships is a moment to be celebrated for they form the life link of all these islands.

B., leaning against the rail alongside me, voiced the question uppermost in my own mind. 'How on earth are we going to get up there?' There is no harbour at Thera, unless one calls the entire bowl of the crater a vast natural harbour. The ship stopped her engines, and with more resounding blasts on her siren drifted gently towards the base of the towering dark cliffs. Directly beneath the village, up the near vertical face, we could see a thin zig-zag of white. Was it a road or just a pathway? There seemed to be no traffic on it. With a rattle of chains the gangway clattered down and one of the boats which had come from the tiny quay nosed alongside. Twenty or so figures surged up the gangway, bags were dumped on deck and amid a tremendous hubbub of greetings, farewells and general chatter, a handful of us tumbled down the gangway and pitched into the caique. As we chugged towards the quay there came another blast from the ship behind us. *Miaoulis* was already on her way, a green and white slash curving from her stern like a comet trail in the deep blue black of the water.

No sooner were we alongside the small concrete quay than an islander in blue jeans, open shirt and cloth cap made a dive at us. 'You want mulo?' I looked around: there were certainly no cars nor road. The other passengers were milling around and there didn't seem to be many mules either. I glanced up the cliff face to where the tiny white houses were dancing in a mirage of heat and suddenly realised that both of us were already dripping with sweat.

'How much?'

'Twenty-five drachs.'

A rapid calculation: that was about thirty new pence and it seemed ridiculously cheap for the two of us. 'Yes,' I said and I saw a look of horror pass over B.'s face. 'There isn't any alternative,' I shouted to her above the din. 'If we don't take a mule now we mightn't get the chance, and I can't see us carrying this bag and the typewriter up there!'

The muleteer was signalling impatiently for us to follow him, evidently hoping to work in a couple of trips if we moved fast. Two moth-eaten mules and a tiny donkey were separated from a motley collection at the back of the quay. I have ridden horses in my life but it was many years ago and the last time will never fade from my memory. On that occasion I ended up between the animal's front legs, my arms desperately wrapped around its neck while it took a low fence. It is not my forte. To my knowledge B. had never before approached a horse nearer than its kicking distance.

But two of the shaggy and long despaired animals were duly mounted if that is how one can describe the act and our bag and typewriter were lashed athwart the third. It was then we began to appreciate the sole remaining pleasure in the lives of these hopeless but devilish creatures—that of pretending at every twist of the ascending steps to pitch nose ears and scrofulous tail headlong into eternity—human cargo and all. What an ascent! B. athwart her diminutive mount was a little nearer to the ground, and apart from a detectable change in colour and a rapid enquiry for a taverna on arrival at the top, managed the ascent fairly well. But my charger—to dignify it by the name—was a few hands nearer to instant death. There was nothing to be done about it; one put a blind faith in the sure footedness of these despised creatures and prayed. It was a horrendous twenty minutes of buffeting and scraping of legs against the rocky cliff face, with sudden bowel shaking lurches toward the low parapet separating us from the void below. But we got there. It cost twenty-five drachmas each animal but it was worth it just to get off the poor things.

The village, which is the island capital, had retired to rest in the heat of the afternoon, the snow white of its houses lying like a blinding sheet which hurt the eyes. Flies began to take an interest so we dripped into the first bar we found open and enquired about getting to Oia. It was a Sunday and there was no bus but a taxi caught us for eighty drachmas, and after a twenty-minute drive across the shoulders and precipices of this magnificent ash heap arrived at a dead end in Oia. We disgorged opposite a deserted taverna in a dusty open space and the taxi disappeared back along the track in a cloud of dust. There was not a soul in sight, and the heat was unbelievable. Eventually I saw a tired figure drag himself from behind one of the houses nearby. 'The Americano?' I asked. He looked at me much as a gourmet might look at a piece of tripe, and ambled on. B. was wilting dispiritedly against a rickety table outside the taverna and I bellowed for the proprietor. Somewhere along the dusty track which is the main street of Oia a dog set up a dismal howling. I searched hard for any signs of life. Up the track and down the track and across the drought-hardened terrain on either side, the landscape was doing a sort of hornpipe in the wavering heat mirage. A white flame that was a church along the far end of the village appeared to be floating in its own shimmering moat. Something—a black spot which grew grotesquely tall then flattened to disappear and reappear again—was coming toward me from the direction in which the taxi had disappeared. It was a human form and this time, I thought, he's not going to escape. In a moment of rash abandon I decided to bypass the Americano and nose out Mr P. direct.

As the figure approached I went to meet him. 'Mr P?' I enquired. He looked at me. 'Mr P?' I repeated. Not a word. B. who was watching the whole circus act came up and repeated the query. A glint of comprehension dawned in the cracked wizened face but still not a word. His hand, however, made an odd scraping gesture which we took to mean 'follow me'. We followed. He patted the table outside the taverna and disappeared inside. Presumably we were to wait. By now it was close on four o'clock and we were wilting badly but the village was slowly waking up. Along the track figures appeared leading donkeys down to the parched barren fields. From a room behind the taverna there came a sound of movement and more figures were approaching from the direction of the church. We were deeply entangled in a completely unintelligible conversation when our friend of the wizened face reappeared and by means of sign language indicated that it was still the time of siesta and Mr P. was sleeping and could not be disturbed until five o'clock. At least that's what we thought he said. We had a cold lemonade from a comely woman who appeared to be in charge of the taverna and went on a long and sticky exploration of Oia returning at a quarter to five to a group of dejected characters sitting around the few tables outside the taverna door and on the far side of the dusty space. I started the enquiries again with a feeling of slight despair.

'Mr P?' I breathed in one ear after the other, and eventually got a response. A hand pointed down the track. Sure enough dawdling towards us was a figure in a slouched cap and as fine a walrus moustache as you'd ever despair of growing. He drifted up, baggy trousers and all, and I seemed to detect a stir among the assembled sleepy company.

'P!' I neighed at them hopefully.

'Nai, nai,' which, being Greek, you may have guessed means 'Yes'. I breathed a sigh of relief and walked to meet the dilapidated figure. 'Signor P?' I said in my finest bastard Italian pidgin-English Greek.

'Nai.'

At last! We shook hands, smiling as genuinely as we could and indicating our good wishes to himself, his mother, father, sons and grandsons including the family mule if he had one. Then the sign language began again. Yes, of course he had the keys to the house of our friend. But what was the hurry? It was hardly the tail end of siesta time and wasn't the sun still playing homogriddles? Have an ouzo; man alive, have an ouzo and be sensible! I had an ouzo and paid for his as well. We had more ouzos, paying for both his and the assembled company's who had so nobly engineered this essential introduction. B. by now was moist, limp and fractious, but I tried to explain that when in Greece one does as the Italians do—and what on earth was the hurry? We were here. P. was here. I had about five ouzos inside me; what on earth was the hurry?

Mr P. was a scream; his long, brown walrus moustache draped lower with each ouzo and his slouch cap fell farther over his eyes. The baggy trousers flowed round his shins and the chair legs like the drapes of an Hellenic statue. Eventually he started to snore. It was a perplexing situation; did one wake him with a tremendous (but friendly) slap on the back? Did one roar some sea shanty to bring about the same effect? Or did one just let him snore!

Around us there came a gentle stirring. The rest of the company conveyed by a detectable tension that something was about to take place. I looked at them and a hand pointed. A figure, upright and smart as any soldier, was marching towards us. It was (of course) Mr P.

But the battle was not yet won. Had we a letter of introduction? This was all by sign language for not one of them could speak half as much English as we could

Corn thresher at Oia

Deserted cliff dwellings at Oia

Greek—and you know how much that was—had we? I asked for the Americano and light dawned in his eyes. We walked half a mile along the dusty track which was now flowering with urchins, dogs and mamas; the place was humming with life. From afar appeared a portly and immaculately white-jacketed and straw hatted figure. Mr P. pointed. 'Americano,' he said decisively.

Americano, who retains the affectionate title by virtue of having lived for some years in the United States, still speaks American with a bewitching Santorini accent. He is a small but well padded gentleman with immense natural authority and a pair of twinkling eyes that reveal the humour behind a rather awe-inspiring presence. Our hearts warmed to him as we handed him the letter, our only document to prove us other than the direst mountebanks bent on robbing another man's house. He looked at it, then looked at us. He then looked hard at the letter again and turned it sideways. 'Spectacles !' he said, and pocketed it. Which was adroit, if nothing else. But the ice was broken and Mr P. was now moderately certain that we were bona fide so we returned to his house where we had coffee and delightful shortbread cooked by Mrs P. We admired the prolific photographs of himself, his mother and father, his wife and her mother and father and the six children, one of whom was taking us in with a depth and profundity we later had reason to regret, he being aged about ten, which is enough said. Dark haired and impish eyed, he weighed us up, and saw possibilities.

Eventually, in the gloaming of late evening, we followed P. back along the ash road which soon became a cobbled mule track on the outskirts of the village. At a derelict windmill, still pointing with its skeletal axle-beam to seaward as though indicating the path of its departed soul, we struck away from the cobbles on to a thistly track which wove round and about derelict cave dwellings. Then, down a steepish grassy stairway descended on to what was the remains of a cobbled terrace, its front side crumbled away and long since fallen down the cliff face. It was backed by a vertical wall peeling with decayed limewash through which—and into the very bowels of the cliff—led three doors. The locks were persuaded open and the doors creaked back.

We had a splendid cavernous living-room off which an ancient wine press made a small double bedroom. From here, where feet had once crushed the grapes, the rich juice had flowed down a sluice into a well where Ali Baba might easily have—

and still could—put the forty thieves! We had a separate kitchen, similarly bur-
rowed out of the resonant cream pumice of the cliff, fitted with bottled gas cooker
and a rickety table. The third door led into the washroom which catered for the
wildest abandon of a bath, bucket-tossed and soap sprayed, all of which the walls
directed inexorably to a central hole in the floor which came out (we imagine)
somewhere in the cliff between us and the deep blue sea six hundred feet below.

But the loo! Great Heaven, words fail me! Where else on earth can one sit
in anal delight and survey six miles of volcanic grandeur across a bowl of pure
amethyst? Without portals of any sort, one was nevertheless as isolated and aloof
as Zeus on Olympus. As one philosophised therein, the strange outline of Nisi
Aspro (White Island) held the eye six miles away across the white flecked water of
the flooded crater. Below and to the left, behind where the door jamb might have
been, dropped a russet-brown cliff the sheer magnitude of which whispered of
earth's beginnings.

Mr P.'s youngest arrived with a mallet and battered to death the riot of
tough scrub which had taken over the terrace, and we brought out the two
great mattresses to air, and sat there breathless as the sun bid 'adieu' in a livid
crimson miracle.

Echoing up from below, came a deep sonorous hoot: a huge cruise liner was
nosing her way like half a matchstick across the crater. She passed between my big
toe and my digital, bound for the quay at Thera. Doubtless she was full of fat tourists, but up there, balanced on the rim of the Universe, we felt aloof; which, if any
of them, would brave that perilous ascent!

*   *   *

We wake at five thirty in the morning. This is no sprightly virtue, but occasioned
by a distant earth tremor. I jump from the wine press in alarm, fling back one
of the large double doors of the living-room. The world outside seems stable
enough; no tidal wave surges across the crater and Nea Kammeni, the latest mag-
matic upheaval, sleeps down there in the centre of the bowl without even a wisp
of sulphur smoke.

Above me, a cavalcade of six sleepy donkeys plods along the narrow track
which leads directly over our heads, their twenty-four feet drumming thun-

derously through the peculiarly resonant pumice ash. B. is comforted, but any thought of further sleep is out of the question so we move to the cobbled terrace with an odd feeling that we are entering the royal box at the opera. Already the void to the east is suffused with a splendour of green. The pre-dawn air is warm as velvet and the world is quiet again save for that loneliest sound on earth—a distant cock crow. We do not talk: words cannot but detract from the awe-inspiring beauty of this scene, balanced on a magic carpet above a waking world. Soon it will be too hot to remain here on the terrace. Make the most of these comfortable moments. With the first clear ray of burning sun B. disappears into the kitchen to busy herself with breakfast. I throw the bucket on its lanyard down into the cavernous fresh water cistern beneath the living-room floor. Its hollow boom when it hits the water sounds like a distant cannon. As I heave the heavy bucket back up, some of it splashes on the dusty concrete floor and I take it outside to the far end of the terrace where the bread oven is. Stripped I hold the bucket high, pouring the deliciously cool water over my face to trickle ice cold down my arms, over my chest and back, tingling down my legs on to the cobbles underfoot to flow over the edge down the cliff into the void below. This is the most vital moment of the day.

Already the sun is burning, a glowing warmth after the cold sluice, and we set the table at the other end of the terrace where the shade will last longest. Soon there will be no shade, but before the hard edge of heat encroaches we have finished the meal. By ten o'clock the terrace is an oven. Nevertheless we leave the cool darkness of the cavern and retrace our steps along the cliff path which smells strongly of horses, goats and sheep. Beyond the windmill is a field of cut stubble. At its centre two threshing rings are being worked—circular cobbled floors with a low retaining wall at the rim. Already the eight mules are tethered side-by-side, the smallest in the middle, the largest and fastest at the rim. A whip cracks, and the mad merry-go-round of toil for man and beast continues. Thirty-two hooves beat the ears underfoot, thrown into the circle from the piled stooks nearby. They will still be turning, those mules, when the sun sinks toward the horizon tonight, the circles then deep in broken husks and ochre kernels. Tomorrow the winnowing will start, women throwing the dusty mixture high, the light husks blowing away, the heavier kernels falling back to the stone floor. Everything to leeward will be yellow with the dust, and the glowing mound of kernels piled to windward.

Along the ash road which is the main street of Oia we walk between the brilliant whitewashed houses to the baker's shop. Its occupant—a dolorous man who seems to be utterly oppressed by the overpowering heat of his task— sits in the corner of a sooty cavern, and there is a low roaring crackle from the deep-hidden oven at the end. Outside in the small yard dried broom and twigs, bamboo and grass is piled high as the roof; it is his fuel supply. He hands us the round hard loaf and we escape from the stifling furnace into the blistering but breathable air outside, blinded now by the whitewashed walls. But beyond, at the extreme north of the village, the houses are no longer white. Many of them have no roofs, the walls are cracked and the windows gape. Successive earthquakes have taken their toll, and it is cheaper and easier to build new than demolish and rebuild the old. Skeleton eyes stare across the crater. Below them, on the steep incline of the cliff face, ghost cave dwellings—long since deserted and fractured by the shaking earth, make a honeycomb of the clinker cliffs. Arches span deep clefts, walls hang over air, waiting for the next tremor to end their perilous days. It makes a sombre scene, and over it all is a film of pumice ash from the huge quarry at the tip of the rim. There the small coaster loads the pumice, a curtain of white drifting back across the crater. Six miles downwind to the south the scene is mirrored in more huge quarries where man slowly changes the face of the island with his inexorable burrowing. There is money in that ash, even after you have stood the cost of loading and transport, for it has the peculiar quality of congealing to a concrete hardness below water.

But there is something else in that ash too. Down at the southern extremity of the island, right at the water's edge on the flat plain of the outer rim an area of some acres is carefully fenced off. Incongruous looking bright new sheds roof over a gully. Down there, dedicated men are burrowing, sifting, dusting and tabulating. Out of the ash, beautifully preserved, are coming the remains of a whole Minoan settlement which was buried when that great eruption took place about 1520BC. This is Akrotiri, a landmark in Eastern Mediterranean archaeology. Already magnificent wall frescoes, still glowing with their original ochre and claret colouring, have been removed and carefully restored in the museum at Athens. Other exhibits are on view in the smaller museum at Thera.

Threshing corn at Santorini

Exciting detective work is taking place here, for traces of Minoan buildings have also been found under the sea off the shore at Akrotiri and these too are impacted in pumice ash. But pumice ash floats, which means that the land on which these subterranean houses stood must also have been above ground when the volcano spewed its lethal layer of thick suffocating ash, burying everything, packing the houses and contents in the preservative material. Then came the explosion, layers of clinker and rock fell on the carpet of thick ash. The land subsided all round the crater and the sea engulfed it, leaving only the rim we see today standing above the water. The pumice ash impacted and pressed down by the heavier layers on top may well have held the houses secure beneath the water. If this is so a new world of speculation may open up. Was it this cataclysm—greater by some four times that of the more recent Krakatoa explosion in Java—that gave rise to the legend of Atlantis? Theories develop, meanwhile the excavating goes on, and the streets of the town which must have been contemporary with the palace of Knossos can be trodden once more by human feet. Was it the wave resulting from this vast explosion in Santorini which brought about the downfall of the Minoan civilisation in Crete? The authorities in charge incline to believe it was.

On the north-east slopes of the rim, terraced vineyards fall in layers down to the sea, the sulphurous soil nourishing the grapes, green and black which already hang in clusters, ripening for the harvest soon to come. Acres of brown dusty soil are spread with bright red pinpoints of colour. The tomatoes too are flourishing. There are few trees on Santorini, though the road from Thera to the south is lined with splendid eucalyptus.

There are two tavernas in Oia, their rickety wooden tables spilling out into the narrow track which is the main street. Who would want to sit indoors when the oppressive heat of the day has capitulated to the velvet warmth of a starry night. You sit on the wall opposite the taverna door, and seven hundred feet below the lights of a tiny jetty wink up at you while the smell of your fish grilling comes floating across from the kitchen. The single electric light bulb on the wall gives all the light you need when the carafe of local wine is banged down on your table, the hunk of rough island bread alongside it. The sweet brittle fish comes with a Greek salad of olives, slices of tomato and onions with flaky white fetta, goat's cheese, on top, all anointed with olive oil. Everybody here knows everybody else:

the whole village is a family. Not many tourists come to stay a month, as we have: we rapidly become one of the family too.

But the period of respite from the meltemi is approaching. September brings a quiet calm throughout this southern Aegean sea, and we must use this month to make our way back up north toward the Saronic Gulf in *Lugworm*, so it is with mixed feelings of regret, and relief at escaping from the baking heat, that we once more board the steamer, this time in darkness, down on the busy quay at Thera. The necklace of lights up there on the clifftop dwindles as we nose towards the crack in the northern rim. There, far, far above us, is the light on the taverna wall at Oia. Goodbye Oia. We shall almost certainly never again set eyes on you, but you and the island have been an experience we shall never forget.

CHAPTER V

THE SARONIC GULF

IT WAS NOON ON SATURDAY the 28th August that, fully provisioned and fuelled, we motored out of Batsi Harbour in a flat calm, glad to be back on the water. Here the five knot wind of our own making meant the difference between sweltering heat and tolerable sunbathing. The ill-famed channel between Andros and Evvia was asleep and by evening we were beaching on Evvia. To gain a lee from a very light southerly wind, we anchored on the northern side of a tiny peninsula right at the tip of Cape Paximadi. We should have known better than to break our rule of always berthing for the night with shelter from the north. It was during supper that the fire smoke blew back in our faces.

'The wind's gone back to the north,' B. commented. 'Do you think we should shift across to the lee side of this spit of land before dark?'

I looked at the sky: clear as a bell with the first stars glowing. There was about two hundred yards of fetch to the north before the sandy bay gave way to rock and swung round in an arc to give us a weather shore. East of us the promontory rose into a craggy headland, and I knew there were off-lying rocks off the point. I was little inclined to shift. We had supped well, and the wine bottle was empty.

'It'll be O.K. here. There isn't enough fetch to get anything of a sea running; still, just in case it freshens we had better sleep aboard ready for any emergency.' I laid out the second anchor from *Lugworm*'s bow, and brought a light stern line ashore, making it fast to a tree stump which had washed up, roots and all, a bleached and grotesque outline at the top of the beach.

We always sleep with our heads aft in the boat; there is more elbow room abaft the centreboard casing, and the working area of the after deck is ready to hand for making the early morning cup of tea or whatever. By midnight the wind had reached force six to seven, and I was wishing I had heeded B.'s comments. To lessen windage I lowered both masts. It was pitch black: I couldn't even see the beach astern and it must have been white with breakers. *Lugworm* was dancing madly, and the occasional spray came over her bow, but she was lying head-to-wind so it wasn't too bad. We spread the waterproof sheet over our two sleeping bags, and hoped. B. was not asleep. At 0200 the spray was getting a bit wetting, dropping inboard just where our heads were. I advised B. to follow my example and turn the sleeping bag so that only our feet got wet, our heads being tucked back against the forward bulkhead in a good lee. She was in no mood to start pulsing about in the now violently pitching boat, and told me so. I settled down the other way round. A few minutes later at least a gallon of water slushed over the gunwale and trickled on to my head, soaking down into the sleeping bag in a freezing cold ooze.

I cursed. 'What's the matter now,' B. wanted to know.

'I'm stowing my bag and moving on to the beach. *Lugworm* won't shift, and it's not worth getting the bags soaking. Come on.'

I sat up, and gave my head a fearful crack on the mainmast which I had forgotten was now stowed fore-and-aft.

'Are you having fun?' she said, rising just in time to receive a faceful of spray.

'Come on, we're going ashore. I'll bring the boat cover; let's stow the sleeping bags in the forward locker.' We couldn't see each other, so I fumbled for the torch. In its light I saw B. crouched and looking over the stern.

'How deep is it?' she asked.

'Not more than up to your hips at most. Jump as far shoreward as you can, and if you're lucky with the waves you might get away with dry knees. I'll bring the towel.' I shone the beam shorewards where nothing but foaming breakers filled the gap between us and the shingle.

'Go on,' I said. 'Don't dither about dear, it'll be all over in a minute and we'll snug down in a lee somewhere.' It was perishing cold standing there in our nothings with the spray painting our weather hides white, but there was no point in donning any clothes until we knew we were ashore and dry. The wind was screaming now, and I reckoned it was all of force eight. The yellow beam of the torch was pathetic in the blackness, and the noise of the breakers on the beach close astern was deafening; we had to shout to communicate. B. dithered a bit.

'Go on, JUMP!' I roared above the gale.

She jumps. I watch her clamber through the last of the breakers up the beach. Fully successful that. Now it's my turn, but I've got the heavy canvas boat cover, and the torch, and the towel with our clothes rolled up inside. There won't be any jumping for me; it's a case of gently lowering myself over the stern, finding the bottom and keeping this lot high above the wave tops while I wade ashore. I ease myself over the gunwale ... God! How much higher is this water coming. Waist high, my feet touch bottom. I grapple for the cover and things, swing them high above my head, turn and step shorewards—straight on to a sea urchin. The agony is frightful. I lose my balance, and a wave takes me and the cover and the clothes up the beach in a shingly heap but not the torch alas. B. is hopping at the water's edge and together we drag the gear up on to the dry pebbles. I'm wet, and in extreme pain from the broken off spines in the ball of my right foot.

We shake out the cover, and dry ourselves as best we can with the wrung-out towel, huddling in the lee of a crag. The painful minutes tick by into hours before there is any detectable lightening of the sky to the eastward.

'Perhaps this will teach us never to beach on a lee shore,' says B. as she probes for the last of the brittle spines in the cold light of dawn. We both look as though we had been dragged through a hedge backwards, shivering with cold and thoroughly fed up. The torch, being waterproof, is recovered in good working order.

Yes, it was good to see the first glint of dawn that morning. *Lugworm*—a forlorn spectacle with both her masts down—cavorted a few yards off the beach, drenched with spray, but the anchors had held well, and though the bilges were swamped and the bottomboards awash there was nothing that ten minutes bailing couldn't put to rights.

As soon as the sun had risen enough to pick out the off-lying rocky dangers that studded the fringes of our bay, we motored with the masts still unshipped up to a golden sandy beach about half a mile to the north. There were low cliffs of white rock at either end of a deep bay, shot with the blood red earth which is so typical of this part of Greece, and in the bright morning sunshine it formed a warm and welcoming haven from the fierce and relatively cold wind.

The apparently rock-free beach, however, was not without its hazards. Keeping a wary eye on the seabed clearly visible thirty feet down, we watched it gently shallow up to five or six feet, changing as it did so from silver sand to dark green weed. This in turn gave way to flat brown rock which continued to shallow up until finally, some twenty feet from the shore, it lay a mere six inches under the surface. Nowhere did it break the surface and from seaward was impossible to detect. Between this hollow rock ledge and the beach the bottom fell away again before rising to the beach itself.

We had noticed this phenomenon on some beaches prior to this, and were to come across it again on almost every sandy beach we used. Examination of the ledges showed them to be hard impacted sand, almost as though a cementing agent had been at work. They were quite rigid enough to stove in the bottom of a dinghy if driven hard aground, particularly since in places the level layers had been broken up by the sea to leave hard sharp edges; but always lying just beneath the surface.

At one end of this bay the hard shelf broke off suddenly to leave a clear channel through which we were able to row *Lugworm* until her bow grated on the beach. It was a splendid spot, clean and free from tar and sharp rocks. We spread our wet clothes and sleeping bags on the white shingle at the top of the beach, weighing them down carefully with heavy boulders against the wind. There was bleached dry driftwood galore for a fire and after a warming cup of coffee and an egg apiece, we set off to survey the land behind for if we were to be weatherbound here for any time we wanted to know what sort of terrain we had landed on.

Behind the beach a flat baked earth plain about a hundred yards across led to the foot of a low hill. A single tree, some variety of oak, somehow found enough sustenance in the barren earth, and behind this the hillside rose in a gradient of thistly scrub and barren rock, studded here and there with tough bushes of hawthorn and a form of small holly. Halfway up the hill a shelter for goats had been constructed by the simple process of piling the loose rocks into a rough wall, then laying beams back to the rising hillside from the top of the wall. The roof so formed was thickly overlaid with dead shrubs to make a rough thatch kept in place by heavy stones. The floor of the shelter, which was not more than four feet high at the wall, was thick with dried goat droppings, but it was remarkably cool inside.

The hill up which we were climbing rose westward to a height of some five hundred feet, then swung north round the wide Karistos Bay and continued rising to around one thousand feet. Nowhere was there any sign of life; animal or human. By now the sun was burning our skins again, and we were glad of the cooling wind in our faces as we picked our way up the sharp ridged rock, dodging the thick clumps of incredibly spiny undergrowth, and the dried thickets

THE SARONIC GULF

0   10   20
Miles

of thistles—everything of a vegetable nature which remained was there by sole reason of its thorns—the goats had accounted for the rest. Once on the shoulder of the hill we could see clear across the three miles of Karistos bay. It was a magnificent picture. The town, compact and neat, clustered like a bright model on the far shore, its houses glinting white and sand brown in the brilliant light. Behind it the hills reared up to nearly five thousand feet in the heart of Evvia, and everywhere the land was brown with scorched undergrowth—a deep red brown shot here and there with grey buttresses of rock. What made it so spectacular that day was the contrast of this burnt brown land with the incredible blue of the bay. We watched this blue fleck with white as the wind seared down the hillsides behind the town, flattening out to fan across the bay in wide fields of foaming breakers. Then we turned west and continued climbing, skirting round the top of a steep valley before gaining a narrow ridge which gave a superb view of the whole coastline. Five miles to the north the Petali Islands were brown and green mounds in a world of white flecked blue. No cloud broke the bowl of sky above us save one sharp white cap above Mount Okhi behind Karistos. We had come to learn that such a clear sky, with white caps of clouds such as this showing on the highest peaks of the islands was a sure sign of strong wind. It was the meltemi's visiting card, and all the signs—including the forecast that morning—were for continuing high wind.

This survey made two things abundantly clear: though Karistos was a mere three or so miles across water, it would be a hard day's trek over the deeply indented ironbound coast which skirted round the bay. Secondly, the country between us and the town was devoid of any life. Not even a goat had we seen. So long as the wind kept up its strength any thought of putting to sea was out of the question, so working on the assumption that we would be here for a number of days, we started to ration the provisions and water.

We carried an outfit of three alloy billycans, each stowing inside the other for convenience in the boat. In addition we had a heavy galvanised washing-up bowl which could also be put on a wood fire, and of course all washing up was done in salt water. We soon mastered the tricks of a nomadic gipsy life, finding that the soot black outsides of the cooking pots came clean as a bosun's pipe when the pan was rotated in the fine shingle at the water's edge. In Skiathos we had bought a wire griddle, a double grid with a handle between which meat or fish could be clamped and grilled over the hot embers. Fish—or the possibility of it—was still much in our thoughts at this time as a welcome augmentation of our diet. We collected small winkles from the rocks, breaking their shells with stone and baiting hooks with the tiny pieces of gristle inside as we had seen fisherfolk doing, but despite earnest efforts we caught nothing. There was no shortage of driftwood and all cooking was done on the beach fire. This method of cooking had another advantage also: the smoke kept the gnats at bay in the evening time. Indeed, we opted to sleep aboard every night rather than risk an onslaught by these pests. I, personally was immune from them, but it seemed as if each biting insect in the locality had its own M1 right to poor B!

The wind did not ease for three days, and it was a wonderful period of enforced idleness for us both. We went completely native. There was no need to wear clothes for there was no living thing in the neighbourhood, and anyway half our time was spent in the water. We walked dozens of miles along the ridges of the hills, exploring steep valleys and basking on the white shingly beaches where they fell down to the western shore. Only one sign of civilisation was evident from our quiet hideout in the bay: the twice daily throb of the ferry steamer plying from Karistos to Raffina on the Attic shore. It was unbelievable how the rhythmic beat of this ship's propeller thumping the water, and the steady throb of her engine, was carried down to us by the wind from Karistos. No sooner had she left the harbour than it would seem she was approaching the mouth of our bay. But the noise would remain, growing steadily, until we could believe she was bearing down on us, and still the sound would increase until suddenly, a blaze of lights in the evening dusk, she would pass well to seaward. Then, once down-wind of us, she became instantly silent.

The nights were clear and starry, and we would sit until the early hours of the morning with the fire blazing at the water's edge, talking of this and that and solving the world's problems while watching the silver reflection of the moon on the wind-whipped sea. No matter how late we turned in, we were always ready to rise when the first sunray hit our faces. While the fire burned up, a pre-breakfast swim freshened us, and then the weather forecast at 0745 would dictate our activities for the day. We were in no hurry to move on, having enough food for at least a week on board, though after the first meal on the night of the wetting we had to resort to tins and packets.

About four o'clock on the evening of the third day the wind had eased enough for us to consider getting afloat again. With the provisions somewhat depleted it was advisable to restock, so we motored into the teeth of the dying wind up to Karistos.

Shopping in these 'off the tourist track' spots was a constant adventure. Meat, for instance, is sold by weight alone, regardless of the choice of cut, and if you buy a good piece of lean, there will be a piece of waste fat or gristle thrown in with it to make up. That evening B. bought lamb chops—they were on the ribs hanging up in the butcher's, and, thinking they appeared to be rather small, ordered four. To her horror, the butcher took down the beast and hacked off a large section of its ribs, with complete disregard to the direction of the bones. He then chopped this chunk of lamb into four pieces, some of them containing the bits of two rib bones, and then proceeded to beat the lumps of meat with a large wooden mallet until they were quite flat, with pieces of splintered bone everywhere. The meat was delicious, but one had to be very careful not to bite too hard!

We never did satisfactorily identify any cuts of meat such as we find at home for the simple reason that the whole beast was kept in a cool-room, and chunks hacked off from the area selected. We found much the same in tavernas when a lamb or pig was being roasted whole on the spit: there was no attempt at carving as such, chunks being roughly hacked off. But we can say without exception that every piece of meat we ate in Greece was delicious.

By now we had become experienced in obtaining methylated spirits for the alcohol stove, and approached the first grocer in Karistos with confidence. But it was not so when we first arrived in Greece. Nobody seemed to have heard of a methylated spirit cooking stove, and we were in turn made to smell diesel oil, petrol, and paraffin and even olive oil. The word 'methylated spirit' only occasioned a blank stare. Finally we got it translated and written down. It was, so far as I can translate Greek into phonetic English, pronounced 'Enopthneptha' but it took us a month to memorise it without looking at the slip of paper. And, of course, it was sold by the kilo! One took along the container which was first weighed and then this weight was deducted from the total when full.

This method of buying by weight appears to apply to all liquids in Greece, except 'benzina'—petrol. Even wine, when bought in the taverna with a meal is sold by the half kilo or kilo carafe. Bread, too, is sold by weight: on one occasion having asked for half a loaf, the shopkeeper carefully weighed this, then cut a thin slice more to make up an exact round figure. There is not, throughout the country, any form of queueing, and in a shop the chap with the strongest elbows and the loudest voice gets served first. Trying to get on a bus is hilarious. Women and children last is the order of the day, and although at first this did appear to be the height of bad manners to us, we rapidly learned that to show any concern for a dear old lady laden with shopping baskets desperately trying to mount the bus steps was merely ensuring that one did not finally get on the bus oneself, for a tight wad of elbowing humanity barged ahead with no concern for priorities. But there was never any bad humour about it. Dig your elbow hard into the chap beside you to force a way in, and he would gasp and laugh good naturedly.

For all the novelty of contacting civilisation again in the town, I was glad to get back to the peace of our bay that night just as the sun went down. By nature I am a recluse, and find my fellow men in bulk a bit of a trial at the best of times, but B. found these contacts with civilisation very necessary in order to strike a balance between the nomadic back-to-nature wandering, and the sophistication of life back home.

The wind freshened again during the night, and was roaring unabated at daybreak with shades of the 'white tempest' lifting off the sea just to leeward. By early afternoon however it eased and so we bid farewell—not without misgivings—to the solitary freedom of that bay. We sailed up to the Petali Group, spending the night aboard in a deep gully below a cliff which gave splendid shelter from any violent northerly which might reawaken. The following day we reached across to the coast of Attica and ran down before a splendid brisk wind inside the incredibly jagged Makronissos before clearing Cape Sounion with its magnificent temple, to round up in the bay just to the west for the night.

We were now nearing the outskirts of Piraeus and Athens, and the twenty-five miles or so of coast from Sounion to Piraeus was becoming steadily more developed and populous. It is an uninteresting area, and we were both disappointed to find that the land around these centres of civilisation was barren and rocky, with little to offer by way of beauty save the scorched brown of rubbly hills and dusty sparse earth. Few trees broke the skyline, and the main road which clings to the coast had brought its inevitable crop of ribbon development, congealing into the modern holiday resort of Glyfada about seven miles south of Athens.

By now we had completed some four hundred miles cruising in the dinghy, and were feeling rather proud of ourselves for having sustained nothing more than a slightly bent rudder post. We have been asked whether we ever felt bored with the constant confinement of the small boat. In fact, coasting aboard a tiny dinghy such as this leaves no time to become bored, for there is the ever changing panorama and always something requiring attention: trimming of sails, checking of one's position, identifying the new landmarks as they appear and keeping an ever wary eye on the weather and the type of coast one is approaching with a view to a safe refuge in case of a sudden need.

There was, in fact, no 'typical' daily routine. That following our departure from Sounion will serve as an example.

*   *   *

It is one of those idyllic mornings when the world is endowed with such harmony that even the bees seem to steal the honey apologetically. Astern, from his gold-pillared temple on Sounion—a lasting indictment of concrete—Poseidon gazes over his domain and sends a soft breeze to caress us up the coast of Attica. There isn't a cloud in the sky and the sea has that misty blue tint, holding in its void the promise of a cool escape from burning heat which will surely come at noon. *Lugworm* sighs and chuckles lazily in an excess of happiness as the whorls under her transom wiggle away indolently astern.

But this morning B. is in a difficult mood. She is in that sort of womanly mood which Rex Harrison—apologies, Professor Higgins—never understood, and nor do I. Since we mutually decided, as we weighed anchor this morning, to give the teeming Piraeus and Athens a miss, she has been remarkably quiet: bordering on broody. But now she has started burbling about washing her hair in fresh water for a change, and harping on about hot baths and large cool hotel beds and exalting all those things which make for an effete life ashore.

It may be that she is feeling a little insecure because, confidentially, I haven't myself yet decided where we're going, but we are certainly not heading for Piraeus thank you, with its clanking polluted commercial harbour. 'Who's going to scrape the oil off *Lugworm*'s hull and wash her down with detergent?' I ask. Her thoughts on this centre round Man's inability to get his priorities right: did I love the—boat more than I love her? How long was it since we had a good night's sleep without some pre-dawn disaster striking terror into our souls? It wasn't that she didn't care for *Lugworm*, but there are times when a girl needs comfort, luxury even. After four days scratching around back there in No Man's Land her scalp itches ... it's time she had a shower ... and so on and so on.

Women are like this. It's something to do with the moon. For centuries psychoanalysts have been wrestling with the complexities of their nature, trying to root out a logical cause of such traumas. There isn't one. The only thing a chap can do is disregard it. I disregard it.

'And when did you last take a fix?' she harps on, not to be fobbed off by strategy. Now this is unkind. I am a very good navigator. I never run aground unless we're having an argument, and have a keen sense of position born of a lifetime's experience of disaster at sea. Not that I wish to belittle B.'s accomplishments here, but she is, on the other hand, the sort of navigator the Admiralty might put in a glass case and label 'theoretically correct'. She's never happy unless the trackline is so thick with fixes it looks like a strand of barbed wire, and then she's got to check it with a sounding and at least two shore transits every five minutes. After that she starts worrying about whether we're in the right ocean.

'Relax,' I soothe her, and for example prop my feet up the mizzen mast and settle my shoulders comfortably against the chartboard which rests on the gunwale. Who wants to frig around with horizontal sextant angles and compass sights on a fabulous morning like this? That blur on the horizon ahead is obviously Fleves Island, so long as I keep the end of the mizzen boom prodding around Gaidero back there I needn't break my neck craning to see where we're going—this isn't Piccadilly Circus. But she needs buttressing a bit, so I chunter on to show, despite the casual approach, that I'm actually 'with it' deep down.

'There's thought gone into this course,' I say, straightening out a donkey's leg in the wake. 'Sure as little apples the wind will back to the north, or even north-west this afternoon. It's wiser to get up somewhere off Fleves before freeing off for the run down to Aegina, or Poros, or wherever we decide to go. Don't want to end up headed with a long wet beat as the sun goes down.'

'Look's to me as if the wind's dying anyway.'

'Bound to, before the change.'

We ghost on for another couple of hours doing all of one knot beneath a blistering sun, and finally *Lugworm* is wallowing in a circle of her own ripples on a sea as smooth as a baby's bottom. The sails collapse. Down goes the outboard.

'If it has to be under power we might as well head direct for Aegina,' I mutter as we hand the limp terylene, and off we throb, making our own cooling wind, out into the great expanse of shimmering blue. There isn't another ship or boat in sight.

Now I'm never completely at rest when the engine is running. The noise and sense of urgency with which the boat surges through the water isn't conducive to relaxation such as when the sails are silently pressing. After half an hour I have to be doing something. The outboard, hot in the sun, is covered with white salt rime where the odd splash from down the outboard well, and the jet of cooling water, have evaporated.

'I'll give the engine a spring clean,' I say to B. 'Just take the helm a moment dear will you while I get the sponge.'

'For heaven's sake, Ken, while we're under way?'

'Why ever not. She's as steady as a rock: I'm not going to dismantle the engine dear, just give it a wipe over.' B. puts on one of those looks I know to mean 'Oh well, there's nothing I can do about it.'

I take the sponge, dip it in the sea and swill off the rime. It makes me feel better. As I wipe around the air intake to remove a sediment therein, the engine cuts dead.

'Don't worry, I starved her of air: she'll start again.' She doesn't. Our throbbing world is reduced to a heavily charged silence as the boat glides gently to rest while I labour with the starter cord. Off comes the head casing. 'It's probably got a drop of water on the plug,' I comfort B. who sits there like a dumb martyr. It's while I'm removing the plug that my very new and expensive adjustable spanner falls down the outboard well. It winks a silver wink at me twice before disappearing for ever in the deep blue void below. My day is deteriorating. The plug is apparently in perfect shape: there is no water evident anywhere. I test for a spark. There is none.

'It's the electrics. There is no juice to the plug.'

'So?'

'Can't start taking the thing to bits here.' I look around. 'Where are we anyway?'

'Ask me, you're the navigator.'

I can see I'm going to get little co-operation from my crew, so start trying to identify features ashore to fix our position accurately. I plot a cross cut on the chart, which puts us three miles west of Nisi Arsidha, a rounded hummock of barren rock with a bit of scrub itching on top. Beyond that is a deep bay giving a good lee from all but the south. It's about five miles from here to the head of the bay. There isn't a breath of wind.

'There is nothing for it: I'll have to row.'

'That's right.'

Certainly there are people who will scull a light rowing skiff five or six miles before breakfast, just for the pleasure. To lug nine hundred odd pounds of beamy cruising dinghy the same distance in the blistering heat of a sub-tropical midday, is quite another matter. A Drascombe Lugger rows remarkably well, all things considered, but one of the considered things is that the eight foot oars with which I am equipped are really a little too short. I have them that way in order to enable their stowage neatly along the foredeck and it represents one of the debits on the balance sheet of compromise. This row is all debit. Poseidon is having his siesta and not so much as a catspaw of help did the Zephyrs subscribe to ease the labour. To make matters worse, along the skyline to the east a heavy black line of thunder cloud is gathering. I'll say this for B., she's keeping remarkably quiet about the engine failure, and I have a sneaking suspicion we would be nearing Aegina now if I hadn't messed about with that sponge. She needs a morale booster.

I can see lining the shore ahead, there to the east of the bay, a largish town. That'll be Fokaia, marked on the chart as a small village, so evidently there has been some development since the chart was printed.

'Tell you what,' I gasp between pulls. 'What do you say to berthing the boat safely at the head of the bay and walking into the town for a slap-up meal and a night ashore in a good hotel? Bath and hairwash and all? I'll deal with the engine tomorrow.'

'Thank God for the engine failure!'

Well, that's encouraging. What time is it? About one o'clock; should be at the island by two if I don't drip into the bilge completely. Be in the head of the bay by three, with luck before that thunder cloud breaks. Phew, but it's oppressive today. Better give B. something to do, keep her mind off things.

'Ship the rudder again, old dear will you. It will make it easier for me if you steer –I shan't have to be concerned about the course. Just keep her to the south of the island.'

To allow B. to move aft to the tiller I stand up, lower the oar looms for her to step over, and turn to look ahead in an effort to judge the distance off land. As I rise B. moves to one side. *Lugworm* rocks gently. Maybe it is the rapid transition from rowing in a seated position to standing as the boat rocked, but I'm caught off balance—a rare thing for me—and stagger side-ways. My knee is behind the oar, and I sit heavily in the cockpit bottom. As I flounder down, there is a splintering crack, and the wooden laminated tiller is there under me on the bottom boards, broken off six inches short of the rudder head. Obviously, this is 'one of those days'—and it started so well! We are labouring round the island in mutual silence when the first raindrop arrives. As we turn up into the bay a vicious squall of wind sweeps down on us from the north, and it starts to deluge. We put out two anchors and a shoreline, push a few moist clothes in a kitbag and walk the half mile round to Fokaia, a bit low in spirits.

B. says she enjoyed the meal at a proper table with decent cutlery and a glass to drink out of instead of a tin mug.

Personally I could hardly hold the knife and fork. The irony of it is, for our hundred and twenty drachmas we had a fine room but we discovered at about three in the morning that we had left the window open and B. was bitten fifty three times by gnats—even through the sheets! She didn't sleep a wink.

No; there was never any time to get bored!

*   *   *

First things first; the outboard had to be dealt with. I took the coil off, and put a spare in its place. It started first pull, so being loath to throw away an expensive piece of gear and being of a mind to find out exactly what a coil is, anyway, I examined the defective part. It was something special thought up by Kiekhafer Mercury to present a spark of colossal magnitude in a modern wonder called Thunderbolt Ignition. Half-round and housed in a neat rubber casing, in another era it might have been put on a pedestal and worshipped. I prised off the casing and with it came a tablespoonful of salt water. Not even I can expect an electrical fitting to work in a salt bath, so after drying it out I replaced the old coil. The engine has been working satisfactorily ever since. It's still a mystery to me how all that water got in there.

But the distant blur of Aegina, and beyond that Poros Isle were beckoning, so we bought a couple of 'Moon Tigers'—coils of tough fly papers coated with glutinous odorous stick—and another fascinating invention like a green snake coiled in a spiral which emits distressing smoke guaranteed to choke only the gnats. Thus buttressed against winged Fate we sped westward, completing the crossing in just three hours with a heaven-sent fresh south-easterly, and rounded up in the Bay of St Marinas on the isle of Aegina in time for a brew of tea on board. Aegina presents a hilly and thickly pine clad aspect when approaching from the east, but as one works southward it becomes more barren. The harbour of Aegina itself, up on the north west tip is on low lying and rather uninteresting terrain. The bay of St Marinas has been developed extensively, and not liking either the shallow beach—breakers were tumbling some twenty yards seaward of the shoreline—or the populous aspect of the town, we sought out a deep secluded gully between low cliffs just to the east, dropping the bow anchor in fifteen feet on a clear sandy bottom, and making fast a stern warp to a rocky ledge on which some thoughtful person had driven an iron ringbolt. The boat, moored like this, was adjusted so that by heaving on the stern warp the transom was brought within a foot of the flat rock which formed a natural quay. But I'm never happy when *Lugworm* is left so close to jagged rocks, so secured a weight to the bow warp about six feet away from the stem. This kept her stern rope taut at all times, and though there was a slight swell, she lifted and fell in safe deep water.

We dined ashore in a sophisticated taverna with psychedelic lights playing on the walls, and the wail of hip music, which formed a profound contrast to the peace of the grotto later that night.

The following dawn brought the battle of the wasps. I awoke looking, as might be expected, at the sky. Across the span of my vision the furled red sail of the main gently swung, for during the days of light airs I frequently left the gaff aloft with the sail rolled tightly and lashed round the spar. Around the upper length of this red

furled mainsail orbited a number of small dots. This again, is not an unusual phenomenon on first awakening, but is generally dispersed by the simple process of blinking. This time they did not disperse. I focused on the odd picture, and immediately realised that each of the dots wore a black and yellow football jersey. There was something about that sail which appealed, for as I watched more of the loathsome wasps joined the mob. By now I could hear the drone too, and watched in dismay as the cloud of buzzing venom thickened. They did not settle on the terylene, but merely circled round at a short distance as though carrying out a detailed survey. What alarmed me was the fact that as the cloud thickened it also dropped lower. I eased myself out of the sleeping bag, moved gently to one side of the boat, then lunged across to swing the mast violently and, I hoped, deter their interest.

Not a bit of it: the cloud broadened, the buzzing rose to an angry pitch, and B. sprang sharply upright with a gasp. I rapidly put her in the picture.

'We're being swarmed.' Vaguely I had an idea that when Queen wasps take to the air all the workers follow in hot pursuit. I may be mixing it up with ants, but maybe not. In the meantime what on earth about my sails could be so attractive to an Hellenic Queen wasp.

'What scent have you got on?' I asked B., who lay ears awash in the sleeping bag, wide-eyed in horror.

'Scent? Don't be a fool. I don't wear scent in a sleeping bag; DO something!'

I must say, it was a challenge. You can't run far in a dinghy; it was my brains versus theirs, so I thought it out. The result was brilliant. If ever you're attacked by wasps in a dinghy, remember this: I softly took the hand-bailer from the after deck and into it tipped about a pint of petrol from the spare container. Taking careful aim I flung the liquid in an arc up the sail. The cloud exploded. B. shrieked and disappeared into the bag. I jumped overboard. When I surfaced it was all over; they'd gone. 'Brilliant,' I shouted to B. 'Come on out, it's all over. But don't strike any matches!'

It's a tip, anyway.

*   *   *

Poros is delightful. We drifted inshore of a rocky crag jutting from the sea just east of the island, watching the incredibly green pine woods thicken up. We ghosted in the calm of the afternoon under a series of ochre cliffs and rounded the southern tip to sight the magnificent monastery, white and red roofed in the green hills, and finally beached in a secluded bay just east of the town. This is a perfect dinghy sailing area. The island gives protection from the north, the mainland from the south, and if the wind freshens too much from east or west you simply take shelter one side or the other of the narrow peninsula which juts down south of the island to almost close off the shallow channel leading into a marvellously enclosed lake. From this lake there is a narrow outlet at the north through which the Piraeus ferries enter before striking east to berth at the town quay. It is a busy little port, and what we liked particularly was the obvious fact that it was a Greek harbour town, and not just a tourist base. There were a few tourist knick-knack shops to be sure, but nothing to match the ghastly sham of Idhra and Mykonos which struck me as being Mediterranean Polperros with everything en-

terprising businessmen think the tourist will expect to find laid on thick as marmalade at a shilling a sniff.

It was in Poros, after we had moved into the lake for the second night, that we
were awakened at dawn by the familiar sound of a rowing eight exercising in the
sheltered water. It was a crew from the naval base, all good-looking youngsters at
the peak of physical fitness, and seeing us anchored in a quiet bay, well away from
the busy town, called on their way back to satisfy the natural curiosity. In conversation one of them who spoke good English noticed our tiller which still had its
temporary lashing. 'Give it to me,' he ordered. Nothing loath, off it came, and
within two hours a splendid new ash tiller, modelled exactly on the original, was
back aboard. We liked Poros, and seriously contemplated taking a house ashore
for the winter, but we still had at least a month of good weather left, so decided to
do a bit more exploring before laying up the boat.

It was here we made a light cotton tent, specially shaped to fit over a taut line
which could be quickly made fast between the two masts. The four corners of
the tent secured to fittings above the side decks. It was small, very light, and not
waterproof, but it gave us just that necessary bit of privacy aboard when anchored
in populous bays. In fact it was a great success. You may wonder what was the
matter with our large p.v.c. tent, but remember that to fit this involved unshipping the two masts and frigging around with ridge poles. The whole evolution,
from setting up the crutches and rigging the hull girdle to which the tent ties were
secured, would take about half an hour, and in the end it was uncomfortably hot
under the waterproof material. Of course when it rained there was no choice, and
we were glad indeed later in the cruise to have this dry shelter, but during the
sunny months the small cotton tent was a great success. Who wants a cabin when
there is a universe of stars overhead?

For four days we cruised in the area of Poros, exploring the length of the lake,
and taking long walks on the mainland and the island. Each night we would return
to our secluded bay just west of the town, but on the morning of the 11th September—at 0200 to be precise—we were awakened by uproar on the beach close
alongside. At dawn we saw the cause: a large party of campers had arrived complete with tents and baggage. They had taken over the beach, and didn't care who
knew it, making the night and morning strident with their din. We sailed with a

fair northerly, motoring out of the lee of the island until catching the wind free of the peninsula, bound for Spetsai.

That is a day to be remembered. We drift dreamily under the quiet pressure of the sails along the lee shore until the coast falls away to the south enabling us to free off. By noon the wind has left us, and we are floating again in a blue world of water and air, the horizon only a misty line with the barren high ridges of Idhra wavy in the heavy light. Halfway across the channel we throw out the sea anchor and dive into the void of cool deep mauve. It wraps itself like velvet round our skins, and once more we peer down into the indigo depths, then up at the burning blur of the sky. It is ours, this world of warm blue silence: ours alone for a brief spell, with no other human to interfere. We drift for an hour, two hours, soaking in the sun, and back aboard take a little wine with the olives and cheese. This is what we have come for: to rise above the rut we had channelled ourselves into, and take another long look at the magnificent stage on which our brief play is acted out.

Idhra is very beautiful in a baked yellow way, her hills rising steep from the waterline, almost bare of trees. We motored into the tiny crowded harbour, berthing with difficulty among the large expensive yachts, and wandered about the enchanted little town. The shops are attractive, sophisticated and very expensive, but they do not present the true Greece. We are reminded of Mykonos, but this place is geared for the wealthier tourists. We motor gently on along her western shore, then cut across to Ermioni on the mainland, anchoring off a low quay at the top of a deep protected bay. The night was memorable only for the strong smell of sewage, and we were glad, with the first light of next morning, to escape to a clean windswept gully about a mile from the harbour where we anchored and had breakfast before passing west of Dhokos Island with Spetsai a distant blur. It was a kind east wind that finally, that evening, ghosted us within view of the harbour— and what a view! Spetsai was fairly palpitating. We didn't know till later that she was celebrating the official anniversary of independence from the Turks and was going it in style. All yachts in harbour were decked with flags. The beat of music throbbed across the water carrying with it the murmur of the crowd which milled along the waterfront of the old town.

We beached quietly under an ageing lemon tree in a corner of Boat Creek, prepared *Lugworm* for the night, and walked round the head of the creek, passing through boatyards where large fishing caiques under construction stood like orange skeletons on the foreshore, past a barrel maker's workshop—the staves and hoops lay all about—and so along the incomparably beautiful waterfront into town. Spetsai has great character, relic of the days when it was a large shipbuilding and trading centre. The elegant, solid houses standing on the high land bordering the waterfront give it almost the appearance of a fortified town. Everywhere there is the look of its past solid merchant prosperity and unlike Galaxidi which we were to see later, it has been well maintained, for there is still wealth in this island, and it shows.

That night, we sat among the jostling throng at a table beneath the trees above the harbour and watched a demonstration of traditional Greek dancing. It was a lively scene, noisy and colourful, with the steamers and car ferries coming and going. We walked back round Boat Creek under the stars, leaving the noise to dwindle behind us, and turned in with only the occasional rustle of leaves ashore and the odd chirrup of a cicada to break the silence.

Four days were spent on this delightfully green, pine-clad isle and once again we were tempted to take a house there for the winter, but common sense prevailed, and reluctantly we tore ourselves away from her secluded white pebbled bays, the deep clear grottos where you could watch the fish all day and live in their green world of waving weed and pure sand. We retraced our steps to Poros, stocked up in the familiar shops, and beat into a fresh northeaster up the east coast of the Methanon Peninsula: an inhospitable stretch of shore. There is little refuge for a small boat along the north shore of this peninsula either, apart from one small fishing port made, so far as we could see, by the simple process of running a small ship on an outcrop of rock and filling her with cement. There were caiques berthed behind this rough protection from the northerly swell, but we were in no mind to dally there, being bound for Epidavros which was somewhere in the dark brown blur of the coastline ahead. Before noon the wind had fallen light, but still a rather ominous swell was running down from the north. Up between two small islands to the west of Aegina we could see it heaving up and breaking in huge rollers of white foam which was odd, for there is a depth of over fifty fathoms there. Most of that afternoon the wind remained light but as we approached the shore it

Building a Caique at Spetsai

freshened from the north giving us a stimulating reach into a small bay just east of the harbour.

There was a collection of small fishing craft at the head of the harbour. They lay in two clusters, with a clear space between. I headed innocently for this open patch of beach, motoring slowly in. Looking over the side we were astonished to see that we were running alongside a sunken wall. With a gentle crunch *Lugworm* came to a halt, her bows reared slightly up. We have grounded, it would appear, in the front room of a house in 'Old Epidavros'. The ancient town has sunk beneath sea level, but its remains can still be seen down there in the weedy harbour bed.

*   *   *

We have stood, long hours here in the bowl of the hills, watching the youths running down there in the vast stadium, listening to the clamour of the crowd thronging the terraced seats, and thrilling to their excited roar as the climax of the race draws near. We have sat silent in this other world here in the amphitheatre, listening to the orators, watching the actors hold their audience spellbound as the setting sun drenches the pine woods with its parting gold. The ghosts have melted into the evening light, and the old winds have carried them away across the barren valley of the years, and blowing back again, have brought us here to sit on these grey lichen covered slabs, crumbled and subsiding where earth herself, remembering, has turned in her sleep. Everywhere is ruin, where once there was nobility of stone. Broken and chipped, slabs strew the grass of the stadium, and the terraced seats are mere banks of earth, thistly and barren. Tree roots here and there have prised up some marble corner-piece from the dusty soil, prised unwillingly back into the hot noon of now, when the new people pay their ten drachmas at the iron gateway, and pass in to conjure up the ghosts.

The road from the ruins of Epidavros is straight and glassy in the afternoon heat. It leads across the floor of the bowl, then falls gently through the long valley to the sea. We take this road, hoping that some traveller will help us back to the harbour, but there are no travellers, and we plod on the dusty gravelled side of the highway. There is a taverna isolated at the side of the hot deserted road where a woven lattice of bamboo roof spreads a welcome shade from the oppressive dry heat. There are two tables and a few chairs. Not a soul in sight. We draw two of the upright wicker chairs back into the shade beside a table and the sharp grate of their legs in the gravel sets a dog barking somewhere at the rear of the building. It is cool here, after the road. The dog continues to bark, and now there is a shuffling from inside. An old woman, her head covered in a shawl, her body wrapped in the black ankle-length skirt of the peasant, comes to the door. Her lined, brown face is resigned and careworn as she looks at us, the skin around the eyes creasing against the brilliance. She is curious, but holds up a hand as though saying 'wait', before returning into the room. Across the road, down by a dried-up watercourse, we can hear the soft ring of sheepbells. A young man is walking toward us. He climbs the rubble bank and as he crosses the road, we see that he is lame in one leg, this young man, and looks thin and frail. The old woman has returned from the dark interior of the taverna, and draws a chair to sit against the wall outside.

'Kali spera,' I say to the youth, and then, 'Do you speak English?'

He makes a sign with his hand indicating 'just a little'. 'Ligo, ligo,' he says. We order fetta, tomatoes and olives, with bread and half a carafe of local white wine. While he is fetching the meal we watch the woman. She is spinning the rough wool of a sheep from a ball held in one hand, teasing it into a yarn which is twisted by the constant flick of a hanging wooden bobbin. As the strands of wool are pulled off the fluffy ball she whirls the bobbin on which the thread of twisted hair is wound. It is natural colour this wool, and doubtless sheared off one of the sheep over the way. Perhaps she will knit a coarse jersey from it, ready for the winter.

The youth brings our food and the wine. As he places it on the table there is the intrusive note of an engine. A motorcycle roars to a halt before us and the rider takes an envelope from a satchel and hands it to the boy who draws up a second chair beside the woman, as the postman roars off to leave us in a welcome silence with the settling pall of dust.

He has opened the envelope and takes out two banknotes which he hands to the woman. She puts these in her pocket without looking at them, then sits calmly listening as he begins to read the letter to her. When it is finished, she nods once, her hands idle now, her eyes fixed on the road, unseeing. The youth rises and crosses the road again, then calls toward the sheep. From the water bed an old man appears, stands looking toward us, then painfully walks over the scrub, up the bank, and across the road.

The three of them talk together, and the letter is read again while the old man listens raptly. After a while the youth comes across to our table.

'Please ... you read?' He places the letter before me, and I am about to explain that I cannot read Greek, when I see at the bottom of the page scrawled in an immature hand, words in English. 'Please, I not read English ... you speak very slow, I understand.'

'Dear Father,' I read slowly and distinctly, 'I want to marry your son. I hope you will be made happy by this and give us your blessing. Please will you send the certificate I need to say that your son is not married. One day I hope to come and see you, but Australia is a long way from Greece.'

That is all. 'Katalavas,' I ask wondering if he has understood.

'Nei, katalava. Efharisto ...' Thanking me he turns and relays the brief message to the old man and woman. They listen intently, their faces two masks without emotion. This, I am thinking, is what written communication is for: the conveyance of stark fact. 'I want to marry your son.'

The old man is speaking now to the youth, who looks again toward me.

'Please ... you write English?'

'Certainly,' I agree, understanding that he wishes to reply directly to the girl. He brings a piece of lined paper and a biro.

'What shall I write?' He calls the old man across, but he seems ill at ease, this old man, and I smile at him, holding the pen poised. When he speaks, he looks only at the boy.

'You write ... Dear Daughter.' The words come, stilted, hesitant, and there is difficulty in conveying to me what the father wishes to say, but slowly it comes.

'Dear Daughter, Your letter makes me very happy, and I am sure you will make my son a good wife. I send the certificate you ask for. One day perhaps you will come to Greece. I hope so, but do not expect me to write often, for I cannot write English and am an old man.'

We pay for the meal, and set off down the road. Behind us the peaks of the hills cradle the ruins of Epidavros. The stage has broadened a little perhaps, but the strings that jerk and bob the actors are the same strings.

*   *   *

Eight miles north of Epidavros is a delightful bay facing due south. At its head is
the tiny hamlet of Korfos, and we reached its entrance in the early evening of the
21st September after a brisk beat up the coast against north easterly winds. We
dined on the dusty quayside watching the small fishing fleet return in great spirits
with a catch of eight huge tunny. The sight of them sawing off their heads while
we ate our 'marides' and salad did nothing to take the edge off appetite, but we
were glad when they took all the heads, which seemed to wear a look of surprised
disbelief on their faces, out of the bay for dumping. That night we beached at the
eastern side of the bay beneath a deserted olive grove and walked up the stony
track into the hills as the last of the evening light fell away, leaving us to a world of
warm scented earth and softly chirruping cicadas. Soon we would be entering the
Gulf of Corinth, for we had decided now to make the Ionian Islands before finding
a roof for the winter.

Morning brought a strong northerly wind however, against which we would
have made little headway if any, so we spread our boat cover on the beach in the
lee of the olive grove adjacent to *Lugworm* and prepared for a lazy day's sunbathing. Shortly, however, we became aware of a figure coming down through the
grove behind us—a tall, gaunt man with a skin like leather and wearing a shepherd's cloak. Over his shoulder was a bamboo pole with something tied to the
end. It looked like a bunch of feathers or rags.

I watched idly as he worked his way over the rocks on to a small promontory right at the water's edge. With a twig he flicked a little olive oil from a
bottle hanging at his waist, flattening the ripples round about, then peered
intently into the depths. After a while he took up the pole and slowly probed
down with the feathery end. For a long time he kept gently thrusting it up and
down a few inches. I had to know why!

Standing beside him I could see, some ten feet down on the seabed, a large
rock surrounded by weed. The end of the pole was jigging slowly up and down
about four feet from the base of the rock, and I could see now that it was a bunch
of grey leathery leaves of the wild Jerusalem sage which was tied to the pole end
down there. He flicked more oil on the water and we both stood watching.

There was a movement in the dark weed near the rock; it could have been a
fish stirring the long green fronds, but then a black shape like an eel slowly un-

Korfos – *Lugworm* with lightweight tent

coiled, lifted above the weed, and sank back again out of sight. It seemed to be about two feet long.

The shepherd tensed. Still keeping the leaves undulating gently he worked them slowly toward where the movement had been. Peering down I tried to make out some shape to whatever lurked there, but the only thing to catch my eyes through the quivering water was a small bright ring of silver. It might have been as big as a wedding ring. He flicked a drop more oil and when the coloured film had spread I saw quite clearly for a moment. I was looking at an eye!

Large, shockingly human, the eye was set near the top of a shapeless brown blob. Gently the bunch of leaves was jigged toward what I now realised was an octopus. When it was about a foot away from the eye a tentacle uncoiled and cautiously felt the water round the leaves.

It as good as said, 'What's this then?'

The man drew the leaves a little distance away, all the time keeping them waving gently. The octopus rose slowly from the seabed, hovered just above the weed, and without apparent movement of the tentacles slid intently toward the pole. When about a foot from the leaves, quicker than my eye could follow, two tentacles flashed out. I saw the bamboo shake as they twined. The man jerked violently upward ...

A jet trail of inky black fluid was coming up from the depths as, hand over hand, the shepherd lifted the pole and with a last quick pull heaved about two kilos of slimy yellow-brown form clear of the surface to slap it on the rock at my feet. There were three huge barbed fish hooks hidden in those sage leaves!

With a grin he wrenched them free, then opened a clasp knife and plunged the blade deep between the creature's eyes. The flailing tentacles which had been desperately trying to attach themselves to the sharp rock jerked and writhed but now all control was gone. Then the shepherd commenced the operation we had heard and witnessed in the dark lagoon at Pelago. Gripping the creature by the body he lifted it high above his head and flayed it violently down on the rock face. Again and again he did this, and as I watched its colour changed slowly to a translucent pearl-grey. Seventy-five times I counted as he beat it down and there was white froth on the rock. Then he turned it inside out as one might an umbrella, rubbing it vigorously with a circular motion on the rough surface. Finally, taking hold of the flesh near the base of a tentacle, he pulled hard. The flesh tore easily. 'Kalo!' he said. 'It is good!'

Octapothi Vrasto (boiled octopus) is a delicacy among the country folk and the fishermen in Greece. The flaying I had now witnessed twice is a very necessary tenderising of what would otherwise be tough and rubbery muscle. But neither B. nor I could ever develop a taste for octopus.

The brisk north winds lasted unabated the next day and it was not until the morning of the third day in Korfos that I thought it wise to leave the shelter of the bay, bearing in mind that the next leg of the trip up to Corinth offered no shelter from the prevailing north easterlies. The chart showed it to be a ragged and rock-strewn coastline, and probably there would be a lumpy sea running near the lee shore. So it turned out, and within thirty minutes it was evident that we would have to wait for the sea to calm before pressing on, for it was too wetting trying to beat up the next stretch of coast. We ran back into a good lee under high cliffs just south of a prominent cape and fished unsuccessfully in thirty feet of water until early afternoon by which time the wind had fallen light and the seas diminished somewhat. Under power we motored up to a deep bay giving shelter from the north but none from the north-east, and spent an uncomfortable night bouncing on the swell. Dawn found us keen to press on, and since the wind was already freshening I thought it best to seek the shelter of the north shore without delay and kept the engine running until at nine we beached in a perfect lee at Kalamaki just east of the Canal entrance.

Nowhere on the trip did we so keenly feel the insignificance of *Lugworm* as, the minimum fee of 320 drachmas having been paid at the dock office, we nosed into the Corinth Canal. Ahead of us towered a large Greek warship, astern, fast approaching from the Gulf behind, was the silhouette of a huge ram-bowed merchantman called Nog. We were like a flea between two elephants. Straight as a die the three mile cutting ran, slicing ever deeper into the sandy coloured peninsula and we, happy that our stout-hearted four horses would keep us nicely positioned between the two giants, sat back to appreciate the awe-inspiring rise of near vertical yellow cliffs on either hand. Until, that is, we remembered that our ship's papers and passports were still lying on the dock officer's desk back at the entrance!

The Corinth Canal

It was a momentous decision. I eyed the black looming form of Nog which had slowed to allow the dock's launch to collect her fees. A tug was already fussing at her bow back there at the canal mouth. I reckoned it would take all of ten minutes for that little formality to be completed. Then the dock official would have to climb back down the rope ladder hanging over her side. The tug had to gather way and line her up. At least, if we contravened all the laws of the canal, turned round in mid-stream and returned to the wharf there was room there to sneak out of the canal and allow Nog to pass: if not ... the alternative was too horrific to think about. We turned. A whistle blew violently somewhere back near the

entrance. B. started to bite her finger nails; to my horror I saw a taut wire rise out of the water spanning the canal ahead: it was a small floating car ferry that pulled itself across with a winch. There was excited shouting from shore as I turned in a tight circle round and round while that tortoise-like ferry winched herself across. At least Nog was still swung sideways out there. If she started to line up for the entrance I reckoned it was time to cut our losses and get back through that canal; maybe we could hire a donkey and return for the documents overland. The wire ahead dropped back into the canal, and as we sped down toward the office jetty a small figure came running waving our large brown envelope. God bless him! Quick thinking there: we pulled alongside the huge piles, I clambered on to one of the tyres hanging as fenders and reached up. He lay flat and handed down the envelope. A quick look at Nog: she was lining up now and a tug made fast to her bow was already nosing into the mouth. Hell or High Water we'll make it. 'Efharisto poli, poli, poli,' I shouted to the grinning clerk above. 'Thanks very very much. How fast does she go?' desperately in English, grimacing at the tug back there. He doesn't of course understand a word. We push off from the quay, the huge bulbous ram at the waterline of Nog has a bow-wave now ... she's coming in.

We putter at full throttle back into the cutting, relieved beyond measure that we are at least keeping our distance ahead of the monster. Neither of us cared to voice the possibility of our engine failing, but I had my eyes on the banks ahead where there were spaces we might possibly row in and hide while the cliff-sided Nog eased past. Thirty-five minutes later with a sigh of relief we spewed out of the western end and turned sharp north for Loutraki. On our port hand lay the blue, green and white flecked waters of the Gulf of Corinth.

CHAPTER VI

THE GULFS OF CORINTH AND PATRAS

L OUTRAKI IS A THRIVING SPA where sufferers from liver, kidney and bladder complaints throng for the curative qualities of the many springs. We, however, were in the fortunate position of requiring nothing more than petrol, bread, and a top up of the two water containers, and by early afternoon were ghosting on enthralled by the magnificent pine clad slopes of Paliovouna—The Old Mountain—towering some three thousand four hundred feet to the north. It was while having a snack as we sat on a wind-cooled rock, that B. started taking an interest in the flora round about.

'You know,' she said, 'no one has any right to be so abysmally ignorant of the names of the vegetation we're looking at every day. I mean,' she went on, pointing up the hill, 'look at it all. There are at least six different forms of shrub that I can make out from here, and I don't know the names of a single one of them. As for the flowers and weeds and grasses ...'

'Quite right,' I agreed, 'and what's more, if we did know the names of half the growths hereabouts I'm sure we could almost live off the land. Look at this mon-ster,' and I uprooted a giant orange bulb with what looked like a beanpole sprout-ing from the top. 'I'm pretty certain this would make a good substitute onion.' We smelt it. It didn't smell one bit like an onion and tasted very bitter. 'Well, anyway, it looks like one, and I'm sure it would be edible boiled. Shall we try tonight?' I asked. B. is cautious at the best of times where food is concerned but I was all set for a Robinson Crusoe life.

I picked my way back to *Lugworm* and ferreted aboard for the book *Flowers of the Mediterranean[1]*, taking it back up beside her. 'We'll identify this bulb anyway,' I said, 'there are three thousand of them in this bay alone: I'm sure we can cut the housekeeping bill by a quarter just for the trouble of picking them up.

'It is, without question,' I continued after a search, 'either the *Scilla Maritima* or the *Urginea Maritima*. It says: "The bulbs are sometimes collected for medici-nal purposes; they are used in the treatment of heart disease, cough mixtures etc., and have been known as medicinal since Pliny's time ... rat poison is made from

---

1   By Oleg Polunin and Anthony Huxley, Chatto & Windus, 1965

the bulbs with red tunics of certain North African sub-species. The Greeks hang the bulbs up in their houses during the New Year as a fertility rite ... "'

'That was a good choice to get started on for an economy drive,' she said dry-ly. 'Any more ideas, or shall we stick to the tomatoes and sardines?'

Not to be deterred I searched around for another likely edible growth. Here was a splendid looking fruity green plant nestling on a patch of dry soil. It had a small yellow flower, and crinkly hairy cucumbers growing from the centre, about two inches in length. They looked succulent. I bore it in triumph to B., who was asleep. 'Look,' I prodded her, 'like to take a bet on this one ... you know it's amazing what can be eaten of these wild plants. Our ancestors had to survive on them, remember,' and I scanned the splendid colour photos in the book. 'Not a shadow of doubt. Here it is—the *Ecballium Elaterium*. Wait while I look that up in the text. "The squirting cucumber"—what did I tell you—"A poisonous rough shaggy cucumber-like plant with small yellow flowers and green swollen hairy fruits which are easily detached from their stalks and explode their seeds outwards to some distance when disturbed ... the root contains a violent purgative and is used for rheumatism, paralysis, dropsy and shingles."'

I closed the book. 'Well,' I said, 'they're all fascinating to look at anyway.'

*   *   *

There is a wonderfully protected inland lake called Limni Vouliagmeni, otherwise known as Lake Heraion, near the tip of a thick peninsula separating the Halcyon Gulf from the eastern end of the Gulf of Corinth. Our chart indicated a narrow entrance of unfathomable depth, but in fact we saw it to be a shallow gully from which a strong flow of water was pouring out to the sea.

Care had to be taken when approaching the shore near the entrance, for it shallowed up gradually to show a bottom strewn with large rounded boulders, and there was a slight oily swell running in from the west. We anchored *Lugworm* in about three feet of water and waded ashore to make a survey. The gully, as we had surmised from seaward, was a mere foot or so deep in parts, approximately fifteen feet in width, and one hundred and fifty feet in length. At some time it had been a controlled entrance to the lake, for a rusty iron grid stretched partway across the inner end, and some distance from this, at the bottom of the mill race of shallow water, was a second gateway lying in a tangle of bent iron girders. The stream was flowing at some eight knots out of the lake.

'If we unship the rudder, raise the centreplate and lock the outboard up, we will just about make it,' I told B.

'But do we WANT to make it?' She looked at me and continued. 'I mean, we don't HAVE TO get into the lake do we ... not at the risk of damaging the boat?'

It was one of those statements women make when they're not thinking. I looked at her incredulously. 'What on earth are lakes for,' I pointed out, 'except to float in? Could you really pass the entrance and leave that area of water unexplored? Look at those hills behind it, and the calm expanse of protected water just waiting to be fished, and rowed in. God put it there for boats!'

So we waded back to *Lugworm* and carried ashore our bow anchor with its one hundred and fifty feet of floating rope, throwing this just beyond the grid at the inner end of the gully, and allowing the rope to drift back down to the seaward end with the flow. Then came the problem. The rope was not quite long enough to extend into water of sufficient depth for the boat to reach it while under power. It was possible that the propeller might hit bottom in a trough of the swell; we couldn't risk that, and the flow of water at the gully entrance was too strong for me to row against. We solved the problem by speeding in, full pelt, for that wriggling rope end, then lifting the outboard at the last possible moment, and with B. poised like a figurehead over the bow, just managed at the third attempt, to get enough way on to make contact.

'Got it,' she shouted, and I rushed forward to help haul the boat against the torrent. Now a dinghy, when weighted down heavily at the bow will not tow happily—and that, in effect, was what we were doing, towing her against that strong current. Applied forces begin to work in strange ways, resulting in violent sheers off to one side or the other, neither of which we could afford, for the banks of this gully were strewn with sharp rocks, old angle-iron, and other unwelcome man-made litter. With the two of us fossicking about over the stem it was enough to set *Lugworm* frothing away like a paravane. The trouble was, we could not ship the rudder, for at best there was a mere inch or so of sea-urchin studded water beneath our keel, and the rudder blade draws eighteen inches.

I left B. straining at the bow, and moved aft, fending meanwhile frantically with an oar as the boat sheered first to one bank then the other. Somehow, in between these wild lunges, I managed to stream our large plastic bucket on a short warp from the centre of the transom, and with this acting as a drogue I sent B. back to the stern with an oar poised at the ready, and moved to the bow where I could heave the whole outfit slowly against that boiling torrent. It was hard work, and the astonished look on the faces of a couple of sunbathers disturbed a little way along the bank of the lake was proof enough that few—if any—boats are seen inside. B.'s only comment, as we shipped the oars and rowed in peace and calm across the lake was, 'Thank Heaven we're not cruising up the St Lawrence!'

It was worth the effort. We spent two days exploring magni-ficent caves in the low range of pine covered hills inland of the lake, and walked miles on the lower land to the east. We collected the female sea-urchins from the gully entrance and spent hours removing their pink roes, a real delicacy when washed down with lemon juice, olive oil, and cool white wine. In fact, I almost forgave the sea-urchin its spikes, so much pleasurable food did it supply, and perhaps it is worth explaining in more detail how one goes about extracting the roe.

Only the female, of course, has the thousands of little pink eggs inside, and she can be distinguished from her male escort by the simple fact that she loves picking up a shell, or piece of weed, or small chip of shingle, and holding this between her many spikes in a form of adornment. Generally the female is larger and slightly browner than the male, but it takes an experienced eye to note this difference. You may be sure, however, that if the urchin has some small article impinged in the spikes, she is a female.

Once she has been taken from the water—with care so as to avoid crushing the thin shell—a small circular 'face' will be found on the underpart, and with a knife point this disc can easily be removed. Inside the largely empty shell will be found a mass of black spongy substance which is easily shaken out. When this is gone one can see, running up the inside of each section of the shell, a rib of pink eggs. We either scraped them out and mixed the accumulated roes with the olive oil and lemon juice, or poured the oil and juice into the shell and ate from that as a natural cup. Eaten with doughy new bread it was food for the Gods.

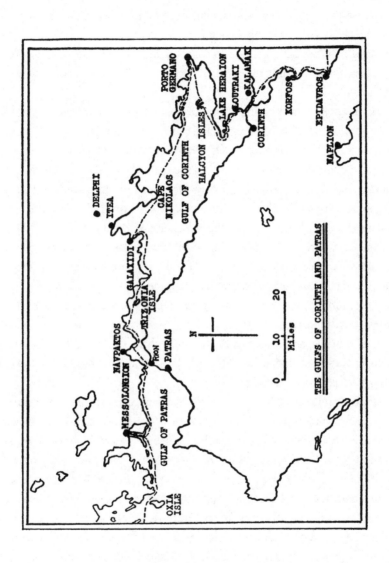

THE GULFS OF CORINTH AND PATRAS

PORTO GERMANO
LAKE HERAION
LOUTRAKI
KALAMAKI
HALCYON ISLES
KORFOS
EPIDAVROS
CORINTH
NAPLION
GULF OF CORINTH
CAPE NIKOLAOS
DELPHI
ITEA
GALAXIDI
TRIZONIA ISLE
NAVPAKTOS
GULF OF PATRAS
FION
PATRAS
MESSOLONGION
OXIA ISLE

N

0   10   20
Miles

We learned that there was no significant amount of water running into the lake from the hills, and in fact the strong flow in the entrance was all resulting from the slight rise and fall of the tide. It changed direction therefore about every six hours, and we had chosen to enter at the worst possible time which is why it was such a challenge.

High water on the morning of the third day occurred at seven in the morning, so we took advantage of the stand of the tide to punt ourselves elegantly back out to sea in absolutely still water, much to B.'s relief. Free of the lake entrance, duly loaded with female urchins, we motored in a flat calm one mile westward, seeking a suitable bay in which to anchor for breakfast and a morning swim, but we never thought to discover the charming little cove with the ruins of shrines and temples which came into view just before the lighthouse on the point. This was Heraion of Perahora where Hera 'Queen of Heaven' had her sanctuary. Remains of a second shrine, dedicated to the children slain by their mother Medea in vengeance against her faithless husband Jason, lay alongside Hera's sanctuary.

That morning, as we breakfasted in peaceful solitude beneath the ruins of the two shrines, we marvelled at the duplicity of Man's nature: to select this enchanting site, conceive and construct the beautiful shrines in which to offer homage, while, on the other hand, creating the very Gods whose mythical behaviour merely reflects Man's own bestiality.

It was a profound soliloquy on a lyrically beautiful morning but we found that the edges of philosophy were soon eroded by an awe-inspiring but dangerous shoreline, so we forgot Man and all his doings in the carvings of nature. Here, viewed from a certain angle, was a regal lion, gazing out to sea, fifty times life-size. There a gryphon, keeping guard over a green luminous grotto, and all the while a constant tingle of danger from the unseen rock carvings which drifted close beneath the hull. Peering down into those depths we were thrilled by the sudden green weed-covered pinnacles towering out of the void to skim a few feet beneath us, but the beauty and interest of the shoreline was too great to be lost by standing far off into safe deep water.

No wind blew that day. Indeed the famed Halcyon Calm lived well up to its name as we crept in a world of misty light straight up to the group of four tiny Halcyon Isles in the centre of the Gulf. At their highest point they rise not two hundred and fifty feet, and the smooth barren outlines, devoid of any trees, suggested little of interest. It was a surprise therefore when, nosing into the narrow channel between the islands, we saw a house above the shore with a vehicle parked alongside, and at the other end of a splendid sweep of pebbly beach, a white yacht moored. Thinking to pass the time of day with whoever had thought fit to settle in such a deserted spot we landed, only to find the yacht in a 'laid-up' condition, and the house untenanted. The vehicle turned out to be a jeep in a state of some dilapidation, and we were left pondering the need for such mechanical aids to transport when the total length of the single dust track on this largest of the four islands was not more than half a mile!

At the eastern extremity of this Gulf the ruins of fourth centuryBC Egosthena, built to protect Attica against any seaborne invasion, stood red-gold on a low hill, its massive square towers deep in the heart of a large olive grove. Pine trees studded the smooth rocks on shore, and we selected a well-protected deep bay for a night berth just west of the little village of Porto Germane. Late afternoon was spent exploring the huge battlements, all in crumbling state, and climbing inside some of the vaulted rooms of the thick-walled towers. We ate that night at a taverna whose tables were set on a high terrace overlooking the fishing boats below, and walked back late through the scented pines. It was at two-thirty in the morning that the sharp rattle of gravel on the side decks awoke us with a start. A brilliant light was moving quietly down the side of *Lugworm* a few feet away, and there was a stifled chuckle of laughter. One of the fishing boats, its vapour lamps at work drawing the curious fish into the circle of light, had had its little joke.

We had of course chosen this north coast of the Gulf of Corinth because it was more likely to afford a lee, and we had made up our minds to seek winter quarters ashore in either Ithaca, Lefkas or Corfu. Since by now the night dew was wetting, nor was the morning sun always hot enough to quickly dry out our bedding, we were keen to make good progress westward into the Ionian.

The forecast next morning suggested variable winds of force three to four so hopefully we motored on hugging a shore which became increasingly barren, the pines giving way to scrub, the scrub to dried grass and fern, and finally to large areas of bare rock. We crossed the mouths of deep bays and passed inside islands which were nothing more than mounds of smooth rock. But the Halcyon calm was still well entrenched, and by late afternoon, still under power, we were approaching Cape Nikolaos, a headland of low orange cliffs, surprised to see a solitary figure in a monk's habit sitting beside the small lighthouse. His long white beard indicated his advanced years and as we slid a few feet from the tip of the cape he raised an arm in lonely salute. We watched him sitting there until beyond range of the unaided eye, then through the binoculars I saw him climb slowly up to the dilapidated building behind the light. We must have been the biggest event in his desolate day!

That was our longest day's run, and all under power, for we had covered forty-eight miles without one breath of wind, before dropping anchor off a protected beach just south of Galaxidi. We supped over an open fire to the distant sound of sheep bells, but dawn light next morning showed us, slashing round the hillside behind the beach, the raw scar of another great road, and before breakfast was completed a team of bulldozers had commenced crashing boulders of many tons down the steep slope. We were quick to escape up to Galaxidi harbour.

This is a charming, sleepy little waterside town basking in the twilight of past prosperity, when it had flourished as an important shipbuilding centre, and the museum there is well worth visiting, with records and exhibits spanning the whole history of its life. Today, however, there is an air of peaceful retirement and decay; the long wharves accommodate nothing more than the odd elderly fisherman sitting patiently with his rod. We were unable to obtain much-needed petrol there, and did so in the larger and very active port of Itea while taking a lightning visit to the hordes at Delphi. It was the last day of September when we reluctantly sailed out of Galaxidi but the wind, alas, again fell to naught before we were well clear of the bay, so we anchored in a small cove and waited hopefully. At noon a light south-easterly set us hoisting all sail. But soon the sky was dark and overcast, and as the wind freshened violently the first heavy spots of rain set us quickly stowing charts and clothing. By early evening we were bowling along before brisk increasing easterly squalls, glad to see ahead a small tree-covered island behind which we might obtain a good lee.

We were not to know it then, but as we dropped sails and rounded-up into a small well sheltered bay, on that island of Trizonia, we had sailed right back out of the twentieth century!

Ruins at Egosthena

Figures came running down the beach despite the torrential rain and quick hands took our bowrope to haul *Lugworm* firmly on to the shingle. 'Where are you from? Where bound? Why have you such a small boat and have you no cabin?' The questions, so far as we could understand them, came fast and thick but we could not stand there in the wind and rain so made our way, surrounded by the inquisitive group, to seek a taverna in that quaint waterside village. We were however not allowed to get that far. From a doorway came the call of a little old woman dressed in peasant costume. One of the group grasped our arms with a laugh and directed us off the path into her small whitewashed cottage. Not to be outdone another ran off to return a moment later with a bottle of cognac. Everybody piled in with us and as we pulled off our oilskins the old woman clucked in distress at B.'s dripping figure; we must have looked like a couple of drowned rats. In a moment we were sat at a rough wooden table, hot strong coffee and small glasses of the brandy before us. As the warm liquor did its work we were again plied with questions and while doing our best to satisfy the curiosity of these charming folk I looked around the room. It was typical of so many other houses we had seen during the trip: the bare wooden beams supporting a planked ceiling, plastered walls, cracking and in parts dropped away from the rough stone. Apart from the table and bench on which we were sitting there was another wooden bench and four upright wooden chairs with wicker seats. A bed stood in one corner with a grey blanket cover and—incongruously, against the wall—a sideboard that looked as though it had come straight from Woolworths with imitation graining and cheap tinted metalwork, the sliding panels of thin decorated glass at the front contrasting hideously with the crude but solid wood of the other furniture.

A doorway, hung with a heavy green curtain, led into what was evidently the kitchen and the floor was of bare cement partly covered with a faded red rag carpet. There was no fireplace. The only decorations on the walls were a calendar which indicated the wrong month below a seductive damsel advertising 'Karelia' cigarettes, and a picture frame in which was displayed an embossed tin sheet, with the middle cut out. From the hole glowed an astonishingly Anglo-Saxon face of Christ, His blue eyes lifted to Heaven, silver tin rays emanating from the crown of thorns. A dog was curled in one corner on a sack and three chickens had scuttered out of the door as we entered.

'Just look at those,' I heard B. exclaim, pointing through the door to where a hedge of brilliant scarlet gladioli, large yellow crown daisies and what looked like purple bougainvillea beamed colour at us from the grey world of wind and water outside. 'Who would think it was October?' Above the door, thick leaves of a vine chattered in the pelting rain.

By now, curiosity was becoming satisfied: no, the boat was not built of 'plastico' but of marine plywood—'ksilo, contra plaquette thalassa', as one of them informed me. All the craft we saw there were of heavy carvel construction and *Lugworm* preened before constant scrutiny—a wonderful topic of discussion among the fisherfolk.

The rain was easing somewhat, so we explored the village, but it was chilly. Indeed, so accustomed had we become to the continual heat that our blood had thinned, and a day such as this, overcast with rain, was enough to set us shivering, though to be honest, it was warm by English standards.

That night, as we walked to the taverna, a boisterous south-easterly was bringing steep seas crashing on the point outside the harbour. I remember the dull glow of the taverna window beckoning a welcome across the rain-splashed quayside where the few fishing caiques chattered, riding gently in the encircling swell. As we open the door only one Tilley lamp spreads its bright hard light throughout the room. A group of fishermen and the proprietor are playing cards at a table drawn to the wall beneath the lamp, and at the far end of the room a counter displays a mixture of edibles: chocolate, cigarettes, dried beans, an opened tin of brinesoaked anchovies, small tins of tomato paste and, of course, the large square cans of olive oil. Behind that, on shelving nailed to the wall, are small coils of rope and twine, and a used net, its cork floats like a crude necklace, hangs from a beam in one corner.

The proprietor rises immediately to greet us; he is one of those who welcomed us on the beach. Soon we are settled at a table opposite the group, and since the light here is dull he brings a candle across; evidently electricity has not yet reached the island.

Fish? But of course. We are led behind the counter to the ice-box where we select two splendid 'barbounia' glowing like pink mother-of-pearl among the ice chips. And 'patates'? But indeed, and perhaps some Greek salad with it? We love these ice-cold plates of crisp shredded cabbage with pickled olives, and leavening of oil and lemon juice sprinkled over a mantle of flaky white 'fetta'. A carafe of local wine perhaps? But of course!

We had brought the chart of the area with us and I draw up another table, spreading the big sheet across the scrubbed wooden tops, for I want to study the coast ahead. While the proprietor's wife busies herself at the bottled gas cooker behind the counter, and the warm smell of the grilling fish begins to enrich the rather chill atmosphere of the place, I get to work with the dividers; fifteen miles from this island to Navpaktos, and then the narrowing waters squeeze through that mile-wide gate at Rion into the Gulf of Patras five miles beyond. Fine once we're through those narrows, but with this easterly wind there will be a lumpy sea up at the western end of the Gulf of Corinth. We will do well to wait for a shift before tackling it. Together we examine the coast.

The game of cards opposite has come to a noisy conclusion, and as we talk together over the chart, we are aware of a keen interest. But the natural good manners of these folk will not allow them to intrude before we give some sign that it is welcome. Obviously our chart fascinates them.

'Poli vrechi, to vradi,' (Much rain this evening) I say, generally to the group. Instantly one of them detaches himself and comes across to our table. He looks keenly at the chart. Trizonia—edho,' (Trizonia—here) I say, stabbing the island with the point of the dividers.

'Nai,' he answers, then casts an interested eye across the rest of the chart where the thin red line of our track wanders.

'Si?' (You?) he queries, putting a stubby finger on the line.

'Nai.' Immediately the remainder of the group noisily join us, doubtless discussing our passage and the size of our boat, for by this time we feel sure every occupant of this small island is aware of these two unexpected visitors.

They look at the chart intently, then one of them attempts to measure the distance from Trizonia to the coast of the Peloponnese opposite, using the span of his thumb and forefinger. I hand him the dividers. Uncertainly he tries to open them, but they cannot embrace the whole distance so I take them from him and measure two miles from the scale at the side before handing them back.

'Dhio milia,' I say. He carefully swings the dividers three times, counting as he does so . . . 'Dhio, tessera, eksi, okto.' There is immediate uproar. The fact is hotly contested and grubby fingers stab the chart as fierce discussion develops. At a call, a small boy appears from the room behind the counter and is sent scurrying out into the night, and the chart is peremptorily removed to their table beneath the lamp. The boy returns with two more swarthies and the discussion flares up anew.

Meanwhile our meal is nearly ready, and the calm faced proprietor's wife brings a clean sheet of white paper, laying it over the table. It is followed by two thick hunks of bread, glasses and a carafe of mild, slightly sweet rose wine made from island grapes. We sit back, sipping the wine, watching the figures still arguing over the chart, their shadows throwing grotesque phantoms on the flaking walls. It is a scene that an old master might have captured for ever on canvas. Outside the rain beats down in torrents, spattering diamonds on the window, dripping off the eaves to trickle in beneath the door where a dog scratches at the panel then pushes impatiently through. I get up and close the door against a cool blast of washed wind while the dog settles under a table near the counter, sniffing the interesting air.

The meal is set before us and I top up our glasses with the last of the carafe, asking for it to be refilled. When it arrives I call to the group under the lamp to join us, holding up the carafe. More glasses are brought and filled, then, in the characteristic way of the country folk our glasses have to be banged against each and every one of theirs with the repeated toast, 'Stin iyia sas!' (To your health!) We drink, and a limited conversation develops. Great fun today: the ferry broke down halfway between Aegion and Douvia. It was at the worst of a wind and rain squall and it was being driven on to the rocks of the island by the east wind, so Takis here put out in his fishing boat and towed it into the harbour. It was hilarious watching those passengers transferring from the ferry to Takis's boat for onward passage to Douvia. Chickens, boxes of fish and vegetables, planks of wood and everybody in their best 'go to market' clothes all drenched in the rain! The tale is enlarged on good humouredly by Takis the hero.

Now the proprietress approaches; shall we be here tomorrow night? If so, there is meat, brought across by the ferry. It comes once a week: shall she get some for our evening meal? I look at B. and listen to the rattle of wind and rain outside. If the weather stays like this most certainly we shall be here tomorrow night, and what a pleasant little backwater to be stranded in, out of the tempo of life and time. 'Yes, please do so, and if it is no inconvenience, we will most gladly come and eat with you tomorrow night.'

We sip the last of the wine, warm now and contented, watching the fishermen still desultorily conversing over the chart. A moth batters against the globe of the lamp, its tiny jerks transformed into darting flights of shadow across the wall. A cat, emerging from under the table where the dog is sleeping, freezes in mid step, its attention caught by the darting shadow. Like a film arrested at a single frame, time suddenly stops. The cat, motionless, concentrates every fibre of its being on that lamp. The figures, sharply delineated in the hard green-yellow light, the candle guttering on our table throwing its soft warm gold across B.'s face, her sun bleached hair throwing back the light ... at once everything seems hushed; it is one of those rare moments when that elusive, incidental quality, happiness, is caught, trapped in a timeless 'now'. Odd, how often it is just ahead, or astern, how seldom cradled aboard here with one.

The moth, inside the glass bowl, shrivels out of life, and the cat, its interest gone, jerks back to motion. 'All right,' I say to B. who is smiling at me across the table, 'I've just had one of those Moments. Are you happy, too?' She doesn't answer, but puts a hand on mine, and there isn't any need.

So, in a moment of lull between the squalls, we walk back across the square, through a narrow alley between dark houses toward the beach. A cigarette end glows under one of the patios and a feeble voice calls to us, 'Kali nichta.' 'Kali nichta sas,' we reply and a bent old figure hobbles out to peer toward the unfamiliar voices. 'What nationality are we?' he asks, and when we reply 'English', follows with the query in stilted phrases: 'That your boat?' Then catching my arm he presses advice upon us. 'You safe here ... not worry. Here good mans, only good mans, no harm!' We thank him for the comforting words and walk on stumbling over piles of rich smelling timber by the boatyard, past the crude wooden sled with its hand-operated windlass where the caiques are drawn up to where the faint white of the tent enclosing *Lugworm* awaits us.

In the night the rain thunders on the taut cloth above us, and though the wind soughs through the olive and lemon trees in the orchard, and our boat lifts and falls slightly on the swell, here, in the enclosing arm of the harbour, we are away from harm—and time.

What will tomorrow bring?

* * *

Tomorrow brought yet fiercer wind, but clear skies, and we stayed on this fairy tale island for three nights and two days, leaving on the morning of the third day. Obviously, the tem-perature and the change in the weather pattern con-firmed our decision to look for a house without much delay. That third morn-ing, a brisk east-south-easterly out of a blue sky was too much to miss, and under full sail we squared away from the island, the whole village turning out to wave goodbye.

There was only one place of possible refuge before Navpaktos in case of need and that was behind a small point, four miles along the coast. After that the coast swung southward giving a lee shore which would, with this wind, make lumpy and difficult going. As soon as we had left the lee of the island I began to have doubts about the decision to sail, which is often the way in a small dinghy. Look from the top of a hill and you'll think there's nothing to it but out there in the din-ghy it can be a very different kettle of fish. However, this morning conditions were not impossible and Navpaktos was a mere fourteen or so miles on. With luck we should make the shelter of the harbour within three hours.

But this day Poseidon laughed and gave us a run for our money. Before we had completed three miles the wind had freshened to force five to six, and be-ing almost on a dead run, we handed the mizzen. I did not like the feel of the weather at all, and to seaward the Gulf was already flecked with angry white. Out there evidently the wind was fiercer; how long would it stay out there? There is a patch a mere twelve feet deep about half a mile south-east of the point I had in mind as a lee. I could see breaking seas on these shallows, and to clear this rather than stand off into the fiercer wind, opted to pass between the breakers and the shore. It was a reasonable decision, the sea to leeward of the shallows was not breaking.

It did, however, put us close into the point itself, and as is common with nearly all points, the waves were building up just to weather. We were evidently going to have a bouncy ride before rounding up into the lee: I did not like the way the swell was banking up into steep short ridges. We were getting to the stage where *Lugworm* was starting to surf for too long at a time down the advancing fronts, and this is a tricky operation not to be recommended in the open sea. We reefed the main, so as to slacken speed and allow the waves to roll under us, reducing the risk of surfing considerably, but they were still building up steeper. *Lugworm* would dip her bow as the stern lifted, surge forward at an increasing speed, throwing up a fine bow wave, then level off as the crest of the wave passed beneath her.

Then she would dip her stern and come almost to a standstill as she slid down the back of the retreating wave. They were still getting steeper, those waves, occasioned by the shallowing up of the bottom as we neared the point. We were, in fact, less than four hundred yards off the beach, but between us and the shoreline the waves were now breaking. I was nursing the boat round the point just clear of the danger area when Poseidon took complete control. A really big one loomed astern and this time *Lugworm* dipped her bow—and kept it dipped! Instead of the wave passing beneath us, we were sliding down that front at the same speed as the wave's advance: *Lugworm* had become a surfboard. The tiller was rigid in my

hand, as a white bow wave sprayed back down either side of the boat. We were doing all of ten knots, and the wave was mounting steeper. Would it break? This was
a possibility which strikes horror into any sailor's heart because of the imminent
danger of being pooped. In such conditions if the wave starts to break it will continue to pour over the stem of the boat and swamping is almost inevitable. It is for
this reason that the early sailing ships, which could do little more than run before
the wind anyway, had such high 'poop decks' aft—to preclude the following seas
breaking over and into the vessel.

Poseidon took complete control.

The tiller, as I say, was rigid in my hand, due to the speed of the water flow
beneath the hull, and we had the centreboard three-quarters up, which probably
saved the day, for once a boat has decided to slide with a wave there is little one
can do save desperately try to avoid 'broaching'. To allow the boat to swing across
the face of the wave can easily result in capsize, and having the centreplate about
a quarter down helped prevent this possiblity, for it gave the rudder something to
bite on. On we sped, two white plumes of spray rising from *Lugworm*'s bow, and
that wave must have carried us all of four hundred yards, for we were clear of the
point when it subsided without breaking and *Lugworm* with her chastened crew
fell back to a rate of travel more suitable to her ample proportions. I must say she
handled magnificently during that horrific minute or so. Many craft when surfing
have to be guided with extreme care to prevent disaster. She did it all herself! But
it was enough to decide against any further voyaging until the wind eased. We
handed the main and turned up into the lee of the point, flying in fine style under
the jib alone until a high bank of eucalyptus trees and a thick hedge of bamboo
took our wind altogether. We had an enjoyable lunch ashore by invitation of a
charming Belgian who had built himself a splendid bungalow near the point, and
found it difficult to believe that we had come from Volos in such a tiny craft—and
gave us up for mad when we voiced our intention of sailing to England in her the
next summer.

The wind did not ease until four thirty in the afternoon, and we sailed before
a slight, and dying, easterly. By five it had died completely, so once more under
power we headed for Navpaktos. Darkness won, however, and in the failing light
at quarter to seven we gingerly poled ourselves, with engine raised, rudder un-

housed and centreplate up, into the reedy mouth of a shallow river, until the pebbly bottom gently grated against our underside and we anchored amid kingfishers, bullrushes and bleached pebbles chuckling in mountain-fresh water to spend the coldest night we had yet experienced.

Dawn brought a fair north-easterly, and regretfully we opted to leave Navpaktos unvisited, using the favourable wind to speed on into the Gulf of Patras which, for us, formed the gateway to the Ionian Sea. Though there is a negligible vertical rise and fall of tide in the Mediterranean, there is nevertheless a considerable horizontal stream occasioned by the moon's pull, and we passed through the Narrows between Andirrion and Rion with moments of excitement as great boiling whirlpools gripped the tiny craft and swept her round helplessly. It would have been a ghastly place to fall overboard, but the tidal stream was helping us through, so it was over in a few minutes. We landed for fresh bread and milk on the northern shore in the lee of Andirrion, and surveyed the coast ahead. It was not a comforting prospect. Klokova Mountain reared nearly three thousand five hundred feet sheer from the sea, and alongside it Varasovon Mountain held its hand. Beyond that—nothing.

From the chart we knew that the coast westward of Varasovon was low-lying, marshy land, and what was more important to us, for a mile off shore the sea shallowed up to a mere fathom or two—in places feet only. It was an indifferent weather shore and the worst possible lee shore to be caught on, and we just had to pin our hopes on the wind staying in a northerly sector. We had become experienced in the sort of conditions we were likely to meet beneath those two towering giants, Klokova and Varasovon: violent squalls and flat calm. However, if we were to make the Ionian Islands there was nothing for it, and frankly there was not much about the terrain through which we were passing at that moment which tempted us to settle there for the winter.

But the fact was, there were thirty miles of inhospitable shore to be left behind before we were again in a position to sneak into the lee of small islands, and shelter from whatever inclement wind might arrive. As it turned out, we experienced fickle winds and increasing rain which persuaded us to put into the flat, muddy and somewhat depressing port of Messolongion, where our stay was enlightened only by the presence of two delightful coloured Americans in their yacht.

We shared a pleasantly intellectual supper in a dismal taverna where, despite the surroundings, we were served with a delicious meal. But, oh! We found it in our hearts to wish that the Messolongions were more aware of the depressing effect of environs.

By noon on the 5th October, having left Messolongion at crack of dawn, we were at the northern tip of Oxia Isle.

CHAPTER VII

THE IONIAN AND CORFU

CEPHALONIA, TWENTY MILES ACROSS a mirror-like sea to the west was a blue whale-back, blowing a puff of white cumulus cloud. Somewhere lost in the blur of that distant outline was Ithaca, for which island we were bound. It was a long stretch of open water, and we kept our fingers crossed for should Poseidon wax tiresome, it would be difficult to wade in one hundred and fifty odd fathoms. We set course 283 degrees by compass, which, with luck, would take us into the Gulf of Molo on Ithaca, from where the sheltered inland harbour of Vathi strikes southward. It is twenty miles exactly to the Gulf entrance, and that meant four and a half hours of open sea crossing. Not much, you may say, but quite long enough for literally anything to come up from the sullen thundery sky that was building up there to the north-west. By two o'clock in the afternoon we were five miles off the Gulf, but the wind was freshening from the north-north-west, and there were thunder rolls from behind Mount Korifi on the northern end of Ithaca. We donned oilskins and once more packed away all perishable gear such as charts and other papers. The wind continued to freshen, and off the entrance to the Gulf we reefed the main and bowled down into the deep hill-flanked harbour of Port Vathi across a cauldron of black wind-driven water. For a splendid hour, after rounding up at the protected north-eastern corner of this magnificent inland port, we managed to dry out the dinghy and get the p.v.c. tent shipped before the rain again torrented. Looking back into the entrance to the Gulf we knew that, had we been much later in arriving, we might well have foundered out there for the sea was now a frothing mass of white, with really savage rollers.

After the barren brown hills of the Gulf of Corinth, Ithaca was green to the eye. Olives in abundance, and lemon and orange groves but now there was some grass—green luscious grass on the odd flat earth tables around the foot of some of the trees. It made a welcome change, for even Spetsai, while verdant in its larger flora, had little greenery underfoot. Ithaca reminds one much of Ireland.

The day after landing we walked the ten miles to a monastery on the North Island. During this cruise around Greece we covered literally hundreds of miles on foot, and believe me it is not an easy country to walk in. But Ithaca will always stand out in my mind as the greatest endurance test of the lot. That morning, when we started out for the monastery, there was a scud of fast travelling cloud coming over the top of the hills behind the little semi-circular township, driven before a brisk south-west wind. The sun had already climbed above the olive-thick heights to our eastward, and, as usual, I was confident that bare feet could cope with the terrain.

Ithaca is virtually two islands which are joined by a thin peninsula, each of them roughly six miles in length, so its total length as the crow flies is a mere twelve or thirteen miles. Although Port Vathi is on the north shore of the southern section, we had already walked over three miles before we had rounded the harbour and struck out of the town on the only road, which follows the deeply indented coastline. Roads in these islands are not always metalled but for about seven miles or so this one was, after which we had to strike off up a rubble and dust track sheer up the hillside for the monastery, for monasteries are generally and reasonably enough built as near to God as possible. From the map it appeared that there would be approximately a couple more miles to do, but as with all these mountain tracks, this one zig-zagged back and forth to make the gradient tolerable, thus increasing the distance fourfold. We were tired and hot by the early afternoon when we finally made the hilltop where the rambling and peaceful old building stood. After the days spent at sea level, engrossed in the intimacies of the shore, it was good to get high again; like taking strong wine after rough cider. To see the crystal tops of distant mountains towering above the veil of sea mist lifts one into a new dimension of perception. The views across to the other islands were breathtaking, seen in the clear afternoon light. Oxia Isle, from which the day before we had first sighted Ithaca, was firm on the horizon twenty miles away, and behind it the whole sweep of the mainland coast, mountainous and deeply indented, stretched up to the north. The islands of Atoko, Kalomo and Arkudi looked like green and brown pimples in a deep amethyst pool. Fifteen miles to the north of the monastery, though we could see little of it for the intervening hills, lay Lefkas Isle, and far beyond that our journey's end: Corfu.

Despite the beauty of Ithaca, we had by now tacitly agreed that we would settle in Corfu for the winter so as to be ready for an early jump across to Italy in the
spring of 1972.

We had covered some ten miles to gain the monastery, four of them on the
sharp flinty gravel of a dust track, and my feet were painful. The thought of
taking that agony of a track back again was too much, and I suggested that we
try a narrow goat path which appeared to lead downhill roughly in the right direction. I should have known better. Goat paths in this country frequently lead
back to the starting point, and are at best a faint impression where hooves have
spread the red soil across the sharp pitted rocks. This one disappeared entirely
about halfway down a five hundred foot hillside, beyond which was an apparently impassable chasm. My feet were, by this time, two lacerated terminals of
hot pain, and each step made me wince. B. quite rightly had little sympathy,
nor did I want any, but at that moment I would have given a kingdom for a pair
of shoes. Painfully we regained the monastery and set off back down the ago-
nising flint path. After a short distance my eye was caught by a bundle about a
hundred feet down the scree of the hillside. At first I took it to be a goat, but
soon it became clear that it was a sack. Two others were lodged just below it,
and one of them had burst open. In disbelief I looked at the contents: shoes!
Black shoes, white shoes, blue and green and yellow and brown shoes; they lay
scattered down the hillside.

'The Gods have smiled upon me,' I said to B. who sat on the roadside waiting as I scrambled down to investigate. They were shoes all right—but all ladies'
fashion shoes, every one of them with high stiletto heels. However, such a gift
was not to be scorned by one in my situation; it was a moment's work to un-
screw the heels of one pair. By sliding four of my toes inside the gold straps at
the front, leaving my little toe protruding outside, I was just able to protect the
sore bottoms of my feet. The shoes disintegrated by the time we had regained
the metalled road. They must have been old stock.

*   *   *

We took the inland waterway between Lefkas and the mainland—passing close
to the incredibly beautiful islands of Meganisi and Scorpio where Aristotle Onas-

sis's yacht *Christina* was moored in the bay. After exploring Port Vliko, a deep protected lagoon with reedy shores, we pressed on up through the three mile canal to Lefkas town, staying in that fascinating busy little inland port for the night, and on the 9th October set off along the rockstrewn shore of the mainland toward Corfu, a light westerly wind helping us occasionally, but mostly under power.

Just south of Parga there are some deep protected bays fringed with clean white pebbly beaches. We were enjoying our noon siesta, after a snack and a little wine, spread out in our nothings like washing day on the hot deserted beach, taking in our daily quota of tan. I put down the *Greek Holiday Guide* obtained in Lefkas and squeezed a hot sticky fig from its wrapper.

'Did you know, Cuckoo, that just behind us there,' and I waved my hand toward the valley somewhere at the back, 'is the famous Mesopotamos, ancient Oracle of the Dead?'

'Of the Dead?'

'Yes,' I said, 'of the dead.'

'What else does it say.' It is difficult to appear knowledgable in one's own right with B. so I didn't try. I just quoted straight from the glossy sheet. 'On a hill, at the junction of the rivers Acheron and Kokitos an oracular necropolis has been unearthed. It is an amazing construction with a series of passages and underground galleries. Those who wished to communicate with the dead came here. The burial ground was surrounded by a polygonal enclosure about 190 feet by 150 feet. In the middle was a shrine with a labyrinth and three arched gates. Adonis and Persephone were worshipped in the shrine.'

'I don't get much of a picture. Is that all you know?' said the sun-soaked voice beside me.

Now it so happened that on this occasion it was not all I knew, for I had by good fortune when in Lefkas met up with a walking reference library in the form of a large Greek lady who spoke excellent English and studied oracles. 'Certainly not,' I said, spitting out a fig stalk. 'It is an ancient example of those distressing human frauds which are perpetrated even in our present day in the form of fake seances. Our ancestors, no less gullible than we are today, came to this Oracle to ask questions of the departed. They signed in first for a sort of "pre-operation" course of dieting, ostensibly to make them receptive toward the profound knowl-

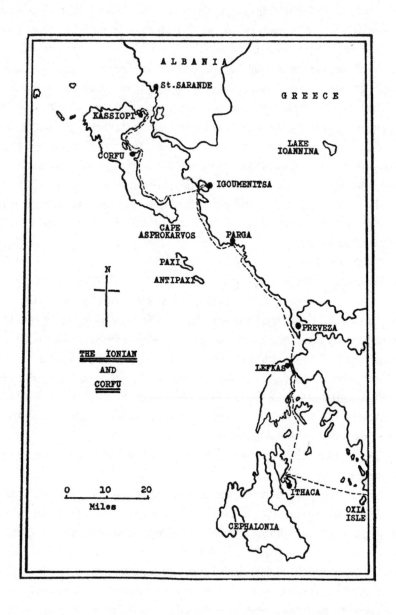

ALBANIA

St.SARANDE

GREECE

KASSIOPI

CORFU

LAKE
IOANNINA

IGOUMENITSA

CAPE
ASPROKARVOS

PARGA

PAXI

ANTIPAXI

N

PREVEZA

THE IONIAN

AND

CORFU

LEFKAS

0   10   20

Miles

ITHACA

OXIA
ISLE

CEPHALONIA

edge which was about to be imparted. In actual fact,' I added, taking another fig from the sticky polythene bag, 'they were submitted to a form of semi-starvation to weaken their faculties a bit before being fed a carefully controlled diet of drugs in the form of a certain seed prepared by the Priests of the Oracle.'

'Fascinating,' B. commented, 'but I wish you wouldn't talk with your mouth full of fig.' She's terribly deflating too on occasions. I finished the fig.

'After they had been drugged into a state of semi-imbecility, they were led down into the dark regions of the underground passages until they came into the presence of the Oracle itself. As far as I can gather this was an actual Priest or Priestess suitably attired in a shroud or some flowing garment, in a darkened underground room thick with suffocating incense, and all very obscure and secret, with gongs quietly beating and subdued wailing voices and suchlike, calculated to arouse awe in the semi-drugged and expectant victims of the hoax. How am I doing?' I asked.

'Fine, I'm getting a picture.'

'But these Oracle manipulators were no fools,' I went on, encouraged. 'During the fortnight or so in which the applicants had been subjecting themselves to the "softening up" preparation, they had quietly been grilled by planted assistants to find out any salient facts about the departed, and most particularly the nature of the requests which the applicants wished to make. Armed with this information it was an easy matter for the 'Oracle' to make the sort of statements which would impress and satisfy the gullible client, for an appropriate fee of course. Just like a fake seance today,' I added triumphantly, and sat up to get the effect. Instead I got a shock. About fifty yards along the beach two large immaculately dressed men were standing looking at us. A third was disentangling himself, incongruously enough, from a thicket at the base of the hill at the end of the beach. Hastily I threw a towel over B. and grabbed my briefs, then stood up.

'Kali spera,' I shouted, for want of something better to shout. They waited until the third man had joined them, and advanced in a line towards us. They looked dreadfully dedicated, these three large men in their black city suits, white shirts and prosaic dark ties. The trouble was, at that moment I had fearful doubts as to what they might be dedicated to. Their black leather shoes crunched horribly on the pebbles. They looked, in fact, as out of place in this setting as three eunuchs at the Folies Bergères. B. was frantically putting on her bikini beneath the voluminous towel.

'Oho,' I said sotto voce, 'we've got a deputation from the Colonels—if it isn't the Colonels themselves,' I added, looking at the three grim faces. But it wasn't quite as portentous as that: one of them, at close quarters, had quite a twinkle in his eye. We passed various unintelligible sounds between us by way of polite conversation, and I noticed that they were eyeing *Lugworm* with rather more interest than she appeared to warrant, bouncing innocently just clear of the beach, our sleeping gear spread everywhere to air, and 'Foogoo' the African Idol glaring in obscene promiscuity back at us from his station at the mast foot.

'Boat-You?' One of them pointed at her and then at me. 'Nai, Ego. Yes, I,' I responded to what seemed a pretty obvious query. One of them was fumbling in his breast pocket and produced what looked like a Banker's Card. 'Polize,' he hissed. 'Ah ! I understand,' I replied, understanding absolutely nothing and wondering what the jails were like in Parga. Then, because conversation was lagging, added, 'Nai, nai, katalava, Police. Yes, yes, I understand, Police.'

'Nai,' he said, and smiled. That was distinctly better. They began to talk excitedly but obviously good-humouredly among themselves, all the while looking *Lugworm* up and down. Finally the one who had a smattering of English at his command approached me again. "We go,' and he pointed to the boat.

'Do you know,' I heard the incredulous voice of B. behind me. 'I do believe they want a trip round the bay!' It was so idiotic, but there just didn't seem to be any other explanation. In my turn I pointed to *Lugworm*, then embracing all three with a gesture said, 'You—in varka, boat?'

'Nai, nai.' they responded together. 'Deka minuti.' This was ridiculous, but clear enough. They actually did want a ten minute trip round the bay. Who was I to deny them this innocent pleasure? After all, it was Sunday. Perhaps they were off duty. But they weren't exactly dressed for strolls through the thickets and joyriding in dinghies. Already two of them had their shoes and socks off. The third followed suit, and all three waded out to *Lugworm*'s transom seemingly oblivious that the waves were lapping above the ends of their rolled up trousers. 'Well,' I said to B. 'Here we go. I hope to be back in ten minutes. Stay exactly where you are and don't get lost,' I shouted as I coiled down the stern warp and heaved up

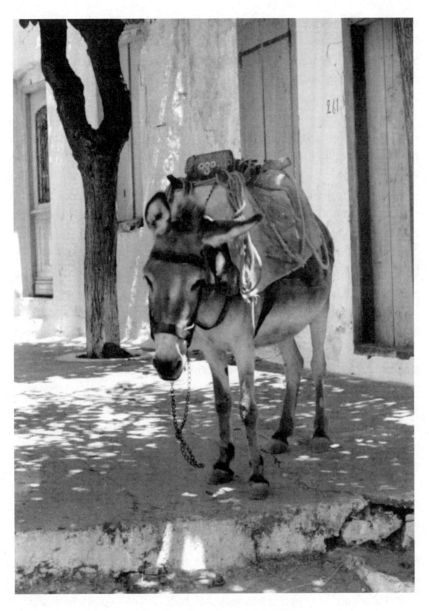

Island transport – it's a hard life

the anchor. The three of them were sitting near the bow, and poor *Lugworm*'s stern was clear of the water. I shifted some of the bedding and the stove, charts and instruments which were lying about, and asked them to move aft so that the outboard propeller could regain its proper medium. Off we went, a very odd looking quartet, sightseeing along the rocky shore.

Suddenly I had a thought. One of those thoughts which always come to me too late. How did I know they were policemen? True, one of them had produced a card, but for all I knew it might have been his ticket to the gallows. How did I know they were not escaped political prisoners, hellbent on beetling to Albania forty miles up the coast. I looked at the three stocky thick-set backs crouched in front of me. I just couldn't believe these chaps really wanted a joy ride because the sun was shining. There was something about the ferocious concentration with which they huddled, peering ahead, that belied the assumption. Already I saw myself casually bashed on the head and dropped overboard somewhere off Corfu,

Lugworm sent to sea with a hole in the bottom somewhere off Albania, sinking and our absolutely everythings going down with her! B. back on the beach doing a caged lion act with her total belongings in the form of a towel and two hankies wrapped round her—not so much as a drachma piece to phone the police!

It sounds quite mad at this distance, but the stark fact had to be faced: it was a very odd situation. Surreptitiously I unlashed the stem anchor at my feet. If there was going to be any trouble, twelve pounds of metal with two spikes would make a handy weapon. If it comes to it, I thought, at least one of these beauties is coming over the side with me!

But they were totally engrossed in the shore. One of them had picked up my binoculars and was studying the rocks closely as we puttered along flat out at four knots, far too heavy laden for my liking. Then I heard a muted 'boom'. It was an underwater explosion, and suddenly, with relief, the whole pantomime fell into place. They were on the track of a fisherman using dynamite to stun the fish. This is strictly illegal, in the interests of long-term fish preservation, and a serious offence in Greece. Obviously they had wind of a culprit in this vicinity and were out to catch him. The whole fiasco became a thrilling hunt to the death; I had been commandeered by the forces of Law and Order, and *Lugworm* was about to become instrumental in apprehending a villain. Splendid. I, too, crouched in true James Bond fashion at the stern. With the explosion a similar, though lesser explosion had taken place among my three passengers. Electricity fairly crackled in the air. Even *Lugworm* appeared to dig her ample nose deeper and growl in righteous indignation, hot on the put-putting scent.

'More, more,' One of them turned impatiently, pointing at our valiant little Mercury already staggering under the load. But it had no more to give. We rounded a headland. The glasses were riveted on the shoreline. There he was—caught in the very act, My God. The telltale bevy of seagulls swooping on the stunned prey floating on the surface. From the rocks, a corpulent figure looked at us in consternation, evidently still undecided whether this obvious pleasure boat could possibly contain anything so un-nerving as the strong arm of the law. We homed in. I thought the three officers were going to swim the last thirty feet, so keen were they, balanced on the stem of the boat, to grapple with the victim. They leapt. The criminal stood frozen with disbelief as two of them grabbed his arms while the third did a neat but fruitless search through his pockets. I suppose they were looking for sticks of dynamite. There was much loud vehement talking, more gesticulating. The victim had now assumed an expression of righteous indignation, his hands spread in a gesture of innocence.

'What, ME!' I could construct from the intonation of his aggrieved outbursts. 'Such a thing!'

But those police didn't give up easily. They knew he had used dynamite—indeed was the proof not there for all to see on the still slightly churned surface of the water—a single sardine, belly up, with a glazed look in its eyes? They pointed, they looked at him, and they searched again. They searched the bushes and the rocks; they peered down into the weedy water beneath the rocks on which they stood. It seemed they even eyed me with baffled suspicion, and then, just for good measure, they searched the now slightly belligerent and feignedly maligned fisherman. Obviously, he had somehow got rid of any gelignite he possessed, and everything that went with it.

Then, out of the corner of my eye, for I was bent double fending the boat off the sharp rocks, I saw him glance, just once, and for only a moment, up the hillside. I too glanced that way. For a brief second, above the top of a thick box bush, appeared a small face, impish, ragamuffin, with a sparkle of triumph in its eyes, then it was gone.

So that was it! He had a lookout. Doubtless he had had just enough warning to throw the whole incriminating paraphernalia of the dynamite and fuses into deep water, but obviously he had already lit one of the fuses. It must have been a difficult situation, with the fuse burning, and suddenly this warning of the approaching boat!

The officers of the law were re-embarking, glumly, their handcuffs, doubtless, burning holes in their pockets. As we shoved off, I looked at the pained face of the fisherman. Was it my imagination, or did there flicker, for the twinkling of an eye, a half wink?

By the time I had made up my mind not to get involved in Greek fishing rights, we were halfway back, and it was a gloomy trio who disembarked, soggy up to the knees and deeply dispirited, thanked me very much, and left.

Meanwhile, the beach was empty. The clock on board showed, to my horror, that I had been away nearly one and a half hours ... but B. had nothing but a bikini and a towel, and you can't go far in that. Then I saw her, dear girl, struggling through the thickets of hawthorn coming down from the top of the hill. I don't know which emotion was winning the day, sheer rage at the discomfort I had caused, or relief at seeing me back safe: for exactly the same thought had crossed her mind as I left the beach with the unlikely trio.

The matter though was not quite ended. We walked inland to try and locate the 'Oracle of the Dead' but failed to do so. In fact, we were probably in the wrong bay, but since we wished to make Parga before nightfall did not have time to explore further.

On return to the beach, as I cast free *Lugworm*'s stern line I heard a squeak of surprise. B. was standing in the boat holding something aloft with a bewildered expression on her face. It was a splendid red mullet, still wet.

We cast a compromised glance up the valley where the Law had disappeared as we bid a hasty retreat toward Parga.

*   *   *

Parga is a fairytale coastal town, unbelievably beautiful as one approaches it from the south, its red roofed houses seeming to climb one on top of another up the lower olive covered slopes of Mount Pezobolos. To westward of the town, bold on its own craggy headland, stands a thirteenth century Norman castle, aloof, seemingly disdainful of the developments which have taken place down below since the Venetians fiercely defended their possessions from within its now silent walls.

We beached close to the town, east of the castle and explored the narrow winding streets, quiet now and empty of thronging tourists. But we chose a more secluded bay just west of the castle for a night berth. When we rose the following morning, it was as though the whole bay were blanketed with white steam. A freshwater stream ran into the sea halfway along the beach, and this colder water from the mountains was evidently condensing the warm air over the cooled bay into wisps of white fog. By eight o'clock it had entirely dispersed, and we continued up this interesting and verdant coast with fickle winds, now giving a boost under power, now coaxing a few knots out of the air until, as we rounded a small headland just west of Parga, we caught our first sight of Corfu. Oddly, this was a rather sad moment, for we were now in sight of our journey's end. Only Italy lay westward, and we preferred to winter in Greece rather than press on so late in the season to a new and therefore more alien country.

The thought of settling down in a house, after the months of wandering free-ly, was strangely disturbing. On a voyage such as we had nearly completed, one gradually falls into a state of mind where to stay in one port more than a day or so makes one restless. Always there is the unexplored coastline ahead, the cape or headland, bay or river mouth beyond which one has not seen, calling one onward. It is the stimulation of an ever-changing landscape and seascape which engen-ders this nomadic drive, and it is, frankly, difficult to adjust to life ashore, bedded down without the freedom of the boat.

That first sight of Corfu was a shock. What first met our gaze from some fifteen miles away was a high line of golden cliffs on Cape Asprokarvos at the southern extremity and behind them was a backcloth of towering mountains. I had always, quite wrongly, thought that the island would be low lying and round-ed, and here we were looking again at the hard tops of what was evidently one more tormented area of the earth's crust. But we could not at that time gain any idea of the verdance on its lower slopes.

Though we were now well away from the meltemi playground, nevertheless the wind was still prevailing from the northerly sector, and a look at the chart made it clear that there would be no lee on the east coast of the island before the actual harbour of Kerkyra (Corfu) about twenty miles up the island. I did not want to sail up the exposed and rock-strewn western shore, preferring to remain in the Straits, so we put into Igoumenitsa—a deep landlocked bay on the mainland from where the ferry steamers operate. Unfortunately we arrived half an hour before a total electricity breakdown plunged this busy town into black-ness—even the ferries had to be guided to their landing ramps by the headlights of police cars and taxis.

Next morning we flitted the nine miles across to Levkimmis Point on a sea so calm that the reflections of Corfu's peaks were dancing a misty pavane on the sea.

Even as we motored gently up the eastern shore of this island, it was obvi-ous that it surpassed in beauty any other we had seen on the voyage. To our starved eyes, there, beneath the thick groves of olive, lemon and orange trees, was dense lush grass: grass as green as that we had said goodbye to in a Cornish lane four months before. But the greatest shock came when the actual town of Corfu came into sight. Instead of the expected white boxes with their flat roofs, here were six and seven storey elegant Venetian style residences. They towered above the old harbour and the surrounding areas, proclaiming with their arches, many shuttered windows and ornate balconies a sophistication and regal way of life which has, alas, almost disappeared from the face of the Earth. High on its hilltop the Achillion, former palace of the lonely and ill-fated Empress of Austria, stood aloof and aristocratic in tumbling gardens the natural contours of which far excelled any landscaping attempted by man. We ghosted in the afternoon sun past the immortal Pondikonisi—Mouse Island—one of the three contenders for the honour of being the petrified remains of the ship in which Odysseus was despatched by King Alcinous after having made an unsuccessful pass at his daughter, Nausicaa. Poseidon, in vengeance for this highhanded action, turned the ship to stone on its return voyage; there it lies to this day, and poor *Lugworm* trembled a little as we skirted its craggy bulwarks.

The silhouette of an armed soldier on the fortress battlements of Kerkyra reminded us that we were now approaching the narrow channel which separates Corfu from the shores of communist Albania.

Tremendous development is taking place to the west of the new harbour, and we were glad to voyage on until free of this carnage where much marshland is being reclaimed. That night was spent in the safety of Gouvion Bay, a deep protected inland lake where modern man, alas, ever keen to mould his environ closer to his own nature, has already spread a scab of shanty development in sad contrast to the elegance of the old town beyond. On the 12th October we sailed up the Northern Corfu Channel, careful to hug the western side lest we inadvertantly stray into communist waters. At noon we put into the tiny fishing harbour of Kassiopi, on the north shore, with its medieval fortress crumbling on the headland and where Nero once sang and made merry at the ancient Altar of Zeus. We did not know it then, but this at last was to be our base for the winter ahead.

*   *   *

One and a half miles out of the village—nearer yet to Italy!—is a small bay the name of which, when anglicised, sounds like 'Seki'. It is just a tiny indentation in the rocky coast but it has its own sparkling white pebble beach like a secret smile on the edge of the deep blue Strait. Behind the bay a deep valley cuts back

into the scrub-covered hills which are almost bare of trees. Not as beautiful in its setting as much of the island, it nevertheless has a view across the Straits the like of which you'll travel the earth to find. Six miles away the hills of Albania glow, quiver and flare into orange fantasies, or dull to a leaden silhouette as the changing weather paints its mood across their barren faces. In winter, snow caps the higher mountains and you can watch the clouds forming, their shadows rising up the bright lower slopes until cloud and shadow join to be combed and shredded by the ragged crystal tops high in the steel blue sky. Across the changing face of the water it forms a backcloth of grandeur which is beyond description.

That afternoon in mid-October we walked idly along the dusty track which meandered round the base of the hills westward of the village, still uncertain whether to return to the town of Corfu or look for a suitable house to rent in Kassiopi. As the track rounded a small headland we saw, deep hidden, this tiny bay. At the water's edge, just above the beach, stood a glitteringly new white house. Its back was turned to the valley and its window eyes gazed across the Straits to those mountains. At the far side of the bay, walking towards us, was a large pink man in a pair of tattered blue shorts. He was followed by a bright flame which materialised enchantingly into a very tanned lady wearing a brilliant orange beach towel. They picked their way along the potholed track, and even at that distance one could tell, somehow, that they were English. At that moment the strap of my sandal broke—B. had at last prevailed upon me to wear a pair of shoes. It was one of those small events which, in retrospect, one sees to have altered the course of one's affairs. I stooped to pick up the leather sole and stood holding it in my hand. As he approached I heard the man laugh, and his first words were, 'Come and have an ouzo, and I'll see if I can find some twine to fix it.' Evidently the recognition was mutual.

We had an ouzo, sitting on the paved terrace above the lawn, watching the water take fire in the late afternoon sun. 'It's a bad road for shoes,' our friend remarked, 'but with luck, by next spring we shall have a splendid tarmacadam highway round the bay. It'll make life a lot easier!' I told him we were looking for a house in which to winter. 'Then you'd better take this one,' he said.

We did.

*   *   *

'This,' I crowed to B. a week or so later as we unloaded *Lugworm* on to the beach beneath the front lawn, 'is our biggest stroke of luck yet.' I looked up the valley behind the house, my eyes ranging over the scrubby hillsides up the deep crevasse of a dried-up watercourse, and on to the distant steppe-grey ridges against the sky. Only the faint tinkle of sheep bells and the quiet sigh of shingle on the beach put bounds to the immensity of peace. What a place to write a book! That evening we walked along the yellow dust road round the headland to the west. Here the hillside was thickly covered with olives, their tops joining hands across the track to make translucent green and shady tunnels. Beneath the trees villagers were already raking the earth clear of weeds so that the black fruit which were soon to start falling might be more easily seen. Before long the great stone wheels of the olive presses in Kassiopi would be turning again, and new baked bread would be dipped into the first yellow-green oil to be savoured with relish.

So, on the first of November, we settled in, B. jumping around the house, 'Oooh-ing' and 'Aaah-ing' with rapture at the hot showers, the splendid bathroom with every mod. con., the superb kitchen with its electric cooker complete with spit, and the vast refrigerator with deep freeze unit. But above all the delight, after months in the dinghy, of instant running hot water.

Meanwhile I was sizing up the place as a possible study for getting on with this book. Bearing in mind that the Greek winter can be cold around February it seemed that a corner of the huge lounge, close against the open log fireplace, would be warm and conducive to relaxed contemplation. That first day I organised the desk and lights and all the paraphernalia necessary for sketching and writing. On the morning of the second day we hauled *Lugworm* high above sea-level on the beach, and chocked her securely for the winter sleep. It was at noon on the third day, as I sat at my desk thumbing through the log of the trip, that a face appeared at the window.

It was a prematurely old, tired face; the face of a man who seemed to have known long suffering. He didn't smile but simply pointed to the east side of the bay, then moved his hands vigorously in a sign which, though meaningless, was oddly disturbing. I called for B. whose mastery of the Greek language was all of two words greater than mine, and together we wondered. But the man was now saying 'Boom, Boom', and pointing to the windows. After a while he came in through the open french windows and started opening all the others. He seemed to be warning us of some danger. We rapidly went through the house opening every window in the place and just as we finished there came a faint 'bang', far distant. I looked at B. 'Was it all for that?' Then came an earthshaking blast and the point of the headland to the east disappeared in an ochre cloud of smoke, dust and flying rocks. The water on that side of the bay turned white with the splashes of falling stone. Our friend said one word: 'Endaksi' and walked sorrowfully away. I looked at B. again, and each of us thought deep unspoken thoughts. Our minds were scanning back across the months. How many times had we seen the searing scars of vast new roads disfiguring the green hillsides, the bulldozers moving sections of mountains in a cloud of groaning dust? Innocent words came back to us, spoken on the terrace that first evening—we, who had seen what it could mean, ought to have known.

At six thirty next morning the pneumatic drills arrived. There were eight compressors, each feeding three drills, twelve of which worked each side of the house. Speech was out of the question, indeed the sheer decibel value of the din made even thought impossible. The ancient Greeks knew what they were doing when they designed their amphitheatres, but no classical playwright ever conceived the sheer sonic force of twenty-four pneumatic drills driving into solid rock up there in the auditorium. Focused as it was on to the small stage on which the house cowered, the effect was unbelievable. Every day for a week it started at seven in the morning, and by nine, deaf and numb, we would stagger up the valley behind—anywhere to escape the brainwashing din.

Then a team of men arrived with long bamboo poles and cardboard boxes containing ominous cylinders wrapped in oiled brown paper. We watched them dropping these cylinders into the narrow holes left by the drills, tamping them down with the bamboo poles, then feeding in a length of black fuse. Our tired looking friend with the long suffering eyes was one of them. We counted the holes ranged alongside the track: there were ninety-six. By eye I measured the distance from the nearest of them to the house: about two hundred yards. It was time to grow alarmed. Taking the tired looking man to one side I pointed first to the house, then to the holes. 'Kalo?' I asked. It was the only word I knew to express the thousand queries rattling around in my head. 'Nai, kalo,' he replied, and then 'Ena, ena, ena,' ('Yes, good. One, one, one.') We breathed again. If that lot had gone up simultaneously we would be picking up the foundations of the house in small pieces, but they were evidently to be exploded one at a time. We ran back to the house and opened all the windows once more, closing the outer wooden shutters as well, just for luck. A man at the far end of the line of holes gave a long wailing cry and everybody drifted round the headland to the west. Our friend indicated that we, too, had best join them. From the safety of the far side of the bay we watched four men hopping along the line of fuse ends.

Smoke began to drift in the still air. They lit the last and nearest fuse, then ran toward us. After about two minutes a single explosion shattered the peaceful air of the valley, a warning blast for the benefit of any shepherds who might have been up there in the shrubs. Then the fusillade started.

At first there were deep muffled underground thuds, but then, among these deeper throbs from underfoot came a stacatto roar followed by another and yet others. Watching the sorrowful man's face I saw him flinch when one of these loud blasts occurred. Those had blown upwards. The muffled booms were doing the damage to the rock down below but these loud blasts were the ones which had found a weakness in the rock above and were throwing lumps the size of footballs high into the air. I heard the musical tinkle of what at first I took to be breaking glass. It was the ceramic roof tiles shattering.

After it was all over we swept the terrace free of broken rock and tried to locate the shattered tiles. There were five of them. 'Well,' I said to B. 'Thank God that's over.' Next morning the bulldozers arrived. Three of them; the hugest brutes you've ever seen. They shovelled the rubble and boulders into heaps then pushed the whole lot over the side of the road to crash down the hillside into the bay. Our drive disappeared under an avalanche. The garden grew smaller. All day the roar of their engines made the air throb and the thud of falling rock shook the house foundations. That night it rained heavily. Next morning the bulldozers started at seven thirty and all the drills had moved round to the western arm of the bay. Down in the lounge, with fiendish selectivity, a steady drip had reduced the papers on my desk to a uniform Mediterranean blue ink-wash. I climbed on the roof and fitted five spare tiles found lying in the garden. The drip moved across the ceiling and fell on to the settee. By now the rain had properly got into gear, falling in vertical cords of grey. More drips started at the back of the lounge and we shifted the furniture around and placed bowls strategically. That afternoon the western side of the bay erupted but this time we stayed in the house, counting the crash of breaking tiles. I replaced another eight in the pouring rain, and just for good measure combed the garden for spares. At this rate we were going to need them! There were fourteen separate drips coming through the bedroom ceiling alone that night and it was impossible to shift the bed so as to miss them all. In desperation I tacked up a waterproof sheet from the boat over the bed and we lay

listening to the musical chatter of water flowing into buckets and pans all over the floor. It continued to rain.

But another, and for me a deeper concern was cropping up. Down on the beach *Lugworm* had received the odd chip of falling rock. How long would it be before she got a direct hit from a boulder? I went into the harbour and arranged with the owner of a taverna for the boat to be hauled on to the shore nearby for safety. I removed Foogoo who had been left in sole command, and next day motored round to the harbour where, with the help of a friendly fisherman we hauled her out, turned her upside-down and securely chocked her. It was a weight off my mind. That evening Foogoo glowered reproachfully down at us from the mantelpiece.

All November and December the drilling, blasting and bulldozing continued intermittently. By Christmas Eve we were stoically resigned to the turmoil, and knew by experience exactly which floor tile we could stand on while remaining unwatered—just! The road and garden was a quagmire of rich red treacly mud in which cars and lorries and even the local bus periodically got bogged with the resultant requests for assistance. The whole house was flushing pink round the edges and the lounge was a swimming pool. B. cooked the Christmas turkey in the kitchen under an umbrella, having baled out the oven first, and incredibly the electric stove still worked. The automatic pump from the freshwater cistern to the header tank, however, gave up the ghost in a theatrical display of sparks and blew a fuse. In fact the only room without multiple leaks was the one room that might not have mattered: the bathroom, with a central drain in the floor.

I wrote the kindest letters possible to the house owners, breaking the news as gently as it seemed wise. Thousands of miles away they could only pray that perhaps, when it was all over, a claim might be made to the responsible authority. One day, in desperation, I stood on the roof ridge after fitting the sixtieth, and last, spare tile and waved my fist (good naturedly) at one of the roadmen. To my astonishment he shouted back in broken English, 'Never mind . . . you'll have a fine road when it's finished!'

Which was one point of view.

Shortly after Christmas we went into the village to take an ouzo and souvlaki with various friends we had made there. As usual I checked that *Lugworm* was safe and sound, glad to think that she was far from the battlefield. There she was, snugged up alongside the taverna door. With six neat bullet holes in her bottom.

Everybody was astonished. The entire village was voluble with offers of help to repair her. The police were delightfully noncommittal, and nobody knew anything. The holes were undoubtedly made by either bullets from a service rifle or a revolver, and had been carefully removed from the far side of the centreboard casing where they had met their trajectorial Waterloo.

The offers of help continued, and so sincerely that it became something of an embarrassment—one felt almost like apologising for the trouble caused. Some drunken 'mother's problem' with a gun had obviously blazed away from the taverna door into the night. Trust an aquatic foreigner to put his rocking boat just where they needed airspace! We clock it up to experience and fate, for we just don't know anyone well enough to have made an enemy!

Meanwhile, up in the bathroom, I press on with this story of the trip, and Foogoo each evening from the mantelpiece surveys us with one of those self-righteous 'I told you so!' expressions that tells us eloquently that we ought to have left him in command, even upside-down on shore in the harbour! Through January, February and March the blasting and bulldozing has continued. We comb the hillsides for wood and sit penned in the alcove by the fire at evening, our Wellington boots slopping a wake back and forth to the kitchen. All the furniture is stored against one wall and occasionally I look at B. and we burst into laughter. Wouldn't it, after all, have been safer afloat?

But we know, despite everything, we wouldn't have missed a minute of it. In fact, looking back across the summer, we are only now able to appreciate how much we have been able to free ourselves from that mental strife engendered by the deplorable rat-race into which we were heading back home. This has not only been achieved through the agents of sun, freedom, adventure and occasional danger. Two contributing factors emerge above all else: firstly the natural honesty of our Greek hosts which would shame our own country's present-day standards. Nowhere while cruising here have we bothered to lock the boat or hide away articles of value. One thing only has been stolen during our visit, and this was luckily recovered the same day—from the English hippie thief. Secondly, we look back with gratitude to the constant help and friendliness of everyone. Most particularly this last five months spent near the small village of Kassiopi has given us a regenerating insight into a pastoral life. Complete strangers as we are, nevertheless we have been accepted without question and welcomed as full members of the village family. It is a good feeling.

*   *   *

April 1972

The irises are out up the valley, and the garden is thick with daisies. The hills are a riot of yellow flowering broom. There is heat in the sun and the mud has caked to a hard red crust. Last week from the top of Pantokrator—Corfu's highest peak—we looked toward Italy. Seventy miles away, could we just make out a darker line?

Foogoo is wearing a contented smirk, once more in full charge of *Lugworm* who dances down in the bay bright and patched modestly concealing her noble wounds. The Tyrrhenian is calling and we shall be off within a day or so. But now that the moment has come we are deeply sorry to be leaving these delightful islands with their genuinely hospitable and kindly folk.

LUGWORM HOMEWARD BOUND

To Bill,
who started it all

CORFU, APRIL 1972

'LUGWORM' IS AN EIGHTEEN-FOOT open sailing dinghy fitted with a four horsepower outboard motor, and she is the other heroine of this book. I had her built in 1969 for £485 and fortunately in the spring of 1971 went potty. It was *Lugworm*'s doing.

'B.,' I had said to my wife, who is mad enough too if caught at the right moment, 'let's pull out of business for good and tow the Drascombe Lugger overland to Greece. We'll potter around there this summer living aboard the boat and then sail her back to England next summer; it'll rout all the hysteria of the old life from our systems!'

So it had been arranged, though in honesty we couldn't afford it, which is why it is fortunate to be mad. The summer of 1971 has been spent fossicking about the Aegean and Ionian Seas getting used to sleeping aboard an open boat and learning to live again. Believe me, the two of us have got so bitten with a carefree nomadic existence that it seemed strange to settle for the winter in this house on the north of Corfu. But it has given me the opportunity to write a book on our Greek wanderings—and I hope very much you will buy it. It is called *Lugworm on the Loose* (Pelham Books) and costs £3.00 which is too expensive, but I haven't yet raised the courage for a row with my Publishers.

Now it is April 1972 and I'm writing this on the lawn looking across Corfu Strait to Albania six miles away. *Lugworm* is proudly bobbing at her anchor just off the white pebble beach below me—I can see the tops of her two small masts from here. She's packed with gear for the voyage and ready in all respects for sea. 'Foogoo', our hideous hand-carved African mascot, four inches of him, hangs by his obscene belly-button at the base of the mizzen mast, belligerently in charge—for have we not placed the responsibility for a successful voyage squarely in his hands? Since B. is in Kassiopi, the nearby village, shopping for the last bits and pieces, I can safely let you into a secret—I'm scared stiff!

Why? Hah! It's all very well in a potty moment to burble, 'We'll sail the dinghy back to England,' but I'll warrant if, like me, you were here and actually about to set off and do it—you wouldn't be seeing the first mark for butterflies either.

'What are you worried about?' I keep asking myself. 'It's only sixty miles across the Adriatic and then another two thousand six hundred or so more around the twiddly bits at the toe of Italy up through France; then, dammit, you're as good as home!'

Trouble is, I'm blessed with imagination—a bad fault in any sailor. I see roaring great breakers dashing our frail cockleshell against black cliffs. I see us skewered by swordfish, buffeted by whales; my dreams fill with oceans of wind-driven spume screaming across uncaring watery wastes, with B. and I clasped in each other's arms, gasping our last. Oh Hell!

No. I must get a grip and try to be responsible. It isn't ME I'm worried about, it's B. I've no right to risk her life like this, she's too young and beautiful. Of the thousand adventures that are going to arise in the next six months, one surely will be disastrous?

Duxbury you're a fraud! These butterflies have nothing to do with responsibility and noble thoughts, love or fear for B. You're just jellified.

So what? You've spent a lifetime at sea; you certainly know a darned sight more about seamanship and handling small boats than Noah and—Oh God!—look what he did!

OF COURSE it's a ridiculous thing to try to do in a dinghy. But if it comes off, won't it be GREAT talking and writing about it afterwards? Adventure—isn't that maybe what life's all about?

Um ... Well ...

But here comes B. round the bay with the last fresh milk we're going to see for many a month. And what's that she's carrying in her other hand?

Heaven above—it's an olive sprig!

I'm going to seal this page at the back of *Lugworm*'s log and alter not one word when—and if—we get home. Odd, but suddenly I've a firm conviction we shall.

Ken Duxbury, the Author

'B', the Crew

Boat and Crew

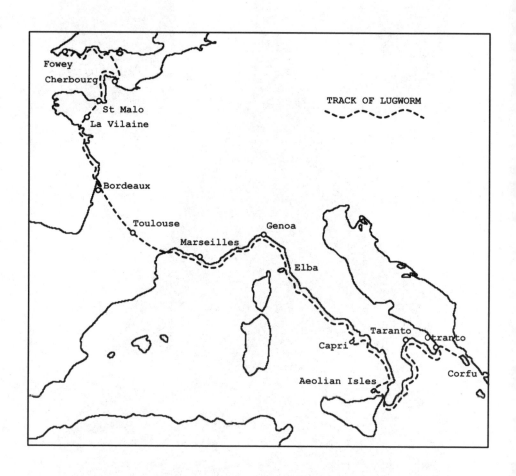

Fowey
Cherbourg
St Malo
La Vilaine
Bordeaux
Toulouse
Genoa
Marseilles
Elba
Taranto
Otranto
Capri
Corfu
Aeolian Isles

TRACK OF LUGWORM

CHAPTER I

THE VOYAGE BEGINS

GLANCE AT A CHART OF CORFU and you will see that there are three small islands off its north-western corner, the largest of which lies some twelve miles out into the Adriatic. Twelve miles, that is, nearer to Italy.

Now you may guess that the prime concern of anyone cruising in a small open boat is to avoid long open-water passages so much as may be possible. A yacht, fully decked and with ballasted keel, if overtaken by foul weather, is often well advised to stand off-shore into deep water and ride it out, but for a dinghy such as ours this could be fatal; she would too easily founder. So it is always wise to have some place of refuge ready to hand, preferably within an hour or so. Of course, this was going to be impossible on the crossing to Italy but it was common sense to make the crossing as short as we could.

That farthest island, called Othonoi, made a handy springboard for the leap, and you may be sure we had taken a few soundings locally. I remember one winter evening in the village taverna tackling our friend Christos about it over a glass of retzina. Christos is the Greek skipper of a fishing caique and a seaman down to his toenails, as well as being the only member of the village community who speaks any English.

'This island here,' I asked him, above the roar of the jukebox, spreading the chart over a table. 'It has a lighthouse but does anyone live there? The chart shows nothing. Is there any sort of harbour?' He elbowed his way across and pulled up a chair.

'You go here, eh? Yes, it is good but is vaary ... how you say ... leetle, eh? Few people there, a vaary leetle harbour and,' he shrugged and made that characteristic Greek gesture with his hands, 'for my boat no good. No water. A few feet maybe but ... how you say ... rifs ... rifts ... what you call those rocks under water?'

'Reefs.'

'That's it, exactly, exactly,' he agreed, using a phrase by which we'll always remember him. 'From a north wind it is good here. Here,' and he stabbed the chart with a gnarled forefinger. 'You anchor in this bay close to the harbour. But if the wind comes south—you get your boat ashore quick, eh?'

201

'What sort of beach?' chipped in B.

'Ammou Bay? All right there; for you good. Small stones, not steep. Your boat, you pull her up maybe, you ask, they will help, the people there.'

Which was comforting. We knew from experience that on the islands, and particularly where there were fishermen, we would never want for help. But it was a problem which was giving me concern for the voyage ahead. On those lonely stretches of coast along the instep of Italy there were few harbours and likely to be few people should sudden need arise. That, however, was a part of the challenge: a problem we would face when it came.

Meanwhile, on that sunny morning of the 19th April 1972, we were as prepared for the voyage as it is humanly possible to be, but—understandably I suppose—when it came to it, the sense of adventure and excitement was subdued by an unexpected sadness. As we walked for the last time across the rock strewn lawn, we glanced back at the house which had been our home for five very momentous months—and our eyes ranged on up the valley behind. It was a riot of yellow broom in the warm spring sunshine, crowned at its rim with silver-grey of the olive grove, and we knew and loved every bend, every ledge and crevass of that place. Our partings were over and done with in the village and now, at last, there was nothing for it but to bid 'adieu' to the house and valley and leave.

As we walked down to the boat, a sound—far away and hauntingly familiar— came floating from the hills and caused us to turn again. It was music which for us will ever bring with it the overpowering essence of Greece; elusive, hidden, seldom located but always there and half-heard—the voice of the very hills themselves, the distant trembling of goat bells.

'Ah,' said B., as she waded out to *Lugworm*, 'I'm not sure I like this much; I didn't think it would be quite so difficult, leaving it all; odd isn't it how you only find the real depth of the roots when you're pulling them up for ever!'

'Oh,' I said, 'we'll be back.'

'Maybe,' she answered, 'but it will never be quite the same again, will it?' And, looking at the raw wound of the great new highway scarring its way ever further along the shore and round behind the house, I knew what she meant. We looked back along the coast where the old fortress sprawled over the distant headland—you could see the bright flash of our secret beach where we found the

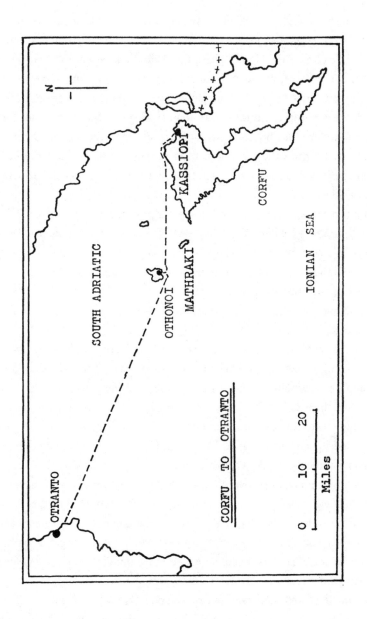

N

SOUTH ADRIATIC

OTRANTO

OTHONOĪ

MATHRAKI

KASSIOPI

CORFU

IONIAN SEA

CORFU TO OTRANTO

Miles

0   10   20

cannon buried—and I saw B.'s eyes swing up the rocky skyline above the village to where the rugged shoulders of Pantokrator, Corfu's highest peak, towered under a cloak of white cloud. There far beyond and above the house was the familiar cypress tree, its green flame still burning the sky, and as we looked our attention was drawn to a small movement. Far up there a tiny figure stood dark against the grey rocks, but there was no mistaking that lean stance, nor the long roughspun cloak and hood; it was our friend Panayotis, the shepherd. Courteous, shy, always withdrawn, he had on rare occasions called at the house to replenish his flask of water and each time he brought some small gift with him, from the hills.

Impulsively we both stood and raised our arms in farewell. 'PANAYOTIS!' I shouted, 'PANAYOTIS ... YASSOU! GOODBYE!' In the complete stillness we listened to echoes reverberating up the sides of the valley, dying away in the hills above, and then incredibly—for he must have been nearly a mile away—we saw him face us and raise his staff in salute.

'Eyes and ears like a hawk,' I murmured, as I pulled in the anchor warp, and there was a long pause.

'Yes,' I heard B.'s soft answer, 'a strange people, so maddeningly unreliable, so infuriatingly naive, yet odd how they can make such a hole in one's armour.'

But *Lugworm* is stirring. Her three tan sails are feeling the first of the morning breeze and the near headland is approaching. It comes slowly up, drifts past, and now gently turns the page to conceal first the house, then the secret bay, then the village and the distant ruins; and last of all Panayotis still standing there in the hills, his staff held high like a benediction.

You must not be impatient. I know full well you want to learn all about *Lugworm*; how we slept in her, how we rigged the tent, stowed all the gear, cooked, dealt with storms, pulled her up the beaches, navigated, blew our noses and had rows aboard; and all will be revealed in good time. But if you're going to share the fun and excitement of this ridiculous adventure, dammit you're going to share the hardships too!

We might as well begin now. In case you don't know I'll tell you that it rains in Corfu in the winter. It rains with such ferocity and so continually that one might be forgiven for assuming it'll never stop. That is why the island is so green and thankful in the summer. April is when the rains finally relent and our moment of parting was one of those first bright smiles of spring.

It was no surprise to us however when, a couple of hours after rounding that first headland, we caught Pantokrator swapping his white cloak for an ominous dark grey shroud. We watched its shadow creeping down the near flanks of the hills to our south, spreading over the beaches and flat marshes of Saouli and Rodha, and already Mathraki island—southernmost of the three ahead—had turned into a black silhouette against the glowering sky. Othonoi, straight over our bow, was now an isolated shining green and white oasis. So calm had our day become, the island seemed supported by its own reflection in a liquid mirror. By noon we were not yet past the rocky Cape Dhrastis at the north-west tip of Corfu and were making no progress. What is more there were ominous rolls of thunder growling up there in the heights.

'I think we're for it,' I remarked to B. We well knew these jests of the weather; seldom did the rain come without a brisk frolic of wind out at sea, and if we were in for a squall, the closer we got to Othonoi before it arrived, the better. 'Best start the outboard and get all the loose gear stowed.'

An hour later we were both standing in oilskins as torrential sheets of icy water deluged from a black sky. When this sort of thing happens, it's far better to stand up because, apart from just not wanting to take it sitting down, you do then offer less actual surface to the slings and arrows. Our world, from being a place of bright warmth and colour, had shrunk to a cold grey circle; even the pale diluted ghost of the land was washed away as we puttered through a blanket of grey water with nothing but the compass to guide us. All about the sea was a spitting, hissing pewter plate, yet still, strangely, there was no breath of wind.

I'm not superstitious, but there are occasions when there's nothing to be lost by offering up a few verbal sacrifices. 'All powerful Poseidon,' I mumbled, peering miserably into the grey pall, for already I could feel that first clammy damp seeping through my oilskins between my shoulder blades, 'have mercy on us. You smiled and favoured us all last summer; have we offended in some way?' B. raised her eyebrows and started bailing. If possible, the torrent grew even fiercer. Then as sudden as the icy trickle that probed down my chest, came enlightenment. 'It's YOUR doing!' I bel-

The voyage begins. Just before the deluge, North Corfu

lowed at her above the roar of the rain. 'When were you born, eh? Pisces! The FISH!'

How clear it was! Discard Poseidon forthwith—was I not carrying in the very boat one of the Piscean shoal? Watery Pisces, so lately clutched to the bosom of planet Neptune; why it was plain as a cod's eye, to Neptune, Roman God of the sea I should shriek, not to Hellenic Poseidon whose domain we were in the very act of forsaking!

'All forgiving, beneficient, omniscient Neptune,' I roared, casting a cautious glance astern, 'Relent, for mercy's sake RELENT! We are but frail humans, lacking the gills to fully appreciate your aweful Kingdom!'

B. stopped bailing and looked at me in alarm. I saw her mouth working and caught, through the hiss of the deluge the words 'for better or for worse' and then—you won't believe me, will you, but that damnable rain fell away before a veil of blessed silence, and ahead, from out of the west, like a smile from the God himself, broke an avalanche of light. It swept aside the hideous dark clouds, bathing and nourishing our steaming forms in the warmth of that after-noon sunshine. And there, close aboard, were two leaping dolphins, leading us away from that awful pall. Oh! The blessing of that heat!

'You little waterwitch,' I admonished B. 'Why didn't you warn me? How can Foogoo and I hope to bring us safely through if the very Gods themselves sport with us?' She said not a word; indeed I believe she was too busy bailing even to hear, but as I pulled my sodden oilskin over my head, I swear I caught the glint of a scaly fish tail fast disappearing up one yellow trouser leg.

We sponged the decks, tossed out the final bucketful and mopped the bilges dry. Everything not actually battened in the lockers was sodden; even the chart which had been stowed in the netting tight up under the side-decks was pulpy with splashes and sagged limply on the bottomboards as we pored over it—for there, close ahead, was the island—and a quick bearing showed that our course would take us straight over the off-lying reefs. I brought *Lugworm* ten degrees to the south and together we scanned its shores.

Islands thrill me. Like humans, no one of them, wherever it may be, is quite the same as any other. It is unfortunate that the poverty of air travel, the isolation of the all-embracing cruise, can present their features as mere distressful repetitions, but this is due to the shallow perception such travel engenders: in fact every island has a flavour of its own, and the finest way to savour it is to approach slowly from afar in a small boat; to be embraced into its arms as a welcome traveller gaining shelter and hospitality.

Ahead of us in the bright sun, the thousand foot peak of Othonoi shone like a beacon, white on the waterline, green up the slopes, and broken with rugged grey outcrops in the higher parts. Already I could make out a straggle of houses, wavering and ridiculously tall in the mirage of the shore, while behind them two valleys probed back, dark with the shadow and translucent green of pine and cypress.

'There are boats in there,' said B., scanning the shoreline with the binoculars. 'I can see the masts; they look like small fishing craft.' As we surveyed the village, we saw that between us and the houses there occasionally appeared a small white line of breakers, and this riveted our attention. A kindly long swell, difficult to detect out here in deep water, was betraying the reefs.

'We'd better nose into the bay from due south,' I told her, 'then scout around and see how the harbour entrance lies.'

'Wait a minute,' she replied, still peering through the glasses. 'There's something coming through the reefs ... a small boat I think.'

Sure enough, dipping one moment completely out of sight, perched the next on the crest of a swell, a tiny rowing boat was working its way out between the breakers. As it approached we could see the figure of a small boy, rowing fiercely, glancing occasionally over his shoulder. When within hailing distance he shipped his oars and stood up, cupping his hands. We heard the call, *'Edho ... edho ...* (here ... here). Follow me!'

I unshipped our rudder from its trunking, hauled the metal centreplate right up, and B. hastily dropped the now dry sails to allow a clear view ahead. Steering with the outboard motor we nosed our way in behind him, and that boy certainly knew his channel. We passed within feet of the underwater rocks, now north, now east, now north again, creeping along and between the lines of white, following the grinning face of that imp, who couldn't have been more than ten years old at most, as he threaded us towards a tiny shallow harbour protected only by a low stone mole.

A group had gathered on a low concrete quay, and the boy indicated that we make fast there. But a long low surge, residue of the swell which crept through the reefs, would have caused *Lugworm* to scrape her golden teak gunwales against the rough edge, which set me searching around for a kinder billet. This is one great advantage of our dinghy: she can float in ten inches of water, and often this fact has secured for us a birth of far greater comfort and privacy than was available to her larger sisters. Eventually we settled stem-to in a depth of eighteen inches with a bow anchor firmly lodged over an exposed rock, and a couple of stern-warps out on either quarter to hold her safe.

It was while I was eyeing the bottom to see that she was clear of any sharp projections that we first caught sight of the captive crabs—tied by strings and crawling about on the seabed all around us for all the world like pets on a lead. But of course this was just the islanders' sensible way of keeping them fresh for when they were needed in the pot. Some of them were huge, and B. viewed the whole situation with some misgiving but as I pointed out to her, 'They're quite harmless unless they bite you.' Which didn't help much.

It was gone 5 p.m. before all was secure. We thanked the child for his pilotage and did our best to satisfy the curiosity of the villagers who were intrigued by our boat, for though neither of us speak Greek fluently, we had by that time enough command of the everyday phrases to make ourselves partly understood.

'And now,' I said to B., casting a weather eye skyward, 'before we do anything else we'd better turn *Lugworm* into a Christmas pudding.'

In case you think me finally off my rocker, I had better explain that this is the term we use for rigging the tent, and indeed perhaps now I should introduce you more fully to this versatile craft of ours.

Lugworm is built of marine plywood, partly decked fore and aft, and with side-decks running down the length of the eight-foot open cockpit. This decking is overlaid with fibre-glass matting bonded to the ply, a fact which has caused many people to think the boat is built wholly of this material. You may ask why just this part of the boat should be so treated, as I did myself when first seeing a Drascombe Lugger, and the answer is because her designer, John Watkinson, is a seaman who has cruised in small boats and knows a thing or two about life aboard. He knows, for instance, that the average dinghy sailor, when forced to

cook on board, inevitably stands boiling saucepans on deck, spills burning methylated spirit over them, allows candles to burn out thereon and stabs them with
sharp anchor flukes; generally misusing them in a way which rapidly reduces any
varnished or painted surface to an unsightly mess. A hard armour-plating of fi-
breglass is virtually immune to all these evils, and I can say as I write this that
Lugworm's decks, after four thousand miles of cruising and over a period of some
three seasons' hard use, remain almost as unblemished as the day we bought her.

She has two pine masts, the after of which—the mizzen—is unstayed and re-
lies for its support on being fed down into a hole abaft the rudder slot, so that its
toe is held in a shoe inside the stern locker, and about twelve inches above this a
strong collar in the deck holds it secure. This mast carries the mizzen sail, which
is very small but quite invaluable to us for reasons which will be obvious later. The
foremast, which carries the mainsail on its vertical 'yard' or 'gaff', is much taller,
and steps on deck in a metal shoe or 'tabernacle'. This mast is stayed by three
wires, one to either side and one forward to the stem of the boat. The latter, the
forestay, is spliced at the lower end into a terylene rope which passes through a
single block at the stemhead, being then secured to a stout cleat on the foredeck.
By easing off this rope lanyard, the mast falls backward to form a low ridgepole. It
was seeing this mast forming a ridge over which a canvas cover was set that first
gave me the idea of a tent.

By removing the bolt on which the foot of the mast pivots, and supporting the
mast there on a three-foot-high 'crutch', at the same time unshipping the mizzen
mast and replacing it with a shortened stump, I realised the mast could lie horizontally about three feet above the deck height to form a ridge pole. It had been a
matter of moments to make the two supports when we bought the boat, and then
a local tent-maker came and measured up for a stout white PVC-on-terylene tent
which fitted over the entire boat.

"You must attach eyelets under her gunwale, or into the hull, to which the
lower edge of the tent may be laced,' he advised, but the idea didn't appeal: I have
a loathing of drilling any holes in boats' hulls for they are meant to keep water
OUT, and any hole, no matter how protected, sooner or later lets water IN! For
this reason I do not even have a drain-bung in *Lugworm*'s hull, preferring to rely
on the well-tried method of hand bailing with a bucket. Suction bailers are good

in racing dinghies, but not for craft which rarely sail at the speeds necessary for them to work, or which are to be left at anchor for long periods.

Instead of eyelets, therefore, I made up a stout terylene warp which can be rigged to encircle the hull about a foot below the gunwales, and it is to this that we lace down the bottom edges of the tent. This warp also serves as a strong girdle for hauling the boat up beaches, and when thus used has the advantage of taking the strain equally all round her hull in a gentle caress, rather than from one hard point such as a ringbolt.

The tent, when rigged, is high enough for us to sit comfortably on the top of the centreplate casing, though I must confess that it was not long before we were leaving the gaff and the mainsail laced to the mast even when it was in use as a ridgepole. Certainly this reduced the headroom a bit but did at least get the gaff and sail neatly out of the way. The mizzen mast, with the sail rolled round it, stows along one of the side-decks—if it isn't left on the beach.

Entry into the 'Christmas pudding' is via the stern where either one or both of the flaps may be rolled back. It all works very well, and of course when the boat is anchored from her bow alone, the open end of the tent is always orientated away from the wind, a point which any camper will appreciate. In a Drascombe Lugger, the outboard ships down a 'well' inboard of the transom, and the boat may be powered with the tent still rigged—a fact which came in very handy on more than one occasion.

I'll sketch the Christmas pudding and you will see that the tent can be rolled towards the bow for any distance one pleases, to uncover a greater amount of the boat.

The whole contraption takes about fifteen minutes for the two of us to rig from scratch and one valuable property of that white PVC tent is that, in addition to being light inside, it also acts almost like a greenhouse: on cold nights the temperature within is always many degrees higher than outside. In Greece we had often found it too hot altogether, so made ourselves a very light cotton tent which secured between the two masts covering part of the cockpit only. Though it gave some privacy, it was of course not waterproof.

The two airbeds, sleeping bags, spare clothes, and my typewriter and papers, went into the forward locker, the hatch of which was made watertight. Provisions stowed in one of two after lockers which are long, narrow and separated by the rudder trunking and the foot of the mizzen mast. The other after locker, on port side, contained the three gallon petrol tank whose feedline passed through a water-tight collar in the deck above. Other non-perishable items such as foghorn, radar reflector, underwater goggles and flippers, containers of spare oil for the fuel, tools and the like, also went into this locker.

On deck, right aft, we carried two two-gallon spare petrol containers making our total fuel capacity seven gallons, and since the longshaft Mercury outboard at cruising revs ran for about 2½-3 hours on a gallon this gave us a range of at least 70 miles at four knots, which is about the speed we would average in calm water. This four horsepower motor, of course, was intended only as an auxiliary for when there was no wind or for shifting around in harbours; if there was an adverse wind it was hardly powerful enough to push us against it, and I do want to emphasise that *Lugworm* is essentially a sailing dinghy. Her centreboard—120 lb. of galvanized steel plate—when fully lowered increased the draught to 3½ ft., and the steel rudder extended about eighteen inches below the hull also.

This rudder is unusual. It slots down through that narrow waterproof trunking you can see below it in the diagram, and the tubular metal rudderpost is attached to the tiller by a brass hinge at its upper end. The tiller therefore may be lifted up vertically out of the way, and when so lifted allows the rudder to swing through 360 degrees. You may wonder why I mention this, but it is very useful, for when the mizzen alone is set and sheeted home, the boat can be left to drift slowly stern-first while keeping her bows into any breaking seas. The rudder blade then 'trails' and thus one may easily steer the boat at the same time. I cannot think of any dinghy in which I would rather have tackled this cruise—and I have spent many thousands of hours in various other small craft.

For 'ready-use' lockers B. had the bright idea of fixing netting shelves, with stout elastic shock-cord at the inboard edge, tight up under the cockpit side-decks. I have attempted to show these in my drawing by cutting away a bit of the side-deck on the starboard side aft. In this netting we kept the chart in use at the time, distress signals, toilet gear and change of clothing plus the ever ready oil-skins. Four gallons of fresh water was stowed in two plastic containers, and these together with a stainless steel two-burner alcohol pressure stove also stowed away under the side decks. With this and a full store of provisions we reckoned to be independent of 'civilisation' for about four days.

For ground tackle we carried two twelve pound Admiralty pattern anchors, one with 150 ft. of floating warp (¾ in. circumference) stowed on the foredeck, and the other with 90 ft. of 1½ in. circumference terylene stowed aft. We also carried an 18 in. diameter canvas sea-anchor, a complete spare set of standing and running rigging, and a spare jib and mainsail. The outfit was completed by a pair of eight foot oars which stowed one along either side of the foredeck. I can tell you when that lot was stowed away in the boat, plus the two of us, *Lugworm* floated an inch or two lower than the designer intended. But she has a very good sheer, with high bow, and even so overladen is a remarkably fine seaboat.

You may guess that wherever it took place, the transformation of a very lovely boat with her black hull and carved teak quarter-badges into a close resemblance to a Christmas pudding caused much amusement among the interested watchers. But she made a snug, dry little home, and the sky that evening in Othonoi gave every hint that we would need one before the night was out.

It rained; by Heaven it deluged again! As we lay on our airbeds, one down either side of the centreboard casing, with two candles throwing shadows in the warm yellow light, the thrumming of water on the tent made conversation almost impossible. It was like being inside a drum. Each of us lay with our own thoughts, that first night aboard of the great voyage home, and I know that I, for one, could not tear them away from the coming crossing to Italy. The night is not the best of times to consider such things; not when there's a first class thunderstorm with all its orchestration of acoustics putting in the background atmosphere. We resolved to stay put until this touchy weather had worked itself to other parts and we listened to the Greek weather forecast in English with much attention each morning and evening. It was just audible on our tiny transistor.

The following day proved clear with a brisk gusty wind from the north west, so together we explored the village and the entire island which is only about two and a half miles in length and less across. There are no roads worth the name: a rubble track leads from the harbour alongside a tamarisk hedge past the Church and the policeman's house and opens out into a wide area bounded on the sea-ward side by the pebble strand, and inland by a miscellany of spartan houses and

CHRISTMAS PUDDING

the typical Greek taverna—meeting place and social centre of the village. We wandered through the village and up the track which climbed the western side of the valley, for through the olive groves we had spied the roofs of a second village. It was just another small group of houses, with a taverna into which we went for a cup of the delicious strong black coffee. The day was warm and the climb had been steep—it was good to rest.

In a small community such as this, the visit of a strange boat —most especially a boat as strange as ours—is an event of note. It is certain that the word had already passed around that these two mad English were sailing home in their cockleshell, and while the Greeks are by nature far too polite and courteous to impose unwanted attention on a visitor, we sensed there was tremendous interest latent in the air, and before we had been seated in the taverna more than a minute or two, three islanders came in, ostensibly to order coffee, but really to size us up.

'*Kalimera,*' we opened the conversation, with the familiar greeting.

'*Kalimera sas,*' came the rejoinder. '*Ti kanete?*'

'Very well, thank you.'

The ice was broken; questions could flow. Was it true we proposed sailing to Italy? Had we come from Corfu? How old were we, and had we any children? What did we think of Greece? Was I a sailor? A navy man?

Always that triggered off reminiscences of the last war, for this subject is still very much alive in the minds of these people. One of the three, a large sensitive man, gripped my arm intensely. 'My brother,' he said. 'You are my brother; my own brother was in our merchant navy and the Germans ...' He was now beside himself with emotion. 'The Germans, in a submarine, they sank his ship, no guns they had, nothing ... they sank his ship and he was drowned.' He broke down completely, tears streaming down his face, and the other two gently piloted him away while the proprietress of the taverna indicated that he was perhaps a little simple, but a good man, and it was very very sad.

We left more than a little downcast that the memories of so many years gone by should still be so near the surface, ready to spring up and raise again the bitterness and hatred which that war had left in its wake. We had heard this tale and similar a hundred and more times in country, town and island as we travelled around Greece, and knew that in one generation at least the roots of their sorrow and bitterness went deep, and there was no forgiving.

But it was difficult to remain sad on such a lovely and exciting morning. We set off up the gravel track towards the north of the island, facing the brisk wind that funnelled down the valley. Soon we were above the village, looking back from the shoulder of the hillside to where the top of *Lugworm*'s tent just poked above the wall in the distant harbour, and beyond that across a stretch of white-flecked sea, the hazy coastline of Corfu could just be seen.

Below us the rich green valley, clothed with pine and cypress, olive, fig and flowering broom, climbed on up to a table land of scrub and rocks. This gained, we wandered through thickets of wild thyme, thistles, and blackberry bushes towards the western shore, and finally stood on the edge of bluff cliffs looking across towards Italy, hopeful perhaps of making out some faint outline of her mountains; but there was nothing.

It was while scrambling up a further rise to view the island's coast northward that we met an islander who, rather oddly, seemed ill at ease and stood in our path as though reluctant at first to let us pass.

'That chap didn't want us to come up here,' I remarked to B. 'It was on the tip of his tongue to say "go back", but he didn't quite make it. Wonder what's afoot?'

PIGEON TRAP

We were not long in doubt. As we breasted the rise, which led to a gentle slope down to more cliff edges, we could see dotted about among the rocks a number of pigeon traps, and they are worth describing for their ingenuity. Each one of them consisted of a shallow hole scooped in the earth and on one edge of this a heavy flat rock was balanced so that, if allowed to do so, it would drop and cover the hole. On the opposite side of this hole another sharp edged piece of stone was placed and over the fulcrum edge of this a specially cut twig was balanced. A second twig sharpened at one end was lodged by its point against the upper end of the fulcrum twig, its far end jammed against the top of the balancing rock. From the lower end of the fulcrum twig two more twigs suitably shaped and sharpened were then jammed against the base of the rock. The slightest touch on any of the three spanning twigs resulted in the fulcrum twig being dislodged which imme- diately let the rock drop. A few beads of corn are put into the hole and the trap is ready. This island abounds in small very quick flying wild pigeons and the bird is a great favourite in the stew pot. When attempting to peck up the corn it inevitably triggers off the trap, and though cruel, they are evidently efficient, for on more than one occasion back in the village, we saw the trapper returning with his booty. I deliberately triggered one to see how difficult it was to reset and it was a tricky task. The object is to stun the bird and pin it down.

I remember as we wandered back later that evening, coming across a riot of white anemones with brilliant yellow centres, and there were orchids, iris (both blue and brown) and a type of mulberry bush. Indeed, some of the sheltered parts of the island were like a natural garden, alive with swallows, and the occasional comical brightly coloured hoopoe, as well as small pigeon.

We ate in the taverna that night—a single room embodying a general store in addition to two wooden tables and a miscellany of hard chairs and benches. The island cooking was, well—distinctive. Apart from the occasional pigeon stew the staple diet appears to have been local fish deep fried or grilled in olive oil, with chips. Always chips; and this night I was strangely unsettled both in mind and stomach. While the meal was being prepared I looked around the room: piles of household wares, brooms, galvanized pails, plastic buckets, twine, and sacks of dried provisions were stacked about. The proprietor, an elderly wizened little man thin as a wraith and the colour of parchment, evidently suffered acutely from ulcers for he constantly groaned, was assailed by spasms of dry coughing, and had recourse to a bottle of what we assume was stomach pills. His wife, a quiet little body, dressed completely in black of the peasant costume, seemed to be in charge, and did the cooking. To our surprise, however, the two plates were brought in by a young man carrying a broken sports gun over one arm, who had obviously just returned from a shooting sortie in the hills, for behind him came an inquisitive black dog of the labrador variety. The sight of two unexpected strangers sitting in the room set him barking at full blast, and only when he had been forcibly removed did I learn that the youngster was the son of the house, and a fisherman to boot. This was fortunate, for we were able to clear up a small, but vital, navigational problem which had been worrying us. Our proposed track from Othonoi to Otranto in Italy, 295 degrees True, was plotted on a very small scale chart covering the entire Eastern Mediterranean. The crease where this chart folded partly obliterated what might have been a small cross, which is the symbol for a submerged rock, and this lay just north of our track line some few miles out to sea. Inspection of local Greek charts in Corfu revealed nothing of the sort in that area, but here was a fisherman who would certainly know if it existed.

Once he grasped my query—which was not easy with our limited means of communication—he disappeared behind the shop counter and shortly emerged with a battered large scale Greek chart of the local waters. Together we pored over this, and I learned much from its more detailed presentation of the island's coastline, but there was evidently no rock out there at sea. We sipped the bitter resinated wine, and picked away at the meal, and the conversation fell into desultory exchanges; but somehow I could not settle to enjoy the evening, and feeling a little sick, eventually excused myself with a remark to B. that I was going outside to have a look at the weather.

I remember sitting in the darkness on the bench under an old tamarisk tree before the taverna, and looking up at the fast scudding clouds. In the bright moonlight they seemed to leap from behind the hills, glance down at me, microscopic mortal that I was, laugh, and hurry on over the wild void of the sea. I looked out across that blackness of water, flecked with the fast moving silver patches which disappeared so quickly and gradually a dreadful weight of doubt seemed to envelop me like a shroud.

'What on earth are you doing here,' the voice of my reason seemed to ask ... 'on this desolate place in the middle of an alien sea? Are you really going to hazard your own life and that of your wife, on that dark and lonely waste, where no man's hand can help if things go amiss?'

'You are a professional seaman,' the small insistent voice continued. 'You know full well that the first and most important rule is never to tempt Providence by taking unnecessary risks; true, your boat is sound and has a stout heart; but you do not need me to remind you of what will happen if the weather turns foul out there halfway to Italy. You know she is too small to take those seas which can rise within an hour to swamp her and send you both to a cold and lonely oblivion: be sensible now while you have the chance; once committed it may be too late.'

I rose, more disturbed than I cared to admit, and looked down at the beach, bright now in a moving patch of moonlight. The roar of the breakers below, and the sigh of a fitful squally wind rustling the trees in the valley behind seemed to voice an insistent warning. Far along the strand, glistening in the brief silver light, I could see the low stone wall of the harbour. Great God! Our boat was too small even to show above it, and as I looked the whole world seemed to expand, and I to shrink, until I was nothing more than a grain of sand in an immense and powerful cosmos which might, with no more effort than an idle shrug, dismiss me and all I held dear to nothingness.

Behind me the taverna window was a small but warm glow in the darkness. Inside there, I thought, was another who had committed herself to this venture simply for love of me, and for whom in this situation I was totally responsible. 'Be honest,' the voice within insisted, 'to risk your own life is your affair entirely; but to deliberately risk another's ...'

I am not ashamed of these thoughts. I am a sailor, and well know the power and the loneliness of the sea. Many times, from the decks of all manner of large well-found ships I have watched grey wastes of water gathering in anger; watched in awe as mountains of energy, rolling invincibly from horizon to horizon, have begun to break and roar before the storm, and I know that a man plays with the sea on the sea's terms, and when his luck runs out, there is no bargain to be struck, no second chance.

The click of the latch on the taverna door broke my reverie. Silhouetted in the light I saw B. peering out into the dark. 'Ken,' she called, 'are you there?'

'Here under the tree,' I answered, and she walked over and sat beside me.

'A penny?' she asked, after a moment.

'Just thinking.'

'Out with it, then,' she said.

But it isn't easy, when it comes to it, to risk calling off a whole planned venture such as this. Still; what was in my mind had to be voiced.

'B.,' I said, 'we have talked of this often before, but I've got to be absolutely sure. When we set off into that void out there, we take a calculated risk, and if things turn against us, it is quite possible that we shall pay with drowning. It is very easy while sitting here safe ashore to feel it's a risk worth taking, but we both know that if it comes to it, we shall be alone to face the fact and there will be no help. It will be up to us and there will be no one to blame but me. Are you prepared to risk it?'

I swallowed hard. If she said 'No', then I knew I was bound to cancel the voyage there and then.

Straight came the answer. 'If that's all you're worrying about, yes, I am prepared to risk it. Of course I'm afraid; I'm terrified of what might happen, but I'm prepared to take the risk this once. To do it often would be foolish, but I think we can make the risk acceptable by watching the weather carefully. It may only take twelve hours—with a bit of normal luck.'

Suddenly my world shrank back to its normal size; I was batting again with as good a chance as the next man, and felt as though a tremendous weight had lifted from my shoulders. So later that night together we poured a small libation of wine over the end of the sea wall—for Neptune—and both slept like logs.

We watched the weather pattern like hawks. Intermittent squalls gave way to short calm periods with sunshine, but I was uneasy at the unsettled quick changes.

The following Sunday, however, our fourth day on the island, broke calm with not a cloud in sight and just a kiss of light southerly wind. A sea, still running from the recent brisk winds, was tailing off, and all looked fair for an evening start. You may ask why we were prepared to choose a night crossing of the remaining 48 miles to Otranto, and the reason is simply that in these waters if the evening is calm there is a good chance of the whole night remaining so, whereas a calm dawn can, with the rising of the sun, bring violent winds by noon. There was a further reason: the probable time for the crossing, allowing an average speed of four knots (which is merely a guess anyway), would be somewhere around twelve hours, and in a dinghy I would much prefer to make an arrival on an unknown coast with the coming of daylight, rather than as night approaches or in darkness. You can then look for a quick lee rather than be forced to keep the sea if the weather turns foul. I therefore reckoned a start around 2100, wind or no wind, would be right and was prepared if necessary to use the motor rather than hang about becalmed far offshore. There were to be no heroics on this first crossing; the object was to get to Italy; plenty of time for disaster after that.

But the 1915 forecast in English from Athens Radio was so unexpected that we looked at each other and could not help laughing; never before during the whole preceding summer or winter had we heard the magic words 'All Greek seas will be calm.'

'Good old Neptune!' cried B. in what I suppose is the twentieth century equivalent of an Homeric Ode. Within an hour we were clear of the bay with a sweet northerly zephyr pressing genoa, main and mizzen as we filled on starboard tack towards the dark horizon.

Ah, but that was a moment! A half moon peered inquisitively down through a thin veil of haze, and the occasional star showed in clearer patches of sky as the outline of our island grew dim astern, finally to merge and disappear altogether in the blackness. Only the moving beam from the lighthouse remained arcing regularly across the sky to assure us there was still solid land in our lonely world of water. Within a couple of hours that too became a faint yellow glowworm, a mere yardstick to dimension, before capitulating to the void.

'Goodbye Greece,' I thought, and noted the time. It was nearly midnight and we were alone, an immense outrageous speck in a void of nothingness that seemed to be considering us quietly, tongue-in-cheek.

If you have never been alone in a very small boat on a very large sea, and at night, then you may never have had the opportunity of viewing yourself in true perspective with the universe. I do not speak of size only, but of values and of such considerations also as human destiny.

In such a situation, and if misfortune should catch you fully aware, you may see yourself as balanced on a tightrope of life, poised unwillingly and precariously between the illusions of Heaven and Hell, Beginning and End. If you then dare to scan that dark ocean which has no shores, you may also have the courage to realise how diverting it is to construct a shadow-harbour called meaning—you may even fool yourself that you glimpse a Hand that jerks the puppet-strings, imagining even that it points out to you a horizon beyond which lies Truth. But that is a disastrous course to lay, for it will rock the ship of sanity too violently for contemplation; and this, after all, is only an account of a terrestrial voyage in this strange experience called life, so bring your eyes to the compass again and try to keep that star ahead in comfortable proximity to the shroud: it may guide us through this night at any rate.

So the long hours went by, the moon swung visibly aside, and still the sea slept, fanned by that soft north wind, and *Lugworm* sang a very quiet song that chuckled and swirled astern, to which a living path of phosphorescence danced.

There was no other ship, or boat, or life on that whole immensity of dark sea, save one small bird that burst with an explosion of wingbeats to settle and share our void for one brief moment, then left us to an even greater solitude.

We slept for an hour at a time, wrapped in a sail and lying on the cockpit floor. After a while the wind fell so light that I started the outboard, and the dull monotony of its throbbing made it all the more difficult not to be hypnotised by sleep, but still the faint breeze gave us a little help from the sails, and it was more than an hour later that, drowsily peering ahead, my attention focused on one spot.

Reaching down, I softly shook B. 'Look,' I said, pointing into the blackness over our port bow, 'and count.' Vague as a wish, a finger of not-so-dark seemed to rise, beckon, then fall again. Time and again we watched; was it three times every fifteen seconds? There was no further doubt: it was the loom of the light on Cape Santa Maria di Leuca—a bright spur on the very tip of Italy's heel down there far far over the horizon. Quickly I took a bearing; if our average speed of four knots was accurate the circle of visibility of the light coupled with our estimated distance run indicated that our position was slightly south of the trackline; we altered another five degrees northward and within half an hour we picked up a second light straight over the bow. It was Cape Otranto, our landfall, over twenty miles away.

I don't really know what either of us expected to sight when Italy first swum out of the lightening dawn, but for me it was a surprise. Accustomed as we had been for the last ten months to the hard rocky mountain-tops of the Greek Islands, bunching almost in defence against the blue sea, this long level coast ahead belonged to a different world. Low ochre-coloured cliffs shone gold in the first shaft of morning sun, stretching either way to north and south. They seemed, wordlessly, to speak of the vast continent behind, where land, land and more land rolled endlessly back. 'I can afford,' they seemed to be saying, 'to lose a few million acres to this tiny sea every year. There is plenty more of me back there.'

We hove up at 0630 in fifty feet of water close under a russet coloured cliff and no sooner had *Lugworm* settled to her anchor than a clamour of black crows launched in protest from scores of holes lining the cliff top. With one mind they swooped, spread their wings and jettisoned a cargo of good luck all over us and the boat.

'Don't fret,' I comforted B., wiping a well aimed tribute out of her hair. 'It's only the ghosts of drowned sailors jealously reminding us how lucky we have been.'

'Maybe, but I think it's a pretty poor entry into the Common Market,' she answered.

It's very hard to be poetic with B. in the boat.

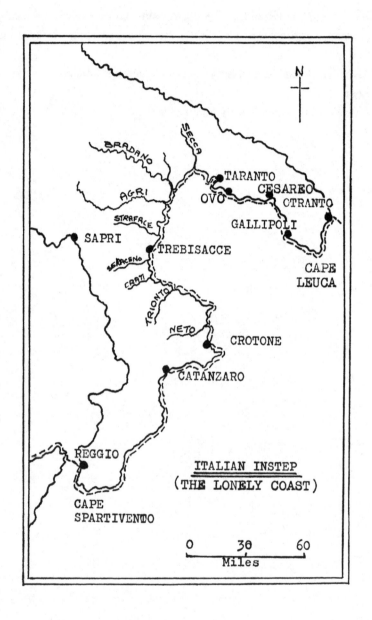

N

BRADANO

SECCA

AGRI

TARANTO

CESAREO

OVO

STRAFACE

OTRANTO

SAPRI

GALLIPOLI

SERACENO

TREBISACCE

CRATI

CAPE
LEUCA

TRIONTO

NETO

CROTONE

CATANZARO

REGGIO

ITALIAN INSTEP
(THE LONELY COAST)

CAPE
SPARTIVENTO

0   30   60
        Miles

CHAPTER II

THE LONELY COAST

OTRANTO WAS OUR NEAREST official 'port of entry' into Italy, hence the need to make a landfall some twenty-five miles north of Cape Santa Maria di Leuca, round which we were bound to sail anyway. It was a great challenge trying to speak Italian after ten months struggling with Greek especially since my own mastery of the language was contained within the first four lessons of a Linguaphone course taken fifteen years before. B. was in even worse state, though later it was she who became more competent; it's something to do with age.

We brewed up a cup of coffee there under the cliffs, wiped the dew and the good-luck off the decks and stowed the boat neatly before nosing into the sleepy harbour. Before long we were confronting the Customs Officers. Fortunately one of these, a tall goodlooking chap, spoke a little English and after glancing at the dossier marked 'Ship's Papers' which I presented, he surveyed us quizzically and then strode to the window through which *Lugworm* was visible.

'You have come from Corfu,' he stated, 'and you are sailing to England.' I nodded. He glanced for a moment at his assistant and then gathering up the folder moved towards the door, beckoning us to follow. 'I must examine your "ship",' he said with faint emphasis on the last word, and my heart fell—not because we had anything to conceal but at the thought of what such officialdom might portend along the vast seaboard which lay ahead. Never once in Greece had we been officially inspected other than in amusement or natural curiosity. It seemed we were now suspect.

Aboard the boat the officer and his assistant sat in the cock-pit and looked about them. I caught the glance of one of them when he came face-to-face with Foogoo—who was giving every bit as good as he got. And then, 'What have you in there?' he asked pointing to the forehatch. 'Clothes, our bedding, my typewriter, paper and things' I replied. 'And in there?' he pointed to the two after hatches, adding, 'I would like to see in them.' The two of them got down on the floorboards and with bottoms in the air squinted into the narrow lockers which were crammed with foods and equipment. They then peered up through the netting under the side-decks, felt the furled sails, examined the outboard, fingered the rigging wires and tested the weight of the oars, chattering meanwhile in voluble Italian. Finally the assistant attempted to lift one of the cockpit floorboards, and this is no easy task. 'Truly,' I said, feeling a thorough criminal, 'really we have no dutiable stores aboard.' Unless B. was engaged in a bit of private dope smuggling, I knew we were innocent of all else. The senior official looked at me. 'But we do not doubt it,' he smiled. 'It is just that we cannot understand—where do you keep the mad dogs?'

After that things were much happier. Back in the Customs House we were issued with our first real 'ship's paper' in the form of a magnificent *Constituto in Arrivo per il Naviglio da Diporto* to put in our folder and I swear *Lugworm* wagged her tail as we filed it away in the ship's office—under the airbeds in the fore locker. Those two officials proved real friends, helping us to translate the weather forecasts, and identifying the stations on our minute tran-sistor against the wavebands on their own sophisticated equipment.

But a rapidly blackening sky portended no good and by noon the wind had freshened a lot. We rigged the tent and set off to explore the coast southward on foot.

Some of the most interesting landmarks right round the coast of Italy are the 'Torres'—watchtowers—built long ago to guard against approaching danger in the form of pirates and the like. These lookout towers formed a chain, usually within sight of one another, from which signals might be passed. Built very solidly of stone, some of them have been kept in fine condition, indeed on occasion we found them converted into splendid private houses, while others are mere mounds with only a few cut blocks indicating their original use. Torre dell'Orto, for instance, a mile south of Otranto, is almost totally demolished, only one section of its circular walls still standing.

We knew from our voyaging around Greece that, taking into account enforced stops due to bad weather and days spent exploring ashore, we could expect to average about twelve miles a day in the boat. Of course, sometimes we quadrupled this distance when conditions were good, but the great safety factor about this voyage was the length of time available; there was no need to rush—and that meant no need to take risks with the weather. I am convinced that this time factor is the cause of many disasters in small boat cruising. When there is a date looming up which must end the cruise, or any urgency to be in one place at a given time, even the most experienced seaman tends to take more risks than he would otherwise.

This is not meant as an indictment of racing—then one must expect to take risks, and long may there be people courageous enough to accept these risks—that's the challenge of it. But when cruising quite different priorities apply. Indeed on this trip home we must have walked almost as far as we sailed, for always when pinned down in a place of refuge we used the time to survey the coast ahead. In our situation it was comforting to know beforehand that just beyond some rocky headland there lay a small beach where the boat might be grounded; or that halfway along a ten mile stretch of unbroken sand was an inlet leading perhaps to a tiny lagoon. So often the chart, in these minor and nor-

mally unimportant details, proved lacking. For us, thirty feet or so of shingle beach jammed between miles of cliffs and rocks might spell the difference between safety and disaster.

The following morning the forecast gave strong southwesterly winds of force six to seven. The sea, so calm twenty-four hours before was already a forbidding picture and obviously it was a day for exploration.

I remember that first long walk in Italy well, and for a most unusual reason. Beyond the lighthouse on Cape Otranto the straight low cliffs gave way to a more indented rockier shore backed by hills. It was while wandering round a small inlet called Porto Badisco two miles south of the light that we came across heaps of dead seaweed, piled up like brown straw just above the waterline. That's what we thought it was until, when taking to a small coast road a few hundred yards beyond we were intrigued at the sight of detached pieces of this 'weed' walking across the metalled surface. Each small piece of raffia-like weed was steering a course unerringly up wind. Indeed, it was clear that no other course was possible, for the trailing fronds of straw, looking like miniature witches' brooms, blew to leeward and the grub, whose perambulating parts were all at the bow, crawled doggedly on totally guided by the air-stream. Whether these creatures had inhabited the dead weed, or whether the whole insect had assumed an identical form by way of camouflage, it was quite impossible to tell, though the latter seemed more likely. The closest examination betrayed no joint of grub and weed: it all seemed to be one. I'll draw it with my toe beside to give an idea of size.

WEED INSECT,
WITH TOE ADJACENT.

We knew that our first place of safety was the tiny fishing harbour of Porto Castro twelve miles from Otranto, and the following noon put to sea under all sail before a light northerly and ran close down the shore to enter this tiny port in the early evening. We found it to lie just west of a small pointed headland snug under the cliffs, and to consist of two quite separate inlets, too small for anything but open day boats. The eastern harbour is formed by a stone breakwater running out almost parallel to the cliff with a quay on its inner side, and it was to this that we berthed, stern-to.

It is interesting to dwell on the reaction of fisherfolk to our appearance in such remote harbours—we came to expect a certain pattern of behaviour, and soon began to understand the causes. Unless we obviously needed help—in which case it was always willingly given—there would first be an almost studied indifference; as though the locals wished to imply that the appearance of a strange boat was of no account whatever, and they would all carry on with their business almost deliberately not meeting one's eye, or in any way making contact. Very shortly, however, when we were safely berthed under the watchful but guarded observation of all present (did this foreigner know how to handle a boat?), and when we had left *Lugworm* perhaps to explore the port, one would see a group collect on the quay alongside the boat. She would then be subjected to curious and very detailed scrutiny. If we returned towards the boat the group would usually disperse, but now faces would not be averted, eyes would meet, a small measure of contact might casually be made. I knew this was the moment to ask for some form of assistance, for there is no finer or quicker way of making friends than placing one's self at a small disadvantage; country people and fishermen, as individuals, are almost without exception, kind. The art lies in knowing how to present an opportunity for the individual to overcome the barrier of fear—fear of a rebuff from the stranger, fear of inviting the censure of his own group by appearing to be too friendly with those who, after all, might turn out to be objectionable. It would be either the strongest character of the group—the natural leader—or the buffoon who volunteered to exchange any pleasantries, or more likely pass some good-natured humorous comment at the expense of the stranger, ostensibly to make his companions laugh, but in reality to sound out the newcomers' reactions. All this, however, could be short circuited by a well-timed appeal for information, or a request for help to moor the boat or an offer to buy something. Show one's self to be a human being, endowed with similar reticences and an errant soul like all others present, and the barriers would fall, questions flood in. From that moment on, the atmosphere would be one of ready help and genuine interest. The fact that one small man and this slight woman (B. never failed to soften the hardest hearts for she has an appealing shyness and delicacy with strangers) had come in this tiny boat so like their own all the way from Greece—Goodness! And bound for Taranto? Could it be true—right round the Cape! To Reggio—NEVER! That was round the toe of Italy itself!

England. England? Where exactly was England ... that was the other side the world somewhere, eh? Again and again in southern Italy astonishment would be shown at the crossing from Greece, whereas our intention of sailing to England brought nothing more than a nod. It was too far away to mean anything.

*   *   *

As you swan southward towards the very tip of Italy's heel the coast becomes progressively more rocky and steep, climbing straight from the water's edge four hundred feet and more up pine clad hills. That next week sailing before a brisk northerly, we were able to run within yards of the cliffs, poking into every grotto and tiny bay hungry for what might be revealed; and it was a surprise when suddenly the domed top of the lighthouse on Cape Leuca loomed above the limestone hillside. It grew taller and taller as we circled the headland until finally the whole eight-sided column towered graceful and white into an unbelievably blue sky for all the world like a colossal needle left sticking in a green and white pin cushion having sewn together the blue Adriatic and the wine-dark Ionian. Banks of terraced steps led from the little harbour up the hillside to the church of Santa Maria di Finibus Terrae—Our Lady of Land's End—for such was the ancient Latin name of this headland from which sailors since time im-memorial have taken bearings when voyaging from Greece to Sicily.

We rounded the point and beat up into the shelter of the mole, well protected from the north but very vulnerable to the dreaded Sirocco winds that come scorching up from Africa. There was no room at the quayside for a stranger; indeed the local fishing boats seemed hard put to find space. So we sailed a little westward towards Punta Ristola and brought up in a small shallow cove with a sandy beach at its head.

I recall that evening sketching one of the fishermen weaving a beautifully delicate but functional lobster pot from thin split bamboo cane. It stood about five feet high when finished and was light as thistledown. He told me that he made one every two days and I believed him for his fingers wove the cane with incredible dexterity. Later we saw boats putting to sea laden with these basket pots piled high and looking rather like floating haystacks.

But a major decision now had to be made; whether to sail the seventy or so miles direct across the Gulf of Taranto to Crotone, or to continue coasting three times that distance round the instep. For reasons already explained, the former course was very risky, especially since this area is noted for its sudden and violent storms. On the other hand, for the next three hundred and more miles, the coast, apart from the three ports of Gallipoli, Taranto and Crotone, offered virtually no shelter until we were round the toe of Italy and into Reggio, Calabria. From inspection of the chart it was evident that rivers flowed into the sea at fairly evenly spaced intervals, but whether these would be navigable even in so small a craft as

THE LOBSTER POT MAN

ours was problematical, and we got very conflicting answers to our queries on this point. Obviously if we did creep round the coast, the two of us alone might need to get *Lugworm* up the beaches if necessary and above the breaker level.

'If we went direct and conditions remained fine, we could be in Crotone within twenty-four hours,' I mused, watching B. to see her reaction.

'Yes, but to get caught out across the mouth of the Gulf with nearest land over thirty miles away would make us look pretty silly,' was her sensible comment. To be honest the weather was worrying us both. For the time of year it seemed all wrong. A choleric purple haze, not to mention intermittent rumbles of thunder back inland was more akin to late summer than early spring, and recent disturbed conditions made us wary of sudden violent storms.

So the decision was taken: round the coast it would be. Now I must tell you that fully laden *Lugworm* weighs something around 1,200 lb. and this is more than one man and a slip of a girl can haul up a beach. While in Greece we had devised a method of getting the boat on to a lee shore above the breakers, provided that this was effected before those breakers became large enough to swamp the craft. Success depended on making the decision to land in good time, but the system itself was simple. Having selected a suitable spot where the beach appeared to slope gently and the waves were not too violent, we would drop our bow anchor and lie head-to-seas just outside the breakers with mizzen alone set and sheeted hard. Our tent girdle of floating rope was then rigged round the entire hull and a double block attached aft. With outboard and centreplate raised, and the rudder unshipped, B. would then station herself at the bow and start checking away on our 150 ft. of anchor warp while I stood at the stern with the second anchor and 90 ft. of terylene warp, the end of which was already rove through one sheave of the double block. As *Lugworm* drifted back I would wait for the first crunch on the beach, then leap ashore taking the anchor and the warp-end with me. Then came the tricky part. You will realise that it was essential to keep the boat bow to sea, for to broach across the waves might easily have meant swamping. While B. kept the bow warp taut, I would jam the stern anchor behind some convenient rock ledge or even round the bole of a tree, then, with a rolling hitch, attach a single block to the warp about halfway up the beach. Through this single block I would reeve the tail end of the stern warp, then take it quickly through the second sheave of the double block at *Lugworm*'s stern: which sounds simple, but try doing it with the boat lifting and sheering in the white water, and often a long surge running up and down the shingle.

Taking the strain on the tackle I would haul *Lugworm*'s stern hard ashore while B., having eased off a suitable amount on the bow warp and turned up, would leap ashore and join me on the tackle. It all had to be worked with a keen eye to the seas and surge and *Lugworm*'s angle relative to both, but having used a surge to get her as high as possible up the beach, there would then be brief periods of respite, for she would only 'lift' at the very top of each following surge. We had time to look around for some likely piece of driftwqod to jam under her keel aft, over which the boat could more easily slide, for you will realise that dragging her across soft sand (this was the worst of all) or fine shingle was, even with the tackle, very difficult. Once a flat rock, or maybe a stout piece of driftwood, was positioned there, we would together get down to the heavy work of dragging her further back. Even with the tackle it was not easy, but half a boat's length was often sufficient, for it was only necessary that she be above the line where the longest surge might float her. Of course, if we proposed leaving the boat for any time we would make sure she was well above the danger line, bearing in mind that an increase of wind might well bring the surge another fifteen to twenty feet up the beach.

It was the first of May before the weather relented from a minor tantrum of squalls and heavy rain, giving us leave to continue up the coast to Gallipoli. We covered thirty miles that day, mooring just after sundown in the shallow western basin of the old port. I shall never forget our first sight of the place as we rounded Punta del Pizzo three miles to the south. It was one of those evenings when the world has lost her brash reality and taken on the gentle miraculous colours of a Turner or Ruskin. Distances grew immense, expanding under the soft rose and green of an evening sky and the old town seemed to float above the edge of the sea, shimmering over the fortified walls, and marvellously heightened by the mirage effect. We were still too far off to make out the narrow low causeway that joins it to the modern extension on the mainland. It hovered there, the last shafts of sunlight glowing on the western walls, and we just sat and drank it in, ghosting silently up before a soft south wind, half afraid that it would evaporate before our eyes like some dream citadel; it was not without cause that the ancient Greeks named her Kallipolis—Beautiful City.

But that magical quality endowed by distance was soon dispelled as we landed on her busy quays, for it was market day, and we were soon lost in the hubbub of stalls, and noisy bargaining. Adjacent to the dock gates were the shellfish stalls, piled high with shrimps, mussels and oysters, to say nothing of scallops and cockles, crayfish and many types of winkles, B., to my astonishment, proclaimed that she had never tasted an oyster, so we bought three each and half a lemon, first getting the exuberant stallkeeper to open the shells for us, watched in amusement by a crowd who quickly gathered. Our arrival had not passed unnoticed from the walls towering over the basin, and the Red Ensign advertised our novelty value. That lively and uninhibited interest which is the hallmark of the Italians was soon unleashed on us, captives as we were, among the crowd. But we took our oysters along the quay, climbed some narrow worn steps directly above *Lugworm* and sat on the very top of the immense stone walls, savouring each mouthful as we watched the last light disappear over the east basin where the fishing boats were busy unloading.

It was exciting to later roam the busy streets of the new town across the causeway. The elections for a new government were taking place very shortly, and loudspeakers blazoned the virtues of various candidates—of which there seemed to be dozens—not without attendant noisy comments from the populace. But we were tired after a full day's sailing, and it was good to return aboard to the comparative peace of *Lugworm*, lulled until the early hours of the morning by the—for us—unusual distant noise of a large town.

*   *   *

A source of some contention between B. and myself is my built-in aversion to guide books. The truth is, I'm a born explorer—in a world where the art is well nigh impossible to exercise. Just show me a hill and I ask, 'Is there anything more interesting than what might lie over the top?' Drop me in the middle of a town and my day will be happily spent poking round each successive corner. So you will understand that, this waffling along unknown coastlines was pure bliss; for I can imagine no greater stimulation than not knowing what lay beyond the next headland. 'In Heaven's name,' I would argue with her, when in one of my more belligerent exploratory moods, 'who wants to wander about a stage, the "sets" of which are already "old hat" before you arrive? Surely, there's more fun in discovering things for one's self. Why ruin all the effect by knowing about it first?'

But this advanced form of philosophy falls on barren ground. 'In that case,' she might reply with decimating logic, 'why have you spent a fortune on Admiralty charts?' Indeed, it is difficult to be ethereal with B. She lives on a more realistic plane than I, and I love her for it, but there is some romantic quality lacking in her make-up—a fact which helps keep us solvent.

Anyway, about ten miles up the coast from Gallipoli the chart showed a shallow saltwater lake with narrow inlet from the sea. It looked interesting, especially since the lake was thicker with crosses than a churchyard. 'That's the place for tonight,' I assured her as we hoisted sails outside Gallipoli. 'If we miss all those rocks and provided we can get through the entrance, it'll make a magnificent shelter.' But I ought to have known better and left that first bit out.

'You mean Porto Cesareo?'

'Uh-huh' I commented, settling comfortably against the base of the mizzen mast. She continued to study the chart with more dedication than a crossword puzzle—and that's saying a lot for B.

'It's got "Occ. 3 sec. 13 M. La Salmenta. 92. conspic." in brackets. What's all that mean?' she queried after a long silence.

'Leading lights occulting every three seconds, visible for thirteen miles. Get them dead in line and they take you into the lake clear of all off-lying rocks. A transit of the two bears 034 degrees True,' I said taking a quick squint over her shoulder. 'Useful for checking your compass. La Salmenta must be a village with something conspicuous ninety-two feet high, probably a church, for taking bearings on.'

But I sensed she still wasn't happy. I had another look at the chart myself. True, it was a very tiny entrance, with no more than a fathom depth at the narrowest neck, which was fine so long as no swell was running, and it wasn't.

'It's a lousy lee shore,' she said after a while.

It was a gorgeous morning, very hot with a light westerly kissing the sails and *Lugworm* chuckling with bliss. We passed the Torres Sabea, Fiume, Caterina and Luzzio, bright against a darker line of hills beyond. I was stretched full length now deepening my tan, idly studying the outline of Gallipoli astern, which still quivered in the heat haze.

'Where do we go if we can't get in?' came the query.

'Oh, we'll find somewhere, there's sure to be some crack in the coast.'

Silence.

'We're heading straight for a wreck,' came the voice.

I never have established the cause, but B. just has these days. The strange thing is that they only occur when the weather is calm, hot, and doling out buckets full of Paradise: but let it turn foul, indeed bring on any emergency situation and she's as cool as a cucumber, competent up to her beautiful eyelashes. Maybe it's just a basic incompatibility of Nordic blood and Mediterranean humidity, but obviously this was to be one of those days.

'Don't worry about it, cuckoo.' I had noted that wreck marked on the chart and we were passing well inshore of it. As for Porto Cesareo I wasn't a bit worried: if the Italians took the trouble to mount leading lights on beacons, certainly they were not there to beguile mermaids; it was a safe bet the lake was used by local fishermen.

'Good God!'

I sat up. From B. that might mean anything, but she was still looking at the chart.

'Have you seen when this was last corrected? 5th February, 1954—nearly *twenty years* ago!'

'All the more fascinating,' I consoled her. 'It shows what the coast was like then—intriguing to see the alterations in the last twenty years.' All the same, I thought, squinting at the chart, that did seem a bit antiquated.

'You're wrong, see, here,' and I pointed to the bottom left hand corner. 'Last small correction was in 1965. 1954 was the last large correction incorporated when the new edition of the chart was printed.'

'So it's only seven years out of date,' came the comment, not without sarcasm. 'The lake could still have silted up in that time: there may be no entrance at all.'

'Cuckoo, DO stop fidgeting. How do you think the early navigators coped when the chart simply ran out on them, imagine it: nothing but a dotted line and "UNSURVEYED" written in with a quill pen and splendid little fat cheeked cherubs puffing all over the place with their backsides obliterating five hundred miles of coastline that might or might not be there; how would you feel about that? Seven years—Hah! The sand hasn't settled on the barnacles yet.'

I might have saved my breath.

'And what's THIS,' she squeaked, unrolling the chart from gunwale to gunwale, 'CAUTION—SUBMARINE EXERCISE AREA. And we're slap in the middle of it!' She was standing now, bristling with alarm as though expecting at any moment to be impaled on a periscope.

'For heaven's sake, cuckoo, any submarine Commander who brought his vessel this near to the coast would need wheels on his bottom, just forget it, lie down and enjoy the sun.'

There was a long pause. 'Torpedoes!' came a faint squawk.

You see what I mean? I started ferreting about in the locker for a bag of tomatoes and the flask of wine. From experience I know the best thing in the circumstances is to feed her. But the trouble with those after lockers is they're long and narrow and in such a locker—have you noticed?—anything you want is always right at the back. I got down on all fours, the helm jammed under one elbow, and squinted into the cavern. Above me there was a flapping of terylene. I leapt up. Over the bow, Gallipoli was grinning at us. B. was sitting with tightly compressed lips, with an expression of long suffering. *Lugworm* was in irons.

'Back the jib please, darling,' I requested quietly. But we were already making sternway. The helm slammed over, knocking the wine bottle off the side-deck, the tomatoes were already spread over the chart, two of them squashed flat.

'Happy now, Vasco da Duxbury?' came the comment as we continued in a silent but profound dudgeon. But you must know that I have a buoyant soul, a soul that is nourished on sunshine, and I cannot respond to pique, even under the most extreme provocation.

Ahead the low coast swept in a splendid curve westwards, and somewhere along there forty miles away in the shimmering haze was the mighty port of Taranto. Exciting to think we would be there tomorrow—and after that? Nothing but the lonely coast, and rivers; truly, this was adventure.

The leading marks at Cesareo stood out clearer than Belisha beacons; two black and white chequered towers, one behind the other, and around them the sprawling chaos of a thriving town. 'See what I mean,' I cried to B. 'What can happen in a mere seven years—the place is throbbing with life. So much for your sanded up wilderness.' Indeed a high powered fishing boat was charging out of the narrow inlet, a white bone in her teeth and the whole navigational problem had evaporated: all one had to do was to stand on until those towers came in line, then steer for them.

We freed off and surged under sail through the narrow channel, the reefs glowering black on either hand, while beneath our keel the white sand was pockmarked with darker spots of weedy rock. Once clear inside the entrance I rounded head-to-wind and we handed all sail, for I thought it wiser to proceed under motor for the first time in this busy harbour. All secure we headed under power direct for a low stone quay. On the far side of the channel, along the sandy beach, a man was running, waving cheerily to us. I stood on the transom and returned his salutation, commenting happily on the splendid welcome.

Inertia is a strange thing. If you've ever daydreamed while going up a store's escalator you will know what I mean; there you are flat on your face in the haberdashery. But you try it balanced on a rocking deck with your eyes glued through the glasses on a running figure half a mile away. I can tell you that acceleration from a relative nil to four knots plus in zero time is devastating. Devastating enough to hammock B. in the foresail and send me crashing headlong in the cockpit.

'Astonishing,' she commented dryly, when the mess was sorted out and we had established *Lugworm* was undamaged. 'Astonishing how fast rocks can grow in seven years. But I do observe,' she added with icy sarcasm, 'that we were about a hundred yards off the transit when we hit.'

Dammit, with B. in the boat, a chap can't be perfect ALL the time.

*   *   *

To be honest, I think I like being lost. After all, one spends all one's lifetime being continuously 'found', getting lost makes a change. Now you might wonder how this is possible along a dead straight piece of coast when you know perfectly well that the port you've just left is back there behind you, and the port you're heading for is certainly within thirty miles or so ahead. But like most things in life being lost is a purely relative state. On that hot and oppressive morning it was relative to Cesareo and Taranto.

The trouble is, all those damned 'Torres' look the same. Oh, their names are wonderfully different: there's Torre Chianca and Torre Lapillo, Torre Colimena, San Pietro, Boraco and Molini all standing guard along that low Apulian coast and which, I ask you, is which? Just miss one, or see a hillock which might—or might not—tell its own sad story of ravage and rape, and where are you? You're frantically stabbing around with dividers and a clock. Not one of them flies a banner with its name blazoned on it, and anyway you can't keep checking when there's toast and marmalade and hot coffee to be made, and one ear clamped to the wellnigh incomprehensible weather forecast.

I realise now that everything was wrong for us that day we left Cesareo: we just ought to have stayed snugged up in that rocky lake, but to tell the truth B. had been so terribly bitten by gnats that it was a relief for both of us to get sails on *Lugworm* and feel a breath of fresh salt wind round our hides.

The forecast had been good: variable force three with possibility of thunderstorms and that was nothing new. If we'd taken any notice of thunderstorms we would still have been back in Otranto. Even so, I soon felt in my more arthritic joints that something might be brewing weatherwise. Inland, over the distant hills, there were the usual grumbles of thunder, but the wind was just too good to throw away; steady south-easterly; even a soldier might have put to sea. We bowled along under genoa, main and mizzen and life would have been blissful had it not been for B.'s continual scratching and the changing colour of the sky.

I must tell you about that south Italian sky, and had best start with a phrase we soon came to recognise as an old and clinging friend: for it was to come regularly out of our radio speaker: *Possibilita di temporale con locale colpi di vento.* Liberally translated, and depending on whether it was before or after breakfast, this had come, for us, to mean anything from 'possibility of thunderstorms with brisk winds locally' to 'watch it! freak storms with gale force winds'. That morning our barometer was steady at 994—indeed it had been steady at 994 for so many days that I took to hitting it, hoping to see the blue needle move, whereas only the silver one fell off. But the sky! It began far inland over the hills, to turn a deep hazy purple. Gradually, outlined in the pyrotechnic display of sheet lightning we saw the hard black outline of thunder clouds seeming to grow without moving perceptibly. The odd thing was that they appeared to infuse into the air against the direction of the wind—calculated to give any sailor the jim-jams.

By 1000 there was an oppressive heat uncommonly like the Sirocco, but I prayed there was too much easterly in it for that. By 1030 that morning the sky all over was puce coloured, like an over-ripe victoria plum, and the wind still steady south-easterly was freshening, but what appalled me was the sudden appearance of a swell, rolling up from our quarter. Now if anything will make my hair stand on end, it is swell, for that spells finis to any thought of landing on an exposed beach, be it a lee or weather shore.

'Here B.,' I said, 'take the helm: I'm going to take a good look at the chart.' Being lost is all very well, but to Hell with it when you need to know where you are. Rapidly I worked back from the last known position; off Cesareo entrance at 0800. At just under four knots that put us about nine miles along the coast; Torre Colimena should be abeam. It wasn't. Mount della Marina, 374 ft., should be on the starboard bow, two miles inland. To my horror I realised that we could no longer see two miles inland for there was a thick wall of grey rain sweeping like an express train along the coast obliterating everything.

I grabbed the glasses and threw B. her oilskin. The beach, half a mile north-ward, was growing dim in the pall, but already I could see massive breakers pounding up the shingle and sand. Perhaps we could get in there, if we had to—but it would more than likely mean losing *Lugworm* for she would be swamped and rolled within seconds.

Hastily we stowed the chart and all perishable gear, battening down the locker hatches. The wind was still freshening as the first portentous splash of rain over-took us. Minutes later we were deluged in the roaring hissing storm, fighting to change the genoa for the small jib. I furled the mizzen sail and unshipped its mast, laying the spar along the side deck to reduce windage aft, for when on the run like this it's not good to have too much pressure abaft the rudderpost. Then, with B. still manfully at the helm, and *Lugworm* fairly creaming down the now foam-ing seas, I started to reef the main. By the time all the reef-points were fast, and the sheet-block snapped into the leech reef-cringle, it was obvious that *Lugworm*, even reefed, would be over-canvassed. The wind was shrieking now, a wild dirge, and a glance astern was enough to set one praying; oceans of charging white crests, streaked and flattened by the screaming wind. Things didn't look good. 'O.K.?' I bellowed back to B. She smiled bravely, standing astride the helm, sway-ing against the roll of the boat, every nerve concentrating on keeping *Lugworm* steady before the rising seas; it was all happening far too quickly for my liking, this maelstrom. We had to get the jib off her, and quickly, but I did not like be-ing off the helm any longer—one bad broach across these waves and I knew that we could be on nodding terms with the squids. I grabbed the helm. 'Get that jib off her,' I roared, 'and try to come back aft as quickly as possible—mustn't keep weight forward!' She cast off the halyard, then lay along the bucking foredeck to gather in the thrashing sail. For one moment I thought she must have cast off the wrong halyard, for incredibly the mainsail, too, was down and flogging across her out over the side. Then I knew: the mast itself had gone overboard.

In emergency you think of many things at once. Two thoughts were uppermost: is B. all right, and how could the mast have gone?

'Are you O.K.?' I bellowed, not daring to leave the helm. There was a muffled cry from under the sail. I could see her struggling to extricate herself. Thank God, she came out, white faced but unhurt. 'Back here,' I yelled, 'Here, on the helm, quick!'

There was no choice now, I had to get that sail and the spar inboard before it filled under water and made the boat uncontrollable. In it came, a tangle of terylene, wire and rope, and I just had time to see the four securing bolts of the tabernacle grinning at me—wrenched up, nuts and all through the massive king-plank, and then I was back on the helm and getting the outboard started, to regain control.

Lugworm, now shorn of all her glory, was riding the seas wonderfully. Astern the creamers reared and seemed to tower over us ready to burst down on deck and 'poop' us. But like a cork she would cock her tail up high, level off, and then as the crest foamed past, sink down again ready for the next; it was superb to watch. But this was no time for admiration: the decision had to be made—to bring her round head to wind and seas and get the sea-anchor out, deliberately stopping her further passage and trying to ride out the storm—or to continue as long as we dared under power and running before the wind in the hope of finding some lee?

When one is actually in the situation, this is a horrible decision to have to make. All one's instincts are to get the boat's bow into that wind, for she would then cleave the waves and throw them back on either side—but this meant staying at sea through whatever was still to come, and the look of the sky astern was enough to fill one with dread. The wind showed no signs of easing and the rain, driving horizontally, now blotted out the shore even close abeam, though we could still hear the thunder of breakers above the din. Believe me, when it comes to it, there is an overpowering desire to find a lee as fast as possible, and in our position that meant continuing to run under power.

Lugworm was still doing well. As long as we could prevent her broaching, and equally important prevent her actually surfing down the steep seas, we would survive; at any rate, I decided we would carry on for a bit, for the visibility might clear enough for us to risk a run inshore—if we could find the slightest indentation in the coast to give some shelter.

I knew from the chart that somewhere about eight miles ahead there was a kink in the coast at the Torre dell'Ovo—the Tower of Eggs. A small tongue of land curved out where the coast swung northward into a shallow bay—and it looked as though that torre held all our eggs, for there was no other shelter between us and it. But eight miles! That meant two hours. If the conditions remained static, it was possible; if they deteriorated more there was a grim choice left—to run ashore and say 'Goodbye' to *Lugworm* or try to ride it out, which I knew in my heart was probably, in our circumstances, the most risky course of all. You see, by running ashore, one does at least remain moving fast until the final moments when the boat either hits the beach in the surf, or rolls over very close inshore; to be swamped half a mile off a lee shore would mean either desperately clinging to a foundered boat (I had confidence that she would remain awash), or making a bid for it to swim ashore —which would have meant almost certain drowning. Both of us, of course, had already donned our life-jackets, but you cannot really swim far in breaking seas, and not at all through surf, with its ever-present undertow just when, completely exhausted, you think you've gained the beach.

No! We would continue under engine, fighting to keep her buoyant.

I can recall vividly every minute of that next two hours. Evidently this was no small passing squall, for the wind continued undiminished and the seas steadily grew steeper. With the engine full throttle, and the wind helping on our port quarter, I reckoned we were making four knots and a bit, for occasionally *Lugworm* would take the reins and go for a long exciting surf down a sea's face. Again I was torn between two choices; to trail a rope and ease the engine revs so as to slow us down, allowing the seas to move quickly underneath—or to take that risk and speed on as fast as possible. We did the latter, but there was one final hurdle to be jumped.

Just to weather of that Tower of Omelettes, where the coast swung north a bit, was a shallow spit of rocks. According to our chart, it extended offshore for about three-quarters of a mile. I knew that the seas would be breaking even more steeply on this, yet the last thing I wanted in this situation was to get farther offshore: we were as close to the coast as I dared go, so that in the event of necessity we could run in within seconds. But there was really no choice—to seaward of these shallows we would have to go.

Little by little I eased her away from the shore, peering ahead desperately to try to make out some sign of the Tower and at last it appeared, a darker patch through the rain. 'Nearly there,' I encouraged B. who was doggedly bailing, for the deluge was filling the bilges. I knew that conditions close to leeward of that spit would be slightly better, for the shallow patch would have taken the brunt of the seas. It proved so, and luckily, since it was necessary to motor more across the seas while heading north into the lee of the point. But as we approached the sheltered basin, a grim picture presented itself. Quite unpredictably the swell was sweeping round the end of the spit to break with frightening strength right across the shallow entrance to the little bay. 'Lord!' I gasped to B. 'We just can't get in through that!'

Desperately we searched the coast farther on. About three cables beyond the bay a short line of rocks probed out from the shore, and close to them on their far side the sea was quite calm. It was also obviously very shallow, for even from our position we could see the green and brown of weeds and rocks under the surface. It seemed our only hope, for the small natural mole gave a good protection from the swell.

'We'll go in there and anchor close up under the rocks,' I bellowed at B., pointing. 'I daren't drive her actually ashore until we have had a look at the beach.' With rudder unshipped and the plate right up, we gingerly nosed round the end of the rocks, watching the seabed shallowing up, closer and closer, until finally *Lugworm* hit bottom hard once, twice, then surged in over a ridge into a small pool only a foot or two deep.

'Phew!' But I can tell you it's a wonderful feeling, to be suddenly safe after an experience like that. We stood in the boat and looked back out to sea. Under the black sky great rollers were thundering along, their tops lifting in a white frenzy of spray. 'Have we really escaped from that,' B. croaked. 'We're lucky,' I assured her, and in my heart sent out a silent message to John Watkinson, designer, and

Brian Nicholls and John Elliot, builders, 'You'll never build a better boat, nor have more heartfelt thanks from any owner.'

But back to work. Our second anchor was laid out, and *Lugworm* positioned in the middle of the pool, as far away from all the rocks as possible, for even in here there was still an uneasy long surge. Satisfied that she was secure, we waded ashore to examine the beach. Both of us were soaked to the skin and very tired, for it had been exhausting work with nerves at full stretch. The whole beach was spattered with boulders and thick with dead weed, rolled and heaped into banks of black tarry muck. Provided we chose the spot carefully, it would be quite possible to bring the boat ashore here—which was preferable to remaining at anchor for still the storm showed no sign of abating.

Curiosity then took over and we staggered to the top of the beach. What sort of a coast was this that we had landed on? Over on the point, the square tower was obviously deserted, but in the other direction we could see a straggle of low bungalows, such as one might find at the small lidos which dotted the coast. Immediately inshore of us, at the end of its own short drive, was a two-storey house which also appeared to be empty. Not a soul was to be seen, and together we stood, palpitating gently like two frogs, then wandered over to a small coast road which ran from tower to village about a hundred yards inshore. We were standing near this in the lee of a small shed, sheltering from the wind and rain when there came a sudden and alarming silence. Gone was the howl of the storm—we were listening now only to the distant roar of the sea and the sudden loud patter of the rain. We looked at one another in disbelief.

'Maybe we shan't need to beach *Lugworm* after all,' B. remarked cautiously. But the sky remained that ghastly black, and off shore we could still see the fast scudding clouds rolling along. Even as we stood there, a lick of wind came swirling across the marram grass—straight out of the west.

We had passed through the middle of these local tempests before in Greece, but never had we experienced the suddenness or fury of that particular wind change. Within a minute we were fighting against a gale-force westerly that slammed at us with even greater fury than ever. We started to run back to the boat for she was now on a dead lee-shore, but even as I closed the beach, with B. staggering in pursuit, we saw her drive ashore, broach, lift to a sea and slew over on her side. The next sea filled her, and in horror I saw her lifted, half by the sheer force of the wind and half by the seas, up on top of a bank of tarry weed. Before I could reach her she had turned turtle. Thank God both masts were already down, or they would have been snapped like carrots. B. arrived, and together we frantically tried to shove *Lugworm*'s bow into the seas and wind, for we were terrified that she would pound on a boulder and be stove in. But it is one thing to shift a heavy boat when she's the right way up and quite another to do it when she is upside down and half buried in great masses of weed. Each breaker—and they were increasing in size by the minute—brought a new morass of weed and sand spewing over her, swirling the sand away from under her as it receded again down the beach, until the poor boat seemed set on burying herself where she lay. Neither of us, exhausted as we were, could do a thing about it.

'Get those petrol cans clear,' I choked in B.'s ear. 'I'm going to try to get the outboard off her.' But the outboard was already buried deep in the filthy weed, its propeller sticking up helplessly, and fast as I scrabbled under the stern to get at the securing clamps another few hundredweights of water, weed and sand would come crashing over us. Desperately I searched the beach for a pole or baulk of wood with which, perhaps, the two of us might lever her back upright, and it was then I saw a figure running from the house towards us. It was a middle-aged man, his dark raincoat flapping wildly. 'Signore,' I roared, and then, because it was quite beyond me to say anything more, I merely pointed to the boat and idiotically repeated the word; what else was there to do? But there was no need for explanations; a backward Bedouin who'd never seen the sea would have grasped our immediate need. The three of us got our fingers under the shoreward gunwale—for that was the higher of the two— and heaved. With relief I saw *Lugworm* begin to tilt over. He was a powerful man, and while he and B. held her balanced, I knelt and got my haunches under the gunwale. I have a vivid recollection of Foogoo, entangled by his belly button in the netting under the side-deck festooned with weeds, as between the three of us we got the boat balanced precariously on one gunwale, holding her against the wall of wind.

'Careful!' I roared, terrified lest she should crash over and down the slope while there was no water there. 'Wait till I say "Now".' Mind you, I don't know who I thought I was talking to, for B. was beyond much in the way of strength, and our friend, up to his armpits in the scrimmage, had his ear jammed against the boat.

I watched till a sea came surging up the beach, then nodded to him and shoved. *Lugworm* tilted gently beyond the point of no return and crashed down, but her fall was softened by the upsurge of water, and as the next wave licked its way under her belly I shoved her head into the wind and tautened in on one of the anchor warps. She was a dreadful sight, half full of weed and sand, plastered with tar, and an indescribable tangle of rigging, sails and loose gear floating everywhere. But she was not holed.

An hour later, with the boat emptied of water and dragged farther up the beach (looking rather like a fly in a cobweb, so many warps had we rigged to hold her against the wind), we were able to pay more attention to our very real friend in need. Who was this man who had risked injury, ruined a suit and mackintosh and a good pair of shoes in the bargain to render help? He had saved *Lugworm*—there was no doubt of that.

'*Lei parla Inglese?*' we shrieked at him above the roar, but he merely waved a hand, indicating that it was little use trying to talk. He smiled, and pointed up to the house, where we could now see a lady standing on the verandah watching us.

'*Questa è la mia casa,*' he shouted, beckoning us to follow him.

Italo and Anna Maria Campa became our firm friends. We stayed in their house and were made most welcome for two nights while sorting out the mess aboard *Lugworm*. The tabernacle, though bent, could be straightened easily enough, and the bolts, fitted with larger washers were still usable. How the nuts and washers had drawn up through the wood without splitting it beyond repair is incredible, but it says a lot for the design and strength of the construction. Our spare set of rigging was fitted, and examination of the broken shroud revealed that the wire had parted at the soft eye which lies over the truck of the mainmast—a point I had deliberately protected with tubing against chafe, and this precaution was the very cause of my not detecting the fracture until it parted, for the wire had gradually weakened through constant flexing at the hard turn, completely hidden within the tube. One learns the hard way.

It was the morning of Friday 5th May that we finally pushed *Lugworm* back over that shallow rocky ridge, and with a farewell wave to our two new friends, set all sail for Taranto twenty miles up the coast.

*   *   *

'Fiume Lato, Bradano, Basento ... Fiume Agri, Sinni, Trionto ... Fiume Neto.' As each river name rolled off B.'s tongue, her small finger stabbed down the coastline on our chart which was spread across a flat stone balustrade on Taranto's waterfront. 'That's seven; we ought to find shelter in one, at least.' Above us a cloud of moths mobbed the yellow lamp-glass half hidden in the branches of a dusty orange tree which helped keep at bay the strident clamour of traffic in the wide boulevard beyond. Between us and the dark Mare Piccolo—Taranto's 'Little Sea'—the busy quays stretched as far as eye could follow.

Scores of fishing craft, their flared bows gaily painted and numbered, were drifting with engines quietly throbbing or shoving impatiently alongside the tightly packed quays, shouldering their way in amid raucous but good natured banter from the crews. Above the hubbub an occasional deep-throated roar of a powerful diesel would assert itself, commanding brief attention as, with lifting bow-wave, a boat shook free of the congestion to sweep into the canal out beneath towering battlements of the old fortress, into the blackness of the Mare Grande.

Behind and above it all rose the impressive squalor of the old city, mellow in the dark night like a backcloth painted on the sky to enhance the bustling activity of the waterfront, where once again her vast fishing fleet was preparing for sea. It was a vital and noisy scene. A hundred yards along the quayside two rival gangs of youngsters were waging full-scale war. Stones flying and fists flailing, the battle surged back and forth across the balustrade, in among the orange trees and into the road, then back again over the busy quay until a stone, wide of its mark, brought a sudden explosion of anger from a tight-knit group of fishermen. As one, the group surged towards the battle area; a shrill cry of warning and, with a last fling, the opposing warriors scattered before the common enemy, their retreat sounded by falling glass splinters from yet another conquered lamp standard. Uneasy truce.

But this evening one sensed another focal point of interest; a new topic was under discussion other than the prices their catch might fetch or the weather conditions out there in the Gulf. Who were these two foreigners in their small black boat with the finely carved teak quarter badges? Where had they appeared from, and what were they doing down there at the end of the quay in the hubbub of this old port? She was no working boat, that was obvious, for though small she carried herself with the airs of a yacht and yet ... why then was she not anchored off the elegant yacht club out there in the Mare Grande, her owners knocking back their Martinis and Camparis under the awnings? There was mystery here. In the line of her sheer and the flare of her bow, the boat had a marked similarity to their own rugged fishing craft; and the two sitting up there on the balustrade studying the chart—English, eh? They neither of them looked much like the dandy yachting folk one sometimes sells fish to at exorbitant prices out there in the Gulf. Too lean and brown and wiry ... can't he afford shoes then? There are sly grins. *'Zuanne,'* shouts a voice, *'Tuo cuggino cha la tua Nana Inglese,'*—roars of laughter— *'Vai a vedere cosa Fanno.'*

'It seems to me,' said B. poring over the chart, 'that the Basento is our likeliest first attempt at a river. It's twenty miles as the crow flies clipping straight across the top of the Gulf; but all these rivers are mighty shallow off the mouth—under a fathom and sandy bottom. It's ...'

'Engleeesh?' came the cheery call. A swarthy dark haired fisherman was filling a bucket from the tap adjacent. 'I spek Engleesh, yes.'

'Amico!' I responded, throwing out my arms as to a friend in need, *'Parla lei Inglese?* We need your help with local knowledge, can you spare a moment?' His face fell, the smile faded and a look of blank incomprehension took its place. From behind him, a roar of laughter arose from the nearest group around the boats.

'No, Signore, io non parlo Inglese,' came the shamefaced reply, but then the teeth flashed again. *'Parla Italiano lei?'*

'Poco, poco,' B. answered, but her reply was drowned in ribald comments from his watching companions.

'Itte sese fattende insarasa, Zuanne, ses-giai proponende a sa brunda, eh! E tue un omini sposadu. Torra ai noghe e narrame itte ase iscrobettu faiddende su Inglesu chi faeddas tue ... la finisi de le faghere sos ogos drucches su maridu este arribbende. Impizzade de sa pisca tua Zuanne ... Mi la presentasa, seu mannu abbastanza.'

Our friend seemed embarrassed. I could guess something of the nature of the shouted conversations taking place and, keen to widen the tenuous contact which had been made, beckoned him over at the same time pointing to our chart. My gesture brought some twenty of his inquisitive companions strolling across as well. We were surrounded by a grinning horde of black-browed, brown skinned fisherfolk, and one of them pointing to my bare feet broke into voluble Italian. To a clamour of approval he started removing his rubber thighboots intending, I feared, to give them to me.

'*Amici, amici,*' I bellowed above the hubbub, in my atrocious Italian, grinning more broadly than perhaps I felt. '*Noi siamo Inglesi ... barca mia,*' and I pointed to *Lugworm*. '*Noi andiamo in Inghilterra in barca. Noi ...* ' I got no further. A stunned silence had fallen on the crowd. From along the quay yet more of their companions were joining us. One and all they turned and looked at *Lugworm*, then pandemonium broke out.

'*Ses navighende subra e custu finzasa a Inghilterra! Suba e custu ... Ma ses maccu ... Passas mare malu subra e custu.*' The amazement was obvious.

'*Noi arrivamo de la Grecia,*' I explained. 'We come from Greece and we are sailing home to England,' and jumping off the wall I clasped two of them by the arm, leading them to the edge of the quay. '*Vengano,*' I invited, and jumped aboard, beckoning them to follow. Four heavy feet dropped on *Lugworm*'s after deck and amid ribald comment she heeled dangerously over from the quay, where the large crowd had gathered to watch. I opened the lockers, showed how our clothes and food stowed, how we cooked, where the clock and the barometer stowed and how the rudder shipped down the trunking, for this latter always caused a good deal of interest in Greece, being quite unusual. '*Plastica?*' queried a voice from on shore. '*No ... legno compensato marino ... Tutto in legno compensato marino, niente plastica.*' They showed tremendous interest, but the whole object of my exercise was not yet accomplished. I needed to show we were friends, as good as they were, unafraid, and that we trusted them; perhaps that was now clear. So what about us seeing over their boats, eh?

I was very keen to examine these boats, for I knew something of their history. They represent the end of a continuous line of evolution lasting more than 2,600 years. Their owners, these 'Tarantines', were descendants from an ancient stock who originally left Greece under the stigma of 'Spartan Bastards'. Illegitimate children of Greek soldiers, tired of being away from home during the long wars of that period, the 'Parthenoi' as they were then known, rebelled at their low social standing and left Sparta to become independent and found their own colony here in Southern Italy. As is so often the case with new mixed blood the stock was virile and intelligent. 'Taras,' as the port was then known, rapidly became one of the richest and most powerful cities of the ancient Magna Graecia, proud in her prime to muster an army of some thirty thousand infantry, as well as the famous Tarantine Cavalry. Now we were sharing their famous 'Little Sea' and proposed exploring their fascinating coastline where even today very few pleasure craft penetrate. We were entirely in their hands, and they were good hands to be in, if friendly, for none knew better than they every contour of this desolate coast ahead.

It is surprising how much can be conveyed despite language barriers, when a common interest is shared. I was shown over many craft there under the lamps of the quayside, and after accepting one gift of a fine little squid, had difficulty in refusing more, but somehow managed to convey that there was one very real way in which they could help us: to tell us which, if any, of the rivers between here and Cape Spartivento we might possibly enter.

Back under the lamp again, with the chart spread over the wide balustrade and dividers at the ready, we systematically eliminated one river after another.

'*Lato?*' I would stab at the river on the chart. '*Possibile di entrando?*' A dozen opinions were voiced: on balance it was 'No'—and Bradano? Yes, that was possible for your little boat, perhaps, but shallow. Basento? So-so, shoulders were shrugged, perhaps, perhaps not. There had been much rain inland, it would make a strong current and shifting sandbanks. Hands were swung to indicate overfalls and current at the mouth ... pericoloso! And Fiume Agri ... ah, yes perhaps, but enter from the north side of the mouth, eh Pietro? Much discussion ... but yes, Agri could be entered ... and so it went on, with B. making notes, and then general discussion and interest returned once more to *Lugworm*. I showed them a drawing of the dinghy with centreplate lowered and rudder shipped, to give an idea of the draught when sailing. There was much concern—general advice was offered; we must beware, with the wind off the land it was good, but if the winds came from the south—take care! We already knew this, but it was good to hear confirmation. Sirocco! Heads were wagged; altogether it was quite clear that we were mad, but interestingly so.

*   *   *

And now Taranto's extensive western mole is far behind us, like a thin grey thread drawn delicately along the horizon. As we watch, it grows more tenuous, breaks, and finally disappears altogether leaving only a blinding white and faintly curving coast which dances in the heat ahead and astern until this too merges into the far-off pearl of sea and sky. Low hillocks of marram grass flank the beach, backed here and there by scrub tamarisk and odd clumps of small windblasted pines. For close on two hundred and fifty miles ahead our chart shows no harbour save Crotone which lies half that distance away. It is a magnificent morning with just the ghost of a south westerly breeze pressing *Lugworm* along, and no other boat in sight; the seemingly endless shore and the sea and the sky are ours alone.

Conversation wanes. We laze in the brilliant sun and watch the beach, some two cables away, drift silently past. A torre, ethereal, and seemingly transparent like a dream castle quivers and flows into the scene ahead. We watch as it solidifies, assumes the proportions proper to an earthbound thing of solid stone, and gazes with empty eyes out to the horizon, quite oblivious of our tiny boat, as though its soul were withdrawn and far away, dreaming of ancient days when it pulsed with urgent warning of approaching fleets. We watch as it slowly dissolves again astern, the only changing object in a never changing shore, and the sun grows ever hotter. Already the two of us are tanned to match our teak gunwales. B. has taken to wearing her sampan hat, a straw circular creation about three feet in diameter. I wear nothing, since it's much better for the constant cooling flops over the side; and then there is the flask of dry white wine, and a dish of olives to idle away the noonday torpor; can you imagine anything nearer to Paradise on earth?

Not if you're me, you can't.

"Do you know,' I say after an hour or so of soporific content, and more to ensure that B. hasn't passed out from sunstroke than from any urgent wish to break the silence. 'Do you know that at this moment there are millions of benighted humans ferreting away in offices in the warrens of vast metropolis,' I pride myself on my plurals, 'Some of them may even glance occasionally at the window—if there is a window, but what need of a window when there are tubes of synthetic neon blazing down on their sickly pallor from the ceiling? Would you not rather be there?' I ask her provocatively.

'Oh,' she muses, dangling a long leg overboard and clasping her hands over the crown of that ridiculous hat, which makes it look like an inverted Elizabethan flower basket, 'there are lots of jobs I would rather be doing than that, like driving a tube train on the Circle Line, or operating a lift in one of those large department stores.'

'Well, there's blessed little fear of that,' I comment. 'Both those occupations require a built-in sense of feeling and expertise. Even with long training I doubt they'd put you in charge.' One of her delightfully irritating ineptitudes is a total inability to push the right knob, or turn a dial the right way at first attempt, and often even a second attempt. This has nothing to do with intelligence—she can sail rings round me when it comes to a game of chess or a crossword puzzle, but give her anything remotely electrical or mechanical and you might as well be ready to dial 999.

This taunt provokes nothing but a prolonged and deserved silence, charged with faint dudgeon. Ashore, a small domed grey concrete gunpost, its slit eyes cocked skywards, sags on the undercut edge of the shingle, forlorn monument to man's eternal inhumanity.

'Have an olive, cuckoo.'

Silence.

There is a distant low rumble of thunder somewhere up there in the hills of Basilicata to the north. The hat jerks upright.

'Yes ... well ...' I comment. Both of us are thinking the same thought. This, more or less, is how it all began back there at the Tower of Eggs. The wind is dying; indeed, now one thinks of it, *Lugworm* too is almost asleep, her three tan sails idly collapsing with ennui. We study the chart again but there isn't a kink worth looking at until it cuts off just south of Cape Spulico and that's forty miles away. 'We could start the engine, but it seems a terrible waste of fuel at sixty pence a gallon,' I suggest. But B. is looking ahead through the glasses.

'There's something dark sticking out from shore ahead there. Looks like a pier, but it may be anything in the mirage ... take a look.'

Sure enough, a dancing line of dark probes out from the beach just on the edge of visibility. We start the engine and stow the sails, and soon it is clear that a low concrete mole has been constructed but there is nothing to suggest why; not a house or tower or any sign of habitation. As we close its seaward end another parallel mole comes into view about fifty yards beyond. They both bury themselves into the sand of the beach. *Lugworm* noses in between the two, where the slight swell that is running fails to penetrate, and we ground gently, taking the anchor up the sand. Together we walk up the hot sand, half afraid to talk lest the sound disturb the absolute torpid silence. Over the ridge of the beach a green shallow pool probes back into luxuriant foliage. Reeds quiver as a kingfisher darts away in surprise. Trees, thick and green, crowd the banks, as though overbalancing in their haste to drink the fresh water.

As we stand looking across the lagoon a faint rumble makes itself felt, but this is not thunder; it is continuous and gaining volume every second. 'Of course,' B. says, 'the railway,' and we sit to await the passing of the train. It thunders towards us, quite invisible somewhere back there in the trees, roars by in a crescendo of sound, then just as quickly dies away somewhere beyond, leaving an even more profound silence. But the sky is turning that familiar purple, as though suffocating with its own heat, and we return to *Lugworm*, mooring her securely with a bow anchor out seaward and a couple of stern warps to prevent her ranging, then rig the tent for there seems little point in motoring on. It is just gone midday and there is no breath of wind. What is more, this freshwater lagoon intrigues us, for if it is the end of a river, either it is a river with no water in its upper reaches or, if there is water flowing in, it must be escaping into the sea by slowly permeating through the sand of the beach itself, for there is no mouth. The latter bodes ill for our hopes of getting into the rivers for night shelter, but this is a good opportunity for exploration; these concrete moles, evidently built during the war for some military purpose, provide a useful shelter should the sea turn wild overnight.

That evening we walked deep back inland through stunted pine woods following a beaten track beside the river whose green water seemed to be quite still though not stagnant, which suggested that in fact there was a slight flow. The bridge carrying the railway appeared within a quarter of a mile inland, and beyond that a long straight road running parallel with no sign of traffic. Here the woods ended and the whole flat land was cultivated for some distance either side the water, and after a while the river seemed to have been canalised, its banks becoming straight and obviously dug out as an irrigation channel.

It was at some forgotten hour of the night that an alien sound awoke me. A steady and unaccountable hiss grew in strength, and across the white canvas of the tent a moving shadow crept, thrown by the approach of a powerful light. The brilliance increased until inside the boat was like daylight.

B. sat up with a startled 'Whatever ... ?' and I checked that my plastic toy revolver was to hand, for while in Greece we had been warned that along this lonely stretch of coast the local 'banditi' might make themselves a nuisance. I had bought the toy gun in case of such emergency. But a soft call, *'Amico ... amico ... '* put my fears to rest. Blinded by the light, I poked my head out of the open end of the tent, to see a small fishing boat with its two pressure lamps approaching. The grinning face of Zuanne shone in the lights and as his companion 'back watered' with his oars a great wet squid was slapped down on to our after deck.

'Grazie, amico... molto grazie,' I called to him, and watched as they pulled back past the mole ends, to gradually diminish until their light joined that of the stars, balanced there over the horizon. It was a kindness and good to know they were evidently keeping a friendly watch on our activities.

We stayed in that unnamed river mouth all next day, and saw not a soul. No breath of wind stirred the sea's face, and the weather remained sultry and treacherous, the sky turning horribly black at early evening. But the following morning—the 9th May—we were off early before a light land breeze. Alas, within the hour the breeze failed, and reluctantly the engine had once more to come to the rescue.

In the late forenoon it was evident that we were approaching the mouth of the Bradano river, for we noticed the water close inshore turning to a muddy brown, with a quite clear demarcation line between it and the clear blue of the sea. Ahead we could see what appeared to be a low line of tamarisk and other small trees growing out into the sea. Sailing within yards of the shore as we were, this 'bulge' of land at the mouth of the larger rivers was most pronounced. It is caused by the gradual deposit of silt brought down with the river water. This builds up a projection out into the sea, and on this fertile bulge trees take root. From the chart it is scarcely detectable, but when viewed along the line of the shore, due to the low-lying nature of the bulge and the heightening affect of the mirage on the trees, it gives the peculiar appearance from afar as of tall trees actually growing out of the sea. As we approached these river mouths, it was impossible to detect depth by eye since the water always became too thick with mud or sand and always this brown fresh water crept up along the coastline to meet us before we arrived, thus revealing a slight surface drift in a northerly direction.

The Bradano river was one of those stated by our friends in Taranto to be navigable, so in view of the lack of wind we decided to call it a day and try to enter: but it was not so easy. To start with there was a strong outflow: about two to three knots. As always happens when a swell meets a flow of water running in contrary direction the height of the swell rapidly increased and the wave-length decreased. This resulted in slight surf some distance off the entrance, but it was a calm day and presented little hazard so with rudder unshipped and the centreplate up, we gingerly nosed under power towards the river mouth. Considering the quantity of muddy water drifting up the coast this mouth was surprisingly small—not more than a hundred yards across at most I would guess. B. stationed herself at the bow with an oar which she used as a sounding pole, while I perched on the stern at the outboard, ready to lift the propeller at a second's warning, for it was clear from the behaviour of the water there was a shallow bar across the entrance. Round my waist I had a warp made fast, its other end leading forward clear of the shroud and fast to the foredeck cleat. This was a precaution in case I had to jump overboard. The problem as we saw it was that of hitting bottom right in the mouth where the current was strongest. In this event the engine could not be used for fear of damaging the propeller, hence the possible need for me to jump overboard and tow *Lugworm* across the bar into the quiet water behind. To lose power at the moment of crossing the bar would simply result in our being drifted out to sea again.

In the Bradano entrance this proved unnecessary, for the minimum sounding gave three feet, and although the breakers were popping us about a bit we got in without trouble.

It was fun entering that first river, and gave valuable clues for use on future occasions. One learns to sense the deeper channels by the appearance of the surface
and soon we found the hidden snags. For instance, when approaching the mouth
it was necessary to aim for that small area where the swell from seaward broke
least. This may sound obvious, but in fact it can be the most hazardous point, for
by virtue of the fact that it indicates the deeper channel it also ensures that when
and if the swell does break therein, it will be a real thumper. Often we would lie
off a mouth, watching the wave patterns for half an hour and more before deciding exactly where and when the least risky approach might be made. Remember
that a capsize or foundering in the entrance would result in our being immediately
swept back into and through the breakers which in such a situation, could prove
very dangerous.

But once inside the mouth, the transition from blinding blue sea and white
beaches to dark green water and the shade of overhanging trees and tall reeds was
like a long cool drink to a thirsty man. We would motor up slowly against the current, exploring the river for a mile or two with a view to a good night berth. Let the
storms arrive; once we were inside the mouth we knew there was no danger, and
this was our constant concern along this shallow harbourless coast. In the early
days we would choose to sleep ashore on some grassy patch perhaps amongst the
scrub bushes, but we soon found that the farther away from the sea the more the
gnats and other biting insects made life difficult. Subsequently, in rivers up the
western seaboard of Italy we would always moor as close to the entrance as possible, anchoring the boat against the sandy banks near to the sea and clear of trees,
for this reduced trouble from winged nippers. My own hide seems to be immune
from the pests, but poor B. was obviously a repast worth flying miles to savour.

They were wonderful days, and we shall always remember this instep of Italy
as being one of the most adventurous and carefree parts of our cruise home for we
are by nature 'loners', far preferring the solitude of country to the gregariousness
and noise of towns and harbours. You may guess that marinas with their barrack-
like parking slots are anathema to us.

The evenings were spent beachcombing for drift wood for the night fire, wandering miles along the shore, stretching our legs after a day in the boat, smelling
all those hidden scents of the land which are denied one at sea. We came close to

that sense of adventure which must have attended the original explorers of the world, for although we had a chart of the coast, we never knew what the terrain just inshore of the beach would provide. In fact, my impression of this stretch of the coast is of scrub tamarisk and tall grasses swept back like hair, bleached and combed by the salty winter gales, while that area immediately around the river mouths would bear every sign of being inundated with fast flowing water. Although parched and dry now, the boles of the trees were wrapped around up to three feet above their bases with dead reeds, grasses and the branches of smaller trees where the flood waters of winter had left them.

We would light a wood fire at the top of the beach, well away from the dry scrub behind, and cook our evening meal as the light faded. The smoke would keep the insects at bay, and afterwards in the darkness our flickering circle of light would be like a small oasis far away from the noise and stresses of our modern world. Sometimes, behind us in the undergrowth or perhaps among the pine forests, we would hear a herd of wandering water buffalo, or the sudden stamp of a horse's hoof, but very seldom did we see any living thing. The beaches were thick with bleached driftwood, and there was never any shortage of fuel.

But the really tricky part of this lonely coast was yet to be tackled. We had now rounded the top of the Gulf and were working southward where the coast is different in character to the northern shores. The hills of Calabria down towards the toe crowd to the edge of the sea, grooved by vast 'torrentes'—mountain rivers— which hold cataracts of water only during the rain periods of autumn and winter. Their dried-up beds, strewn with boulders that have been washed down by the force of the torrent, look like grey wounds down the green face of the mountains, and the shore tends to be of shingle and boulders rather than sand.

It was shortly after leaving the Fiume Agri on 12th May that we anchored just north of Cape Spulico, close ashore to miss a nasty swell and sea which was bowling up before a brisk heading south-west wind. I was undecided at midday whether to leave this small lee and tackle the next stretch of coast, for I was doubtful whether we would manage to enter either the Straface or Seraceno rivers with the amount of swell which was running. In the event the wind eased somewhat by 1600 and since our chart indicated (it was a mere suggestion of a line) that there might be a small protective mole off the coastal town of Trebisacce eight miles south of the Cape, we took the risk and started a quick nip under power into the teeth of the wind. It proved to be a mistake, for instead of dying, as we had expected, with the evening, the wind freshened. Indeed, so strong did it become that we unshipped the mizzen and lowered the mainmast in an effort to reduce windage and ease the burden on our tiny outboard. To make matters worse the wind had taken a slant southward which, though not allowing us to sail along the coast without the need to tack frequently, had made it a lee shore. By 1730 we could see the tiny mole ahead, but to our dismay it turned out to be a pier, mounted on pylons which gave no protection whatever from the swell and sea which was rolling up the coast. Two choices were open to us: we could either turn tail and sail back round Cape Spulico, or we could beach the boat at Trebisacce. The beach here was of medium sized pebbles, but steep.

Our approach, however, had not gone unnoticed by the small town. As we closed the pier a crowd of interested fisher-folk collected. Their own boats were already drawn up high on the beach, and when one of them—a large powerful man in thighboots—waved to us to go ashore the decision was made. We anchored a few yards off the beach, outside the line of breakers, and rigged the rope girdle attaching the lanyard for rigging the tackle. This was observed with great interest by those on shore, who had been joined by many of the townsfolk. I stood in the stern and pointed to the place I had selected to run ashore. Instantly the fishermen lined the beach, beckoning us in. With B. easing out on the bow anchor I put the engine full astern, then just as we entered the danger area of the breakers lifted the unit and locked it up. Willing hands rushed into the sea. I threw them the sternrope and so expert were these folk at hauling boats out of surf that B. and I were still in *Lugworm* as thirty or so powerful arms lifted and carried her bodily up the shingle.

We did not know it then, but this was to be our billet for seven days as the swell increased, breaking farther and farther up the shingle banks and quite precluding any thought of launching. In company with the fishing boats, *Lugworm* was drawn progressively farther and farther back up the beach as each day brought worse seas, and we began to wonder whether in the end we would not have to be hauled right across the coast road. They were a grand lot, those fishermen. We came to know many of them well, and as in all these seaside communities found that one of the older men was a sort of 'father of the beach'. Gaitano, or 'Poppa' as we came to endearingly refer to him, would come down each morning to enquire after our welfare. If anything needed doing, he it was who would organise it, such as dragging the boat farther away from the encroaching surge, arranging a free supply of drinking water from the communal fishermen's store—and seeing that we were informed of any arrival of fresh fish from down the coast, for at the moment the entire fleet of Trebisacce, with *Lugworm*, was pinned on shore by this weather.

We walked scores of miles back up the hills into the small hilltop towns, now largely deserted by the youngsters who preferred to move to the coast where more money was to be made.

Always we were happy that *Lugworm* was in safe hands. The natural courtesy of these folk would eliminate any embarrassments due to the lack of privacy aboard. No one would approach in the mornings until one of us had shown a head through the after tent flap; thereafter there would be the welcome greetings, a survey of the weather, and various forecasts. As the days went by, we began to feel one of the community, and evidently the word was spreading about these two oddities in their remarkable boat who were sailing to England. Much advice was offered, with repeated warnings to beware of such and such a community farther down towards the toe, for these were 'bad men'—'banditi' who might steal from us. It was the same wherever we made contact with these small shore towns—always we were warned against the inhabitants of the next town down the coast; always we found them wholly delightful, considerate and helpful. It is human nature, after all, and the same this world over.

We learned much of their methods of fishing while shore-bound at Trebisacce. One day, while walking along the beach about five miles to the north we came across a figure running towards us just above the waterline. He was towing a long line, some three hundred feet of it, and must have run a full mile as we watched. Suddenly we saw him stop, anchor the inboard end of the line with a boulder and proceed to haul in slowly. There were about thirty hooks with spinners attached at ten foot intervals, and we helped him land a whacking big fish—some four feet in length of a type we could not identify. What interested us was the method of keeping the line out in deep water. Attached to the outboard end was a sort of

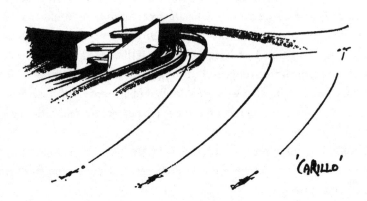

orange box without top or bottom made in the shape of a paravane so that it constantly pulled away from the point of tow. He called it a 'carillo', and it gave us ideas for when we arrived back here at home in our own estuary for fishing during the winter when *Lugworm* is laid up.

The Trebisacce fishermen operated a small fleet of boats about eighteen feet in length, strongly built and some of them with long sweeps, others with outboard motors. All the boats were 'double enders' so a small transom had to be rigged on which the outboard might be housed. The night before we left they launched the boats just after dark, each with its powerful pressure lamp lit over the stern, and it was fascinating to see them being hauled down the beach, the outboard already running before they hit the water, ready to take them instantly clear of the breakers. On one or two occasions the boats without outboards—those with oars alone—were knocked back by the still considerable swell before the oars could get sufficient grip to take take them clear into deep water. It was great fun, undertaken with a tremendous sense of humour and comradeship, not without sarcastic banter when things went wrong and a boat ended up broadside on shore with half its crew up to their waists in the breakers.

We were both sad and glad to get launched again on the 20th May early in the morning, all our friends giving us a welcome shove down the beach. The residual swell from the recent bad weather was still causing a lot of white water along the shore, but as we worked south past Fiume Crati the coast began to swing eastward, enabling us to free off somewhat before the south-west wind, and giving us a spanking sail along to the Fiume Trionto, the small and shallow entrance of which we entered at 1430, just west of the lighthouse on the Cape. We were rounding Alice Point and heading due south towards Crotone in the early afternoon of the following day, and put into the Fiume Neto eight miles north of Crotone that evening.

I shall remember that entry. We stood off and watched the wave patterns off the river mouth for a while, the wind being light from the south, enabling us to make the entry under sail. But alas things did not go so well this time. Of course the rudder had to be unshipped, and steering was effected with an oar through the stern rowlock, but there was a strong outflow and lumpy overfalls on the shallow bar. *Lugworm* hit the bottom solidly, coming to a halt just as a breaker hit her stern. I jumped out, attached by the lanyard to her bow, and was pulling against the current while B. steered. But that current was shifting the sand under my feet, and if I stood in one place for more than a second or so found that I was gradually sinking lower and lower into the riverbed. Finally, I hit quicksand, sinking down to my waist when the strong current immediately carried me and the boat back into and through the breakers again. Oh, it was tremendous fun, and we made it on the second attempt, by the simple expedient of using the engine, but not before losing a lot of paint off the propeller blades, the tips of which were bright metal from the sanding-down they received. Last month while completely stripping down the engine here at home, I found a great deal of sand inside the cooling water system, much of it I'm sure, came from the River Neto and brought back memories.

Crotone was hovering just over the horizon to the south. We sailed from Neto next day—an exciting exit through large breakers—and headed under all sail before a brisk north westerly which was building up the seas off the harbour entrance. By the time we made the entrance we were surfing more than sailing, skidding down the large waves which were beginning to break some half mile from the harbour mole. It was good to get into the shelter of the Porto Nuovo, the new north harbour, but we found it too commercial for our liking, and later that evening, when the wind and seas had eased, motored round to the Porto Vecchio, the quieter old south harbour.

Most of the small coastal villages were little more than fishing settlements in this area, often poverty stricken and squalid. Many of the houses, shanty-built on the beaches, were dilapidated and ruined. This may have been due to earthquake tremors or merely to the undermining of the foundations due to their proximity to the sea, for they appeared to be erected on sand. There were no harbours, the boats being drawn up the beaches, and as we approached often the inhabitants would run to the water's edge and imperiously wave us in. But unless we needed provisions we kept our distance. One pleasant surprise; having rounded Cape Colonne and Cape Rizzuto we came across a newly constructed port at Marina di Catanzaro, spending a pleasant evening there.

But we were now in the heart of the infamous 'Gulf of Squalls' and the sooner we could get down south and round that big toe the better. In the event it turned out to be easier than we expected. We sailed from Catanzaro early on the 24th May, but before noon the wind fell away light. Under the outboard we pressed on down to the toe, rounding Cape Spartivento at midnight. It was fascinating taking compass bearings on the lights of hilltop villages. A flying fish came aboard with a great clatter, but apart from that the calm night passed uneventfully. Dawn, however, brought a rising north wind which found us beating wetly up round Capo dell'Armi to drop anchor in the lee of the Bay of San Gregorio just south of Reggio at 0600 on Thursday 25th May.

Ahead lay the Straits of Messina.

CHAPTER III

SICILY AND THE AEOLIAN ISLANDS

IN ITS STRUGGLE FOR SURVIVAL the swordfish, poor innocent, has fallen into the trap of adopting inflexible habits. About the end of February each year this fish's thoughts lightly turn to love and having chosen a mate the couple stay together with utmost fidelity. Moreover, they then leave the colder northern waters and swim south to honeymoon in warmer areas. From early June they may be found in the Straits of Messina lazing around just beneath the surface. One more mistake they have made is in being very good to eat.

Long before Christ, the predator Man had detected these fatal flaws in their pattern of behaviour. But the swordfish is one of the fastest moving creatures of the sea. Sensitive and alert, it is known to take violent alarm at the slightest alien vibration of water. It was observed, however, that this intelligent creature had learned to a fine point exactly how near a stealthily approaching boat might close before the need to take flight. By mounting a pole in the boat up which a lookout—called a *guadiano*—might climb, the fish could be seen some distance off. By further fixing a stout plank over the bow of the boat a skilled and agile harpoonist called the *allanzatore* could, with luck, strike a split second before the fish's alarm system said 'flee'.

With the march of progress in the form of steel girders and high tensile rigging wire, the gap in time between 'harpoon strike' and 'flight alarm' has been extended and today, if you are lucky enough to be in the Straits of Messina you will in summer see the swordfish boats, or *ontri* as they are called, erratically probing about with the most incredible lattice girder masts some sixty feet high at the very top of which is perched the guadiano who, I'm told, now communicates with the helmsman below by a sophisticated intercom system of microphone and earphones, all aimed at maintaining the utmost possible silence.

Out over the bow is another slender lattice of equal length, stayed to the top of the mast like some brain child of Emmet's, and at the tip of this you will see the allanzatore with his two-pronged harpoon. Watch carefully through binoculars and you may well see this man very smoothly raise his *triccia*, as the weapon is called,

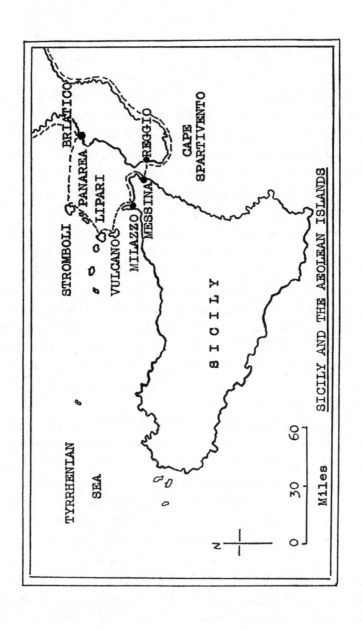

SICILY AND THE AEOLEAN ISLANDS

TYRRHENIAN
SEA

STROMBOLI
PANAREA
BRIATICO
LIPARI
REGGIO
VULCANO
CAPE
SPARTIVENTO
MILAZZO
MESSINA

SICILY

N

0   30   60

Miles

taking care not to jerk or make any sound, then spear downward with tremendous power and accuracy. More often than not, once this strike has been made the water below will erupt in violent protest as the impaled fish fights to free itself of the horribly barbed spear. Its mate likewise will frequently swim frantically round in desperation, trying to find some cause of the companion's anguish, itself thus often falling prey to a second harpoon. Thereafter the ever-weakening fish will be 'played' on the end of the stout line which is attached to the harpoon, finally to be brought alongside and hauled aboard the ontri. When you consider that an average sized swordfish may weigh around one hundred and ten pounds—sometimes much more—you will appreciate that this whole recovery process is not easily undertaken, particularly if the fish has not suffered a seriously disabling strike.

Like most hunting, it is all a deplorable and beastly occupation but, as we all have to learn, such unnatural human concepts as morality bed ill with natural human appetite, and when like me you sit down to an exquisite swordfish steak, grilled in olive oil with a liberal sprinkling of lemon juice, oregano and finely chopped mint, Satan, no doubt, has a good belly laugh.

We sailed from San Gregorio fully provisioned and watered, beating against a brisk north wind and a southerly set of current, using the coastal indentations so far as possible to gain to windward up the narrow Straits until abeam of Reggio, then reached across to the Sicilian shore, picking up a useful northerly set of tide which helped us up past Messina where we anchored for the night close under a palpitating funfair on Punta Paradiso.

On looking back, this passage through the Strait marked a distinct change in the ambience of our cruise. It were as though we had passed through a doorway into another room; a room where Man had again taken over Nature, and was solidly in charge. Islands and lonely places there were in abundance on the rest of the trip, but always Nature had been tamed, the land cultivated, the sea used, the rivers fished, bridged and boated upon; unlike those desolate untamed stretches of Italy's instep.

'The last time I crossed this Strait,' I remarked to B., gazing up at the white tipped peak of Etna smoking far away in Sicily, 'was in a Landing Craft in 1943. We ferried George Formby and his wife Beryl, complete with piano and an ENSA group across to a delightful little marble jetty at Reggio which has now disappeared. The war stopped while we unloaded the damned piano; funny how you remember the inconsequential things.'

I looked north to where the colossal pylons elegantly draped their high power cables across from Italy to Sicily. 'And I can tell you why it was that Scylla and Charybdis, those two horrific whirlpools, stopped tormenting sailors in the narrow mouth up there, though nobody else knows it. We dropped a bronze offering in the form of a valuable propeller blade; it was a great sacrifice too—the ship nearly fell to bits with the vibration, and it put us in dry dock for a week. But it was evidently appreciated.'

Indeed, it was strange looking into the harbour of Messina and remembering how it had appeared thirty years before. The figure of Christ was still perched up there on the column at the mole end, but gone were the deserted quays, the ruined silent grey cadavers of the badly bombed town. Gone was the rusty and burnt-out shell of an enormous cruise liner, heeled over on her side on the beach just outside the harbour, her funnel lapping the waterline. I looked across to the hills of Calabria in Italy: tonight there would be no red glow of forest fires up there, as there were in 1943. No fat grey shape of a Monitor would glide silently down the Straits, her massive long range guns ready to pump tons of high explosive into enemy positions, softening up the interior after consolidation on the invasion beaches.

Ashore the hurdy-gurdies of the funfair blazed into the night, their clarion music echoing across the Strait. Lean hydrofoils, like angry wasps, darted from the harbour, bound for Reggio. Ferries lobbed past, their wakes making *Lugworm* roll mightily all night, and on the coast road the roar of traffic with its urgent horns proclaimed the tenacity and resurgence of human spirit.

We motored beneath the pylon wires in a dead flat calm the following morning within feet of the shore to escape the tremendous southerly flow, turned west to skirt along the north Sicilian shore, and rounded Cape Peloro at 1000. The Ionian lay behind us. Ahead was the five hundred odd miles of Italy's Tyrrhenian seaboard and we knew that up there the summer winds prevailed light from the north west, which boded ill for our sailing. But first, there were those enchanting Aeolian Islands dotted about out there off the north coast of Sicily; it was impossible to look at a chart and by-pass them, but in the event it turned out a hard battle to make any westing along that north shore. It was a fascinating area, long sandy beaches being backed with low hills behind, and I remember the sea was thick with pumice chips and there was, alas, a lot of tar on the beaches.

Before noon the wind had freshened into a dead header and clear of Cape Rasocolmo was knocking up a nasty wetting sea. We put into the lee of the Cape and anchored close to the beach, up which a long surge was beginning to run. Shortly after our arrival four stalwart brown Sicilians hove up in a fishing boat which they promptly ran ashore, and hauled up high and dry on a small sled attached to a hand windlass.

It was pretty obvious we weren't going to make Milazzo in the lee of the promontory fifteen miles ahead under sail that day and the opportunity was too good to miss. I bellowed at them, pointing to *Lugworm* and the sled. Within minutes we were high and dry up the splendid sandy beach, alongside the other craft. It was always like that, everybody was only too willing to help.

*   *   *

There are times, I suspect, when B. is convinced I'm mad. This is one of them. You had better know that when the hours drag—and they've been dragging on this gritty beach under Rasocolmo for too long, with a high wind and sand in our molars—I'm given to standing on my head. This in itself is not particularly odd; I know a lot of intelligent people who do it and a lot of politicians who ought to. It flushes the brain, keeps the scalp healthy, nourishes the roots of the hair, and relieves the circulatory valves. It also presents the world in a different light, which often helps.

In fact, I'm pretty good at it, managing before meals to bring my toes down to touch the ground, then springing them up again vertically, and it goes well about nine times out of ten. This morning was the tenth, and there I was rolling in the tinned tomatoes with the cooker upside down and a billy of good tea libating the beach.

I can see B.'s point of view, but there's no need to keep harping on.

'As if it isn't bad enough,' she splutters through the muslin turban she's wrapped round her head and face, 'to have sand in one's ears, one's nose, one's throat and the b— bed, without having it mixed with breakfast by the pound.

What idiot other than my husband,' she goes on, 'would try to stand on his head while cooking breakfast? Just look at the butter.'

'I'm off to fill up the water canisters,' I retort, rubbing a very sore vertebra, and rattle off with the two jerrycans. Now the 'farm' which was the home of our beach host is about a hundred yards back in an apricot orchard. It is a quite delightful old place and the father of the family does not appear to be in residence. The mother, who presides, keeps house for her two stalwart sons, one of whom helped us pull *Lugworm* up the beach. He is a fine athletic young man, dark, well-proportioned, and susceptible to beauty. I know this because I happened to be watching his face when he first looked at B. yesterday. You know the sort of thing I mean—natural bonhomie tinged with the belligerence which operates between two male strangers can be seen to capsize and grow spongy round the edges when it comes face to face with glamour. Not that I'd call B. glamorous, but she has a certain something.

I like Alphonse, for such we have come to call him, having no idea of his real name, but suspect that he looks upon me as being something of a pity. Anyway, I found Alphonse sur-rounded by hens sweeping up what looked like the leftovers of battle, hundreds of purple squashed mulberries dropped overnight from a magnificent tree outside the farmhouse door—and here am I presenting myself with the two empty water cans.

'*Buongiorno, Signore,*' I address him. '*Per favour e... aqua fresco?*'

He surveys me for a moment looking a little glum, and disappears into the house. '*Un momento!*'

I sit under the mulberry tree with the hens. After a few minutes he reappears with a wheelbarrow and an empty five gallon drum. '*Vieni qua,*' he beckons. I follow him a little puzzled.

'Is there no water in the house? *Aqua ... non ... in casa?*' I query in my atrocious Italian. With a jerk of his head he indicates up the hills behind. '*Sulla salita,*' he says, and trundles on.

It is a long trundle, but interesting for all that. The gravel track winds through orange and lemon trees, olives and vines, then turns inland towards the hills; and I begin to feel more than a little embarrassed at having put our host to such trouble.

'Scusi.' I say, trying to convey my feeling. *'Non lo so non c'e aqua in casa … pardone … quanto chilometro in monte?'* I might be speaking Greek for all he understands, and probably was, so we just trundle on in silence until the track, which has now deteriorated to a narrow footpath bestrewn with boulders, ends at a small but fast flowing spring. A length of rigid plastic pipe lies nearby and this Alphonse places in the spring source, putting my jerrycans under the far end. There is enough fall to make the water flow. It is clever—but slow.

Meanwhile we sit and think, but not for long. From somewhere above us in the hills comes the distant wail of a siren. It increases in volume, finally arriving in a crescendo round a bend of the road, and there goes the top of a police car for a fleeting moment before it wails away with a ghastly Doppler effect on up the coast. This is shortly followed by a quite incredible sight: hordes of bottoms, jerking like puppets, flash into view, preceded by heads bent low. A holocaust of cyclists pedalling as though Hell were in pursuit, legions of them, interspersed with police motorcycles, the occasional siren blaring, radio phones crackling; endlessly they stream round the hillside above, and I look at my host questioningly.

'Vicino la Sicilia Internationale race di bicycletta,' he says, and seeing my incomprehension tries it in English. 'Beechicletta Internationalie', and then, continues, 'Chuko Vin Sore … you hear?'

I ponder that one. Chuko vin sore? Chukovin, Sore? Chu kovin sore? Chuko vinsore … ?

Blankly I look at him. He tries again, putting tremendous emphasis into the words … 'CHUKO VIN SORE … YOU!'

Suddenly it clicks. DUKE OF WINDSOR! It must be. But what on earth has that got to do with a round Sicily Bicycle Rally? Can it be—and I look up the hills to where the last broad backside is palpitating away in the distance—can it possibly be that the old boy is heading the Rally? No … it's just ridiculous. Perhaps sponsoring it; well, it's possible I suppose; good old Royalty, they really are getting democratic; but somehow it seems doubtful. Alphonse is standing now, looking frustrated. Once more he tries.

'YOU … CHUKO VINSOR … E MORTO OGGI,' He stamps the ground with exasperation. 'MISSUS SIMPSONE AT QUEEN. CHUKO VINSOR E MORTO.'

Morto! There is a bell clanging far away down in the village. Can it really be that cracked, or is it just the effect of distance?

Morto! Is this Sicilian youngster trying to tell me that the Duke of Windsor is dead and Mrs Simpson is at the Palace?

Soon it is quite clear that this is precisely what he is so desperately trying to make me understand. But why, I am wondering with half my mind, why should he bother? I look away up the hills. Below me the cracked bell is still ringing—why, I wonder? Behind us the cicadas are making the midday heat crackle with their strident chirruping, and the Duke of Windsor is dead.

Goodness, I wish that bell would stop. What memories are floating slowly up this far-off hillside with that distant sad cracked note. So the young King Edward the Eighth is no more, and the woman he loved is finally accepted at the Palace.

Bizarre, kaleidoscopic world. Here on this hot Sicilian hillside, strangely enough I just want to sit down and cry.

*   *   *

If you happened to be working your way north before a brisk westerly close under the lee of that remarkable promontory which ends in Cape Milazzo on the north Sicilian shore, as we were that morning of the last day in May, you would see on the horizon a truly impressive sight. The volcanic cone of Stromboli, balanced like an inverted pudding basin, seems to tower into the heavens, over thirty miles away. Dark pewter against the incredible blue of the sky, it wears round its peak, like a monk's tonsure, a white fringe of cloud. The nearer islands of Vulcano, Lipari, Salina and Panarea are hidden behind the end of the promontory, and Stromboli alone rears like a forbidding sentinel ahead. There is something strangely brooding about the hunch of its shoulders and the regular incline of its three thousand foot high slopes, but the most impressive thing about this natural vent is the small plume of smoke and steam which, regular as clockwork, every half hour or so, fingers its way vertically above the cone, to disperse quickly in the clear sky.

It is as though one were watching a vast sleeping monster which, now and then, exhales a long and sulphurous breath. The mind boggles at the possibility of a cough, sneeze, or more violent awakening and the eye can become hypnotised by the sight, counting minutes till the next horribly portentous puff. Totally absorbed in this phenomenon as I was, you might just excuse me (B. never will) for ramming the rock which brought the noble *Lugworm* crashing to a standstill—anchored firmly by the bottom of her rudderblade.

In fact, so firmly was she pinioned that her after parts were lifted six inches or so above her normal water-level. We leapt forward, in an effort to bear down on her bow, thus allowing the stern to float free, but to no avail. I looked cautiously over the side. Sure enough, there was the weedy top of a large rock, towering up from the depths, and here was *Lugworm* staked like a banner to its crest. You may wonder why I did not simply lift the rudder from its trunking, but alas, this was impossible for the violence of impact had bent the sprung steel rudderpost beyond removal. There was nothing for it: I gingerly lowered myself on to the weedy pinnacle and with B. perched at the bow, I forcibly shoved her ample quarters inch by inch until she finally slid off the pinnacle and floated free.

A dive under the surface revealed the worst—the post was badly bent. It presented problems, for while it was still possible to move the helm and thus steer the boat, she could no longer be beached, since before doing so the rudder has to be unshipped. If possible, the post would have to be straightened while the rudder was still in position, and with womanly logic B. suggested that, since we had bent it the one way by impact in a forward direction, surely the obvious thing was to bend it the opposite way by impact in a reverse direction.

I thought about that. There seemed no harm in trying and, after all, the post might not need to be straightened completely in order to be withdrawn. If we could just bash it somewhere near true we might be able to unship it, beach, and finish the job properly. We dropped all sail, relocated the rock, and lowered the outboard. In principle the problem was easy—all we had to do was to hold the helm roughly amidships and ram the rock with the back of the rudderblade stern-first. But things are never as simple as they appear. To begin with, in order to get sternway on we had to use the outboard motor, and maintain a high degree of steerage in order to strike the rock correctly. That meant the outboard had to be stopped and locked into the up position just before impact, otherwise there was every chance of wrecking the engine.

Meanwhile, on the shore close by, people were beginning to take an interest. The obvious fact that a boat has struck a rock is enough to attract anyone's attention, but the chance of seeing a circus act such as we were putting on was drawing an interested crowd.

'This way,' a voice cried, beckoning us into the beach. Others took up the cry, and free advice was offered as to the best channel in through the off-lying rocks. Of course they could not know this was the one thing we dare not attempt until the rudder had been unshipped. Again and again we reversed on to that blessed rock, while the onlookers, gathering verbal momentum became enraged at the sight of what must have seemed deliberate boaticide.

It was no use. Poor *Lugworm* staggered repeatedly under the impacts, but that steel rod laughed at our efforts and remained just as bent. There was only one thing for it, the tiller head had to be taken off and the rudder dropped down free of the keel from underneath and obviously, this had to be done in fairly shallow water, or there was every chance of losing the blade and post complete. We anchored in a depth of six feet and I dived under her stern, making a light line fast to the blade with a barrel-hitch. Then, by easing back the tiller head clamp bolt the blade was lowered until the top end of its post came free of the keel. After that, we were able to nose our way into the boisterous group and explain the complexities of our problem.

But how were we to straighten that post? Sicilians and Italians as a people tend to be warm, open-hearted and helpful, but they are also highly volatile and hold very firm opinions. If these opinions happen to be at variance with one another it is quite possible for the fact to spark off physical violence; even about helping to straighten a stupid foreigner's bent rudder post.

I started with the best will in the world to clout the bent post with a heavy rock, but such was the quality of that steel that the rock simply sprung out of my hand on impact, singing its own glad song as it went.

This intrigued the crowd, who quickly grew impatient at this obvious ineptitude and finally a powerful man strode forward, tapped me on the shoulder and took the rudder out of my hands with an air of a father quietly taking charge from an incompetent child. He took it, followed by the crowd, down the beach and carefully selected a narrow crack between two massive boulders. Jamming the

— IF A SICILIAN COULDN'T...!

post firmly into this crack, he grasped the blade between both arms, braced his feet against the base of one rock and gently started to apply force. His muscles bulged, the veins stood out on his neck and a suffused red glow spread over his determined face. At the moment of full effort, the blade, under tremendous stress, sprang round and flung our friend full length in the shingle; the rudder remained bent and juddering gently in the crack.

Undaunted our friend picked himself up, took a deep breath and advanced again to the task, encouraged and goaded by the advice and criticisms of the crowd. The business was now completely out of our hands—the straightening of the rudder-post was a matter of personal if not national prestige, and if a Sicilian couldn't bend back a bit of paltry English steel, what was he good for, eh?

Again the post was firmly jammed between the rocks, and this time a friend of the friend was positioned to preclude that blade swinging round under stress. Again muscles bulged. An awed silence fell on the crowd, as gradually one rock separated from the other, the crack widened and the post, still just as bent, claimed a second victory. But now the entire crowd was clearly on its mettle. Somebody appeared brandishing a car jack. Loud discussion took place, most of it quite incomprehensible to us, and the offending rudder was carted across the road to a nearby garden where a high stone wall abutted the end of a house. At the end of this wall was a slot—a sort of vertical drain hole—left between the solid boulders of the footings. It was ingenious, the whole idea. The blade was hammered, not without trouble, deep into this slot, leaving the offending post sticking from the wall. Thus jammed, and firmly held, the blade could not twist round, and the jack was then positioned under the post. The garden was crammed full of people. B. and I were awed watchers of this clever ruse. The house owner smiled at us; the jack owner's lips were thin and determined, the friend and the friend of the friend just glowered.

Slowly the jack was tensioned; the post was seen to start bending like a clock spring, in a graceful curve; a hush fell on the watchers. Little by little that inch and an eighth diameter steel post bent up and then, unbelievably the slot elongated, its lintel stone rising up to carry the entire wall with it. Seconds later we were looking at a gaping hole, and all Hell was let loose. Everybody was shouting at everybody else.

The friend and the friend of the friend were rolling about with laughter until the houseowner actually hit one of them. I extricated the still triumphant rudder and together we withdrew, making every kind of apologetic noise to anyone who was prepared to listen; but nobody seemed interested in us any longer. Why should they be—wasn't there a full scale war getting into gear back there in the garden?

We re-embarked, and motored gingerly out through the rocks, the still bent rudder grinning at us from the bottom boards, and it took me two solid hours in a secret place with a borrowed eight pound sledgehammer to persuade that post back far enough for it to once again be inserted in the normal manner. Aha! I would give a lot to know exactly where that rudder and tiller is right now. But that is another story which will be told in good time.

*   *   *

Vulcano, which rose from the sea in 183BC, is famous for its therapeutic mud. It may be famous for other things as well, but so far as I'm concerned the mud's enough-it's quite splendid. One earthy ambition of a friend of mine is to watch well proportioned women wrestling in mud, and I quite agree with him; there's something wonderfully erotic about the whole idea. It may be why I'm sitting up to my neck in this boghole.

We sailed the fifteen miles to the island yesterday evening after that fiasco with the rudder, and really life has been hilarious since we anchored here in the Baia di Levante. To begin with, the sea is constantly belching; it leaves no shadow of doubt that we're fossicking about on sufferance here, and it makes you appreciate the present. Sulphurous gases pop up from the bottom and *Lugworm* has spent the night anchored in the bay with her belly being tickled. It sounded pleasant enough inside, like floating in a glass of champagne, but the smell takes a bit of getting used to. You either like it or you don't; I'm not sure myself.

These mudholes are like small lakes, scooped out of the low-lying shore not far from the sea, and they look as though they have been messed about a bit by man, but don't think the mud is black—far from it. White would be nearer the mark. Battleship grey is about the right colour, and the occupants are totally disenchanting. One sits and hopes, but so far the nearest thing to a sex symbol is two obese German Fraus down at the far end who, with appalling concentration, are laving themselves with hands full of the stuff.

Apart from a dreadfully ill-looking Italian paddling about in another hole, that's it. And me. But I'm just a head sticking out. The heat is terrific, you have to prod about carefully to select a tolerable spot and lie full length to get completely covered because it's quite shallow, but if you're going to get in you might as well get right in not friggle about. I've been gently simmering here for half an hour and there are still no well-proportioned women, much less any chance of a wrestling match so I might as well go and give B. a shock. She's still turned-in.

I drag myself out, all slimy grey and shining, and flap along the beach, slap sluppy slop it's DELIGHTFUL! If I stick my elbows out, it doesn't make so much noise. 'B.,' I yell from the beach. 'Quick, look at this.'

I know what a shock it was; a near black head sticking out from a light grey mudpack. I have the photo beside me as I type. You want to see it? Well you can't—it's positively revolting.

B. is not impressed. But the mud is drying. Even as I stand in the sun it's beginning to congeal.

'I'm going to run round the island to see what happens,' I call to her, and set off. It's fantastic; have you ever run fast completely encased in a thick layer of drying mud? No, I bet you haven't. I blunder into a family emerging from a chalet and a small child screams and sits down suddenly. The mother rushes over protectively and the whole group stands gaping as I disappear. Better not to stop now, they might think I'm mad. On I go, but it's hardening quickly—almost like glue. When my thighs hit each other they stick together and it's most uncomfortable—better to run with my legs apart.

Have you ever tried running with your elbows out and yours legs apart? It's hilarious. Dammit there's another group right across the path; a portly gentleman (Lord, he could be English) grabs a beach brolly and freezes at the head of the column, like Napoleon. What does he think I'm going to do: attack him? It's difficult enough running like this, never mind getting belligerent. Why do they all stare so—you'd think I was stark naked. The mud is cracking and dropping off in cakes. It's getting a bit uncomfortable so I stand on my head just for fun, and I bet you've never done that, either, caked in mud. Oh, it's quite a morning one way and another.

I run right round Vulcanello at the north of the island to have another look at Stromboli. Then take a swim in the hot bubbling water, wipe the lot off and join B. for breakfast.

Halfway through coffee she pokes her head out of the tent. 'Why are all those people standing on the beach looking at us?' she enquires.

It's true; there are dozens of them, standing in groups gaping at us.

'Maybe they've never seen a boat like *Lugworm* before.' I comfort her, and carry on with the marmalade.

Yes, it's been a surprisingly different morning, one way and another. Better than the eight-fifteen.

*   *   *

It's no distance at all from Vulcano to the Island of Lipari—half a mile across a twenty fathom strait and you're there. This is the island which in ancient times was known as Meligunis and is the largest of the archipelago, famous of old as a trading centre for obsidian, the dark vitreous lava that looks like broken glass bottles. Today its most remarkable sight is the quarries in the pumice hills, above Canneto on the eastern shore: for all the world like our Cornish china clay mines. The sea round these isles is thick with floating pumice, you can scoop up knobbles of it everywhere.

The sixteenth-century Spanish fortress above the small port is magnificent. If you want to float back in time, just drift around the narrow streets of the town behind the castle; no hideous din of internal combustion engines and at night, when the litter from the tourists seems less obvious, it's quite enchanting. After you have lost yourself in the history of the place you may wander out and lose yourself in the deep valleys that run up the steep hills behind. On the western shore the small road runs high on the cliff tops and one can look from Quattrocchi (four eyes and well-named for you really need them), down at a superb coastline with magnificent off-lying rocks. It's great fun to wander about looking at the coast then to be able to say, 'Come on, let's go and sail round there!' But yesterday *Lugworm* got her anchor jammed under some massive boulders thirty feet down—we could see it for two hours while we tried every conceivable way of recovering it other than hiring an aqua lung. After that it just came free, but it was a good opportunity to explore the depths with our snorkel gear and flippers. Phew ... but it's hot on this hillside and the sulphurous smell everywhere seems to make it even more humid, one begins to feel over-ripe if you know what I mean, like a soft tomato. It would be good to have this scenery and sunshine with an occasional bracing Cornish wind, but one can't have everything and I mustn't grumble, we're doing pretty well.

I think the most noticeable thing about these islands is the peace. We have forgotten what life must have been like before machinery was invented. No noise, and none of that hysterical rushing about that internal combustion engines engender. A good place to escape and be happy in, these Aeolian Isles. It's a strange thing, happiness, people say you can be happy anywhere —I can't. To be happy I've always thought I had to be surrounded by beauty and tranquillity, but is this really true? When you look at these islands they are not very beauti-ful. Great lumps of volcanic ash probing up from the sea have little grace. Grandeur, yes. Tranquillity? Perhaps, but it is a brooding tranquillity—unimaginable power at rest. What makes them so enchanting is the colours. You have to experience this to know what I'm talking about. The sky in the evening is indescribable. It almost lifts you out of reality into a dream world of fantasy: you see the evening light on the western flanks of the hills, infusing a luminous glow into the subtle greens of the fig, cypress, olive and cactus, and behind it all is the dark reds and violets of the lava and black volcanic ash. The powdered ash of the beaches is that pure matt of lamp-black, it takes a bit of getting used to. Of course there is novelty value for northern Europeans like us, the warmth alone tends to wrap all other experiences with a blanket of content. But one wonders how long the indolence and non-action, the sheer hedonistic pleasure of sunbathing and swimming here, divorced from all the roots of one's own culture, the stimulation of the colder climate, the very scents of England, could withstand a dreadful ennui; a vacuum of non-creativity.

Pondering on happiness, I remember a thought from somewhere way back in my schooldays, which for me seemed and still seems to capture something of its meaning. I am an Englishman, wondering in a far off place whether I could really remain happy anywhere else than at home. It runs:

> Happiness … ?
> Happiness lies in the crook of a willow
> Down near the pool where the cows stand at dusk
> Deep in the heart of a wood fire at night.
> Happiness lies wherever the green of a hill meets the sky
> Where leaves that are new can tremble and shiver
> And wind lifts the song of a lark on high.
> It lies in the warm grass whose breath has been freed
> By the soft swinging low singing glide of a scythe
> and comes with the river
> the reedy rush river
> the watercress river
> … and sun in my eyes.

Well … is that England? Or is it perhaps the ghost of England? How often today does one catch the scent of meadow grass drying in the sun, freed by the 'soft swinging low singing glide of a scythe' on the banks of 'the reedy rush river, the watercress river?' It is still there in odd corners of course, but mostly it has been overtaken by the characterless face of 'progress', buried beneath the concrete and tarmacadam of the motorway systems, with their foetid breath of carbon monoxide. Can one still, I wonder, ever catch a fleeting shadow of it in our darkened homes with the stark flicker of the 'box'—watching the hysterical animal violence of the crowds at soccer matches?—listening to the eternal reports of union wrangling with management, political squabbles, violence?

One wonders sometimes what is the value of our 'gains' compared with the price we are paying in terms of loss. One wonders sometimes if England really exists any longer, if soon there really will be any roots left to go back to.

But these are sombre thoughts for a sunny hillside on Lipari, altogether too close to reality for pleasantness, so come on, let's go down and get some sail on *Lugworm*; it's a fair soft silent south wind and we can ghost up to Panarea before nightfall.

*   *   *

Panarea is delightful, for my money the best of the islands we had yet seen; no cars, just a few three-wheel drays for delivering stores from the boats that ply out to meet the inter-island steamers. What development has taken place is in good taste, nothing even remotely trippery. Long may it stay so. There is no real harbour, just a mole on the north-east shore giving protection to a beach of large boulders, and there is a small sandy beach to the south-east. The western shore has dramatic steep cliffs and the rest of the island is really a natural garden with rhododendrons, figs, eucalyptus trees and a riot of geraniums. There is a form of hollyhock too, and cactus. It is interesting to see that all the fishing boats, some of them a lot larger than *Lugworm*, are regularly pulled out up the stony beaches, sliding over wooden baulks like railway sleepers.

We had a delicious evening meal ashore in a quiet and homely restaurant overlooking *Lugworm*; fish soup and *spaghetti con pommodoro* in company with the twelve apostles hanging on the wall—a picture of the Last Supper. Before turning in we shifted *Lugworm* to the other end of the bay, and though the weather generally remained calm, the night was made remarkable by the most peculiar violent gusts of wind coming off the island. It made sleeping afloat with the tent rigged most intriguing. When the wind hit her, *Lugworm* ranged about, chuckling to herself, which B. found most disturbing, imagining that we were adrift and disappearing out to sea. 'That would be fun,' I comforted her, but she didn't seem at ease.

The early forecast next morning gave the sea as *'poco mosso'* (slight) and sky as *'sereno o poco nuvoloso'* (clear or slight cloud) with winds light from the north. In fact, at 0930 a splendid north westerly came fanning along. We reached, under genoa, main and mizzen, out past the offlying islet of Basiluzzo and there was Stromboli, much larger now, eight miles to the north east. 'We seem to have been looking at it for a long time,' B. said to me after breakfast, 'Are we actually going to land on it today?'

It was a spanking good sail. I remember we reached across with genoa set, arriving about midday close to a tiny concrete slipway hidden in the rocks just west of Punta Monaco on the south shore. A small dinghy lay on the slip but swell and sea was churning the narrow approach into a foam bath. We continued running goosewinged up the eastern shore, losing the wind progressively as we edged into the lee of the island. Soon we were ghosting lazily within feet of the black cinder beaches, and it was while silently studying the high shoulders of the volcano that we first heard the awe-inspiring far-off rumble, like a reverberation of distant thunder. It echoed and re-echoed, dropping gently down from the heights like a suppressed growl from earth herself. We looked at each other and remained silent, awed by the sheer power of it.

By early evening we were becalmed off the north-east shore just to the south of the village. There was no harbour, nor even a mole—just the incredibly black beach sloping to the water's edge, then plunging on down for more than a thousand fathoms; a terrible place to be caught in bad weather. But the barometer was steady and all seemed fair and set calm so we decided to remain afloat and dropped our bow anchor a few feet from the beach, taking the stern anchor well onshore. One or two dirty white box-like houses were straggled about a hundred yards back, and beyond these we could see a few more scattered dwellings rising up the fields of vines, and the deeper green of a lemon grove, while higher up we could see the dried coarse grasses and broom, gently merging into the brown and reddish solidified lava which towered on up into the sky itself. No sound broke the oppressive silence other than the long gentle surge of the sea along the beach, and then, again, came that distant hollow and all-pervading rumble.

'I don't like this place,' B. whispered, looking up there to where the faint echoes of the sound still lingered. 'It makes me feel too vulnerable, too small to even matter; it's frightening.'

'True,' I agreed.' But in a way it's salutary for we microbes who think ourselves Lords of the Earth and the Universe.' I was remembering Santorini, that relic of a volcanic cataclysm in the south Aegean where we had recently spent a month living in a pumice cave and where 3,500 years before, eighty square kilometres of mountain top had blown sky high leaving the sea to flood the vast crater, wiping out the Minoan civilization in Crete and bringing death and destruction along the seaboard of the entire Aegean with the resultant mountainous waves. In our position, at the foot of this other monster, it didn't bear dwelling on.

'Still,' I said out loud, 'if an entire village can live their lives here, I'm prepared to accept the risk of one or two days. Come on, let's have a brew of tea and then find out what's going on up there?' Within half an hour we were ashore enquiring as to the best ascent.

The village was a pleasant surprise, there was a tranquil charm about the narrow lanes which led between the small houses, each with its little garden bursting with red geraniums. As usual there were no cars. We passed a sleepy white church and the occasional donkey dozing in the late afternoon heat, and one or two small shops which seemed to differ little from the private houses, save for the wares displayed in the windows. An elderly man, hacking patiently with a broad bladed adze at a small field of dry black soil, stopped his work and, with quiet courtesy indicated the best way to the summit, pointing towards the far end of the village. We wandered on following the lane until it escaped from the confines of the houses and stretched itself, a wide stone pathway now, zig-zagging up the gentle lower slopes, and giving the impression that one was wandering through hanging gardens, so thick and rich with yellow flowers was the broom.

After about half an hour of steady climbing, the path, which was beautifully made of cut stone blocks, became narrower and more unkempt. About five hundred feet up we sat and looked back. Far away, over the distant village we could still see *Lugworm*, a mere dot on the fringe of black shore snugged close under the foot of this vast cinder heap—a ridiculous speck in an eternity of blue sea and sky which stretched out to a horizon made vastly more distant by our height.

But there remained more than two thousand five hundred feet to be climbed, and having no fancy to be caught on the slopes in darkness we hastened on at greater pace while the path became more haphazard, carried away in places by small landslides. It wound through a bamboo grove, broke clear and snaked across a steep shoulder of low scrub, finally shaking off all semblance of respectability as a man-made track to become a lithe impatient beaten cinder path, ever steeper as it attacked the slopes in a more direct line to the top.

Another hour of this, and B. decided she had had enough. We had spent it clambering across the loose metallic sounding clinker, clinging to the illusive path then losing it again. For every step forward we slid half a step back. Both of us were hot and growing tired, but the view lifted us high above such mundanities. We had reached a point where a ridge dropped vertically about fifty feet. Below this the slope inclined away at a steady sixty degree angle of black clinker scree sheer for two thousand feet before plunging under the blue-green sea. It was an awesome sight, appalling for anyone who suffers from vertigo, and it was here that B. sat down and stated that her legs had gone to jelly and she intended climbing no farther. 'You go on,' she said, I'll regain my breath and then start slowly back down and you can overtake me when you've seen the crater.'

At that moment the volcano 'blew' again. But this time we heard it building up, now frighteningly close, like the approach of a mighty wind, then I swear the ground itself shook and there came that spine chilling roar which left us looking feebly at the white plume of smoke rising so tantalizingly near up there.

'That's it,' she said. I'm off; this is no place for a girl with imagination—good-bye, and please be back before dark. I shall worry.'

With that she started scrambling down and I watched until her tiny figure disappeared over a bluff, far below, and then I again looked upwards. The clinker slopes, broken here and there by outcrops of contorted purple lava towered into the sky. There was another thousand feet still to go and I had no idea whether it was possible to get to the crater edge or not. For that matter I didn't know whether I was on the right path or whether this apology for a track finally disappeared up there in a mountainside of scree. What happened after that? Would the clinker get too hot for my bare feet? When the crater 'blew', did it blow out a bit more lava and ash as well—and where was I going to be if it did? If I was not to be scorched alive and buried it would have to be well outside its range, and how far was that? In nothing but a swimsuit, it was all a bit disconcerting and quite exciting really. Odd what a difference being alone makes to one's courage. I was fighting the desire to scoot down there after B. and call it a day, but couldn't think of any reason for doing so other than being a coward, so I started climbing again to stop the thinking.

If it gets too hot, I thought, I'll have a good excuse to go back. Now do I, or don't I hope it gets too hot? My mind bumbled on to itself as I scrabbled over the loose resonant stuff. A thousand vertical feet is an awful lot of clinker. Suppose my weight starts an avalanche—just a few billion tons of it sliding down. I suppose they'll cast an idle glance up from the village and carry on milking the goat and that'll be that, with me just an undetectable redder splodge on the hillside of congealed magma. Would it matter?

At last the infernal slope began to level off. I stopped scrabbling about like a monkey on all fours and stood erect and there ahead of me was another entire mountain. Have you ever had that experience? When you're certain you have finally reached the peak and there you stand again looking up from a new lot of foothills! Dammit, I thought, unless that Admiralty Chart is lying, there cannot be more than another seven hundred and fifty feet left before I'm flying.

But gently, as I rested there to regain energy and breath, there stole across the scene a remarkable change. The vanguard of that monk's tonsure came creeping silently round the slope alongside to envelop it and me. The effect was dramatic. Gone was the oven hot bright limitless world, the blazing distant blues and nearby cinder reds and browns; instead I was in a dreadfully cold closed twilight of greys and blacks, with the damp swirling mist goosepimpling my hide, and as I shivered there a strange lurid freak of the thin light began to take effect all round. It was as though the black slopes of the volcano were glowing with a green luminescence. It may have been the damp glistening on the sulphurous clinker, or it could have been something to do with over-compensation within my eyes adjusting to the sudden change of light, colour and intensity, but the whole swirling cold and hollow world up there in the heights took on this lurid luminous green shimmer as though the ash were carpeted with glistening moss. But this was not just the effect of the light and cloud; the dark slopes were actually smoking, or it may have been steam rising where the mist touched the hot ashes, but the green glow was reflected from acres and acres of rising tongues of mist, like green flames, and over all there hung a suffocating oppressive smell of sulphur.

I wanted to drop down, quickly, and get out of that cloud level, back to the bright real world below. Visibility was down to a few hundred yards in this subterranean world of the sky, and then a thought came to me; maybe I was an idiot, but wouldn't it be as easy to break up above that cloud level, as it would be to drop below it? I knew, having seen the volcano from afar, that there was almost always a small peak standing proud of the clouds.

Shivering with the cold, I picked my way steadily upwards. The world seemed to be getting darker, and there was a wind now, drifting the cloud perceptibly past. To my right there seemed to be an overall gloom and through a sudden slight rift in the mist I saw that I was in a valley, a narrow black valley with a thin line of path along the bottom. I started to run, and the path began to incline upwards away from the valley base, sloping round the shoulder of the hill. It was dank and cold and the smell was overpowering.

Suddenly, as though dark curtains were being drawn aside, my closed world grew bright again, its boundaries rolling back and away. I was still running hard up the path, round the shoulder of a small hillock of ash when I broke free from that fast retreating cloud.

But how can I describe the scene? I was alone in the sky on a tiny black smoking island surrounded by a sea of snow white cloud. Down below me on all sides, obscuring the horizon of the real sea, was a swirling ocean of fast moving white billows, and there was nothing else in the whole world save this small island which appeared to be flowing along through its billowing sea, floating in a universe of intensely dark blue sky. I stood on the peak of a small hummock and spread my arms to the wonderful warmth of that sun. Truly, I felt I could have flown at that moment, alone up there above the world on this magic carpet in the sky; indeed, I seemed to be flying as I ran on, following the thin winding track. It balanced along a knife ridge, the slopes of which plunged down on both sides to disappear beneath that misty sea; I knew how many thousand feet it went down, down, invisibly beneath the cloud, but that world down there no longer existed for me. I ran, light as air, through a rainbow of steam, up a rise and down a long gradual incline, breasted the brow of another rise—and came to a halt, aghast.

Fifty yards ahead, standing on the very edge of the great crater, were two women dressed in heavy tweeds, thick stockings and tough brogues. One carried an open umbrella and the other had a guide book under one arm and a camera round her neck.

'You looked exactly like Eros,' the woman said, in a horsey English voice. 'Running down that hill, with practically nothing on. How ever can you do it in bare feet, I don't know?' and she looked me up and down as one might view a cod on a fishslab. Obviously, I was quite beyond her comprehension. But she was talking still.

'You're only just in time if you've come to see the puff. It's due in precisely one minute—that's why we've got the umbrella.' Her friend smiled weakly, adjusted her spectacles and examined the camera.

'We must leave immediately it's over, Agatha,' she burbled on. 'We simply must not miss the evening boat. And I must say I'll not be sorry, they really ought to put a fence round this hole!'

I stood there, and I swear I could actually hear the fabric of my world of light in the sky crumbling and collapsing around me. Suddenly, there came a quite unreasonable anger welling up. Damn and blast and damn you, I shouted silently in my mind, smiling sweetly at her. Is NOWHERE on earth free of bloody tourists, here, of all places!—and I turned away, lest my eyes should give me away.

Hell's bowels, but I was angry.

From the ruins of another world, I started to laugh. 'There's a good flat place for a car park back there,' I commented. 'They might allow, perhaps, a slight discount for coaches?' I added mildly, to be met with an uncomprehending stare.

Suddenly, I didn't want at all to stand there while mother Earth did her little show for the clicking cameras of the tourists. Somehow it all seemed beneath her dignity. I hoped she would belch a gurgle of molten bowel and vaporise the screaming tweed, socks, brogues, me and all.

'I'm off!' I roared and they both jumped as I pelted back up that path, round the shoulder and back down the gloomy valley. I was halfway through the cloud layer when the earth herself began to roar too. I heard it grumbling up from somewhere deep in her belly underfoot, rumbling closer and closer with a noise like a small hurricane, and then with a booming akin to a thousand express trains neck and neck in a tunnel she spewed again. A cloud of warm ash began to rain down, and I was covered in ochre grit. But oh, I was so angry—angry with myself, the world, and everybody in it. Fool, Duxbury, I fumed within, don't you know that you're living in the twentieth century, not some greater ideal Homeric world of another age. Come down to earth you idiot; they've as much right to be up there as you have.

But I wish they hadn't been. I was so angry I ran all the way back down, one and a half hours aided by gravity, and was still fuming when I overtook B. just outside the village.

'You've been very quick,' she said, startled as I came padding along. 'Did you see the blow?'

I sat down on the path and told her exactly how it had all happened, how it had all been so wonderful, and how it had all suddenly collapsed in a packet of English Tweed.

'Oh B.,' I groaned, still fuming. 'I really got very very near to Heaven up there; for a moment it was unbelievably wonderful.'

I sat and regained my breath there on the path, until a strange sound made me look aside. B. was lying full-length in the grass, holding her sides and rolling about, with laughter.

I suppose it's why I love her so.

*   *   *

Our earth has long since turned this face from the sun, carrying us here on Stromboli far into the lee of night. Only the glow of our candle under the cotton awning traps a pale memory of day, and the sea, whispering softly on the ash beach, begins to lull us towards sleep.

But we are roused by the crunch of footsteps. Two figures have left the village and now, at the top of the rise they have lit a fisherman's pressure lamp which hangs over the stern of a boat hauled high. They carry wide rakes, and when the lamp is burning well, move down to the water's edge nearby and commence raking the black beach flat, forming a level highway up to another boat which rests on wooden sleepers well above sea level. Two or three more figures emerge from the village, and then a drift of ten or so in a group, some of them carrying rucksacks, some with rolled bedding across their backs. Teenagers mostly, young men and women, they gather at the top of the beach round the boat with the lamp. Their figures cast long moving shadows which drift across the distant dim faces of the houses, erasing them to join the blackness of night for a fleeting moment. There are more groups forming behind the lamp, and we see a rope being led from the boat on sleepers down the beach.

Amid the hum of conversation a voice rises. The murmur dies for a moment, then rises again as a surge of people move down the beach to grasp the rope. A figure—it is a girl—leaps on to the boat with the lamp and puts a tin whistle to her lips; the thin reedy notes come floating across, and a voice picks up the tune, followed by more and more as the crowd take up the ditty. Soon everybody on the beach is singing lustily, and with the swing of the tune they put their weight on the rope. Others crowd round the boat, which begins to slide towards the sea.

Two black shadows vie with one another to collect the sleepers from astern and thrust them again beneath the bow of the moving boat, forming a ramp down which she can slide to the water, and the singing rises in tempo as the crowd begins to catch the rhythm.

But above it all now comes another sound; it is a deep regular throb, like a quick pulse from somewhere out there in the black sea, and as we look across the water two bright eyes, one red and one green, can be seen making towards us. It is the ferry steamer from Milazzo approaching.

The haulers on the rope have now reached the waterline, and fold back to join the willing hands ranged round the boat. With a last cheer she is pushed forward, the crowd running alongside, until she plunges into the sea, while a dozen or so islanders grasp another line trailing from her stern and check the way, then pull her gently back to the beach. A plank is rigged and the still singing crowd begin to embark. The throb of the ship's propeller ceases suddenly and as the ship swings slowly round, the deck lights expand into a long bright necklace a quarter of a mile off, throwing their own faint light on the tableau on shore.

Now the boat is full, and amid shouts of farewell is shoved off from the beach, the long oars gripping the water as four lusty islanders pull towards the ship.

Twice the boat returns, and each time she departs the figures on the beach thin out until, finally, only six islanders stand there waiting her final return in silence, their cigarettes glowing in the night. As the boat casts off for the last time from the ship, the vessel's engines throb once more into life, her lights swing away, and gradually disappear into the darkness.

I wade ashore and join the waiting islanders. A block has been overhauled to the water's edge, its tackle secured to a massive stake up the beach. And as the boat crunches into the ash this is hooked to her stem. Two each side, we keep the boat level on her broad keel as she is hauled slowly back up the beach. I drag the sleepers from the stern and thrust them under the moving bow. When she is far enough up, the tackle is unhooked and two stout chocks placed beneath her bilge. The pressure lamp is dowsed.

'*Grazie, Signore ... buonanotte,*' one of the islanders murmurs to me, and they drift back into the sleeping village. The ship is just a pale dot of light on the horizon.

Our candle glow leads me back to *Lugworm*, and the sigh of the sea on the ash beach lulls us both off to sleep.

CHAPTER IV

THE LONG COAST NORTH

WAS IT GEORGE BERNARD SHAW or Caesar who said that the art of life lies in gathering memories? I do not know, but I do know that memories, like good wine, last longer and remain clearer when stored in the right container—and what pure magic can lie enshrined in a chart! Sitting here writing late in the February night, with a log fire crackling and the good old English sleet slurrying on the window panes, I look at this battered faded sheet. Creased, scribbled on, stained with coffee and with the clear imprint of five small toes spread across the title, I trace the familiar names, each rich with memories, of that Calabrian coastline; feel again the blazing heat of the sun, shade my eyes from the blinding light on untold beaches, and see the faint silhouettes of the distant islands. I turn the page of our log, and begin to read.

It is forty-three miles from Stromboli to Vibo Valentia on the Italian mainland. The first thirty-odd are across open sea and then you connect with that carbuncle on the Italian toe which comes to a head at Cape Vaticano. It's far enough in a dinghy—one is well advised to pick the weather carefully and Ye Gods, we couldn't have bettered this day if we had rigged the Heavenly computer.

Stromboli still looms twelve miles astern, crowned with that ridiculous wisp of mist, but now the blue haze of distance has robbed the volcano of its power. If it erupts at this moment we shall merely be entertained by a firework display and, being totally human, it no longer seems to matter much.

But the sea—how I wish you could be here! From horizon to horizon is a tranquil plate of blue with no trace of wind to so much as ripple the surface: no single puff of cloud is mirrored there from the high blue bowl of sky, and the monotonous throb of our outboard thrusts *Lugworm* gently on, making the tiny whirlpools swirl from under her counter where deeps of ten hundred fathoms paint a darker mauve-blue void. The whirlpools spin, flatten and grow irregular down either side of the wake, finally dissolving in limpid ennui as they too give up the struggle and pass into oblivion. Indeed, we are finding it hard to fight off sleep in this baking blue world of sun and sea and sky.

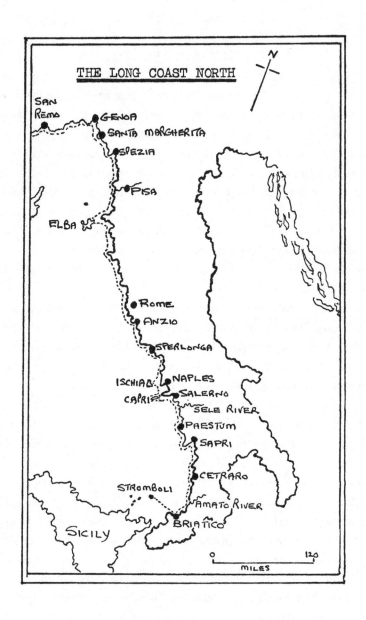

THE LONG COAST NORTH

SAN REMO
GENOA
SANTA MARGHERITA
SPEZIA
PISA
ELBA
ROME
ANZIO
SPERLONGA
ISCHIA
NAPLES
CAPRI
SALERNO
SELE RIVER
PAESTUM
SAPRI
CETRARO
STROMBOLI
AMATO RIVER
SICILY
BRIATICO

0   120
MILES

I count the crystal beads of water strung like diamonds on our fishing line astern and for the hundredth time haul it in hopefully. The spinner winks idly at me. 'Do you really think any damned fish will make the effort to give chase on a day like this?' it seems to say, and I drop it back, half envious of its silver path through the cool silent depths. We stretch out in our nothings, settling down to a soporific stupor as the sun mounts higher, adding yet another shade of tan to our already mahogany skins.

All things considered, we are keeping remarkably healthy and fit on this venture. It's surprising really because the fresh water is becoming a bit of a problem. Plastic cans are perhaps not the best containers for storing drinking water in a hot climate, but at least they have one big advantage: if they're thin and white like ours they do allow one to detect the colour of the contents. Some weeks ago we found a green slime coating the walls and having long since exhausted the purifying tablets bought in Corfu I've taken to dropping in a handful of small shingle each time just before refilling to scour the insides. Shaken around vigorously with a quart or so of water it comes out like pea soup but, as I remark to B. (who always seems to be watching at the wrong moment), 'Better out than in!'

We find also that *Lugworm*'s bilges must be swabbed with fresh water and dried completely at least once each week, for if the salt damp is allowed to lie there on the spare warps and rigging, they soon start to smell abominably. Today we have removed them all and are towing them astern to freshen up. The floorboards are piled on the foredeck meantime, and we've emptied all the lockers as well to give them an airing. Tins, packets, rigging, bedding and clothes are spread all over the boat; she looks like a Chinese funeral with we two strips of leather stretched out among the chaos. One wonders idly what would happen if a hurricane arrived out here halfway across the Tyrrhenian—maybe we'd see it coming, but life would be hectic for a while.

For want of something better to do I squint through the handbearing compass. The tip of Stromboli bears 274 degrees. What else is there to take a sight on? That faint grey pimple to the south-west must be Panarea—248 degrees. It's not a good 'cut'; a bit too small an angle but it'll do, and the 'fix' puts us a sniff south of our trackline. Better alter course a couple of degrees and we should hit Vibo on the nose. I settle down comfortably with my back resting against the base of the mizzen mast, eyeing the flat steering compass strapped to the top of the centreboard casing and gradually become hypnotised by the blessed thing; but wait a minute! Isn't that something other than sea and sky fine over the starboard bow? A thin line of cloud, or land perhaps? I stand up to get higher, blink, and run my eyes slowly along, just above the horizon—it's the best way to pick out anything that isn't there.

'Stop wobbling the boat,' comes a sleepy voice from under the sampan hat, 'you'll upset the coffee.'

'I'm navigating!' I retort. A chap has to justify himself at times.

'Where are we,' she asks. 'Are we lost yet?'

B. has a peculiar approach to navigation. Unless she can say, with no shadow of doubt, that we're balanced exactly on the head of a pin in precisely THAT position—so far as she's concerned it's an emergency. She could be lost on Bodmin Moor on a fine day. For my part, as long as I know which ocean we're in, what matter? 'All right, cuckoo,' I mumble, 'we're somewhere between Stromboli and Italy, maybe a bit farther south than I thought but nothing to worry about.'

That does it.

The hat wobbles and two long brown legs unfold to start slithering about on the sloping hull bottom where the floor boards aren't. She tried to stand and sits down heavily again. A box of tools and a half full tin of varnish slide off the side-deck. The coffee is already in the bilges. I continue looking, steadfastly, towards Italy.

But it's no use; it's one of those hot days again and the pressure is high. I start thinking about ducks. Did you know they have a more or less airtight skull, and are prone to bouts of sudden flapping about and fits during summer thunderstorms? Something to do with rapid variation of atmospheric pressure on a small brain box.

Odd, because there's no thunder today.

'Where's the rag?' she says.

There's varnish, coffee and the tools all becoming intimate down there, but I stare unblinkingly towards Italy. 'The rag, quickly,' she squeaks, fossicking up under the side netting. My newly dhobeyed white jersey joins the sticky mess in the bilges. 'Oh God!' she shrieks, 'don't just stand up there like Eros, DO something!'

'Come back here, cuckoo,' I hiss, soothingly. 'Just take the helm and leave it to me. I'll clear up the mess and stow everything.'

She steps in it—then on to the chart. Honestly, sometimes I wonder if it wouldn't be simpler opting for the hurricane.

*   *   *

We never did make Vibo. Neither would you had you rounded Cape Zambrone and seen that crumbling golden ruin of the watchtower of Briatico and the gay fishing boats drawn up on the beach behind the tiny mole. It was a perfect little harbour half way along the carbuncle, just made for *Lugworm* to bury her nose in, and being about six in the evening we were ready for toast and honey and a refreshing swim to wash off the torpor of the day.

The fisherfolk were boisterously welcoming. We buried our anchor under the ample backside of Madonna di Pompeii and poodled around among the brilliant greens, golds and reds of Stella del Mare, Santa Gerardo and Rosa Madre, all bestrewn with nets, lines, buoys and boys, for each boat seemed to harbour its own small explosion of children.

'See!' One of the fishermen calls impatiently to us, 'FISH TV!' and he leaps aboard his boat to proudly uncover an expensive echo sounder, a trace of the seabed still faded and purple on the paper roll. 'Fish TV.' he grins again delightedly pointing to a faint shadow about twenty fathoms under the surface which may or may not have been a shoal. He is buoyant this one, and well he may be, for didn't he bring back two spendid tunny this morning, forty and sixty kilos each. So far as I can gather they'll reap a good harvest in lire if he's shrewd in the bargaining. 'And he'll have to be!' growls a companion, sotto voce as he mends his nets, 'to pay for that costly bit of nonsense—there's six months good eating mortgaged in that box.' A tinge of jealousy perhaps, but we wonder more and more at the economics of this fishing; we've been trailing a line now for more than six hundred miles and even the damned spinner complains of being lonely.

We wandered inland with the cool of the evening, up the dusty road and through the little village which lies about a kilometre from the harbour, resting our eyes on the green of the hills with their deeply wooded valleys which back the splendid sandy beaches. Northward round the Gulf of Eufemia we could see the coastline to be flatter, but about fifteen miles away beyond Cape Suvero it rose in a more continuous mountain range which sloped steeply to the sea. From the watch-tower it looked appealing.

And so it was. We set off on the morning of 5th June to skirt round the Gulf, using the lightest of westerly zephyrs until she, too, dropped off to sleep leaving us to anchor under the beautiful fortified headland town of Pizzo where we replenished our petrol supply. There was nothing for it but to motor gently on within feet of the beach, which became more and more shingly. By early evening, sated with sun and the blinding beach and sky, we were off the mouth of Fiume Amato and making a difficult entry against the strong outflow boiling over a shallow bar.

But it was well worth the effort, if only for the delight of bathing again in cool sweet fresh water. We washed all our clothes and spread them to dry on the pebbles, then walked inland along the deserted banks. Merely to use one's legs after hours in the boat is a delight. You cannot know the pleasure and contrast of wandering through reeds, bamboo, eucalyptus trees, grass and green scrub bushes after a day of blinding beach, sea and sky. To hear the sudden swift beat of a bird's wing, and glimpse the blue flash of a kingfisher as it darts along a leafy lane of green water. Breathing becomes a new delight, for there is always some fresh scent, a rich green breath of growing things, nourished by the river, and above all these is shadow—flickering pools of relief that come rustling with a million leafy voices bringing balm after the heat of day.

That night we cooked supper over a blazing log fire on the pebbles, listening to the quiet whisper of the sea, while a herd of oxen, attracted by the glow, ranged curiously back and forth on the opposite bank. But we slept aboard *Lugworm*, for the water and the tent deterred the insects, and somehow we always felt safer with a moat.

There remained more than five hundred miles of this Tyrrhenian coast before crossing the border up there into the French Riviera. The prevailing winds in this area are light north westerly, and every sailor knows that around the first or second week in August there is generally a period of violent weather. Our average of ten to twelve miles per day would see us in the region of Genoa by late July, and this was fine, for then we would be coasting along a weather shore which would offer the chance of a good lee from the northerly winds. But *Lugworm* bless her is

not at her best beating to windward in light airs, particularly when heavily laden as she was, and we were quite prepared to motor much of the way.

I remember the next morning having ghosted round the lighthouse on Cape Suvero in a near calm, we passed through a shoal of dead tunny floating belly up on the surface. Large fish these, there were some fifty of them in varying stages of decomposition, and we never did unravel that mystery, for the flesh of this fish is highly prized. It may be that the long tunny nets—they stretched as much as six miles out from the shore—had simply caught too many fish for the boats to cope with, but it seemed unlikely. Yet death by pollution seemed even less likely so far south, for there was little heavy industry on this coast.

That was an interesting day's sail, some of it under power to fill in gaps between fitful gusts of wind. The hills, as we had expected, sloped quite steeply to the shore and a strange result of the many small mountain torrents was that during their brief winter cataract down the valleys they had over the years brought much rock and silt to build up a river bed which was actually higher than the surrounding low fringes of the beach. The road and railway which cling closely to this coast appeared therefore often to tunnel beneath these raised riverbeds: it was an odd sight and of course the rivers were now quite dry, but what happens when the winter torrents flow is anybody's guess; perhaps they were contained by man-made banks of shingle and rock for the last few hundred yards before plunging into the sea.

Late afternoon found us still south of Cape Bonifati and to our surprise — for it is unmarked as a harbour on our chart — the little coastal village of Cetraro proved to have a fine mole. It gave excellent protection from the north, west and east, but would not provide much peace when wind and sea came out of the south. Another good thing Cetraro gave us was the finest pizza we had throughout the whole of Italy, and I refer not only to the taste, but also to the sheer entertainment which accompanied its production, for I must tell you that the proprietor of the small and unostentatious Pizzeria just beyond the mole is an artist and a show-man — and he knows it!

You may be acquainted with pizza, that popular round flat wedge of cooked pasta with its various highly seasoned fillings? It formed our staple diet, together with *spaghetti con pommodoro*, up the whole of this coast, for our bag of shekels, one year since leaving England, was becoming an embarrassment. Pizza and spaghetti is cheap. So also, thank God, is the local wine, and frankly we were both willing to forego the more attractive menus in exchange for the protracted freedom and adventure of our voyage. But join us for this memorable entertainment, sorrowing as you do so for that drear invention of the infra-red grill with its instant and expensive banishment of all flavour. Suffer instead a meal prepared and cooked entirely by hand, each ingredient of which is added, so it seems, by pure inspiration; for Guiseppe the proprietor, as I have said, is an artist.

He is also immensely large. Indeed, as he appears beaming from behind the raffia curtain his gaily striped apron advances like a spinnaker drawing full and gloriously on a dead run. One's heart, already warmed by the kindly, happy and totally wholesome giant, forgives the fact that the superbly flourished pasteboard menu contains but one item: Pizza Napolitana. The wine, in simple clarity, is local. But we spy a dish of anchovies among the clutter of utensils against the far wall.

We query the exact contents of the Pizza Napolitana, asking if these are included. 'But, of course,' beams Guiseppe clanking down a bottle of golden plonk and two thick glasses, 'and, Signore, you will be surprised!'

Against the back wall, which in fact is solid rock of the cliff face, a huge brick oven is built, and its wide mouth is glowing from a wood fire within. Guiseppe approaches this, looks inside at the inferno, and begins to sing. His voice is quite simply magnificent—how could it be otherwise, born in that great barrel chest? Indeed, it is the sort of voice that in sheer quality of tone and power, spurns instrumental accompaniment. He sings a popular Italian ballad with pure joy, and as he does so takes up an iron-handled rake, plunges it deep in the oven and withdraws Hades—spitting, flaming and astonished—out on to the stone floor where, to the accompaniment of a victorious crescendo, it is banished sizzling to a damp corner.

A galvanised bucket stands to one side of the oven. Into this he dips a massive hand to withdraw a dripping rag which is pulled expertly through the closed circle of his forefinger and thumb to remove excess water, and then with practised skill he knots one corner of it to the end of the rake handle. 'It is good—the wine?' he beams, and ashamed we realise we have not yet poured ourselves a drink, for the show has been too enthralling. Guiseppe bears down on us reproachfully and fills our two glasses then pours himself another and together we take the first portentous mouthful. *'Salute!'* he carols, rolling the liquid around in his cheeks. 'Ah ... but is it not like the milk of the Madonna herself?' With this benign giant standing there, so open-heartedly, so very sincerely waiting for our approval—it is.

He returns to the oven, humming with a deep rich satisfied rumble and takes up the rake with the wet rag attached. Then begins a truly masterly piece of syncopation. The long handle of the rake, endowed now with all the magic of a conductor's baton, is coaxed back and forth, in and out, and the spitting hissing rag rolls itself into a rope and begins to revolve like a Catherine wheel over the circular brick floor. Ashes spin to the walls as this steaming centrifuge first sweeps, then washes, and finally burnishes the cauterised bricks. Startled gouts of steam, matched cloud for cloud by swelling volumes of song spurt from the door to escape thankfully up through the rattan roof; and Guiseppe is obviously happy.

There is a large enamel bowl of the pasta ready mixed to hand, and adjacent are smaller dishes, the contents of which are not yet clear. He flicks a sprinkle of water on to the now dark oven floor, listens to the instant vaporisation with practised ear, and nods approvingly. The oven is ready.

I have seen my mother rolling pastry and kneading dough for bread, and marvelled at her skill. But I have never, nor ever shall again, watch such a miracle of dexterity as now took place. The pasta—one almost hears its sigh of resignation—is withdrawn in one lightning swoop from the basin, and quicker than eye can follow flattens of its own volition on the cold marble slab alongside. Then two great hands—living embodiment of those cataracts of sonic joy—imbue that limp pancake with a life of its own. It rises, apparently inspired by the mere proximity of those fingers, and spins in the air like a conjuror's plate to drop, surely destined for the ashy floor, only to stop in mid air, fold itself neatly in two halves and flatten once more on the slab where some—to us undetected—imperfection is already liquidated in a fresh and waiting embryo. We watch those hands, hypnotised, and so catch the quick glance from his happy eyes, the glance of a master who knows he is perfect and has totally captured his audience.

With a fresh outburst of song the favoured cake, crimped now at the edges and circular without flaw finds itself on the blade of a broad wooden shovel. A flick of the wrist and Guiseppe sprinkles its astonished face with chopped tomatoes. *'Tommodori,'* he roars between stanzas and then, in neat order and each accompanied by its own appropriate grimace, *'Mozzarella, olive, cipolle,'* and on went a spluther of finely chopped onions. Capers, black pepper and garlic followed and then, with a dreamy expression accompanied by ecstatic sniffs, *'Origani sulla montagna!'*

And finally, *'Oho!'* he shouts, *'Tacciuga,* much anchovy, eh? And more, for the smile of the Signora!' as another shower of the salty fishes flushes the startled pizza, to be followed by olive oil, liberally sprinkled from a watering can—and into the oven it goes.

Guiseppe turns, raising his hands in a gesture of feigned horror. *'Signore!* But …the wine!' And sure enough, the bottle in some miraculous fashion has become empty. It is a moment only for another to take its place and with it comes Guiseppe to sit with us, bringing added warmth to a world that is already glowing round the edges. 'And that is your tiny boat there?' he asks, pointing to *Lugworm* who is still visible in the dusk. We tell him our story and he listens, his fluid face registering astonishment, incredulity, disbelief, and then softly, his eyes wide with genuine wonder, 'but such happiness! To sail our lovely coast in such a boat, the two of you alone like … like … the Odyssey!'

There is a rich scent of roasting anchovies. The giant rises, takes the wooden shovel and slides it neatly under the bubbling pizza. He draws it towards him, gives it a quick twist and once more it is lying dead-centre in the oven. No trace of ash nor charred splinter of the pungent sweet smelling wood flaws its browning crust, but it is not quite ready and Guiseppe lights two candles and places them on our table. He stands then for a while looking down at B. 'The Signora's hair,' he says at last, 'I have been looking … you do not mind? It is like a Mass!' I glanced across to where the candlelight is catching her blonde curls. They seem to glow as though returning something of the sun's radiance that has soaked into them all day, and I look at him more closely, this gentle giant; he has a strange turn of phrase. A Mass!

But the pizza is ready—and we are more than ready for it. Guiseppe retires behind the raffia curtain as we savour every mouthful washed down with more 'Milk of the Madonna Herself'. And there are still some five hundred miles of this enchanted coast, and then all the canals of France, and the whole summer lies before us. Lucky, lucky us!

Maybe if we had to choose one memory only from this strange quixotic experience called life—one memory to last the whole of eternity—well, perhaps that night at Cetraro would be our choice.

We were content.

*   *   *

Yes, as we slowly worked our way up that coast it was easy to imagine ourselves by some strange alchemy transposed in time from the legendary days of Ulysses. Acciaroli, which you will not find on the map for it is a mere oversight of the coast scarce large enough to protect its own small fishing boats, opened its sleepy eye one evening to see *Lugworm* nosing into its narrow entrance and kindly bared a few feet of its dusty beach to accommodate this stranger from the sea. And even as she was drawn up, aided by the hoary old fishermen, to nestle between her tarry smelling sisters, the sky became black and overcast and that well-known brooding calm enveloped us, forewarning of the inevitable storm. Watched in silent amazement we rigged the tent and it was during the next blustery three days, pinned on that beach, that we became entranced with the place, and largely through the medium of a window.

You might not think that a window could capture the imagination and hold one spellbound, but that is because you have not laid as we did hour after hour under *Lugworm*'s tent listening to the searing breath of a gale that came hounding up from the south—with nothing but that window high in the crumbling wall above the harbour peering down at us, a square black hole with peeling green shutters glowering in through our turned-back flap. It was there in the morning, gazing over the harbour and beyond to the distant sea, and it was there in the night, a flickering square of golden light until the eyelid shutters closed, but never face nor form did we see giving soul to the eye. No, I doubt whether you would find another window such as that if you searched the whole world, for what other window is there which peers across the harbour mole where the gale-blown swell fumes and bursts in a storm of driven white, filling the uneasy boats with weed and grit, lifting the dust and sand from the beach and blasting the tight-shut doors with its breath of utter disdain.

And then, from that window, when the storm has eased one might hear the drone of the bent old forms mending their nets down below, and the account of how there had been so many tunny that scores of them had to be left, for the boats could not hold more with safety. So last week, under the Torre Guardia down Diamonte way, the stink of the blown fish cleared the village for a whole day until they sent for a boat to tow the carcasses to sea again. But at night from behind that casement, when the voices from the Albergo drone and lift in a murmur of argument, that eye in the old cracked wall looks at the church across the piazza aglow in the ochre light of the street lamp, and braces itself as it watches the great bell in the campanile begin to swing even before it roars out to the drowsy paese its rolling reminder of the evergone moment, echoing across the listening sea to where those brilliant beads of light dip and twinkle on the horizon, and the women of the village watch, and hope.

No, you may find many another window in many another crumbling wall, but this window knows Acciaroli, and we have known it too.

The weather grew calm again and we slowly worked our way up towards the Gulf of Salerno. One hot afternoon, happening on a small cluster of houses at the waterside we witnessed, amid great excitement, the landing of a large tunny. It must have weighed some three hundred kilo for the boat, unable to pull the fish aboard, was obliged to tow it to a small jetty. There it was with difficulty hoisted by block and tackle to be gutted on a mobile dray, bespattering the jetty and many of the excited onlookers with blood. *'Presto! Presto!'* shouted an impatient fisherman as I clambered atop a pile of boxes to get my picture and then, laughingly, I was offered the entire severed head, its open mouth and staring eyes a picture of astonishment.

Shortly after, nosing alongside an early morning mist which lay thick over the low-lying shore, we dropped anchor and landed to stretch our legs along a dusty track which led directly inland through the woods. A ruined wall of gigantic stone blocks soon appeared to our left, and scrabbling with the lizards we climbed this to look across what, five hundred years before Christ, had been the precincts of Paestum, that religious centre whose remains today contain nothing but three Doric temples. But in their magnificent isolation these are claimed to be the most perfect Doric temples in existence. Looking at them that morning, before the last of the mist had dispersed and before even the first of the tourists had arrived, we believed the claim, and just stood and gazed in silent awe — until a movement in the grass at our feet revealed a thick black snake, coiled and surveying the two of us in anything but silent awe. We removed ourselves, pondering the fact that this entire city which was once a great trading port should have been so completely deserted by the sea.

It was the fifteenth of June when, seeking to refresh ourselves again in river water, we surfed into the Fiume Sele to the south of Salerno; it might have been better had we not. We swam and washed ourselves just inside the river mouth on a deserted pebbly beach flanked by tall pampas grasses, and then emptied *Lugworm* entirely, washing out her lockers and the bilges. All our gear was spread about the beach to air, and evening was coming on before every-thing was re-stowed. There seemed no point in carrying on up towards Salerno that day; indeed we preferred the peace of this lovely river to the bustle of a busy harbour. So thinking to break the spell that decreed we catch not a single fish, we set off up river under sail, steering with a stern oar for fear of damag-ing the rudder on any shoals or under water obstructions. It was a still calm evening, and I remember as we ran silently under mainsail alone up the huge green river, being startled at what appeared to be a section of the surface sud-denly lifting skywards.

It turned out to be a colossal fine-meshed net all of sixty feet square which, by a clever arrangement of poles and pulleys, could be lowered horizontally down to the river bed and hoisted at a moment's notice by means of two taut overhead wires. There was no sign of any fishermen, and so intrigued were we with the mechanism of the thing that we quite forgot that the top of our gaff was some eighteen inches higher than the sagging centre of the net.

Lugworm was brought-up all standing, pinned by the top of her mast until with a twang like a snapping banjo wire the main halyard parted to bring gaff and sail crashing down. The effect ashore was alarming. A group of vociferous Italians exploded from the bushes, gesticulating wildly and leaving us in no doubt that the cause of their concern was only that madly swinging net and certainly not our own fate. Luckily there was no real damage on either hand, and concern rapidly turned to laughter as we closed the bank to pour oil on troubled waters.

We saw many more instances of these 'skyhook nets' as we came to call them and it is worth describing them in more detail. Two poles of wood or metal are erected about seventy feet apart on both banks, each pair opposite the other. Be-ing in the region of thirty feet tall this calls for a deal of complicated rigging, and through the blocks at the top of one pair two stout wires are rove, led across the river, and secured to the top of the opposite poles. The running end of these wires is then led down to a windlass which has to be firmly anchored to stand the con-siderable strain, and this windlass is sometimes hand operated or it may be driven by a small electric motor. By bringing the two wires down to each end of the same windlass drum, easing out on both wires will automatically ensure that they sag at an exactly equal rate into the river. The net is then attached by two of its sides to

Doric Temple, Paestum

'Skyhook' fishnet, River Sele

the wires about halfway across the river, and from its centre hangs a short umbilical cord, knotted at the lower end.

You will appreciate that the span of the wires can be as much as three hundred yards, and the net (large though it is) takes up only a small section of the middle of them so that when the windlass is eased off, the resultant curve is not very great out there halfway across the river. Down sinks the net to rest on the river bed. No bait appears to be used, but every fifteen minutes or so a quick turn of the windlass and up it shoots bringing with it anything which might have been floating or swimming above it. We saw one fine fish plucked from its element wiggling madly up there in the net and working itself down to the centre as it did so. A small rowing boat was immediately despatched from shore and by the time it was beneath the net, that fish had obligingly worked itself down into the umbilical cord. The rower simply undid the knot and the fish fell into the boat. We saw modifications of this type of net rigged out on ridiculous overhead gantries from clifftops, piers and beaches as we worked northward, and it was evident that fish formed a valuable part of the local diet. It never did ours.

That night we anchored about four miles up the Sele river and it was next morning that disaster struck. I must explain that our usual method of leaving these rivers was under power, so as to shorten that tricky moment of crossing the bar with its attendant breakers. We would therefore leave the rudder unshipped, have the centreplate hoisted, and steer with the out-board. Remember it was necessary to watch carefully before heading over the bar, for the waves nearly always occur in cycles of large, then small, and it's important to go through them when they're small. Of course, the whole procedure is much faster when making an exit, for then one has the strength of the outflow working with one, not to mention the safety factor of the boat's bow being presented to the seas rather than her stern which is the case when entering.

An onshore wind had developed during the night bringing a bit of a sea with it, and this was breaking three or four lines deep all along the width of the bar. We poodled around just inside the mouth, choosing the right moment, and then set off to pass smartly through the breakers. It was not until we were through and I had set mizzen and jib, lowered the centreplate and moved back to ship the rudder that we became aware that there was no rudder to ship. Can you imagine it? We looked at each other, appalled, and slowly the fact became clear: we had sailed and motored the boat four miles up and four miles down that festering river, fished un-successfully, slept aboard—and not once in all that time had either of us twigged the fact that I had left the rudder on that beach when cleaning out the boat.

Well, there was nothing for it; back into the river it had to be. But this was quite another matter for now we would have to present the boat's stern to the breakers and be working against that strong outflow. I looked at the exposed beach and all hope of landing there faded immediately—the waves were too big. So we waited outside the bar for the critical moment, and then with the engine full throttle headed in again. This time we were not quite so lucky. The outflow was slowing our speed over the bottom to little more than half a knot and the time we took to move through the danger area was sufficient for another series of large waves to overtake us. I could see them building up astern, and it's not conducive to peace of mind, believe me, when you watch them shortening up, rearing, and then just as they reach the boat, crashing over with a roar. Realising we were go-ing to be caught right in the thick of them, I yelled to B. to hold on tight and kept *Lugworm*'s stern true into the line of breakers. As the first hill of water crept upon us she cocked her stern up, lunged forward at a terrifying pace, then balanced for a moment on the crest and slid down the back just as the wave broke ahead of her. But not so with the second wave; this broke just astern.

Oh crumbs; anyone who knows the way of a boat held in the grip of a wave will know that ghastly feeling as she lifts aft to remain poised in the jaws of that creaming line of foam. *Lugworm* was surfing. In a crazy minute of wild uncontrol she lunged in on the advancing face of that breaker, and Heaven alone knows how she didn't broach—it was certainly nothing to do with me, for remember I had no rudder. One can only assume that the skeg of the outboard was sufficient to hold the stern into the seas, for we were going twice as fast as that engine ever achieved. Yes, it was quite a moment but *Lugworm* made it and while B. bailed out the water which had squirted up through the outboard well, I scanned the beach hopefully for the rudder. I knew exactly where I had laid it on the pebbles—but it was no longer there.

This was a serious blow. 'Drascombe Lugger rudders,' I remarked to B. as we closed the beach to start searching and think things out, 'are very sophisticated bits of equipment, not to be lightly "knocked up" from a few bits and pieces.' No; this was a real disaster. I couldn't see us sailing another fifteen hundred miles or so using an oar to steer, yet at the same time the complexities of having a complete unit despatched from the builders to some forgotten outpost of the Tyrrhenian seaboard made one feel weak. 'We've just GOT to find it, even if we have to cause an International Situation; and who the blazes could want to pinch a useless bit of equipment like that?' I fumed.

'Brass,' she answered, and of course that was it: the top hinged fitting on the tiller was solid brass and worth a small fortune to a scrap dealer.

You may be sure we searched the banks, waded out into the fast flowing current (thinking children might have thrown it into the water), and finally in desperation combed the pampas woods, but to no avail. So finally we spent the whole of next day locating a policeman and the proprietor of a farmstead we found back in the hinterland—and I leave you to imagine the hopelessness of trying to describe our loss, we who didn't even know the Italian for 'rudder'. By the following evening it was quite clear that it was gone for good, and somehow we had to get a replacement made. Obviously, Salerno some fifteen miles up the coast was the best hope, so we sailed there next day, steering with the oar, and great fun it was before a brisk quartering wind, but to tell the truth we were somewhat downcast, for that tiller had been fashioned for us by a good friend in Greece after an episode in the Saronic Gulf, and it was rather like losing a limb of *Lugworm*, entirely through our own negligence.

*   *   *

Our approach to Salerno was somewhat daunting. It is a large and flourishing harbour imbued with that sense of hectic bustle which characterises most Italian seaports, and we were a little overawed by such activity. But in a situation like this, I'm a firm believer in going right to the top and working down through the hierarchy of authority to the chap who is actually going to get on with the job. A replacement had to be obtained. It was a complicated bit of mechanism for which there would be no template available. Only I knew exactly what was needed. We would therefore sail right into the biggest yacht club present—if any—and ask for the Commodore.

We did.

The *Circolo Canottieri Irno*, or as we would say the Irno Yacht Club of Salerno, is a splendidly active, crowded and sophisticated establishment jammed between the busy Via Porto and the sea, flanked by the arms of the Molo Manfredi and the Molo Gennaio. Its floating pontoons are crammed with large racing dinghies, fast runabouts and elegant cruisers. It does not really cater for visitors, being hard put to find room for its own members' boats. We sailed into the thick of them, spotted one slot conspicuous by its emptiness, and tied up. Our Red Ensign flying from the truck of the mizzen drew polite attention, and in response to a query from an adjacent yacht I asked if the Commodore might perhaps be available for a word? I was led into a building on the quayside, up a dark cool flight of stairs, past some offices and on to a large roofed balcony overlooking the yacht harbour. It was cool, altogether pleasant, and there was a very active bar. Eventually a large gentleman in a white shirt and grey flannels, followed by a retinue of what I assume were club officers came forward. 'Signor Capone, Presidente di Club Irno,' he said, extending his hand. 'Can I be of any help?' Through an interpreter I explained my predicament, and the need to employ an intelligent metalworker, preferably from a boatyard, to produce under my direction as near a replica of the lost unit as possible.

Signor Capone walked to the edge of the balcony and surveyed the crowded boats below. 'Which is your yacht?' he asked. 'There,' I pointed, adding 'actually you cannot see her at the moment, she's behind that Flying Fifteen.' The group peered down to where the two masts of our dinghy showed above the other boat's hull, then the President looked at his fellow officers and again at me. 'Let us go and examine your boat,' he smiled, and together we all proceeded back down the pontoon. I introduced him to B. who, looking totally gorgeous in her wide straw hat and a flowered shimmery sort of vest—she might just have stepped from the Isis after a morning's punting—smiled appealingly and apologised for the trouble we were causing. 'It is OUR pleasure, Signora,' the President replied, offering his hand as she disembarked, and then, turning to me, asked, 'And where, Captain, have you come from?'

'Greece,' I said. 'We are sailing to England.'

There was a moment of evident perplexity and then, as though all had suddenly become clear, he exclaimed 'Ah, I did not understand. This is your tender.

Your yacht then is perhaps at anchor outside?' and everyone peered out to sea as though looking for signs of a funnel or masts.

'No, Signor President,' I replied through the interpreter. 'This is our yacht. She is called *Lugworm* and is a very noble stouthearted boat and is taking us to England—if we can get her a new rudder.'

There was an incredulous murmuring among the group, and suddenly the whole atmosphere changed. Away went the slightly formal approach, the polite but distant hospitality. In its place came interest, curiosity, and informal good natured questioning. Jackets and shoes were removed while members boarded *Lugworm* to be introduced to Foogoo. I explained our commodious living quarters, the staterooms either side the centreboard casing, the private wardrobes and the separate engine room. I showed them the marquee which we rigged at night, and word meanwhile had flown far and wide, so that our pontoon became quite unstable with more and more interested members. Finally Signor Capone (relative, we were jokingly assured, of the infamous Al) having held consultation with his officers, announced that from that moment on we were honorary members, that the entire facilities of the Club were at our disposal for just as long as we needed them, and that the member who spoke fluent English would gladly conduct me to a 'man who matters' who would know exactly how to manufacture a new rudder and tiller. Meanwhile would the Signora and myself not join them on the balcony for a drink, where we would be presented with the Club Burgee? In the meantime the club crane would be prepared for lifting our 'yacht' from the water in order that vital measurements might be taken.

It was all rather overwhelming, after the weeks of roughing it up rivers and behind rocks, constantly on the alert for hazards from a dozen different quarters, to find ourselves most hospitably sunk in settees knocking back the cooling drinks while under our feet, the astonished *Lugworm* was already dangling high above the water, encircled by two stout slings, while workmen danced attendance rigging chocks on the quayside to hold her ample belly.

Overwhelming perhaps, but it was a very real relief to know ourselves among sailors and friends who, in a metaphorical if not literal sense 'spoke our language', felt for our predicament, and were openly and genuinely prepared to give every possible help.

Meanwhile I was asked to make an accurate drawing of the lost rudder, which I produced instantly, having thought of little else since the awful discovery. In company with our good friend the interpreter I was conducted out of the club, up some broad steps on to the busy Via Porto where, at risk of our lives, we dodged the onslaught of traffic. We plunged from the blinding light into the dim cavern of a warehouse and our ears flinched before the shriek of metal in torment.

The 'man who mattered' turned out to be a small gentleman of some forty years of age, with a sallow face, blue chin, oily hands and dressed in a grey overall. While the interpreter explained the situation my eyes grew accustomed to the darkness and I looked round the metal shop. It was obviously part of a ship builders' premises and my heart lifted as I spied, in a far corner, scores of gleaming steel rods. They looked just about the right size for *Lugworm*'s rudder post, and that, I knew, was going to be the stumbling block if there was one; metal plate was always for the having, and for that matter I could make the tiller myself; it was the post and the welding and the metal cutting which was beyond us. My drawing was examined. Our friend from the Club explained the technical details and in company with a young apprentice we all four trooped back to *Lugworm* for further discussion. Returning back across the Via Porto the 'gentleman who mattered' stopped in his tracks, caught hold of my arm, and in a conspiratorial whisper hissed: *'Urgente?'* I looked at him and weighed up the situation. *'Molto urgente!'* I replied, looking just as rich as I dared.

'Domani!' he said, and we parted.

I shall never forget that *'domani'*. The apprentice, a powerfully built blond-haired youth with brilliant blue eyes, had been placed in total charge of the job, told to get on with it, do anything I asked and make it snappy. We started at eight. By eight-thirty we had made the discovery that my rudder trunking diameter was not of any standard size. By nine o'clock we were carrying a fifteen foot length of solid twenty-seven millimetre diameter steel rod across the Via Porto, to the strident anguish of a queue of lorries and other traffic. By nine twenty we were carrying it back again, it was a millionth of a something too thick, and the morning was growing hot. The apprentice thereupon wanted to start cutting into a 24 mm rod but I'm a great believer in what is called 'offering it up' first, and so for a third time the traffic in the Via Porto ground to a noisy halt, while that incredibly heavy rod was manhandled over to *Lugworm*, and since the rods were preserved in a thick coating of axle grease, the day was becoming sticky, to say nothing of *Lugworm*'s after deck.

But the rod was too thin; it rattled loosely in the trunking and would drive us mad when sailing. Somewhere, it was clear, we had to get a bit of 26 mm rod, but the apprentice was looking glum. Once again we stopped the traffic, and then all work in the factory too while the foreman, the 'gentleman who mattered' and half the employees searched for that odd piece which had been left over from … you know the bit … surely that was 26 mm in diameter? Eventually it was unearthed from behind a pile of metal plate and the calipers applied. It was 25 mm. It also had half a ship welded on to the other end.

Again the traffic ground to a halt while the contraption, reduced in size but still awkward and very heavy was manoeuvred across, down through the Club, along the pontoon and aboard *Lugworm*. The rod was loose, but for want of better it would have to do. By now it was late morning and I was learning that the south-facing quays and highways of Industrial Salerno bear an all too close affinity with Inferno. We were both running with sweat and caked in grease. As a precaution B. had disappeared with our fast dwindling Traveller's Cheques to find a bank. By noon the blade was cut, shaped, and welded to the post. By mid afternoon the complicated hinged tiller head with retaining collar was completed and also welded to the top of the post, and a very clever engineering job it all was too. But it didn't fit the rudder trunking. The welding between blade and post, stood proud and prevented the blade slotting down between the trunking plates. By teatime the apprentice and I had a deep and mutual admiration for each other's determination. The weld was ground off, other adjustments made, and … Eureka! The rudder sank down through that narrow slot. But it would not turn. The distance between that top collar and the highest point of the blade was a micro-something or other short, and it jammed. Yet again we cavorted up to the factory where I observed, a little apprehensively, that all the workers were preparing to leave. 'You …' and I looked at the apprentice with despair in my heart, for I was determined to get that rudder finished on one day … 'You—go?'

'*Marbor,*' he replied.

Marbore? Marbo? What the devil did he mean?

'*Zigarette Marbor,*' he enlightened me, and whistled softly as he doodled with his finger on a dusty oil drum top. I'd never heard of the brand, but scuttled off to find a tobacconist's shop. '*Zigarette Marbor,*' I gasped, having tracked one down in the town.

'*Marbor?*' exclaimed the tobacconist, looking blank.

'*Marbo ... Marboi ... Malbo ...*' Desperately I tried all inflexions in an attempt to reproduce the sound, scanning the shelves the while. There were Players, Philip Morris, Gitanes, Nationale and Marlboro ... MARLBORO!

'Marlboro,' I exclaimed, pointing to the red and gold packets.

'*Si, si ... Marbo,*' replied the proprietor, and of course, they were quite the most expensive in the shop. Frantically I scuttled back along the Via Mercanti, down the Lungomare Trieste and into the Via Porto to surprise the apprentice who hastily slipped a packet of Nationale into his back pocket, while holding out his hand for the six packets of Marlboro. Negotiations were resumed. The 'gentleman who mattered' surveyed the situation also, looked pointedly at his watch, accepted the two packets of Marlboro with thanks and disappeared back into the now silent factory muttering 'Molto Urgente!'

The blade was ground down a thou or so and once more we wore that groove back to *Lugworm*. B. was back aboard cleaning up the mess. 'Cuckoo,' I said, feeling a bit faint, 'I think we're very nearly home and dry!' She looked at the rusty blade with the carbon-crusted weld, the great iron collar on the top, and the heavy bolt and nut which protruded from one side, and said 'Strewth!' Which could have meant anything.

'Have you got the cash?' I asked her.

She had. I bought a pot of grey paint and weakly sat down for a trifling financial calculation with the 'gentleman who mattered'. I left feeling positively limp, but the job was done. Crude maybe, but it worked and we could sail again.

'One thing troubles me,' said B. early the following morning as I penned an appreciative letter to the President of the Club 'what happens if we bend THIS rudderpost—we can't drop it through the bottom of the boat like the other one; that top collar is welded on.'

'There's only one possible answer to that,' I replied. 'This one we JUST DON'T BEND!' And we motored past the end of the mole and set course for Capri.

*   *   *

Capri was both magnificent and horrific. We circumnavigated the island, marvelling at the awe-inspiring cliffs, the wooded ravines and miraculously beautiful bays, keeping the while a cautious distance from the throbbing beaches and jostling tripper boats. No glimpse could be gained of the entrance to the famous Blue Grotto for a fleet of hire boats swarming there. B. dodged ashore for some urgently needed provisions while I remained with the boat, standing off into deep water to escape the hordes of clamouring swimmers who threatened to swamp her by their sheer numbers.

Lugworm distinguished herself by sailing through the *Sottopassaggio di Mezzo*—a colossal natural arch through the rocks off Punta Tragara—only to escape annihilation by the bloom on her topsides from a thirty-knot gin palace with similar but reciprocal intent.

We were glad to leave. These middle latitudes of Italy's western seaboard are incredibly beautiful but, as B. sadly pointed out, 'There are just too many of us; we're annihilating the very thing we come for.'

It was near the end of June that we found the delightful little port of Sperlonga, unmarked as such on our chart, and since the small harbour was jam packed with pleasure craft we anchored outside just east of the new mole. We spent three days wandering round the streets of this lovely headland village and here too, one hot morning after coffee in the piazza high in the fortified village that, as was my custom, I casually made my way to a vantage point from which, far below, I could see *Lugworm* and check that all was well.

I looked, and blinked. She was bristling with small children. They were crawling in under her tent, diving off her bow, and walking the slippery pole of her boomkin. I could see one of them through my binoculars attempting to wrench off the lock of the forward hatch, aft another was busy rifling the netting shelves. I handed the glasses to B. and set off down the zigzag path from the citadel faster, I'll warrant, than anyone before or since. I feared mightily for the boomkin, which was never intended to be used as a diving board, being but a pliant spar. But my approach, hot-foot and flying, had not gone unnoticed; those ever watchful eyes twigged me before I so much as got to the beach—and overboard they all went, like a slippery shoal of fishes, swimming madly to the end of the mole. I caught them—it was a tactical error on their part for I now commanded the only escape route since they could not remain swimming around for ever. Maybe they did not expect a visiting boat's captain to break the four minute mile and still have fight left afterwards, but it was a very sorry band of ragamuffins that eventually faced me, cornered. One of them was bleeding profusely from his foot. I approached slowly, looking as fierce as possible, trying not to laugh at the dejected band and then, with a roar that I swear could be heard back up in Sperlonga bellowed, 'Va via!' aiming a feigned kick at the backside of the largest. They went.

Lugworm was in chaos. Blood was spattered over the decks and gear, our clothing strewn about. Obviously they had been after two things: cigarettes and money. Since we were both non-smokers and broke, they chose badly, but it served to make us more wary in future. Hitherto, throughout Greece and the extreme south of Italy, we had no qualms about leaving the boat and gear. But now, approaching the more populous and affluent metropolitan areas, the usual lowering of standards was becoming evident.

Indeed, a subtle change was taking place in our attitude towards the cruise. We found, alas, as we crept northwards, that we were no longer hungering to know what lay round the next headland, nor looking forward to landing on deserted beaches to explore a wild and barren hinterland. We began to talk with nostalgia of days spent beachcombing and sitting round driftwood fires alone and at peace long into the night. Indeed we now knew only too well, as we picked our way through growing flotillas of luxury cruisers and floating gin-dens EXACTLY what lay round the next bend and behind those immaculately raked beaches with their ranks of sun brollies and their 'NO LANDING' notices. And I will pass the opinion now that if mankind had conspired to kill stone dead any last vestige of sea-fever in his soul, he could not have devised a more effective means than his invention of the marina.

A lonely cove just south of Capri

Night berth up the Sele River

Neptune preserve me from the mass development of mass facilities for mass sailors. We were to slot on occasions into those vast and jam-packed soulless parking lots in Northern Italy and along the French Riviera—and paid handsomely for the privilege. But the supermarkets and plush restaurants at the end of the pontoons, and the casinos and knick-knackery shops close ashore and the whole way of life of a large proportion of the populace began to awaken old base desires. We were in danger of growing effete and tired of life and even began to view the sea with a patronising air. Oh Heaven forbid!

Until one day when casting about in the bilges, I came across a letter from my Bank Manager and I don't know which frightened me more; that or the deplorable state of affairs into which we were in danger of sinking. There was only one remedy for both; to get to sea immediately and to stay there as long as possible.

But even that now had its additional hazards. It was, I remember, on the glorious fourth of July that, after a short stay at the marina on Cape Circeo just south of Anzio, we were ghosting in baking heat before a very light land-breeze some hundred yards seaward of the Pontine Marshes. The beaches here are formed of low-lying sandy dunes with occasional ducts into the lakes behind, all of which are inaccessible from the sea, and four hours of blistering heat was beginning to take its effect. For a pleasant respite just south of a small headland we anchored and took a swim. A crumbling Roman viaduct which must have originally carried the road to the ruined Torre Astura on the point, lay behind us, and we spent an hour or so exploring the submerged traces of houses and fortifications around the foot of the tower before gently idling on under the outboard, for all vestiges of wind had died.

We were both in a very soporific state when B. gave a small gasp and sat bolt upright. 'Did you see that?' she hiccupped pointing seaward. 'Over there. It must have been a large fish jumping, there was a tremendous splash and a spout of water shot upwards!'

'LOOK,' she squeaked, 'there's another.'

I stopped the engine, since its noise prevented us hearing anything far off. Sure enough, my eye caught the end of a shower of spray about half a mile seaward of us, but there was no sign of a fish, nor any sound.

Together we stood peering about in a silent world of baking heat under that sultry sky, listening and looking, for there was something strangely alarming about those spouts of water.

Then we both heard an unearthly throbbing whistle, and I felt the bristles on my neck quivering. Anyone who has ever heard shells whining overhead will know the sound, for that is precisely what it was, and some two hundred yards on the bow another shower of water shot skywards with a staccato 'slap'.

'B.,' I said, hastily pulling on my shorts, 'we're being shelled!' There didn't seem to be much point in trying to conceal the fact, since another howling banshee was lobbing noisily across.

'Shelled!' she gasped. 'Don't be ridiculous, who would want to shell US? We're not at war are we—well not with Italy, surely? Oh, no, it's just ridiculous. Anyway, they aren't exploding are they?'

It was true. Apart from the whine of their trajectory as they zoomed past, there was no other sound, but this, as I pointed out, was rather academic; I didn't think it would make a lot of difference if one of them actually hit us, and told her so.

We were about half a mile offshore and with the glasses I scanned the coast. About a mile back there was a tall white tower with what looked like a large water tank atop, and from above this I could just see a limp red flag drooping. I ranged the glasses along the coast and there, about a mile ahead was another. In between the two were a succession of squares, some twenty or so feet in height and made apparently of solid concrete. But they were in horrifying stages of disruption, with jagged ends of reinforced steel strands sticking out like hairs on end. Quite clearly, we were poodling around slap in the middle of a firing range, and what was more, the heavy artillery either didn't know or just didn't care. There was no sign of any boat, and we were alone on a sea calm as a millpond, except for those goosepimpling splashes.

'Well, what do we DO?' squeaked B., as another banshee zoomed past, and it was a good question.

There were four simple choices. We could either turn back, go on, go straight out to sea, or beach immediately. I looked at the beach. The thought of landing at the foot of those gruesome tombstones was horrifying. If we puttered out to sea at our full four knots we would simply ensure that we remained squarely in the danger area for at least another hour; and even then a freak overshoot could quite possibly send us to the bottom just beyond the horizon in splendid isolation. No: we either went back or went on, as fast as possible.

Since the risk was equal which ever we did, it was logical to go on, but at the exact moment I gave a tug at the outboard starter cord the air above and around us exploded. I cannot otherwise describe the sheer stunning 'crack' of that sound; it were as though the noise came from within one's own head instead of outside. B. shrieked, and I sat down dazed, holding my ears, wondering if perhaps we had suffered a direct hit and were already dead. Nothing happened. There was no sign of a shellburst, no gout of water, no smoke even in the sky, nothing. Just the ringing echo of that tremendous sonic 'crash'. It was quite ghastly.

'What on earth ...' came B.'s frightened voice and together we again took stock of the situation.

Another gout of water shot skywards dead astern. That did it. With the outboard at full throttle we nosed on, eyes glued to those horrible squares on shore. Twice more we nearly jumped from our skins as the electrifying blast shattered our ears, but no aerial nor subterranean explosions took place, nor was there any sign of hits scored on the targets.

I can only conclude that there was some form of beamed warning sound system meant to attract the attention of boats which strayed into the danger zone, but how this was effected remains a mystery. Suffice it to say that, a quarter of an hour later, and well clear of the second white tower, a highspeed military launch came speeding towards us. On its foredeck stood a portly Italian officer—whether he was Army or Navy was difficult to tell, for he wore grey uniform trousers and a white shirt rolled to the elbows. It drew impressively alongside and the large gentleman, who was obviously very hot and appeared to be not quite recovered from his siesta leaned importantly over the rails and pointed back to the firing range.

'No' he said wagging his finger admonishingly. No, no ... you not go there!'

'No, Signore,' I answered him, with equal authority. 'We not go there ... we come!'

This seemed to take him aback somewhat. He looked us over for a while, and then his face broke into a smile. 'Yes?' He beamed holding back a chuckle. 'I see.

You come, that VERY good!' And he was still roaring with laughter as the power-ful launch purred into life and swept effortlessly off.

Well, it was one way of looking at it.

*   *   *

By mid July we were in Elba, spending far too much time snorkelling underwater to examine the rocky bottom for nonexistent fish, and by now were quite accus-tomed to being an object of open curiosity as we had worked our way up past the entrance to the Tiber, past endless populous beaches and lidos. Fleets of twin-hulled pedallos would come out when the weather was suitable, to pedal along-side until the lusty occupants tired. Huge tripping boats, painted a riotous cam-ouflage of colours and crammed with camera-wielding holiday-makers, throbbed from the beaches and circled us. It was becoming more and more difficult to ob-tain any privacy or peace for the night anchorages.

On 1st July we entered the river Arno and ran before a kindly west wind un-der genoa alone, negotiating an incredible complex of 'skyhook' fishnets before eventually berthing at the Canottieri Arno in the town of Pisa. This sophisticated rowing club very kindly placed their facilities at our disposal—and how welcome were the pilfer-proof jetty, the cold showers and ice-cold drinking water!

Yes, of course we went up the leaning tower, and listened to that chap's heav-enly voice echoing round the Baptistry, and sat looking at the Cathedral while drinking an extortionately expensive glass of ice-cold beer in a nearby bistro, and it was all tremendous fun.

I think on looking back at this voyage, it was our sense of complete independ-ence and freedom which made it so memorable. We were shackled by no timeta-ble. There were no boats nor coaches to catch nor planes with which to connect; no hotel mealtimes to interfere with one's wanderings and always there was the challenge of finding a safe berth for *Lugworm* against any inclement weather; al-ways the possibility of returning to her and escaping to sea, or farther up a river, or into a lake. She was our constant security and, though small, supplied all our very moderate needs, for by now we were quite drunk with wandering, and used to the life aboard. We would not have changed it for the most luxurious hotel suite. Indeed, four days spent exploring Rome from the comfort of an hotel merely left us breathless and bewildered, for the tempo of that lovely city was too traumatic for a pair so completely attuned to a tranquil life.

One thing which did worry us as we entered the Ligurian Sea north of La Spezia was the alarming amount of pollution. No longer did we care to swim, for the water had turned an oily green-brown, and the ever-present litter in the sea spoke of the more industrial and tourist nature of the coast.

We had made the mistake of arranging cash withdrawal facilities at Genoa, so were forced to enter that highly industrial port. I remember on the 27th July after a torrential early morning deluge which overtook us in Santa Margherita, that the water, as we approached Genoa, was turning a sickly brown-grey. The smell of sewage was overpowering, and so unhealthy was the atmosphere that I stood out to sea again as quickly as possible having left B. to nip ashore to the bank. It was evening before we were able to escape westward and the sun had sunk when we anchored for the night just outside the charming little harbour of Arenzano.

The end of July found us in San Remo, involved in custom formalities for checking out of Italy, and in celebration of the event, we wined and dined ashore that night altogether too well. I remember down in the crowded harbour, *Lugworm* was jammed between two vast and opulent cruisers, the cigar ash from which was constantly having to be removed from her side-decks. The trouble was, her transom failed to reach the quay level by six feet or so, and on returning late that evening B. expressed some doubts as to whether she or I could manage the drop in safety.

'Nonsense, darling, I'm as sober as a Methodist,' I retorted.

'Maybe it would be best if we went for a brisk walk first,' she replied, hesitating.

'Tell you what, I'll run six times round that hut, stand on my head, then kiss you without missing,' I promised her.

I did. But I broke my toe on the hut in doing so. Still, you don't need your toes much in a boat.

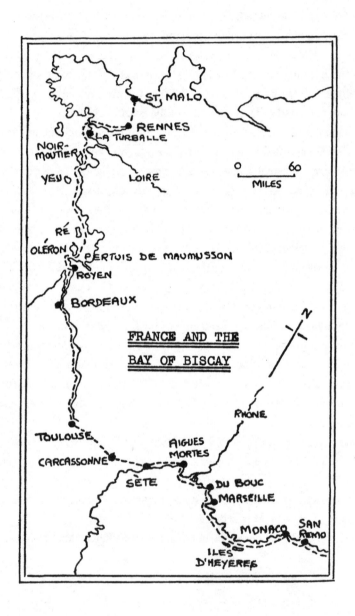

ST MALO

RENNES

LA TURBALLE

NOIR-
MOUTIER

YEU

LOIRE

0   60
MILES

RÉ

OLÉRON

PERTUIS DE MAUMUSSON

ROYEN

BORDEAUX

FRANCE AND THE
BAY OF BISCAY

N

RHONE

TOULOUSE

AIGUES
MORTES

CARCASSONNE

SÈTE

DU BOUC

MARSEILLE

MONACO   SAN
REMO

ILES
D'HEYERES

CHAPTER V

FRANCE AND THE BAY OF BISCAY

'JUST EXACTLY HOW MUCH MONEY HAVE WE?' I asked B. as we sipped our cups of coffee beneath the awning of the Cafe de Paris in Monte Carlo. 'Not nearly enough.'

I looked across the shady square where palms threw cool shadows on the grass and the gorgeous flowerbeds. The sprinklers had stopped watering the lawns, pigeons fluttered about the pavement at our feet, and the morning sun was just getting into its stride, awakening the Principality of Monaco to another uninhibited day of pleasure. 'I know,' I commented 'but in French Francs how much have we left since withdrawing the cash five days ago in Genoa?' She did a long calculation.

'Three hundred and forty-five.'

'Francs?'

'Francs. And if you're thinking what I think you're thinking, we'd better get back quickly to *Lugworm!*'

I took another pensive sip at my coffee. That was the equivalent of about £30 sterling and it had to last us until Marseille. My eyes wandered across to the imposing doors of the Casino. An important looking uniformed gentleman was fidgeting about on the elegant steps. Between the two domed towers the large windows looked dark and expensively empty.

'I won five pounds in there once long ago.'

'You were far luckier than most,' she commented. A Mercedes had drawn up at the Casino steps. The Commissionaire descended to open the door, and a dark-suited gentleman emerged to ascend buoyantly and float into the foyer. The Mercedes drew silently away. I began to count the Rolls-Royces and Bentleys and other expensive cars gently circulating with the traffic past the gardens. Some of them had little flags on them and were so highly polished I could see the reflection of the palms in their bonnets. It was all very pretty. I'd counted up to fifteen before B. asked (as I knew she would), 'How did you manage it?'

'It was very cunning. I had a friend who, like you, was cautious. I was keen to go in and have a flutter and he told me I was a fool. Finally, to teach me a lesson, he bet me a fiver I couldn't come out with more cash than I went in with. I took him on.

'In those days,' I continued, 'you had to be wearing a suit to get in the place. I borrowed one of his, since the most elegant apparel I possessed at the time was flannels and a sports jacket, and armed with my fiver went into the *Salon Ordinaire*. I had only one object—to come out with more cash than I took in. I spread the whole handful of 'chips' all over the table except for three numbers, reckoning it would be exceptionally bad luck if any of those three came up. They didn't. I recovered my stake plus a winning of about sixpence. The croupier was a bit perplexed when I demanded all my chips back, but I went straight to the desk to cash them and walked out with about £5 and sixpence.'

'So you risked losing a fiver to win sixpence.'

'No, I risked losing the fiver to win five pounds and sixpence. Which I did.'

'And lost a friend instead?' she commented. I thought about that.

We paid for the coffees, and to recover idled down to the harbour where, rising like a queen above the riot of exquisite luxury yachts was a magnificent white ship called 'La Belle Simone'. Her stern which was some fifteen feet away from the quay, had cleverly opened up and from it like a wasp sting projected a long elegant companionway complete with guardrails.

We watched, fascinated, as the end of the companionway hovered a few inches above the level of the quay. With each gentle surge of the sea, her stern would slowly lift and fall, and with it the companionway, but strangely its end never once actually touched the quayside. Always it hovered magically a few inches above. I drew B.'s attention to this. 'Do you know,' I pondered, 'I think it must have a photo electric cell or something hidden in the end to keep it always just that distance above the quay. Isn't it quite marvellous?' And so it was. We sat in the sun and watched the goings and comings, listening to the idle chatter aboard the boats, and slowly began to feel enormously rich. Rich.

'You know, with just a bit of luck we could recover the expenses of the whole cruise to date,' I mused. 'Just one lucky spin of the wheel up there and ...'

It was quite a thought.

We had a packet of crisps for lunch. About three o'clock we were wandering among the flowerbeds outside the Casino and finally I couldn't bear it any longer.

'Look, cuckoo, here we are actually standing outside the most famous Casino in the most famous Principality in the world, and what are we doing? Admiring the tulips! We'll never be here again, ever, you bet. Don't we owe it to ourselves just to have one little flutter … don't we? Just for the experience? Have you ever been inside a Casino anyway? Just imagine … with one fifty-fifty chance we could double our stake and I'll take you to the poshest restaurant in Monte Carlo this evening and we'll blue the lot on a magnificent dinner!'

That did it.

I put ten pounds in a back pocket, and she took ten pounds and I took ten pounds and in we went, all of a quiver. It was a bit awe-inspiring really: a uniformed man was approaching everyone who entered and at first we thought he was frisking them for guns, but he was only asking that cameras be left, please, at the cloakroom, no photographs inside. I don't know why, but we started talking in whispers; everybody seemed to be *sotto voce* and tense. The *Salon Ordinaire* had not altered much since I was there thirteen years before. It was just as huge and wonderfully stimulating. We had twenty quid to stake, and with one bit of luck could walk out with forty. 'If we win,' I cautioned B., 'we come out at once. No second chance to lose the lot—not us!'

I'd completely forgotten how to play and B. had never known, so between us we circulated round the tables, our pockets full of plastic 'chips' and our hearts full of hope. 'Why are some of the women wearing gloves?' came B.'s hushed whisper.

'It's to hide their fingernails, they've bitten them down to the quicks.'

'Suspense … anguish … despair. Blood.' I enlightened her and she seemed to shrink a little.

Twenty quid.

I watched a tall well-dressed aristocratic chap standing palely beside one of the tables. He was taking no part in the play, his hands thrust deep in his pockets and his eyes seemingly focused on some other world. Another man emerged from a large door which led through to the more suicidally serious gaming rooms. The newcomer looked around the tables and then, seeing the figure palely loitering, walked quickly across to him. He didn't say a word; just looked at the other fellow and there came a faint whisper in response to his silent query: 'Everything … I've lost absolutely EVERYTHING!'

We didn't like that very much, so wandered off to another table and concentrated on the faces of the winners. There always seemed to be a winner, no matter which table we stood by; it was quite encouraging if you looked at it the right way. There was a winner every time that horrid little ball clackety-clacked into either a red or black slot on the wheel; every time the quiet voice of the croupier droned *'Faites vos jeux'*.

Not once did NOBODY smile.

After about an hour of this we felt brave enough to take the plunge. I drew B. gently to one side and we sat together on an ornately upholstered settee beneath a romantic mural. I recall that in its background Diana was hunting an elk or something, and I swear she seemed to be looking at me as she drew her bow. It appeared propitious.

'Now, listen,' I cautioned B., 'It's all quite simple to understand : if we place our cash on one number only there are enormous odds against winning, but of course if we do win, we win a fortune. On the other hand if we simply place our stake on red or black—Rouge or Noir—we have a fifty-fifty chance of coming up trumps since there are only those two colours ... but only double our stake.'

I looked at her, and really, put like that it seemed quite hopeful. She thought for a while, and I could see her mind working. 'Ken,' she said. 'If that's the case, it's quite simple: put ten pounds on red and ten on black, and that way we've just GOT to win!'

It really took me aback for a minute, it seemed so simple, but after a while we got it all sorted out and she could see that it didn't work like that. 'Anyway,' I murmured, taking a deep breath, 'the great thing about this game is not to fossick about; we'll put the whole twenty quid on one colour and take the fifty-fifty chance of doubling it, eh?' She seemed to physically shrink a bit more. Diana winked.

I took her by the hand and led her to the nearest table. 'Give me all your chips,' I hissed, sweating. I put her's and mine in a ghastly little pile, on red. 'No!' came her small voice, and I felt her hand contract in mine. 'Put it on BLACK, please put it on BLACK!'

But a man has to be decisive. Indeed, perhaps the thing I admire most about me is—I'm decisive.

Honestly, I heard that elk groan as we staggered, cold as death, out into the foyer and back into the brilliant daylight, shaking off the dark pall of that brooding malignant place.

But Oh! *Spaghetti con pommodoro*, with the occasional bag of crisps, is hard— VERY hard—to stomach in Monte Carlo; and Nice, Cannes, Raphael, St Tropez and ... well, we lasted until those magnificent Îles d'Hyeres off the Cote d'Azur before decimating our dwindling traveller's cheques once again.

*   *   *

The fifth of August found us coasting close along the northern shore of the Île Levant, where clusters of fat pink nudes could be seen festooning the rocks, which wasn't surprising, this being a nudist colony. That night we fetched up in the delightful little bay of Port Man on the Île du Cros, in company with sixty-four other craft of varying size and fascination, so we were able to spend an enjoyable evening observing the aquatic habits of the Frenchman afloat.

It would seem that the average French yachting family will not consider taking to the water without the full range of pets aboard. This presents problems when it comes to the call of nature. We watched in admiration as, with sundown, dinghy after dinghy frantically rowed ashore, its feline or canine passenger straining at the bow, poised in anguish for a desperate flying leap long before the boat grounded. We found ourselves holding our breath in sympathy, exhaling with a real and shared relief as the business was satisfactorily completed. The return trip was a triumph of 'one-upmanship' as other boats in the earlier stage of the drama streaked shorewards. And do not think this drama was entirely confined to the lower species. I watched fascinated at five-thirty next morning, as head after surreptitious head peeped from cabins and then, assuming the fleet to be safely slumbering yet, a wide variety of human shapes in the altogether lowered themselves quietly over the side, floated around with an entranced expression for a minute or so, and then clambered back aboard to towel themselves in vigorous satisfaction at the success of their morning 'dip'. And what, you might ask, was I doing at five-thirty?

Well, we put into Bandol for replenishment of fuel and provisions, and at the end of that first week in August were coasting along the magnificent shore

— TOSSED IN ANGUISH —

towards Cassis. Cliffs, lined with clear layers of light and dark browns, towered
sheer from the sea to as much as one thousand feet, and so it was one morning
that we saw the awe-inspiring 'Bee de l'Aigle' rearing like a hooded predator
above a thick blanket of fog, and it is a sight we shall remember for the rest of our
lives. The port of Cassis was altogether too crowded for our liking so we sailed on
gently westward where the cliffs became snow white, and then those incredibly
beautiful 'calanques'—flooded ravines—with their wonderfully green pineclad
slopes, offered shelter for a night. I remember, as we drifted silently up one of
these ravines, espying an exquisite bare-breasted siren calmly planing a mast to
shape in a small boatyard. Ah me ... what a WONDERFUL thing is sex.

And what hellish trouble it can cause.

But I don't recall a more inspiring sail during the whole trip than that morning
Lugworm spanked along from those Calanques to Marseille, with the white cliffs
towering a few hundred feet away and the sea so clear and deep blue that one
could check by eye there was nothing for at least ten fathoms below her keel. The
islands of Riou and Caleseragne, Jarros and Maire, floated like burst meringues
on a sea of sapphire jelly, and Marseille—from a distance—shimmered white and
unreal along the whole sweep of the Bay.

From previous experience I knew that the Rove Tunnel which used to connect Marseille with the inland lakes had collapsed years before, so we ignored the
information supplied in Nice that we could enter the canal system there. We did
however accept in good faith the tale at Marseille that we could enter the canals

at Port de Bouc a bit farther on in the Golfe de Fos, and we entered that port hopefully on the 9th August, only to find the canal closed for reasons nobody could supply.

Nothing daunted we sailed on across the mouths of the Rhone where heaving green shallows proclaimed the strength of the outflow which was meeting a slight north-running swell. We were alert at this time for the fearful 'mistral', particularly since we were finding the French forecasts impossible to translate due to their being read so very quickly. But our luck held, and after a night in the mouth of the Petit Rhone we carried light easterlies right up to Aigues Mortes, that fascinating thirteenth century fortified port from which the sea has since receded some three miles. It was here that we finally bid adieu to the Mediterranean, not without very mixed feelings, to enter the canals. *Lugworm*'s mast was stowed permanently on the crutches and we began motoring along that incredible waterway system, working westward into the great Étang de Thau, a vast salt water lake north of Sète.

The transition from months of blue sea and sky, and blinding beaches, into those reedy canals with their tree-lined banks and limpid water was like a tonic. We passed into another world—the Province of Languedoc—whose marshy coastal lakes hummed each evening with a million mosquitoes and turned poor B.'s nights into a torment. Luckily, malaria has been stamped out in this area, and my own hide proved too thick—or distasteful—for the pests, but you may be sure we pressed on fast as possible. It was while trying to motor into a freshening northerly out of the port of Sète that we at last fell foul of the 'mistral' which, within half an hour, set us frantically searching for a lee, for otherwise I believe *Lugworm* might have foundered, so short and steep were the seas which were knocked up in these shallow lakes. We spent three days tucked up behind a spit sheltering from this vicious cold north wind, and used the period to collect armfuls of the rushes which line the lake banks. With these we made thick fenders, sewing them into canvas cylinders fashioned from an old boat cover we had aboard, and they protected *Lugworm*'s sides from the ravages of the scores of locks we were about to pass through. We also learned the art of that very French game of 'Boule' from a strange youngster who spoke no English, but appeared to be living in a straw hut and surviving entirely on unlimited bottles of Anis, a particularly intoxicating aniseed drink. So it was not until the 19th August that we finally entered the Canal du Midi, bound for Toulouse and Bordeaux.

Life now became pastoral. The tent, when weather permitted, was unrolled each morning and stowed, but the ridgepole of our mast was left in place against sudden need to take shelter again. No night navigation is allowed on the canals, the locks being operated from seven in the morning until six each evening, and there was almost no commercial traffic and very little pleasure boating along these first southern stretches. We would motor gently on after a protracted break-fast, sometimes taking it in turns to walk along the towpath (when there was one) to stretch our legs, covering perhaps fifteen or twenty miles each day. It was very pleasant to moor up at evening and explore the small villages, taking a meal perhaps in some rustic restaurant and comparing the local wines. This region of southern France is known as the Herault and stretches roughly from Aigues Mortes along the seaboard to Valras, extending inland to north of St Christol and Lodève. The rivers Lez, Hérault and Orb form the main irrigation for the district and it grows wonderful vines. We particularly like the heady Muscat which comes from the St Jean-Minervois region.

The country here is truly beautiful. Most of the villages still have that gra-cious air of early French architecture in the houses and gardens, there being few recent additions by way of modern 'boxes'. We passed through thousand upon thousand of acres of vines and the occasional olive, fig and apple orchard. To my way of thinking these southern sections of the Canal du Midi are the best because, being rolling countryside, one often found one's self floating round the shoulder of hills and therefore having superb views across the adjacent valleys. As we worked north the views became more localised, and often we would have to leave the boat and climb the canal bank in order to gain some idea of the coun-try through which we were passing. Unfortunately for us, the grapes were still not quite ready for picking.

By 24th August we were in Carcassonne, wandering round that fairytale town by day and night and marvelling at the bygone way of life it portrayed. By now we were thoroughly used to the locks, passage through which is free, and therefore placing one under obligation to take some of the burden of operation off the shoulders of their often elderly war-disabled keepers. B. would jump ashore

The prize tunny catch

Low bridges were no problem: Sète

some hundred yards before arrival and run ahead to start the procedure. If the lock was full of water—and remember that in these first stages of the system we were climbing and therefore always rising in the lock—the far gates would first have to be closed and their sluices cranked shut. Those in the near gates would then be opened to reduce the level in the lock. Once this reached the level of our section of the canal these near gates could be opened and I would take *Lugworm* in, throwing up a stern-rope first, which B. placed on the bollard, and then a head-rope. It paid in such a small boat as ours to keep well back against the rear gates, so that when these were shut and their sluices closed, the onrush of water from the opening sluices at the front gates had a chance to subside a little before reaching the boat. I always kept the centreplate right up, for this underwater turbulence might otherwise have made her unmanageable in the early stages of the flooding. As the level rose, so I would take in the slack on the headrope to keep the boat against the lock side, and as soon as the level had reached that of the canal ahead, B. and the lock keeper would start to winch open the forward gates while I cast off our ropes, skimming past B.'s gate so that she could jump aboard as the boat left the lock. We carried a supply of good quality French cigarettes, handing two to the lock-keeper as we parted from each lock. Often they would be pleased to sell us eggs and fresh vegetables. B. always refused point blank to remain aboard *Lugworm*, preferring by far to help work the locks.

It was at Castelnaudary that we came across an Oceanic Catamaran, the crew of which regaled us with frightful tales of high seas between St Nazaire and Bordeaux, expressing the opinion that we were doomed if we so much as poked our nose out into the Biscay seaboard. We sat in their cabin late that night while they related accounts of mountainous swell breaking on the reefs miles offshore, and hazardous entanglements with oysterbed stakes close behind the islands; for them it was all tremendously stimulating since they had just left it all behind.

But both of us were well aware that the next leg of our voyage—up the western seaboard of the Bay of Biscay—was going to be the most dangerous phase. We had purchased a French tide table ready for calculations once we had locked out of the canals into the tidal River Garonne, and from this moment on I began thinking and living tides and Atlantic weather forecasts to get acclimatised to that great ocean once more, after two summers in the non-tidal Mediterranean. People often ask me whether we didn't get tired of the constant travelling on, day after day, with the routine of life aboard such a small boat. But to be honest, this voyage of ours brought such a rich variety of experiences that each new phase arrived before we had really got saturated with the last. The ever changing scenery, and gradually altering climate as we worked north was refreshing in itself. Add to this the constant need to assess navigational risks—and they were infinite in form, from hunches as to the effect of swell on some harbour-less coast (resulting from storms which might be ranging far away at sea), to dealing with overhead entanglements of masts in the branches of trees—all this, plus the changing language from Greek to Italian to French, and the totally different makeup of the people with whom we came into contact, formed a constant stimulation.

Once more the entire rhythm of our lives had changed. Those weeks of cat-and-mouse hopping along the desolate shores of Southern Italy already seemed a whole lifetime away. The transition from that miraculously beautiful coastline of Western Italy, south of Elba, and the excitements of the French Riviera, to this green meandering life of the inland waterways was total. Let the winds rage—what matter? The farthest we could drag would be a few hundred yards up or down the dappled canal, and suddenly from being sailors we became campers. Camping admittedly aboard a boat, but the style of life we were now living was much akin to hiking through the country, for we really did quite as much walking and exploring those charming little villages as we did boating. Moving so slowly, we had ample time to become integrated and absorb the subtly different atmospheres of the areas through which we passed. We were able to compare their individualities. Castelnaudary, Toulouse, Montbartier, Moissec, Agen and Damazan all had their own distinctive characters; I have particular reason to remember the first of September for it was that evening we moored under the towering hillside atop which perches the delightful village of Meilhan and it was here, for the first time on the voyage, I began to feel distinctly unwell.

To tell the truth, ever since our overindulgence in underwater swimming at Elba, my right ear had been giving trouble. It was a recurrence of an infection I had caught during the war, and pleasant enough at first—a mere itch which could be gratified with a stiff blade of grass or some twig of a bush inserted and twizzled about inside the ear passage, and I ask you is there anything more pleasant in life

A lock at Beziers, Canal du Midi

The Calangues near Cassis

than the assuagement of an itch? This one had kept me happy for hundreds of miles. But somewhere along the line this happiness reawakened an old trouble, an infection which had laid me low thirty years before. It's not surprising really, and I got scant sympathy from B. when, during the last week in August the ear became inflamed and the inflammation spread to my neck glands, and finally my whole head became so painful that I wrapped it entire in a towel and groaned continually and things began to swell up. I couldn't move my head on my shoulders and was in frightful agony and quite ready for death.

It was (of course) B. who finally dragged me to salvation in the form of a saint—there are one or two of them about still—whose name is Docteur Girol; he lives in Meilhan, and I shall certainly send you a free copy of this book, good Docteur, for you saved my sanity if not my life—you and your young son who so patiently interpreted our troubles. Thank you, both of you, from the bottom of both our hearts, for your ministrations. Within three days, by dint of a crash course of antibiotic injections, oral ingestion and externally applied salves, the fearful malady was quite overcome; and a firm and lasting link in the *entente cordiale* of France and England was forged, especially since the good Docteur, aided by an excellent *sage femme*, refused point blank to accept any fees whatever for his services.

So, thanks to them, we were refreshed and keen to tackle the ebb and flow of the mighty Garonne when at 0800 on the 5th September we finally dropped through that enormous lock at Castets-en-Dorthe and hand in hand with the fast-flowing current set off down the river under power. Five tumultuous brown swirling hours later, having somehow avoided multiple bridge supports, shoals, submerged trees and horrifyingly powerful barges, we turned to stem the current and desperately lassoo a bollard at the Sport Nautique Club just north of Bordeaux. Had the line missed, I doubt if our stouthearted outboard would have been capable of regaining the pontoon and we would have gone backwards beneath the imposing suspension bridge. But we didn't miss, and before nightfall old Lucien, custodian of the Club, had persuaded us that the safest place for *Lugworm* was resting on an antediluvian cradle drawn up on a muddy slipway clear of the frightful current and massive wakes from passing barges and ships. So we slept that night on wheels, attached to an archaic winch by a rusty steel cable, and I put chocks under those wheels just in case somebody should accidentally take off the brake.

So it was that we came to know Bordeaux, and were able to stand and gaze from the Vieux Pont, and eat exquisite things we could ill afford in some very fine restaurants; it was all totally enchanting and quite like being on holiday. Honestly—has anyone the right to enjoy life quite as much as we two?

But dammit! Isn't that what it's for?

*   *   *

There is no doubt whatever that the river Gironde, from its yawning mouth up to the Garonne and on to Bordeaux—some sixty miles—is tidal. We used that torrent of water sluicing out to sea to make Pauiliac before it halted in its mad onslaught, turned and rushed back up the river. On the 9th September that current again swept us relentlessly seaward until, at noon, we managed to deflect northward and hitch on to Royan, near the entrance. We made all secure in the small marina there and walked ten miles out to the Pointe de la Coubre. There we found a fine lighthouse two hundred and ten feet high which flashed its characteristic signal far across the sea to guide incoming ships into the river through a narrow channel leading between the Banc de la Mauvaise on the north side and the Battures de Cordouan southward.

It was a fresh morning, brisk with scudding clouds which rode a healthy wind from the north-west, and this added a clean scent of pinewoods to the salty tang of the sea. The birds were singing all along the lovely road that winds through the Forêt de la Palmyre. But behind their song and above the sigh of the wind there was a new and strangely disturbing background pulse—the distant mighty roar of surf. Still subdued and far off, yet it was there always in the lulls, and alien in the ears of two sailors fresh from an inland sea; yet wonderfully stimulating.

'Now,' I remember thinking to myself, 'the navigation and the seamanship begins in earnest.' In earnest it was, too. Don't imagine from this somewhat lighthearted account of our adventures that we took the business of seagoing without due care. Believe me, every heave of those equinoctial tides was calculated, every treacherous drop of a millibar noted, and so far as mortals were able to be, we were prepared for our emergence back on to the bosom of a real ocean, but even so ... even so we were still not psychologically adjusted to that traumatic switch from a blue Mediterranean to the hoary grey wastes of the Bay.

On the Canal du Midi

We stood at the base of the lighthouse, shielding our eyes from the spray that came driving over the dunes, and looked seaward. The sky northward was now turned a leaden grey and even the gulls, swooping above the shore, seemed to be crying a warning. Swell rolled down from the horizon to gather up, lift, and thunder down on those 'Evil Banks', and we each kept our own thoughts as we turned inland again to continue walking northward up this fearful 'Côte Sauvage'. I was concerned about a certain passage called the Pertuis de Maumusson five miles up the coast which led in behind the Île d'Oleron, for I wished to pass inland of the isle, the seaward coast of which is rocky and ironbound, offering no succour to a small boat which might need immediate shelter. But it is a dreadful passage according to all the pilot books and the local fisherfolk; indeed all authorities advised strongly against its use in any circumstances. For me, however, as is the case so often at sea, it was a matter of choosing the lesser of two evils. Despite everything, that channel was the better choice in our circumstances; but I feared it horribly. We walked to the Pointe d'Arvert on the south side of its entrance and sat in the marram grass on the dunes.

It was a scene fit to turn a sailor into a stockbroker. As far as the eye could see, heaving mountains of grey spume-wracked ocean piled up and burst in roaring fury across the Banc des Mattes at the opening of the channel. Over the years an exceptionally strong outflowing tide has built up a tongue of sand and shingle off the channel's seaward end, and this reaches out to trip up the huge Atlantic swells which roll along this coast. In the heart of the maelstrom we could occasionally glimpse a tiny black object: one of the channel marker buoys. So we walked south again, turning our backs on a thin driving rain, climbed the lighthouse and spent a fascinating hour or so chatting with the keeper, of shipwreck and drowning.

But of course, we knew that all this splother and fury would eventually die down, and I will say again that our biggest insurance against disaster on this voyage was the fact that we had time. On the 11th September we nosed cautiously from Royan along the coast into the Bonne Anse—a shallow sandy bay under the foot of the lighthouse—and our friend the keeper crossed himself on our behalf when he saw the mighty size of *Lugworm*.

The following morning, with a clear sky and a light northeast wind, we caught the tail end of the ebb to help us out to sea through the *Grande Passe de l'Ouest*, and though the fury of the wind and sea was long since spent, nevertheless poor *Lugworm* had a hard fight not to founder in the short steep overfalls. Five miles out to sea, and clear of the Banc de Mauvaise we set course north east for the Maumusson channel. It was calm, as I say, but even so there must have been a very long low oily swell still rolling in, for about a mile off the entrance to the passage there was a sickly feeling of unease about the sea, as though Neptune were sleeping very lightly and might at any moment turn over in bed, and fling us all to Hades.

We lay well off for a good hour, waiting for the tide to lift a bit and start strongly flowing in. Then, judging it safe went through hellbent under the outboard with the swirling flood behind us; it is a dreadful place for one who knows the way of the sea and swell, and it is a risk I would not lightly take again; once lucky is enough.

But now we met an unexpected hazard which besets the sailor navigating close inshore along this coast—withies. The French (like some of we English) have a weakness for shellfish. It would seem that every Frenchman within motoring distance of that shore lays claim to a patch of the seabed on which he cultivates crustaceans. This patch he marks with a multitude of tall stakes. Branches of trees, slender and bending, are thrust deep into the black ooze and there they remain, offering little resistance to wind or waves. There are forests of them as far as the horizon, and through them thread narrow straight channels which the local fishermen know well. These are quite evident if you happen to be looking straight up or down them, but once you get out of the damned channels you can freckle about for demented hours in a sort of aquatic woodland—as we did—expecting every moment to be impaled from below. I'd hate to try coping with them at night; it was bad enough in broad daylight and we had a guilty feeling as of trespassing, which seemed a bit odd at sea.

We sailed beneath the long bridge which joins Oleron to the mainland and beat up to Le Chateau on the island's eastern shore to spend a calm night in the little harbour. Next day we passed inside the Île d'Aix and made up through the narrow Rade de la Pallice between Île de Ré and the Charente region, putting into l'Aiguillon by early afternoon. It is difficult to convey the different world in which we now found ourselves. Gone was the sand and sun and baking heat, and the green and leafy waterways. Instead we were left, as the sea withdrew, to bed down on mile upon mile of black mud, and the wind—from being a welcome cooling friend—was becoming a bitter icy enemy. No doubt our blood was thinned from the months spent in the languid heat. We bought a balaclava each and an extra blanket to add to the spare sails atop our sleeping bags each night, and slowly life aboard became more difficult. It's astonishing what a difference warmth and sun can make to this primitive life we were living. Back in Greece and Italy any clothes washed in the morning were dry enough to wear by noon. But now once things got wet they remained wet for days, even after hanging in the wind. We unearthed our small gas heater and it made life more tolerable aboard in the evenings. This, with the guttering flame of two candles kept the temperature inside the tent at a bearable level and we would turn in early, listening to the flurry of wind against the canvas tent, matched by the chuckle of a fast flowing tide on the hull until, at some dark hour of the night, *Lugworm* would gently heel as she settled in the mud.

But it was still fun. In fact there was a heightened sense of adventure now we were dealing with the real sea again and we would spend hours together por-ing over the charts, listening to the forecasts, and absorbing all available data on the tides and currents that might be encountered on the following day's sail. Of course we worked the tides all up this coast to help make headway, and we were very lucky with the wind which remained mostly light north-easterly off the land, for which we gave thanks. By mid September we were entering Les Sables d'Olonne after a very wet cold beat against a brisk north-north-easter, glad to take shelter inside at the pontoons of the Sport Nautique north of the harbour. That night was memorable for a magnificent meal we took in *Le Dragon d'Or* restau-rant which cost 80 francs and was worth every centime. Now that the weather was so much colder we were finding that we needed these hefty meals to keep up strength and morale.

The fifteen miles up the delightful coast to St Gilles-sur-Vie was completed in one day and then came another tricky stretch across the shallows inside the Île d'Yeu where the wind went foul and headed us from the north-north-west and began to freshen. It's a ghastly shore to have to leeward and I was thankful when, approaching Les Marguerites bank the wind eased. We were also now gaining protection from a long northerly swell by the bulk of Noirmoutier and those terrifying off-shore reefs which lie west of the island. In fact, in different conditions that narrow channel leading inside Noirmoutier could have been every bit as bad as the Maumusson, so we were lucky to have this fortunate protection from the swell, flying through without mishap, to once more become enmeshed in a forest of withies.

By 20th September we were in Pornic and reunited with an old friend who, it seems, had been scouring every grotto on this Biscay coast on the chance of finding us. It was a wonderful feeling, to make that very first contact with one from our own culture again, and we spent a hilarious day exploring in his car—almost forgotten luxury, a car—over the region of the Loire Inférieure. As we parted and slipped once more from the pontoon he thoughtfully threw aboard two thick horseblankets and a sou-wester.

So we worked slowly up across the mouth of the Loire, playing cat-and-mouse with the weather and finally took shelter against an unkind wind at the tiny fishing port of La Turballe. We shall remember the place, for it was here on the morning of Sunday September 24th that we happened upon a sight the like of which I doubt we'll see again.

The bay southward to le Croisic is a sweep of magnificent golden sand which flattens to run shallow out to sea in vast areas of shingle which become exposed only at very low water springs. On this day of all days—Sunday and equinoctial too—the temptation for those shellfish-orientated folk was too much. Viewed from a distance the entire bottom of the bay seemed to be crawling with black ants. We approached, and as we did so there came a sigh as of the sea stroking a shingle beach—but there was no sea. It was those thousands of humans raking the shale for cockles; but it was the manner of their raking which held us spellbound. We all know that Time and Tide wait for no man, and at most I suppose there was a short hour in which that rarely exposed seabed could be harvested. So with a concentration which was almost demented they raked, shovelled, sifted and bagged millions of flat, round, twisted and scalloped shellfish. There were Demoiselles, Coques, le Couteaux and Escargots de Mer being shovelled into plastic bags and carted with intense fury up that beach to waiting vehicles.

One and all they were far too busy to engage conversation with two ignorant foreigners, but we did spend a delirious ten minutes stalking a thighbooted hunter who was pouncing on tiny bubbles which appeared here and there, to thrust downwards deep in the sand with (you'll never believe it) a HARPOON. It was a slender steel lance with hinged barbs on the end and there, each time he withdrew it, was impinged a tubular rubber Couteau whose shell had evidently been discarded in the chase.

But WHAT in the name of baggywrinkle, I hear you groaning, has all this to do with sailing a dinghy from Greece to England? Very well; if you must have the how and the why of it all I'll give it to you. While I'm at it I might as well purge my soul and admit to an event which—quite rightly—all but put an end to our wanderings.

Anyone familiar with this coast will know that off Castelli Point just south of Piriac there is a rash of off-lying rocks and shoals extending a mile and more to seaward. It is marked by Les Bavonelles buoy. The wind was brisk from the north-north-east when we left Turballe bound for la Vilaine river and we had a splendid reach under the lee of the land with main, mizzen and genoa set. Once free of Castelli Point, however, the increase in wind decided me to hand the main. Before we had reached the Bavonelles buoy it had freshened enough to make a change to small jib advisable. I did nothing about it.

Why? Because I was getting idle and sick of changing sails and anyway we were so near to the river mouth that to hold on for another hour with that genoa couldn't matter. But the truth of the matter is I didn't want to get soaking wet, and fossicking about at the bow changing sails would mean just that.

So we cleared the point on starboard with genoa set and then I committed one of the oldest and most terrible crimes at sea. I tried to cut the corner in order to gain the lee of a headland up to windward more quickly. I TACKED INSIDE THE BUOY—for which I expect to spend a year at least in Purgatory. Within minutes I realised two things; we were in very disturbed water and we were carrying too much sail forward. I gave the helm to B. while putting myself up in the nose to change to small jib—and can you imagine anything more crassly idiotic?

The inevitable happened. We were beating over shoals which humped the seas into short steep chops and with my weight forward poor *Lugworm* just couldn't rise quick enough. I heard B.'s startled warning, looked up and got a hogshead of solid water in the chest which swept me aft of the cockpit and knocked some sense back into my addled head. For a moment it was all Hell with both of us bucketing the sea back where it belonged and *Lugworm* staggering manfully, her cockpit awash. I hardened the mizzen and she kept her nose into seas and looked after us while we drifted stern-first out of that shoal into safe deep water, praying meantime that nothing more would come aboard, nor up through the bottom as we did so. And why do I tell you all this? Because maybe I can brush off just a bit of that salutary lesson which nearly stopped the hearts of myself and my crew— namely NEVER to get careless and take the sea for granted.

We bailed her back to safety but I can tell you it was touch and go for a while. And then we rounded Castelli again with mizzen and small jib set, OUTSIDE the buoy this time, to have a hard wet fight up to the Vilaine river. We were thankful to get in.

*   *   *

One day when we are senile as well as old the two of us are going to get on our bicycles and pedal off to Plymouth where we shall board the Roscoff Ferry and set off to potter in the peninsula of Brittany. We made this vow during the next ten days of our voyage through those delightful canals, for we quite fell in love with the area. There is something subtly different about them for they are narrower and more overgrown; more like our own small inland rivers as they meander quietly along, and there is also a great affinity between the Breton people and the Cornish folk from back home. The Vilaine river, which until recently used to flow into the sea just north of the Loire, has now been dammed at Arsal about five miles up from the mouth. The lock there is huge, but once through it one moves into a different world where the river winds through a wide flat valley between reedy banks, and fat cows graze in green meadows. There were few vines here, the cultivated land being used mainly for growing maize. Roche Bernard, a sleepy little village with a small inlet where floating pontoons are available for berthing, is a good point from which to explore the area and it was there, after a superb meal in the auberge *Les Deux Magots*, that we took our first hot bath since the disaster at the Torre dell'Ovo in the Gulf of Taranto five months before.

The next four days were spent idling through Redon, Besle, Messac and Molière and on Friday 29th September we passed through Rennes. I would strongly advise any voyager to avoid its waters if possible, so polluted are they from the industrial city. On the last day of September in the early dusk we made fast to the left bank just beyond the St Germaine lock and wandered up a hill to the small village in search of a meal. The place seemed asleep and no sign of any restaurant was to be found, but a matronly lady from whom we made enquiries assured us this was not the case. 'Est ce que vous avez visité la Crêperie de Madame Lecoq Oubret?' she enquired. We assured her we had not and forthwith she gave us directions, asking that we please inform the good Madame Lecoq that it was she who directed us there, and none other, much less chance fortune.

We followed her advice and soon stood before a large establishment combining, it seemed, a crêperie, restaurant and shop. But alas, it was securely locked. Inside, however, there was movement, and without seeming too inquisitive we could make out the figure of Madame amid a display of confections. She was ironing a pair of trousers—and looking occasionally at us. Still loath to give up hope we remained, examining the contents of the window and before long saw her spit on the base of the iron, survey it for a moment, then place it carefully on a folded cloth at the end of the table. With that she came to the door opened it a fraction and raised her eyebrows.

'Madame,' we explained, in doubtful French. 'Nous sommes voyageurs avec un bon appetit. Mais calamité! Ici dans St Germaine c'est evident qu'il n'est pas possible à manger. Et vous, recommendé par la bonne Madame ... êtes aussi fermé!'

At this the good Madame, who must have been approaching 70, cocked her head sideways, looked us up and down, and then in a surprisingly resonant and manly voice which seemed to be operating under great pressure exclaimed in French that indeed she was shut, and the season being over she feared there was nothing in the house; and she took another look at us; but wait a minute; she would have words with Pierre, for after all perhaps she could knock up a little something if we did not mind sitting among the groceries and keeping an eye on the iron while she looked into the matter?

After a while she returned with the news that if we were prepared to accept such miserable fare she might manage perhaps a little melon with port to start with followed by homemade paté, hamburgers in savoury rice, washed down with a bottle of Chambertin (rouge). To end the meal, alas there was only chocolate caramel, cheese, coffee and grapes.

We did in fact manage to accept this offering and before long, Pierre himself came to examine these odd late foreigners. Soon, the three of us were engaged in animated conversation, round the board table while Madame continued with the ironing of Pierre's trousers. By now it was known that I was an ex-Service man. Of the Navy, it was true, and therefore not perhaps directly connected with the land fighting which had raged in the area towards the end of the war. But as soon as he knew that my elder brother had lost his life in one of the assaults south of Caen, we were like blood brothers, Pierre and I. Ancient war maps showing the invasion beaches and the main assault routes were soon laid over an adjacent table which was drawn up to ours, and between the paté and the cheese I learned more of the strategy involved during those perilous months than any history book will ever supply, in-terspersed with a recipe for apple pie from Madame, the whole lingered over with a second bottle of the excellent Chambertin.

But it's strange, isn't it, how the little things stick in the memory; like lingering down on the canal bank in the night after we had parted from this very lovable couple, watching the swarm of furry moths on the bridge above battering their brains out against the glass of the glowing lamp.

Just because it—and they—were there.

*   *   *

It was on the morning of Monday the 2nd October, lying alongside the quay at St Domineuc which is close to that delightful little town of Dinan, that a sort of depression set in. Of morale, that is. The night had been one of torrential rain and everything in the boat felt damp including our sleeping bags. Came the dawn with a continuing fine drizzle percolating through a grey morning mist, and suddenly all the horror of returning to our indescribable climate; the coming winter and the undealt-with Tax Returns and accumulated overdue National Health Stamps— the whole lot loomed like a desolate dreary battle field ahead, and suddenly it seemed a hell of a long way from Corfu. Add to this the fact that I'd upset a full carton of milk on the after deck while brewing up the morning cup of tea, most of which had gone down my neck and into my sleeping bag. Things, one way and another, were in a bit of a mess and dammit there are times when you can be joyous and times when you can't.

At such moments it's not a bad policy to deliberately set about boosting one's ego. 'Cuckoo,' I addressed the nose on the far side of the centreplate casing, 'don't you think I'm...'

Wait a minute, I'll start again.

'Cuckoo, don't you think we are brave?'

There was a long pause while one eye extricated itself from folds of bedding, opened, swivelled about and then focused on me.

'Brave,' I repeated. 'Don't you think we're very brave and ought to be famous? Dammit we've voyaged over three thousand miles in *Lugworm* since we left Fowey last year. Don't you think when people hear all about it they'll think we're brave; I mean, in a way aren't we in the same bracket as Cabot and Raleigh and Vasco da Lopez; just on a smaller scale?'

The eye continued looking at me. The rain began beating down another tattoo on the tent above. 'Think of all the perils we've survived. Shipwreck, strandings, sunstroke...' I couldn't think of any more and anyway the wooden rib halfway down *Lugworm*'s cockpit was cutting a slot into my starboard liver and it hurt. I turned over and drew up one knee (it was just possible to do this without widening *Lugworm* amidships). The bruise on the other hip started boring a hole into the bottom boards. Long ago had we given up the useless task of inflating our airbeds; they were flat again within minutes, in fact the whole of the Riviera had been a succession of breathless nights.

'Courageous,' I said. 'Empire Builders!'

'I think I am,' she said.

Suddenly the sleeping bag felt damper and the Tax Returns much worse.

'You're a sailor, born and bred,' she went on (which wasn't true anyway), I never profess to be one. For me the sea is a vast unknown peril; it's ME that's the truly courageous one. Real courage is doing a thing even though you're scared stiff; yes, I think I AM brave.'

I thought about that. 'OK' I came back fighting, 'So I'm a seasoned salt and the sea holds no terrors (Oh, Ha Ha!) for me, but I'm courageous in other ways surely? Remember when that festoon in the thirty-knot gin palace rocked the boat

IT WASN'T ALL JOY

off Cannes and a litre of boiling water went all over my foot? Did I shriek? No: I simply dunked my foot over the side.'

'And I did everything else for the next fortnight,' she chipped in.

Things were bad. It wasn't going the way I'd planned, this dialogue, at all. It was bad enough to be wet and miserable, but to be wet and miserable and unappreciated was intolerable. I told her so.

'It isn't that you're unappreciated, it's just that you're quite intolerable when you're wet and miserable,' she retorted. Hell, things were getting worse.

'When we get ashore I'm going to tell somebody all about what we've done,' I mumbled. 'I'm going to see the local newspaper proprietor and sell our story to the highest bidder.'

'In St Domineuc?'

'When we get to Dinan, then.'

'In French? That should make good reading.'

You can't win.

We went ashore, moist and hungry to search out the local breadshop. They had no bread. The village was a long straggle of depressing houses either side of a busy straight road that came from somewhere and went, I suppose, to somewhere else; it didn't seem to matter much where. We walked about a bit and bought an umbrella which was slightly damaged.

No; it wasn't ALL joy.

But spirits tend to rise with the barometer, and by the following morning, when we dropped down into the tidal River Rance through another huge lock, L'Écluse de Chateliers, we both felt better, and even a bit dry, which was a good thing for it was low water in the river with oceans of thick black mud everywhere which wasn't uplifting. By midday, after picking our way carefully downstream we were approaching the colossal hydro-electric barrage which uses the rise and fall of the sea to generate a great deal of electricity, and we felt rather like a flea in a coffin as the gate clanged shut on us in that gigantic lock and the water level began to fall; and when the other gates opened, there again were the hoary grey wastes of the Atlantic. By early evening we were locking into the basin at St Malo and—Hah!—Fame at Last—a reporter with a camera made us turn round and come in again to look as if we'd just arrived, and our photograph (looking as if we'd just arrived) was in the next edition of the *Ouest France* with a remarkable and slightly accurate news item beneath.

'I look a bit thin,' I said to B., thumbing the photo over a coffee in the old town.

'My hair looks as if it could do with a good wash,' she replied. 'Do you think ...'

'Mon Dieu!' came the exclamation from alongside. A wild looking figure in a mackintosh was reading the same paper. 'C'est vous!' he added, looking from the paper to us and back again. 'Merveilleux! But in such a little boat ... and to take so long ... you must be very rich!'

'I am,' I replied as we pooled our last centimes for the coffee. 'Immensely. In fact I have shares in a goldmine!'

And I took her hand as we walked out.

CHAPTER VI

THE FINAL STRETCH

IF YOU LOOK AT THE CHART of the approaches to the English Channel you will see that in distance there is really not much to choose between Guernsey to Start Point or Cherbourg to Portland Bill.

We had been weighing up this problem while pottering through the canals, and at first we were inclined towards going up through the Channel Islands, then shooting across direct from Guernsey to Start Point. But we had spent too long eating, enjoying ourselves and being ill and the weather had turned unsettled. Mists, sea-fog and autumn squalls were not uncommon, and I knew the power of the tides and swell between those rocky off-lying reefs and islands, so finally we thought it safer to stick close to the coast of the mainland, work up round Cap de la Hague, and then strike north from Cherbourg.

Another alternative, of course, would have been to work eastward along the north coast of France until the Channel narrowed at Boulogne, then nip across to Newhaven, but this would have involved more than two hundred and fifty more miles before we had clawed back westward again to Portland, and now, for the first time on the cruise, we were becoming concerned with the lateness of the season.

The early morning forecast on 5th October (we were now picking up the BBC transmissions) gave a probable easterly force six to seven, which is no good in a dinghy, so we spent the day exploring St Malo, cashing traveller's cheques and buying a series of large scale Blondel's French coloured charts of this coastline.

I quote from my log for the following day, to indicate how the hour by hour details of the trip were recorded -without which it would have been impossible to write this book.

Friday 6th October 1972
Barometer: 1002 Rising slightly.
Forecast: Easterly force 5-6 becoming south-east.

0630 De-rigged tent and rigged boat for sea. Approached lock entrance but had to await the 0800 opening. 0800 Locked into exit. Bright clear sunny morning with light S.E. wind. Tide flowing west approx. one knot.

0900 Off the Petit Bey island set course under all sail 050 Compass for Pointe de la Varde. Wind light E.S.E. 1015 Anchored in entrance to Rotheneuf Bay to await easing of adverse tidal stream which was now running westerly approx. one to two knots. Wind remaining light E.S.E.

1130 Weighed and proceeded under power, wind very light easterly.

1245 Anchored in Anse du Verger and went winkling on the rocks for lunch.

1445 Tide now slack, wind very light easterly. Weighed and motored toward La Fille buoy off Pointe du Grouin.

1520 Off La Fille Buoy. Tide setting 115 degrees True at 2¾ knots. Set compass course 030 for Granville (allowing 35 degrees offset for strong tide to make good 065 degrees) and using transit of the Herpin Lighthouse and the Pointe du Grouin to check trackline. Visibility a bit misty, but allowance for drift seems about OK. This inset to the Baie du Mont St Michel is tricky.

1600 Sighted faint white houses above horizon. Granville. Wind fallen to nil.

1700 Wind coming in very light north east.

1715 Came to buoy inside harbour to await lock. Many fishing boats also waiting.

1745 Entered inner basin and berthed at very crowded marina. Shopped for fillets of fish and supped aboard with fish and white sauce and sweet wine, mashed potatoes and fresh watercress.

The notes for that day, which I always kept on the right hand pages of the log read as follows:

The strong tide (approaching three knots) ran 115 degrees True off the Herpin Light then swung to 090 True about three quarter way across the Bay. A marked overfall was visible all along the shallow bank off the shore. Gannets and shearwaters are here in abundance, also shoals of tiny fish which

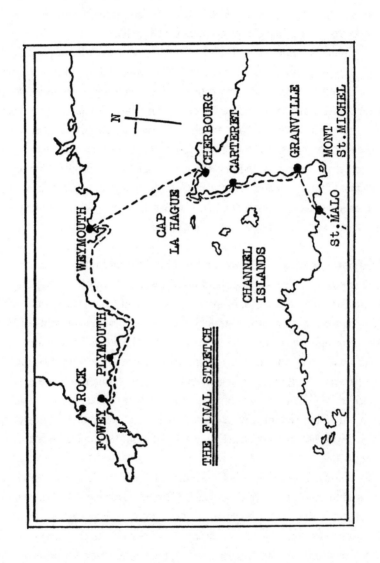

THE FINAL STRETCH

dive on our approach giving the appearance of raindrops in the water. Sky is absolutely free of cloud but visibility a bit misty. Wind disappointing, but came in from north east about two miles off Granville.

Granville is a flourishing fishing port with inner dock basin (single gate only) in front of a busy shopping centre. Behind this, and climbing up the hillside is the old fortified town the western end of which appears to be a military barracks. We closed Le Loup tower off the entrance, leaving it to starboard and entered the outer harbour which is surrounded entirely by quays, and as soon as the influx of fishing craft were through we followed them in and berthed at the very crowded marina. We are the fifth boat out! A notice on the Yacht Club door states that due to overcrowding visiting yachts cannot be welcomed by the Club after the 27th August. However, we do not consider ourselves a yacht, and nobody has come to molest us, yet.

We had now completed two thousand two hundred and thirty-six miles by my reckoning since we left Kassiopi, and the crew was, to put it mildly, becoming somewhat weathered. Foogoo, from being stained a hideous green of the African jungles, had taken on a sort of grained soapstone colour, with veins of brown showing through where intense heat had cracked the wood. He remained, however, as belligerently in charge and competent as ever. We other two members having passed through that mahogany-bronze stage of sunburn, were now turning an Oriental yellow; the sort of deep sallow colour of boiled leather soaked in curry powder, and reminiscent of retired Indian Army Colonels. The health of all aboard was, however, unchanged, and I really think we were both as wiry as two centipedes.

The following morning, 7th October, we left Granville at 0700 and sailed before a light south-easterly up towards Carteret, carrying the ebb stream up the coast until about 1345 when we had to motor against an hour of adverse flood, the wind having once more deserted us. By 1445, after a run of 34 miles, we were anchored off the entrance which has a long stone breakwater jutting out from magnificent sand dunes with the shallow entry channel on its eastern side. The sand dunes to the west soon give way to rocky cliffs off Cape Carteret. The entrance channel is long and bottomed with shingle, swinging to the east as it goes in, and the flood stream scoured in like a mill race. Inside, and past the little town which lies all on the north bank, it opens into a huge shallow marsh, somewhat muddy and grassy. We found the town unprepossessing, being mostly modern houses with no character, but the environs might well be worth exploring more fully.

The next day was hilarious. The wind remained nonexistent, for which, frankly at this point I was thankful, for the chart in vivid red lettering off the Cap de la Hague, has the warning 'VERY VIOLENT CURRENTS, DANGEROUS BREAKERS WHEN WIND IS CONTRARY TO TIDAL STREAM', and as it turned out had there been a fair breeze from the south (which would have been the one we wanted) it might have been a tricky rounding. I have to admit to a complete navigational bish-up here for which I've still not found the cause. My tidal stream calculations for 8th October 1972 taken from the inset tidal stream atlas on Blondel's chart gave me to think that at midday we would have a comfortable north-east running stream of about one knot to help gently ease us round this dangerous Cape. On arrival, however, it soon became evident that abeam of La Foraine beacon, with the outboard running at full revs and little help from the wind, we were making half a knot backwards. The tide had thrown Blondel's predictions overboard and we spent a frigid half hour homing-in on a bearing of 040 degrees for the light-house which took us clear of the appalling off-lying rocks until we were free of the main strength of the tide. Thereafter we were able to nose gingerly into a tiny little crack in the reefs called Goury where *Lugworm* was carefully positioned to dry out on just about the only few feet of flat bottom to be found. The scene at low tide looked rather like a Martian landscape, so prolific were the fangs of barnacle encrusted rock all around.

It was evident that we were not going to round that Cape until the tidal stream turned, and in some perplexity I made enquiries at a row of coastguard cottages close ashore, to receive totally wrong information once again, which finally led to our motoring in a flat calm round that cape against a three knot adverse flow. Our experience was that the stream regardless of flood or ebb ran in a south-westerly direction close under the light. Maybe it was a local back-eddy, but certainly to the north of the light it remained running in a westerly direction all the rest of that afternoon, and in desperation we motored into St Martin's Bay having failed

Goury, Cap de la Hague

to find a berth in Port Racine, which must be the smallest harbour in Europe; the berthing warps of the few fishing boats therein quite precluded even *Lugworm* finding a niche.

That night was spent uneasily off an exposed beach—a thing I never relish—but the following morning with a brisk southerly we hoisted all sail and set off for the Bréfort Buoy. Once more, however, the stream predictions on Blondels proved quite wrong and we met an adverse flow of great force which was knocking up a nasty sea with an easterly swell on top of it all. So we tried again that evening and succeeded in rounding Bréfort buoy and making a bit of southing past La Coque and Le Hoquet rocks to round l'Etonnard Beacon and enter Omonville harbour very wet and thoroughly chilled through.

You will have gathered that the tides in this tricky area were determined to beat us, but we were more determined that they should not. On Tuesday 10th October, we closed a local fishing boat just off Omonville entrance and enquired when, if ever, the stream ran towards the east. 'But immediately after low water!' came the surprised reply, 'When else?' So it may be, but it certainly did not run eastward close inshore where we were and once again, with a forecast of freshening north-easters we battled against an adverse three knot tide with sails and engine giving everything they could for I was keen to enter Cherbourg before the arrival of a predicted 'low' which might pin us up a beach somewhere on an exposed bit of the coast. At 1700, after a hard fight we gained the lee of the Grande Rade breakwater of that superb harbour.

The yacht club proved shut for the 'vacances annuelles' from 2nd to 16th October, but we learnt at a temporary office, that our stay at the pontoons would cost six francs a day which was reasonable enough, even though there were no toilet or shower facilities. So we went ashore and ate at the Cafe Theatre: Moules Marinière and Côte du Pore followed by cheese and caramel pudding with a bottle of reasonable red wine and it cost us forty francs which, at eleven francs to the pound was a bit shattering, but worth it.

Yes, it was a triumph, but oddly disturbing, to arrive at Cherbourg. It meant the end of our foreign travelling and in a way was a climax to our adventures and yet, when we thought about it, the 'hop' that now faced us was a greater challenge than anything which had gone before. Seventy-five miles as the crow flies north to

Weymouth may not sound much, but for *Lugworm* it represented some eighteen hours sailing across open water and directly across all the major traffic lanes.

Torrential rain beat down all that first night and by morning the winds had swung northerly and were beginning to knock up a nasty grey sea over there towards England. We explored the town and earmarked the likely cheaper back-street restaurants for evening meals ashore, spending a small fortune in the 'launderette' getting our wet and dirty gear cleaned and dried. Thursday 12th October saw that particular 'front' pass over with the usual gusty clear skies following on, and a forecast of force four to five north-easterlies which was little use to us. Our plan was to await a southerly slant and fair forecast, but we took this opportunity to lighten *Lugworm* for the crossing by off-loading a heavy bag full of unwanted gear such as clothing, snorkelling equipment, books, charts, and this typewriter, to a friend in a large yacht with whom we arranged a rendez-vous at his home in England. It was wise to bring *Lugworm*'s freeboard up a bit if we could, and I looked to the watertightness of her hatches, checked the rocket flares and daylight distress signals and generally reviewed all the safety meas-ures, working backwards from the ultimate disaster of a complete swamping, or being run-down. Over and over again in our minds we went through the exact action to be taken in the event of emergency.

Meanwhile the wind increased from the north. Yachts came running in with blown-out sails, their crews red-rimmed about the eyes, and salt grimed. They would surge down under headsails through that narrow channel from the Petite Rade and make fast quickly to any empty slot on the pontoons. For the next four hours or so they would die, and reports came in of leaving England with fair fol-lowing winds only to encounter ever freshening conditions as they made more southing, until the last twenty miles or so proved a bit of a pounder, with splendid seas running. We stood on the weather end of the quays and watched as ever in-creasing swells rolled down and burst over the top of the breakwater to weather of the Grande Rade, and wondered if, after all, we were not biting off a bit more than we could chew.

All Friday and Saturday the wind remained force five to seven from the north-east and the seas steadily built up while the temperature dropped. We al-ways seemed to be cold, slightly moist, and found it hard to keep up morale, now that we were so near home and yet still so far away. All that Cherbourg had to offer was sampled, and then we took to making sorties farther afield along the rather distressing suburbs but it was all rather lacking in uplift. The *Patisserie Paris* on the corner of the Place de Gaulle was a constant but expensive relief from approaching boredom, and the *Prisunic* supermarket claimed much of our time wandering around the counters; at least it was warm and dry, which is more than could be said for *Lugworm*, bless her. Our berthing warps were becoming very oily and somebody burned a hole in the tent by dropping a cigarette thereon. Things were a bit depressing, and still the wind kept up its constant howl from the north. Forecasts of gale force nine in the adjacent areas kept us pinned to that pontoon and by 13th October we were so bored that we began to think terrible thoughts of shipping *Lugworm* across on the ferry steamer.

'It's not a bit of use risking our necks just for the vanity of saying we sailed right home,' I remarked to B. one horrible wet evening as we sheltered in the port harbourmaster's office watching the rain and fast scudding clouds. 'This is just the sort of situation that leads to disaster, going against one's better judgement simply to "pull it off".'

I looked through the gathering dusk to the ferry terminal. Above the sheds we could see a funnel rearing; evidently the Townsend-Thoresen ferry was berthed. It would do no harm just to wander over and make a few enquiries. The wind was soughing through those huge deserted sheds, banging the doors and rattling windows, and the squalls of sleety rain pattered in grey sheets along the empty quays. We hugged one wall for shelter and B. looked up at the ferry's sides, towering above us. 'I'd no idea,' she remarked, 'they were quite so big!'

'It's just the contrast after *Lugworm*,' I told her. 'They're tiny, as ships go, but they're a damned sight bigger than we have been used to for the last eighteen months.' As we idled along the quay we could hear the deep humming of her generator from somewhere within.

Then I felt B. catch my arm. She had stopped, and was pointing upward. 'Er .. . darling,' she said. 'Look!'

It was *Queen Elizabeth II*.

*   *   *

By 22nd October we were both thoroughly fed up with Cherbourg, and despairing of the weather. But finally the wind swung out of the north-east and settled in the west though it kept up its strength of around force five, and the seas kept rolling in. 'But it just MUST ease off soon!' B. kept saying, as we trailed in and out of the very excellent and helpful Harbourmaster's office where a daily weather chart was posted. And of course it did. It happened very suddenly and really caught us a bit unawares. We'd just completed a long and enjoyable evening meal of shellfish in our favourite lowdown 'dive' and when we came out into the street in the darkness a strange feeling came over us; something was missing. The howl of the wind had ceased. We both looked up to where, palely through a layer of mackerel clouds the moon was glowing. We just looked at each other and started running, calling in for a quick last minute check in the Pilot's Office where a kind official telephoned the local Met. station and confirmed that for the next twenty-four hours nothing violent was on the books. In fact the immediate forecast for the night was calm variable winds.

We raced back to *Lugworm*, dropped 100 francs into the Clubhouse box for outstanding dues, and got the boat ready for sea. She was fully fuelled, and within twenty minutes we were coiling down the tarry warps and nosing northward into the Grande Rade. It was 2300 as we cleared the end of the outer mole, and started dancing in the seas which were still running from the recent winds. With all sails set we steadied before a light southerly breeze on a course of 338 by compass, and the lights of Cherbourg winked 'goodbye' astern.

Oh, but it was an exciting moment, that parting from France. If fate willed, we would be hearing English spoken again all around us by the following night, and really be home! It was hard to believe. As the Cherbourg lights grew dim astern we picked up the farewell flash of Cap de la Hague and then it was just a case of praying that the winds would stay in a southerly sector and behave themselves for a while. I knew that, striking across the tidal streams as we were, we would be carried first one way and then back again, and my calculations indicated that the ebb would just about cancel out the flood. We took it in turns sleeping for an hour at a time and keeping a good watch for the constant traffic up and down the Channel. Like necklaces of lights the ships crossed ahead and astern, but only twice was there danger of collision or swamping from too-close approach to the huge wakes of tankers—and then the risk was easily avoided. I feared that our tiny navigation lights might be missed, and frankly the radar reflector clanging up there on the starboard shroud was more for morale than anything else. I think on that crossing *Lugworm* really felt smaller than at any other time on the cruise; maybe it was just that we were again sailing in home waters and the true perspective of what we were doing and had already done suddenly came home to us.

The wind remained kind, light from the south-west, and we helped it out a bit at times with the engine. There was just a small and violent whirlwind which funnelled the clouds down to meet the sea at dawn on 26th October as we peered ahead, keen for the first sight of England; and at 0810 we sighted Portland Bill fine on the starboard bow.

Crumbs ... but it seemed incredible. How many lights had we sighted, how many headlands had we approached, how often had we watched as the land beyond slowly materialised ... again and again over the last seven months of the voyage home? But not one of them looked like this.

We just keep looking, and slowly the land became clearer, and we could actually see the Dorset hills. Then, for us, a very splendid thing happened. Out of the north the long lean grey shape of a warship came speeding down. With a white bone in her teeth Her Majesty's Frigate 190 hove up at full speed, circled us, and sped off again on her business. It was like a welcoming handshake reaching out even before we had made port, though I suppose they were really just wondering what the Hell we were doing out there in something that looked like the Captain's gig.

Feeling rather self-conscious I tied the yellow 'pratique' flag to the shroud as we nosed into Weymouth at 1500 and the Customs Officer was on station ready and waiting at the base of the quay steps. No sooner were we moored safely up in the harbour than the television crew and reporters hove-up and we had to leave again and sail back, looking as if we had just arrived. It was all very exciting really, watching it on colour TV that night in the local pub, and we kept saying to each other at odd moments 'Hush ... remember these people can tell what we're talking about!' And 'We've done it—we've really done it, haven't we? Doesn't it feel a bit queer?'

So we booked in at the local concert hall and basked in the music of the Bournemouth Symphony Orchestra, and late that night ate fish and chips sitting on a bench on Weymouth Prom ... and felt dreadfully English, and glad of it, arrogant beggars that we are.

On the 8th of November, drenched with sea-fog we entered Fowey harbour and grounded gently on the beach up Mixtow Creek. The round trip was completed, and suddenly there were Brian and Shirley—those two stalwarts who had towed us overland from this port more than two thousand miles to Volos in Greece. It seemed an incredibly long way back to that dusty hot morning when they had waved goodbye just south of Mount Olympus.

But, for me, the oddest thing was—there was finally nowhere else to go. I looked around for a bit, feeling strangely unsettled, and then I kissed B. very long and hard, for it seemed as good a thing to do as anything.

And really, I think she deserved it, don't you?

Thoughts

It wasn't a 'Do or Die' venture, this, though it had its moments, and really I know we were very lucky to get *Lugworm* back more or less intact. A thousand ill chances might have resulted in complete disaster.

People often ask us what, if anything, we might alter in the planning should we with hindsight do the same voyage again. It is a difficult question to answer for it all depends on what one is seeking from such a venture. For instance, we now know that from the purely sailing point of view it would have been better to do the whole thing the other way round and sail from England to Greece. That way we would have been able to use the light north-westerlies right down the coast of Italy, and no doubt the time taken would have been shortened. But from our point of view that would have been a sad loss, for it was just the fact that often we could not gain ground northward that kept us pinned for days at a time in many really fascinating out-of-the-way harbours.

Again, people have commented that it was odd to arrange our arrival in Greece just as the fearsome northerly 'meltemi' was getting into its stride for the summer. But again I reply that dealing with that wind was, surely, half the challenge of that fantastic summer in 1971 when we were playing cat-and-mouse with the elements around the Aegean. Had it not been for that wind we might never have spent the incredible month in Santorini living in a pumice cave, or known the sheer elemental roar of a near hurricane for four days on a beach under Andros Isle; and such memories are worth more than money and will be with us all our lives.

Would we, with hindsight, have chosen a different boat? Bigger perhaps, with a cabin? The answer is no. *Lugworm* fulfils all that we needed on this voyage. A larger boat, while providing more comfort, would have denied us entry to all those rivers, and innumerable scrambles up beaches. Believe me there is a tremendous sense of satisfaction to be got from sitting in your boat at the top of a shingly beach listening to the thunder of the waves a few feet away —knowing that, no matter what the wind and the sea care to brew up you're out of their reach. You can't do that in a larger boat; you're just kept desperately buzzing about looking for harbours and often, on a trip like this, there aren't any. Who wants harbours anyway?

Of course on such a venture you have to be fit. Really fit—and we both were. But after all, if you're going to enjoy life haven't you got to be fit anyway? One couldn't enjoy this sort of trip nearly as much unless the sheer joy of using one's muscles hard, and then completely relaxing afterwards, was a normal routine. I think the constant hard physical work would soon exhaust a slack person. Being small helps too.

Experience? Of course thirty years spent handling small boats in all conditions breeds a margin of safety through sheer instinct, and this undoubtedly stood us in good stead and it's something which cannot be acquired otherwise. But I would say that a less experienced person planning the same sort of venture would run little greater risk of disaster provided he was not a fool. And that means simply taking a sensible stock of the situation each day before sailing, carefully weighing up the risks, and then not being ashamed of deciding to stay ashore, even when the decision proved groundless. That's good seamanship; it gets you home.

There is nothing by way of equipment we would have changed; our two-burner meths stove worked excellently, and you really can't beat candles for lighting—they're waterproof and non-rusting and will light when taken straight from waterlogged bilges. Two anchors and plenty of warp are essential, and though we never set them the spare suit of sails kept us warm on many occasions.

As for the engine; well, four horsepower is little enough, but again doesn't this make for a greater challenge? After all, if you can simply turn a switch and speed at fifteen knots to the nearest port—well, that's motor boating. The great thing is reliability; you've got to KNOW it's going to work every time you need it, and our Mercury did this without fail, omitting the time I filled the coil with salt water which is a bit unfair. You have to weigh up the fuel situation too; our seven gallons was good for seventy miles or so pottering along at four knots. No; I'd have the same engine if doing it all again.

One thing I would strongly advise, and that is to make sensible provision for cash withdrawals at selected points before leaving England. We did this through Lloyds and the machinery worked very smoothly. To be able to go into some unpronounceable place at the back end of beyond and calmly cash a cheque is very satisfying, and it was only when the Pound Sterling was 'floated' halfway up Italy that we were ever denied this facility—and then only for two days. But of course you've got to have the cash and this entire trip cost us about £1,600 excluding the cost of the boat and engine. It could have cost us a lot less of course but we spent more and more cash on meals ashore as the weather got colder in France—and that's expensive. One can argue that it would probably have cost that living at home anyway over a period of eighteen months; and we were fortunate enough to rent our house for the entire time which paid the rates.

Finally, the crew. Complete compatability is essential if one is going to get the most from such a jaunt. It is more important than natural aptitude, provided the skipper knows what he's doing. B. is, frankly, not a sailor, the sea for her is an alien thing and she is not really at home on it, which speaks volumes for her very real courage in tackling this voyage.

I would not have done it without her.

So together we did it, and now *Lugworm* is upside-down on the lawn behind the house and Foogoo glowers from the mantelpiece. Just occasionally we find ourselves out there looking at her scars; and suddenly one of us will say: 'Do you remember where that happened! What was the name of that idiot who …' And off we go into dreamland.

It's fun!

LUGWORM ISLAND HOPPING

To John,
who lent me his house on Ensay

CORNISH WIND

Unfettered, free, an ocean's breath
* – you come,*
Knife-edged laughing Cornish wind,
You shock the cold dew-misted land to life
Flinging a spray of screaming gulls high on the cliffs

And we, poor earthbound mortals, stand
* with feet of clay.*
Reading your message in the waves…
I went that way…
… that way…

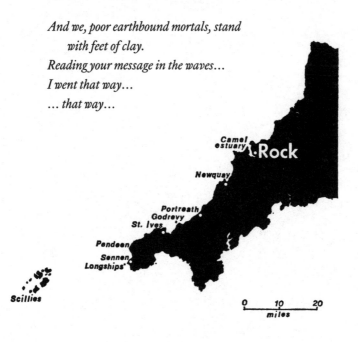

CHAPTER I

THE EYE OF THE WIND

THANK GOD FOR THAT WEST WIND!

From a thousand miles of ocean, pure as an Angel's breath she comes, gusting free until WHAM! Baulked by the great cliffs of Cornwall, she bowls keel-over-truck. And here are we, ripping our spinnakers in greeting and drawing in great lungfulls of virgin air—with the rest of the Continent down to leeward getting all our stale vapours, and good luck to them!

Make no mistake, it's a good place to live, out west on the northern shore of this rugged peninsula, and if you happen to own a dinghy—a dinghy as fine and noble-hearted and adventurous as the immortal *Lugworm*—and you happen also to be potty about islands, why, I tell you there's no better place to be on this earth!

Not that we're overbestowed with islands. The nearest to this Camel Estuary where *Lugworm* lives is the Scillies, and they're forty-five horrendous miles down this iron-bound coast to the Land's End. After that you've still got another twenty-two miles of heaving ocean past the bones of *Torrey Canyon* on the Seven Stones reef before the daymark on St Martin's Isle beckons you in to safety; and it's no place to be in a dinghy unless you're tired of life.

Or in *Lugworm*.

'Come on,' I said to my wife B. the spring after *Lugworm* had sailed the two of us back from Greece, 'the disease is breaking out again. Shove the tooth-brushes in a bag and we'll sail down to the Scillies for a month just to get the feel of it all again.'

'Uh-uh,' she commented, nibbling the Ryvita. She was looking at me hard and I knew immediately it was a tactical error to have broached the thought at breakfast. I ought to have learned from experience and waited at least until lunch-time.

'We've already done over three and a half thousand miles bouncing about on the seas—and *Lugworm*'s tent is getting leaky. For glory's sake, haven't you had enough yet?' And she nibbled on, deeply disturbed.

Of course, you've got to know B. to understand what I mean by that. It isn't that she's not besotted with *Lugworm* and wouldn't hesitate to ruin her best bod-

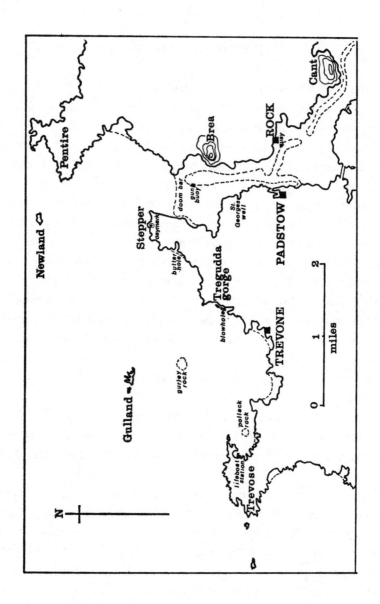

ice under the bilges scraping off the barnacles but... it's a sort of 'love-hate' relationship she has with the sea. 'It's caused me more sheer torment than anything else in my life,' she'll state. 'More plain discomfort, more wet, bruised, downright misery than any girl has a right to expect.' And of course, she's right.

But as every sailor knows, that has nothing whatever to do with it. All such things pretty soon get lost in the rich tapestry of memories that gild even the most frightful event with a golden halo of remembering.

There was that pre-B. day on the Doom Bar, for instance, back in 1957. Every besodden second of it glows as brightly now as it did eighteen years ago. I see it all again, the sweep of the blue summer sea out there to the north beyond Newland Rock, and a raven-haired girl called Jo with me in a boat even smaller than *Lugworm*, looking out past the sandy beaches under the golf links. Three frustrated hours we'd spent towing a maggot hopefully up and down that stretch between the bar and Rock quay with neither bite nor jiggle to raise a hope, and we both felt there were better things to be doing.

Then I caught Jo's eyes wandering seaward toward Newland. 'Wouldn't it be more fun if we went out there to the island?' she whispered. 'I mean, we might catch a mackerel or two outside the bar, it's so lovely and calm, and there are so many people in here.'

I knew what she meant.

But I was older than she, and responsible to boot. I had to put up a resistance. 'Not likely. Not over that bar.'

'The tide's rising,' she answered, quietly. I looked again at the bar. Not a whimper of surf was there, and she was quite right, the tide was rising. We were getting into deeper water with every minute! But I knew that bar backwards, knew it was just when you felt certain that the danger was over, just when you were balanced in innocence halfway over that sandbank stretching across the estuary mouth that Neptune would heave up a drencher. And a drencher in a fourteen-foot sailing dinghy is more than enough.

'Nothing doing!' I stuck to my guns and we stooged back again past Ship-my-Pumps point. She fretted. On the next leg toward the entrance it started again.

'Wouldn't it be grand to disappear behind that rock out there, I've never been out in the real sea in a small boat before, couldn't we just...?'

Now I had been watching the bar like a hawk since she first voiced the idea. Not a heave, nor whimper nor fret of white had there been this last hour, and with the rising tide the estuary was becoming more crowded; there was at least one other boat plugging up and down getting in the way of our lines. I had been over the bar often before in that dinghy, but I knew there was some heavy weather frolicking about out there to the westward, and sooner or later that meant there would be a swell running up the Bristol Channel. Still, as I say, there was no sign of it that morning; even the gulls were snoozing, so soporific was the heat and the peace.

'Put on that lifejacket,' I ordered. Remember this was in pre-marital days and I had an image to keep up. Rugged responsibility if I remember rightly. Her eyes flashed.

'Oooo... Ken. Are we really going?'

'The lifejacket,' I repeated. 'And blow it up.'

There was a sweet zephyr of a south wind and we ran up goosewinged past St George's Well close to the western shore, then struck out to the centre of the channel, leaving Gun Buoy to port as we ghosted on toward Stepper Point. Neptune acknowledged our presence with a gentle sigh as our shadow slid over the sand of the bar a few feet below, and seaward the world was bright and blue, full of hope and mackerel and...

I saw it coming.

Halfway in innocence isn't really honest; I was halfway in experience, but could do nothing to stop that swell advancing. Round the point of Stepper and across the broad mouth of the estuary it stretched, the ghastly smooth ridge of a silent, menacing mountain.

We watched it undulating toward us, pregnant with intent, rearing up inexorably as it began to feel the shallowing seabed, and the hair on the nape of my neck wriggled.

'Jo,' I croaked, 'whatever happens, HANG ON TO THE BOAT—DON'T GET SWEPT OFF!' I'll never know whether she had an inkling at that moment what I was talking about, but it's certain she did seconds later. That great mountain of swell reared up, glared us in the eye, curled over with a fiendish grin not twenty feet away and plunged down its own face with a roar fit to split your eardrums.

THE EYE OF THE WIND

'Hold on!' I shrieked as the wall of foam hit our bows, and I have a lifelong recollection of the boat's stem swinging vertically above us, her stern plunging down into a white cauldron of threshing water and then a green silent world of bubbles. Something hit me in the teeth. I think it was the rudder which had come unshipped in the maelstrom—and then I was gasping for air and clawing at the half-submerged bottom of the boat which had turned turtle, pitchpoled backwards, and there was Jo, bobbing about like an orange cork, enmeshed in a tangle of rigging and sails, all aspluther with foam. I looked frantically seaward: another like that and the two of us would be needing gills! There was another, but, Neptune be praised, not quite like that. It rose, teetered, and then changed its mind. We rose with it, balanced for a hideous moment on its knife-edge, and then slid down its back as it rolled on inexorably to lose its energy farther up the estuary without actually breaking.

Half an hour later the flood tide had drifted us and the mangled dinghy into water shallow enough for us to get a foot on the bottom, and then we pulled the boat on to the beach and sorted out the mess. As we were collecting all the bits and pieces together, oars, sails, bottom boards and our loose gear, down comes the lifeboat tender fairly bristling with Padstow fishermen—and I got the telling off I shall remember all my life, and fully deserved!

But why am I telling you all this?—it's nothing to do with *Lugworm*, still less with B. It's just that I remember it so well; only now, as I have said, the event has a rosy halo of romance about it which was lacking at the time. Where was I?

Islands. No: B. didn't take the bait as I hoped she might, but in the end we hit on a compromise. 'You sail down there,' she said, 'and after I've thinned out the lettuces I'll fly over and join you for a week or so; but I shall have to get back to pick the beans!' So that was it. Just *Lugworm* and me.

It could be worse.

*   *   *

Now I must tell you, because it is pertinent to the adventures which follow, that the previous winter I had built a garage. Resulting from this I had fifteen thin bendy deal planks left over—offcuts from the rafters—which I had to pay for, and what else can you do with fifteen wafer-thin planks save break two of them, swear, and build a skiff dinghy with the remaining thirteen lucky ones?

So *Ben Gunn* was born, light as a feather, skinned with an old bedsheet and painted white to keep the water out. I tow her behind *Lugworm* and she rides the seas like a mermaid, albeit in a permanent quandary regarding her sex. Nine feet in length and three feet in the beam she is, and just for good measure I carved a hideous face on the bow with a black eyepatch, and brought the painter out through piratical teeth just to make *Lugworm* go that bit faster, being permanently chased as it were. Why call her *Ben Gunn*? I can't remember, but it seemed appropriate at the time.

That spring morning Phoebus was virile with glory. I'd launched *Lugworm* and *Ben* the previous day and spent the night aboard up the estuary hidden in behind Cant Creek to sort myself out after the chaos of a winter ashore. There are a thousand little things you forget about living under a tent in a dinghy: long since, for instance, both B. and I had given up the idea of airbeds. No matter what quality they are, after a week or so of squashing in between the knees of the centre-plate casing and the side of the boat, they develop a death rattle. You spend half the sleeping hours giving the kiss of life and for all the good it does you might as well save your breath and go to sleep. Far better to spread out the spare sails, jerseys, towels and whatever—anything that will separate your haunches from the ribbed bottomboards—and you sleep like a log!

Lugworm's main mast pivots at deck level. It's only a moment's work to unship the mizzen then hinge back the foremast, remove the hinge bolt and support the whole mast complete with gaff and sail still lashed thereto, on crutches to form a stout ridgepole. A white waterproof PVC tent then ships over this and laps outside the gunwales for the entire length of the boat, securing with short tie-lines to a strong rope girdle with which one encircles the hull. The after-end of the tent has flaps, and depending on the weather the tent can be rolled forward to expose any amount of the afterdeck you require—it's remarkably convenient and has the added advantage that when at anchor the boat naturally faces into the wind, so any rain sweeps back and away from the open end. *Lugworm* is one of the original wooden eighteen-foot Drascombe Luggers, and the design very cleverly ensures that any water slopping on to the sterndeck flows aft to disappear down the outboard 'well', which is inside the transom. Two lockers stretch back under this sterndeck, one either side of the rudder casing, and we use one for food and the other for the petrol feed tank and spare chandlery. Clothes and bedding go in another capacious locker under the foredeck, while odds and sods like hairbrushes and charts and bars of chocolate stow up in elastic-fronted netting beneath the two sidedecks. It's all very shipshape, and you always know where everything is—either somewhere in the boat, or gone for good!

I'd kissed B. goodbye the evening before. 'If the weather heard the shipping forecast, I'll be off before high water early tomorrow and catching the first of the ebb from Trevose to help me down to St Ives,' I told her.

Do you know this north coast of Cornwall? From the Rock Estuary to Land's End it's just as God left it when things cooled down: rugged off lying islets—not really islands—more like headlands that have fallen off and then changed their minds. Cliffs: you'll not better them this side of the Hebrides, and in between lie those glorious and often inaccessible sweeps of strand. It's a lotus eater's paradise when the sun shines—and enough to curdle the blood when the storms come.

Now it's thirty-two miles to St Ives from Stepper Point and there's only Newquay in between. Both these ports spell disaster in a dinghy if a northerly swell starts running, for the surf breaks well off the harbour entrances at low water springs.

'Remember I love you, and take care of *Lugworm*,' B. had said as she blew a kiss from the Rock wall; and here I was, off.

Off!

Is there ANYTHING to equal that first chuckle of water under your hull at the start of a new summer cruise? The thrill of response as the boat heels under the press of her sails, free as the wind itself, and all the cares and tribulations of life ashore falling away like nightmares from a waking man!

Glory, but what a morning that was!

The flanks of the estuary were brilliant with sand glowing in the first shafts of the rising sun. Behind them to eastward rolled the washed green of the golf links, and beyond that the balding head of Brea hill folded the colours gently back and up into that pure unbroken blue of a Cornish spring sky. I could smell the young gorse as I beat out against a light northerly, tacking close under the old quarry south of Stepper, and *Lugworm*'s wake gurgled and rippled a paean of happiness astern. Before we were over the bar I was stripped to the minimals and awakening again to that delicious tingle of sun and wind and spray on my skin, looking to all the days ahead, endless days of freedom, with summer just over the horizon!

'Nobody,' I bellowed to *Lugworm*, 'nobody has any right to be as happy as this!' And she dipped, and shook her mizzen, and laughed with me, for she, too, was feeling the roll of deep blue water again, and had caught a first sight of that incomparable sweep of coast down to Trevose, with Gulland and Newland set like emeralds in the amethyst sea.

We freed off to the west close under the daymark on Stepper, reached down past Butter Hole and headed for the blowhole at Tregudda Gorge, that great buttress of cliffs which has cracked off close north of Trevone. It was here I mined my first amethysts for an ill-fated engagement ring for Jo, and since you've been introduced you might as well know what befell.

You can get down to sea-level from the land at Tregudda Gorge, provided you're lithe as a mountain goat, young, and mad. As I say, it was for Jo I did it, before pitch-poling on the bar. We used to go courting out there on the clifftops, backalong, and I knew from past experience that at low tide springs it was possible to cross the bottom of the gorge by leaping from rock to slippery rock until you clambered on to the base of that vast chunk that has cracked away. There is a vein of quartz there, and if you are lucky you can find a bit of it that's beginning to turn blue. I called it amethyst, and Jo believed me.

'What's your favourite stone?' I asked her about a month after we met, and to show which way the wind was blowing. 'Amethyst,' she said, and that was that. Why fossick about with jewellers when you can mine the things all a-virgin on your own doorstep? So there we were one sultry noon at dead low water springs with a coil of spare halyard and a hammer atop the cliffs looking down into the gorge.

'Sure you want to come down with me?' I asked her.

'As long as you hold tight to the other end of that rope,' she replied, taking a cautious look over the near vertical cliff. So together we went to where a peculiar natural slope leads halfway down the cliff face, like a ship's gangway without any steps. After that—about sixty feet down—things get a bit difficult.

There are places to get a hold of, and cracks to jam a foot in, but you have to look hard for them.

It was fine to start with. Jo went first, a bowline hitched under her bosom, and I stayed a bit behind jammed firmly and keeping the rope taut so that in the event of mishaps there would be no disastrous jerks. But by the time we reached the end of the slope, Jo had got the wobbles. There was still a long way to go and the swell was booming into a gulley vertically beneath with terrifying power, launching a shower of rainbows just to leeward. It was fun.

'Sure you want to come on?' I asked.

'Expect it'll be all right after this bit,' she answered, glancing apprehensively back from where we'd come. But of course it wasn't. Things got progressively worse and it developed into one of those classic situations where the lesser of two evils is undoubtedly to go on straight into the jaws of Hell. Before we were near sea-level, Jo was a lump of raven-haired jelly.

'There must be some other way out of this,' she squawked above the roar, quivering on a ledge just out of the sea's reach. Along the narrow crack of the gorge the dark sea heaved and fell in predatory surges like some slow-breathing monster. Close under us the swell crashed in to send a million frustrated spouts cascading up the cliff face. The water close aboard was turned into soapsuds and everything was echoing damp.

'No,' I shouted. 'Tell you what, you stay right here and I'll go on across the gorge for the amethysts. Don't worry, we'll work our way back up in our own time, won't take long, the tide's turning anyway so I must be quick, just stay there darling.' I blew her a kiss and inched along the rocks to where the gorge was narrower. Farther in I could see the smooth rounded top of a boulder which broke surface occasionally some halfway across the gully. Two good leaps and a bit of luck, and that islet was mine for the mining. I got to a point from which I could lunge out and down on to the boulder, waited for the sea to breathe out again—and leapt.

It was like Yul Brynner's scalp with butter on it, that boulder. Perhaps I landed on it but I remember nothing save the sudden cold of the water beyond, and marvelling how deep it was so near to the cliff face. In I went, to the crown of my head, but I was wearing only the hammer so there wasn't much to worry about and being totally immersed it seemed just as sensible to carry on over as come back. By the time I'd swum to a convenient ledge the sea was breathing in again—up I was lifted, graceful as a bird—and seconds later the water was cascading from all around leaving me and the hammer high if not dry, scrabbling across the barnacles clear of the next surge. I looked back for Jo to give her a comforting wave, but the haunch of the islet hid her, and there was no time to waste.

I know that climb well. The southern flank of the islet rises in a sixty degree slope, then breaks into crags and crevasses higher up. The top of the slope is yellow with flashing quartz crystals—maybe it was the original fault line which broke away from the land, for the vein is quite exposed and, as I have said, if you search, there are pockets where the crystals turn mauve and bluish. If you search.

I searched. They're not two-a-penny those pockets, but I found one at last about halfway up and battered it to a powder trying to remove one tiny piece that might look like an amethyst. So I went up higher and found another in a small crack. Time stood still as I worked at that cavity. I hacked all around it, breaking away the incredibly hard rock and working in behind to prize off just one piece in a solid chunk, and eventually it gave in. I had a piece big as half a brick and it looked just like Jo's eyes. In a paroxysm of passion I scrambled up to the very top of the islet, lay full length and peered over the precipitous northern face. Down there, maybe a hundred and fifty feet below, a tiny figure was crouched against the cliff face. She looked oddly damp and paralysed. I waved and shouted but the booming seas below drowned my voice and anyway the dear girl was so shortsighted I doubt she could see the islet, never mind this palpitating dot on top. So I piled a few more chunks of stone on to the cairn I'd built there the summer before, just for good measure, and started back down, clutching the precious jewels.

Of course, the sea hadn't waited. In fact as I took stock of the situation it was evident that it had risen a few feet since my moist crossing, and really you'd be surprised what a difference a few feet can make. Asleep and heaving peacefully it had been when I floundered over, but now it was wide awake and yawning with breakers crashing into both ends of the gorge. Yul Brynner had sunk and every minute things were getting worse. Suddenly I felt cold.

There was now one place only to land on the cliff-face opposite—a narrow ledge that afforded handholds from which one might reach up and grasp a crack above it. From there, with luck, I could inch along hand-over-hand until my feet came within reach of a shelf. There was nothing else for it: clutching the hammer and stones in my left hand, I jumped.

Have you ever tried swimming with a hammer and a brick? They don't help. Lopsidedly I clawed across to the ledge and waited for a sea to lift me up. At the critical moment I grabbed the wet ledge, dropped the hammer, lost my hold and crashed back into that perishing dark water, shuddering now with the cold, but still clutching those precious stones. There seemed little else for it but to swim right along the gully toward Jo, hoping to gain a footing on the way. Halfway along I clambered out, teeth chattering, to claw and slither slowly under the cliff face, in a world that had suddenly grown twice as big, four times as cold, dark echoing and noisy to boot. But, at last, there was Jo, cowering exactly where I'd left her, drenched through from the spray and crying.

'Darling,' I gasped, appearing over the top of a slimy boulder, 'I've got them, they're beauti…'

'Ah!' she jumped, 'Oh… you… YOU WRETCH… you…' She was sobbing and spitting with venom all in one. I'd never before seen a woman really angry and scared stiff at the same time, and it was puzzling.

'You FIEND!' she sobbed. 'You've been hours. I'm drenched, and cold, and miserable, and frightened to death. I hate you… I thought you'd drowned… oh… JUST GET ME OUT OF THIS HELLISH PLACE!'

I showed her the stones.

'Oh, DAMN THE QUARTZ,' she croaked. 'Just get me out of here. It's all right for you—you're a man,' and she glared at me hard before adding, 'and an exhibitionist at that!'

So I got dressed and together we clambered somehow back up that cliff face, but we were both pretty depressed 'ere we regained the top. No, the amethysts were not a success. I can't remember which disintegrated first, the jewels or the engagement—but it was the bar that finished it all.

Never mind, I was coming up to that blowhole. It works only when the tide is at a critical level, and only then when a long swell comes running in from the north-west. Then Tregudda takes a really mighty breath—and bellows! It's awesome and deafening to watch. There's a subterranean cavern underneath amethyst islet whose entrance, on the seaward face, is just high enough to clear sea level at half tide. As is usually the case with these blowholes, the cave expands into a sizeable cavern inside, and at a certain sea level the air gets trapped as a heaving great swell rolls into the entrance—and you can guess what happens then. The pressure is enormous: all the power in that swell, baulked by the cliff, compresses the air inside the cavern and out it comes through the very top of the entrance with a blast like a hurricane. It roars as it comes, a deep sonorous organ note like the explosion of the foghorn on Trevose Head, and it squirts a geyser of water out with it for good measure! I tell you, it turns you into a jelly to get near when it's really enjoying itself, and the spume goes flying up the cliff face like some primaeval sea-monster's breath. Then it hisses and gurgles as the swell retreats and the air is sucked in again ready for the next performance. No place to be in *Lugworm* when that little frolic is on, I can tell you. But this day, as *Lugworm*, *Ben* and I headed down the coast, all was quiet—indeed the top of the cave was well beneath sea-level, being high water springs, so we just blew it a kiss and checked that the stone cairn was still up there atop the islet, and thought a bit about ravenhead.

So we reached down toward Trevone. But something was wrong with the weather. From a nice northerly that would have made bliss of a broad reach right down the coast, the wind had fallen away, dithered about a bit and set in a drift from the west, with little more than a sniff of north in it, if that. The sky, moreover, beyond the horizon to the westward looked like most westerly skies hereabouts—frontal and rain-laden. My heart sank. *Lugworm*, bless her, isn't the best of craft when working up to windward. She's built for seaworthiness and it's asking too much of her buxom shape and rig to expect her to cover much ground on a dead beat. The sensible thing was to anchor under the lifeboat station north of Trevose Head and wait.

Now, I must tell you that the tidal stream, close inshore between Stepper Point and Trevose Head, does peculiar things. It swirls round in a vast circle, the north-east-going stream begins by running northward, then swings east-north-east and finishes in an easterly direction at a rate of about one knot springs and half a knot neaps. The south-west stream starts roughly in that direction, then swings round toward the north-west, its greatest rate being attained when it's running south-west. I had counted on gaining the advantage of that westerly stream, but, as is

so often the case when rock-hopping within yards of the shore, found a contrary flow which, coupled with the now adverse wind, left *Lugworm* stooging about off Trevone with nothing save a raging appetite to goad her on to an anchorage, so I brought her alloy topsail into use and chugged at a steady four knots under the Mercury outboard, skirting south of Pollack rock (which is a thing I'd never do when there is much swell running) and brought up close under the new lifeboat slip.

It's a grand anchorage this. The prevailing south-westerlies can ramp and roar and churn the seas into frothy pea-soup, but you're O.K. snugged under the high ground to weather. Provided you're well clear of the launching slipway, all is well, but mark that: for when that lifeboat rattles down the slip it stops for nothing and the bow wave alone is enough to capsize a tiddler if she's too close. At anything but highest of springs there's a sweet little beach at the foot of the cliffs where one can while away pleasant hours sunbathing with a maid. Mind you, it's no place to be caught when the wind turns east!

On this occasion, however, something alien was in the air. At first I couldn't make out quite what was afoot, but gradually I located the seat of it. The seabirds which normally nest on the off-lying rocks just north of the slipway were whirling in a cacophony of distress. Now this, while to be expected if one starts clambering about the rocks, is most unusual when you're half a mile off. Something was wrong, and I was examining the area through the glasses when I first caught a whiff of the trouble—a faint but horrifying smell of corpse. This, coupled with the activity of the birds, was puzzling, for the air hereabouts is sweet as nectar. No sooner had I dropped anchor just clear of the lifeboat buoy, than *Ben* was alongside and taking me over to the tip of beach which was showing with the first of the ebb. You can't flirt with rocks in *Ben*—one glance from a barnacle and she's sunk—but I gave her a stout protective wooden strip of keel that allows her to be dragged up beaches—provided she's held level.

So off to that craggy outcrop I hied, agog with curiosity, and swam across the insulating gully of water which makes it such a favourite breeding ground for the herring gulls, being out of reach of marauders generally. But I could wish I had not. No sooner was I climbing the fifty-foot crags than tragedy declared itself. Newborn chicks and mottled youngsters just ready to take wing were lying dead by the score, evidently rotting a week or so, for the stink was unbearable; and out

in the bay the parent birds continued to set up a dismal wail of alarm and despair. To this day I don't know the cause: rogue black-backs possibly, but unlikely in such wanton massacre proportions. Man more likely, but pollution most probably, for none of the chicks appeared to be mutilated. Anyway, I collected as many as I could reach and threw them into the sea to reduce the smell, but the event cast a sad air of gloom over the day, and I was glad to get back up to weather in *Lugworm* and rig the tent, for the sky was turning grey.

With the ageing day came rain, and a freshening westerly. It drummed on the tent like a machine-gun, and *Lugworm*, caught by the swirls of wind bowling over the cliffs, chuckled as she ranged about, until I lowered the heavy metal centre-plate which kept her steady and more or less head-to-wind. It's good to be inside her in this sort of weather. With the stern flaps wide open she remains quite dry under the tent, for as I have said the wind and rain sweeps past no matter from what direction, for the boat always lies bow-to-wind. You can sit for hours just watching the changing scene as she slowly describes an arc, bringing now this, now that bit of coast or sea within view. Come darkness, you light the candle and brew up some supper on the small camping stove, then wash it down with a strong coffee laced with a tot of something to keep the warmth in; and there's the stars, and perhaps the moon, sweeping across your real live cinema screen out of the stern.

But I remember as that afternoon wore on the rain increased and a dismal swell started rolling into the bay, residue of the previous day's northerly wind, and since I was anchored in little more than six feet of water at low tide it was feeling the bottom and throwing *Lugworm* about quite a bit. I don't mind this all that much, considering it better than being farther out where there was somewhat less swell but a deal more wind and sea; so there I was, listening to the rain, curled up in my sleeping bag and *Ben* sinking fast under the deluge, when disaster smote. I'd set off without my hairbrush! I'd also left behind a spare can of petrol, a tin-opener, and my metric chart of the Scillies, but these were minor details; the hairbrush brought me up all standing. An itchy scalp is one thing I can't stand before breakfast and I've got one of those splendid rubber padded things with bristles like steel: the day begins with it. Truly it was a disaster.

Ashore, the swell was now booming against the cliffs just south of the slipway and the surf around the bay eastward was fit to turn a sailor into a bath attendant; no place to land in *Ben Gunn*, and lifeboat beach is inaccessible save from seaward, so telegrams were out of the question. I'd sunk into one of those blank states of mental absence which only real sailors can achieve hour after hour with the boat all but standing on her head when a deep-throated roar penetrated the gloom. Squinting through the tent flap I saw the fangs of a high-powered cruiser bearing down on me. It drew abreast, throttled back, and started a hideous *pas de deux* with *Lugworm*.

'What the hell are YOU doing here—trouble?' came the hail. It was friends.

'You bet,' I roared back at them. 'I'm outward bound for the Scillies, but I've forgotten my hairbrush. Tell B.' They looked at me as though I were some sort of phenomenon, then throttled up and flew off into the pall. Fine friends!

Next dawn found me just lying there itching and listening to the thunder of rain when that familiar roar hove up again. A heavy object skeetered into the tent and the roar was just an echo before I'd split my sleeping bag. I picked up the parcel. Inside was a tin of beans and my hairbrush. That's what I call friends! There were also five separate letters from B. all in capitals: IDIOT. On the back was a big cross which made me feel much better.

The tide was ebbing, the rain had stopped, and since my scalp had stopped itching there was nothing to prevent *Lugworm* spreading her wings again, except a total absence of wind. So I stepped her masts, set the mizzen to help digestion and lowered the outboard. Together we puttered off westward with *Ben* in tow.

*   *   *

If you don't stop to pick winkles you can just about fetch St Ives from Trevose on a fully stretched ebb. But my scalp had accounted for nearly an hour of that tide, and when a brisk westerly began to draw breath we still had some twelve miles to go, and the seas were wearing that certain look.

'It's Godrevy or bust!' I encouraged *Lugworm*, thinking we could gain a lee under the islet on which the lighthouse stands, for we could make it out some eight miles ahead. With the wind bang on the nose I knew it was engine or noth-ing, but set all sail just to help—which is why, I suppose, after a sniff or two the blessed engine stopped. Dead cut and not a spark of life. We eased off a point to make the sails do all the work and first tack brought us up under the ruin of Wheal Coates Mine, Chapel Porth. We put about, and there we were all set back to Wales! Meanwhile the sea was, well, like any sea that's rubbing the wind up the wrong way: bouncy and wet. It was raining again, too, and morale was falling for I knew that before Godrevy we'd be bashing both wind and tide under sail alone—and there was no future in that. The alternative was a dismal run back to Newquay ten miles astern. Determinedly we put in a few wet tacks, close under the towering cliffs, and found ourselves looking at Portreath.

Now Portreath is a place I've never before in my life so much as noticed. On my chart it's not marked as a harbour, so it's had scant attention on previous pas-sages down this coast. But under the circumstances we were foraging about with greater interest than usual on shore; and there under the foot of a horrifying black cliff poked the end of a tiny stone mole! Moles generally mean holes, and any hole was acceptable rather than regurgitating all those hard-gained miles, so in we went, hell-for-leather on starboard, and freed off wonderfully just to make a show.

There were some dedicated fishermen on the end of the mole, and—have you noticed?—it's an odd thing, but shore-side fisherfolk seem to think that boats which come in from sea are ethereal things with no substance whatever, gossamer visions that can float through a cobweb of maggoty lines like a politi-cian through pre-election promises. We sheared that lot like a scythe but I was

far too busy ploughing into that dark and narrow crack between mole and cliff to more than note all the stomping about and frothing ashore. It was too shallow off that entrance for good health and a rapid build-up of seas was becoming far more alarming than the furore on the mole, for suddenly there was *Ben* up above me, balanced on the crest of a real thumper. He winked once, the fool, gripped the painter firmly between his teeth and surfed full pelt into *Lugworm*'s backside! I can tell you it was froth and pandemonium for a while, with nobody ashore trying to help one little bit.

But, of course, once within the lee there was nothing left bar the lolloping about with the sails flapping, so to ease the general tension I rowed mightily, following the line of that astonishingly long mole round a bend in the cliff which revealed a marvellously calm little basin, backed by yet another! It was just too good to be true, and I sang a little song as we gently took the bottom and started removing all the fishhooks, floats and trailing lines from *Lugworm*'s underparts. Nobody came to see us, so I dripped about in the rain and finally accosted a lonely traffic warden. 'Where do I find the Harbourmaster?' I enquired. He looked me up and down, blew his nose, and replied in fervent Cornish, 'There ain't been no 'Arbourmaster here since Lord knows when, back-along they was rummagin' for tin, shouldn't doubt!'

'Well,' I explained, 'I've just come into the harbour. Shouldn't I notify somebody, maybe?'

"Tell 'e what,' came the answer, 'go see old Jim down along the whelk stall, end of the car park there; e'll put 'e right.' And with a friendly pat he drifted off to book somebody.

Jim was stacking deckchairs disconsolately, the rain dripping off the ends of his moustache as I told him of my arrival. 'You'm in the 'arbour?' he asked with raised eyebrows. 'Yes.'

'Then you'm all right, then.' And he turned back to the chairs. Which seemed entirely satisfactory.

To be truthful I'm not really in love with that next bit of coast, some twenty-five miles down to Land's End. Nothing wrong with the coast—magnificent to look at—but from a dinghy it always gives me the impression of being, well, disinterested. Nothing to suggest it might help much if things went wrong. Those ghastly Stones a mile seaward of Godrevy, heaving and baring their teeth, and then the swollen knuckle of Cornwall's finger at Pendeen, where all the waters in the Bristol Channel sluice on the ebb round and out to the Western Approaches, as though Neptune had pulled the chain; it's enough to give you the willies, and a fine old turmoil it can knock up just north of the Brisons with nothing but the fangs of the Longships to chew any bits of you that may be drifting to oblivion.

Then there's Sennen Cove. I know all about Sennen, having spent a week drawn up with the crabpots while the harbour turned into a maelstrom: it's no place to be in a northerly or nor'easter, and bad enough in a nor'wester when there's any swell running. But you can't make the Scillies, twenty odd miles beyond the end of the Land, on one ebb from Portreath. So Sennen it was next day on the morning ebb with a congenial pint in The Old Success while the cistern filled up again with the flood, and it was late afternoon on the top of the tide that we were nodding with the Longships and waiting for the ebb to help us out to an empty horizon. A sweet nor'easter came ruffling down from Wales and the sun even smiled once or twice: it couldn't have been fairer if we'd rigged the heavenly computer.

For those who sail westward, Reality proffers her visiting card at the Long-ships. The finale of that play, already rolling to its climax, finally dissolves in a crescendo of spume and froth on those last off-lying reefs. Jagged and drowning under the onslaught, the iron jaw of the land flinches and gives slow ground before a relentless and ever encroaching sea.

The lighthouse rises, a monument to the changing of the scene. Behind, lies the hysterical half-real world of Man, totally wrapped in the Play, set at odds with the universe by his ego and diverted by his own shrewd activity. Ahead lies…?

So the magic begins there and the Overture is an orchestration of silence. For most surely as our ears throw off the clamour of shore, so gradually do they become aware of that stillness which is an absence of all artificial sounds, all hysteria, all pressures. Only then can we begin to listen. So we ghosted away from the land hand-in-hand with the ebb, and set course toward the southern shores of the group, for that way we knew we would carry a favourable stream for longer, and sail in less troubled waters than up northward of the isles.

'Have faith,' I said to *Lugworm*, for I sensed her apprehension as we headed for the empty horizon. 'Have faith, as I have faith in you, for we both know they are there, the islands, and we have but to trust our compass and the sea and the wind, and believe me, we shall arrive!'

So the sunlit hours passed. Astern, the world of man grew remote, and the lighthouse stood lonelier still, seeming to reach out as though yearning to voyage with us across that vast ocean whose edge it is condemned to watch—for ever. A single herring gull wheeled and circled, swooped and rose above *Ben* who was leaping and dancing astern, agog at the wonder of such a mighty sea, for the most he had known until then was the confines of the estuary and those frothing edges of the land; so slowly the evening light grew mellow, and the sea grew dark and still, and quietly gave us its promise to behave.

'*Buggerlugs*,' I whispered, for in moments of bliss such is the affectionate name to which she responds, 'Now there is nought but your thin skin 'twixt us and a merging back with that ocean from whence we both came, and to which we shall both, soon or late, most certainly return.' She chuckled quietly, for her soul understands these things, and above us the vast dome of the universe crackled into a thousand tiny points of starry laughter. It rippled down through the darken-

Author

Crew

Sennen Cove – no place to be in a northerly!
Lugworm with tent rigged, drawn up on the slipway.

ing eastern sky, and even Ben, doggedly biting on the painter in determination not to be left behind, seemed to wear a roguish grin as though he, too, were enjoying the thought.

So it was, there crept into us that gradual expansion of awareness which is beyond expression. Have you known this? Because I am a sailor I suspect such may only be experienced by mortal man when he is alone, under sail, in a very small boat on a very large ocean, and perhaps only in the timelessness of evening after the immediacy of day. Then, and even then only sometimes, may we drift upon reality all unsuspecting and glimpse her true expression.

The western sky took fire with a luminous green and the mirror edge of the sea over there burned the eyes. We voyaged in a dimension which is a hurt to mortal senses, and shadoward the sea grew dark, and *Lugworm*'s tan sails danced with their own ghosts in the moving water.

Three hours passed—what strange yardsticks we do use—three limitations of eternity took form, and northward against the luminous farewell rim of sky we saw the black silhouette of the Seven Stones lightship, and heard the sighing of the sea over that sunken continent of Lyonesse, and we floated in a world of half light, balanced delicately in a tension of in-between which spans polarity and gives rise to consciousness.

Lugworm was poised just midway between the light and the dark and stayed steady on that course, careful not to strain too much for the one nor the other, for as I have said, her soul understands these things and she knew that, at this time, to seek either in its entirety meant losing awareness of them both; and at another point in eternity we became aware of something other than sea and sky ahead. It was the daymark on St Martin's isle.

At first we both thought it to be the bridge of some supertanker, hull down, so bright did the tower gleam in the fading light. But it stayed on a steady bearing and grew clearer and nearer with the passing moments, and soon we could make out the sloping green top and bluff northern cliffs, and behind them the jagged outcrops of White Island, and shortly, beyond that, the boulder-hump of Round Island with the lighthouse sending its welcoming red beam every few seconds to greet us.

So calm was the sea, we altered a point northward straight for the daymark, and gradually the islands grew in form and size, yet faded in detail, for the night was nearly upon us. Slowly the Hanjague—stark eastern sentinel—drew closer, breathed gently with the lapping of the sea around its base, and slid quietly past to our south. The warm scent of the isles came powerfully to us as we crept north of Nornour, and the black silhouettes of Chimney Rocks stared, but passed no comment on our presence.

The wind finally bid us adieu under the rise of Brandy Point and the sails were already asleep as we rounded up under oars so as not to flout the silence. So it was that the gentle crunch of *Lugworm*'s keel on the sands of St Martin's came as both a sigh of content and an audible expression of thanks to the sea, and the wind, and the darkening sky, for a safe and perfect crossing.

CHAPTER II

THE SCILLIES

CAST A GLANCE AT THE CHART. You will see that the isles span a maximum distance of nine miles across their longest axis, roughly south-west/ north-east from Bishop's Rock lighthouse to the Hanjague. Depths decrease quickly from some seventy metres a mile or so offshore to a mere metre in the shallow channel which sweeps round north of St Mary's isle. At low water equinoctial springs, between St Martin's and Tresco in that area south of Tean, there is no water at all other than isolated pockets, and the same applies in the wider southern part of the channel between Tresco and Bryher.

When making the isles from the eastward, the main and obvious approach to Hugh Town, capital of St Mary's isle, is through St Mary's Sound which is buoyed and carries a minimum depth of ten metres in the channel. You sweep round south of St Mary's, thence northward and eastward into the harbour, which is well protected from winds in the southerly and easterly quarters, but no place to be in a northerly or westerly gale, for in the latter case, added to the obvious sea and wind hazards there can come a rolling great swell which makes life aboard quite unromantic.

Scillonian, the ferryboat which plies between Penzance and the group, makes her low-water approach by this means, but at high tide she and other craft often choose to enter through Crow Sound to the north of St Mary's. By far the best anchorage for deep-keel yachts, in my opinion, lies off New Grimsby Harbour on the western side of Tresco. Here there are minimum depths of 2.4 metres nearly as far south as the quay wall, and excellent protection from the prevailing winds and swell with a permanent exit channel at all states of the tide up northward when the weather serves. Admiralty metric chart number 34, scale 1:25,000 covers the whole group, and anyone attempting to navigate in this area without it is asking for trouble.

The range of the tide generally is around 5 metres (16.5 feet) at the top of springs and 2.3 metres (7.6 feet) at neaps, and the stream around the group is complex, directions swinging clockwise. High water at the isles may be taken at a

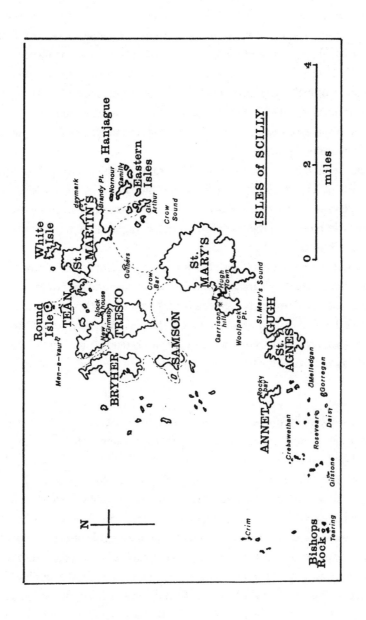

ISLES of SCILLY

rough average of five hours after high water Dover. At local high water the stream runs east-north-east then swings southerly, running roughly due south two hours after local high. Six hours after high (at local low water) it has swung generally in a westerly direction, swinging gradually up through north by three hours before the succeeding high water time, thereafter swinging gradually to an easterly set by the following high water. Such is the general flow around the group, but of course in between the isles a vast variety of directions is experienced depending on the configurations of the land.

Rates tend to be stronger north of the group, reaching four knots at springs just north of Tresco as opposed to around one and a half knots south of St Mary's, but in the narrows and over the shallows between the isles it can reach considerably more, and there are some fiendish races and overfalls up there off the northern shore.

For *Lugworm*, of course, with her minimum draught (plate and rudder up) of ten inches, virtually all areas of water are accessible provided there is no swell running, and she draws only eighteen inches with the outboard lowered. She is therefore the ideal craft in which to explore the isles, and there are few coves and grottoes that have not harboured her in the two extended summers I have spent there, camping aboard the boat.

*   *   *

That first morning after arrival, awakening with the rising sun, there came to me again a wonderful sense of wellbeing, of completeness, which islands always bring.

Lying in my sleeping bag on the cockpit bottomboards of *Lugworm*, I watched a rippling flow of reflected sunlight playing on the tent above. She was afloat—I could tell that, not from any lapping of water against the hull, but from the fact that she was on a level keel and the bright shimmering side of her tent would alternate first on port, then on starboard, as she swung slowly in an arc at the end of the anchor warp. Apart from this, we were in a motionless and soundless world, for there was no breath of wind, nor even the cry of a gull, so still was the dawn.

I lay there, watching the play of light for the best part of half an hour—which is the best way of waking up I know and guaranteed for putting you in fine affinity with Mother Nature and the whole world. After a while I raised myself on one elbow and peered aft through the open tent flaps. Two miles away, across a steel-bright mirror sea, the hump of Menawethan was silhouetted against the eastern horizon. Close northward and nearer, its southern flank part hiding Menawethan, was Great Ganilly, largest of the Eastern Isles. I watched awhile, willing *Lugworm* to swing her stern more southerly, and it seemed she must have sensed my wishes for very steadily my window on the world swung, scanning first a blaze of brilliance right beneath the sun and then taking in the humps of Little Ganilly, Great Arthur, Great and Little Ganinick, about half a mile away. There she stopped, the tent interior still irradiated with the direct rays and then gradually the stern swung slowly eastwards back towards Nornour.

'A north wind coming, if anything,' I told her, for she needs to know these things. 'That means we will have another day such as yesterday—and it'll be too good for wasting in the metropolis.' (A name we use when referring to Hugh Town, capital village of the isles).

Now I must tell you that over on the northern end of Great Arthur, there is a perfect little crescent-moon bay, fringed with a laugh of sand and flanked by granite boulders capped with Hottentot figs and marram grass. In fact it forms one side of a very narrow peninsula which joins Great Arthur to Little Arthur so that the two of them are really one island, though one should never tell them so. Only at very high springs does the peninsula become a shallow ford, with the stream swirling across and proclaiming aloud the lie to anyone who doubts their separate entities.

We know it as Hottentot Bay, on account of it being thick with *carpobrutus edulis*, or Hottentot fig, and the best place to go when it's really hot, for you can run around naked as an aborigine if you choose, so thick is it with the absence of other souls.

'It's Hottentot today,' I proclaimed. 'We've potatoes aboard, fresh water, tea-bags, and if we can't hook a pollack 'twixt here and there we'll know we're growing rusty in the art.' So I started sorting out the trolling lines.

By the time it was all shipshape, the tent rolled forward about six feet to expose the afterdeck and a bit of the cockpit, a billy of tea brewed and drunk, why, that sun was giddy with height and laughing down on the world with a promise of glory. Ashore the island was waking up. A tractor engine puttered into life and there were echoes of distant voices far away over the hill.

So we motored, pollackless, over to Little Arthur. The tide was just past high springs and beginning to fall fast. I eased *Lugworm* gently on the rim of the beach and hooked her anchor securely behind a boulder to hold her safe while the tide drained out, then stripped to the sun and set off on the first voyage of exploration of the season. Not, mark you, that there is a great deal to explore, for the full length of Great and Little Arthur together is little more than three cables and half that in width. But they had everything I needed that day; most of all solitude and peace.

I ran across the peninsula, over a heather-swarded saddle where a Bronze Age grave gapes emptily up to the sky, and on up the grassy slopes of its eighty-foot pinnacle, highest point in the isle. The air was like sea-wine, so clear and fresh did it cut the lungs, and the dew on the shady side of the hill was still ice-cold on my bare feet and legs. But sunward the rocks and heather and grass were dry and warm, full of promise of long lazy hours to come. I tell you, it was a morning to remember.

Three blackbacks, startled from their sleepy perch on a rocky outcrop, launched vociferously off, swung in a wide circle and settled over on the barren sides of Ragged Isle away to the east. A colony of cormorants, alerted at the gulls' flight, stretched their necks enquiringly on the southernmost tip of Arthur Head and eyed me with suspicion. But the danger was not immediate: they kept a close surveillance on my movements, decided the time for flight had not yet arrived and settled once more to drying their outstretched wings, holding their arms out wide as they faced what cooling breeze there was to evaporate any moisture between their feathers.

From the top of the islet I could see the whole panorama of the isles laid out. There was a white yacht anchored off the old Blockhouse on Tresco two and a half miles away; I could see the reflection of her hull shimmering in the sea over there, and the masts of local craft moored off Goats Point to the western end of St Martin's. Apart from that, the world seemed empty of folk, save me, which was just fine. I strolled back to Hottentot Bay, selected a soft grassy spot on the face of the dunes, inclined to the sun, took a blanket from the boat and settled down to enjoy the moment.

Have you ever listened to a small island waking up and adjusting to a hot summer day? It takes half an hour or so for the mind to empty itself. Round and round go the thoughts, darting out at a tangent, separating and taking 'you' off with them to environs quite out of harmony with the moment. But slowly it all subsides. You lie in the marram grass, breathing in the deep salty tang of its roots, with your eyes closed, and the warm sun glows gently hotter and hotter; a faint wind swirls down through the spiky fronds, caressing your skin all over; and silence takes the place of thought.

Silence.

So you gradually begin to hear it all. The whisper of grass above, where the marram fronds rustle in the air movement. A crackling nearby that's the very sound of growing things, stretching roots, splitting sheaths, and everywhere the faint awakening drone of insect life. At first it seems more like an overall murmur, unidentifiable until a singular quality of sound intrudes; a scratching, urgent, methodical, as a black beetle unburies itself from the landslide of dry sand you disturbed while fossicking about with the blanket. Out come the front legs, waving in strange fashion as though belonging to a mechanical toy. A delicate feeler emerges, followed by another and then a head. For a moment it holds still, save for the trembling of the two feelers, as though taking stock of this upper world again after the sudden shock of burial. Then the action begins in earnest, slow flailing legs work awkwardly at the sand, pushing the hard shiny body up, up, until at last completely emerged, it stands, sensing what's afoot. Now off it sets up a spike of grass—a hundred-and-fifty-foot tree, bending under its weight, falling scrabbling, on its back, a determined steady heaving of the heavy body as it prises at the shifting sand to right itself, and again the mechanical onslaught up the grass. What will it do, I wonder, when it reaches the tip? But it never does; it deflects along another spike and slowly makes off through the boles of the forest—after what? Why do I ask? Perhaps unknowing, it's completely content simply just being a beetle.

Somewhere down on the wet shingle of the peninsula, where the receding tide has forsaken it, a crab is scuttling. You hear its tiny 'plopping' like bursting bubbles—I'm sure crabs belch!—and the exposed weed, drying in the ever-increasing heat, keeps crackling and popping. The sound of a myriad winged insects forms a background to the play, and far distant there is the occasional strident call of a gull. A bee buzzes urgently past, there is the sudden startled flurry of wings as an oystercatcher, about to alight on the beach, sees this alien form and sheers off in surprise. But you lie perfectly still, merging into the isle itself, and gradually the wild things become accustomed to your intrusion.

A couple of gulls wing across, in desultory conversation. There is a steady zephyr wind now, flowing over the dune above you, swaying the grass in a moving green pattern against the pure blue of the sky, and the sand is warming up, absorbing and radiating back the heat. You turn over, exposing your back to the sun, burying your nose into the roots of the grass over the edge of the blanket, and breathe the pungent air deeply. Things get hazy in a warm cocoon of content.

Waking up is a surprise. Have you really been asleep at all? Or were you just partly switched off? There's a parched dry feeling on the back of your neck, down your back and in the soft part of the backs of your knees. You wriggle gently, stiff and aching from lying so long in one position, and slowly your limbs flow back to life. Up on one elbow, and the world is a blinding hurt, too bright to open the eyes fully. Everything looks flat and white in the brilliance. You feel like a lump of wood, stiff and hard-jointed. Slowly you grow more flexible as you sit up, on an alarmingly sore bottom, and there is Alphonse staring at you from a circular predatory gull's eye, turning his head first to get a view from the left, then the right.

He is the only large moving thing in the scene, apart from yourself. You continue to eye one another, in mutual curiosity.

'Morning, Alphonse.' He turns his head quickly sideways and brings the other eye into use, a degree of suspicion hovers about his pristine white and grey form.

'What's it like being a herring gull?'

He pecks himself quickly under one wing, then brings the other eye to bear: 'What's it like to be hungry? That's what it's like to be a gull!'

'Are you always hungry?'

'Always.'

'Life's one long search for food then?'

'Nothing but.'

'Boring?'

'Certainly not. It's never boring searching for food. Appetite is everything. Without appetite life would be pointless. With appetite you've got a purpose for living; assuagement of appetite. It's very satisfying, very pleasant; are you, then, so very different?'

I think about that. Somewhere far off in another world comes the drone of the morning helicopter from the landing pad on St Mary's. The tide has withdrawn, leaving the isles robed with a skirt of damp seaweed. It lies like drowned hair in long fronds over the top of the still water.

But Alphonse seems to be waiting for an answer.

'I've got intelligence,' I tell him.

'I've got instinct,' he counters. 'Instinct for survival—that's worth a bucket-ful of intelligence.'

'You miss the point,' I tell him. 'Intelligence can be more useful than instinct alone. Look at me, I'm a human. My brain is many times greater than yours. I can THINK. I have modified my environs not only to survive, but also to suit myself. I have tilled the land, tamed the face of earth, built up a technology that takes the slavery from mere existence. I'm capable of depths of sorrow, heights of bliss. Life for me is more than simple survival. It has subtlety, poignancy, exquisite deli-cacy of feelings. It's a rich tapestry of experiences. It's brought greater freedom of action –'

'Freedom to destroy yourselves,' Alphonse interrupted. 'You haven't learned when to stop.'

'To stop what?'

'To stop raping the earth, to control your own propagation and appetites. You think you're free, but you're in greater slavery than I. I have no problems like that, I leave it to nature, she takes care of it. With your so-called intelligence you've interfered with the order of things and you're exploiting your environs on a short-term spree. Using up earth fast. Is that intelligent?'

I thought about that.

'I'm not sure I like you much,' Alphonse continued. 'Things were fine before your species came along, and now look at it. Things are different in a sick sort of way, and getting sicker. As a species, you humans are a cancer in a limb of the universe. Grasping, overrunning, transforming everything to the exclusive advan-

Top: St Mary's harbour with French barquentine and baggywrinkle galore. *Left:* Alphonse in *Ben Gunn. Right:* ... even caught a thumping great pollack. *Below:* Hottentot Bay, Great Arthur isle with Nornour in the middle background and St Martin's on left

tage of homo sapiens in fine disregard for the balance of the total organism. Like a cancer you're thriving at a suicidal rate. Like a cancer you'll eventually kill the organism. I give you thirty years at the most, and you'll be the end of us all. Intelligent... huh!'

I thought about that too, and suddenly I was annoyed. I didn't want to look truth in the face this morning—I'd come to the isles to escape all that for a week or two and here was this blasted gull reminding me of it. I sat up and hissed. Alphonse squirted off.

It hurt, sitting up quickly like that. I'd overdone it a bit and roasted myself behind, but I can take any amount of sun, really, never peel much or go rotten, just brown. My father had malaria, blackwater, yellow water and every damned fever you care to name back on the Gold Coast and passed on to me some pigmentation in the skin that's burn-proof and gnat-proof. Mosquitoes loathe the smell of me: it's splendid.

Lugworm was high on the rim of the dried-out beach and roasting hot under the tent. I rolled back a foot or two of the canvas at the bow to allow a free circulation of air. Even *Ben*, upside down on a bank of Hottentot figs, seemed to be gasping: the day was turning into a scorcher. I stood on my head for a moment, just for fun and to get the blood recirculating, layered myself with sun-oil and took stock. Eleven a.m. and getting hotter: only one thing for it—fresh fish for supper! We had been unsuccessful on the trip across, so what better than a quiet, predatory hunt to pass away the stuporific hours; and wasn't *Ben* gasping for coolth? I hooked a fat juicy winkle, sorted out a line, carried *Ben* down to the bottom of the bay and pushed him quietly off, careful to soften any sharp sound of oar on rowlock. Outside the entrance of the bay the weed strung out in twenty-foot streamers, like green mermaid's hair trailing on the surface. The bottom, five feet down, was a limpid world of wonder: tall trees waved softly above fields of water ferns, deep pools of shadow harboured ghost shapes that dissolved by the mere act of inspection.

Have you ever lain timeless in a coracle-skiff with your nose half an inch above the mirror surface, drifting silently with the stream, your eyes probing down into the quivering green cool littoral below? You haven't? A pity. It's magic. Like floating in a silent balloon, peering down on a fantasy landscape, you drift effortlessly

above the filmy transluscent tops of green forests. Shafts of light, toned from surface brilliance to muted blue-green depth, sink down into fields of levitating forms,
spreading their many coloured shapes to catch the life-giving light. Gossamer-thin
curtains of opaque green hang undulating slowly in the stream. Devoid of brute
gravity, forms akin to those ashore float in serene weightlessness. Here there is, in
microcosm, the towering conifer, but its trunk is glowing gold and the tips of its
needle branches radiate pale-blue light. Cliffs of pink and cream rock drop from
immeasurable heights to bottomless pits of dark nothingness, their crevasses holding the tenacious fronds of some strange aquatic gorse, and here, from a dense
undergrowth of gently waving tendrils, come the boles of pampas grass. But their
cylindrical trunks do not branch or taper, but rise like thick snakes up… up… up
from the depths to within an inch of your nose, and then, at the extremity of their
supporting world, turn and bask, yard after yard of them, on the sea's face.

You hold your breath, so as not to stir the window surface and destroy the
clarity of this magic world, and gently, as you drift away from the shore, the forests recede. Deeper, darker, the colours fade and the forms become strangely
more primaeval; thick rubbery arms clutch up at you from dark gorges, their extremities spreading into grotesquely frill-fingered hands of mauve-brown kelp.
Macabre contorted roots, spotted, twisted and fungoidal peep through the leathery foliage, and… AH!

A movement. Quick, dartlike, you see movement down there beneath those
slimy leaves. Carefully you ease an arm over the side of *Ben*, squeeze a trailing
line of the green mermaid's hair, and wait. The hairs gently incline, tauten, and
you are anchored, moving now silently through the water but motionless over the
bottom. Yet even that slight, scarcely detectable tautening of the trailing weed has
transmitted an alarm. A swirl of water in motion betrays the flight: yet you see no
fin, nor shiny scale, simply the quick kick sideways of one small frond of weed
down there near the roots. That is all. So somewhere nearby, the cause of it is still
there, waiting, hiding in the water forest, and you watch.

Ben's shadow shafts down on the kelp. It has an etheric aura of blue lining its
rim, a halo of light caused by some freak of refraction, as his movement against
the stream forms a tiny ripple. This, too, must be signalling an alarm. But so long
as it stays constant, without change, the alarm systems will cease. You lie still as

the floating weed, and watch. The sun is burning hot on your back but the oil is doing its work, soothing the slight soreness. Somewhere up and far away, beyond the rim of your present world, an urgent beat startles the silence. The sharp rapid slap of wings on water. A cormorant eases its ungainly form into the air. You don't move; this is a natural sound that will not trigger off any alarms, but one thought-less twitch on your part and the quarry will be gone. Minutes pass. Your sight wan-ders slowly through the weed, looking without looking, as though the mere fact of concentration will somehow transfer itself to alert the sensitive form below.

Then you see it!

A shape, dark and smoky brown, the exact colour of the kelp. Isn't that a head? You scan the form of it, motionless down there, and there is something too regu-lar in the matching of those slight bulges, one at either side. Are they not eyes? A faint, scarcely discernible rhythmic expansion and contraction—the gills quietly working. A pollack? The long body is hidden back in the kelp roots; what size is it? Difficult to guess, size is misleading under water, but well worth catching.

A tingle of excitement runs through every fibre of you as quietly, slowly, with-out any jerks, you lower the winkle-baited hook. It streams infuriatingly away with the tide, then gently filters down toward the kelp. There's a tiny lead weight about two feet from the hook. You let it reach the bottom, keeping your eyes on the winkle, then gently ease it up a little, jigging it very, very gently up and down. The winkle lifts and falls, dancing down-tide from the weight. Pollack is aware of all this, but lying doggo, still as the weed roots.

You jiggle on. About six feet up-tide he's watching, curious. Can he smell it? Can fish smell? How well can they see? Will he see the line? You keep your arm inside the boat, so as to throw no moving shadow down there. Your neck is stiff with the effort of watching, motionless. Nothing happens. You jiggle on. He's watching, too.

Watching!

Your left hand is cramped with holding the weed, your arm aches with the rigidity but you dare not make a single twitch. Sound travels through water too well: he'd be off. This is the critical moment... he's being lulled. Nothing is happening and that means safety. You watch those gills, hypnotic in their gentle expansion and contraction. Are those eyes looking at you? How does a fish see?

He's alert, that's for sure: something in the way he's holding himself tells you that. Is he aware of that winkle? Strange: he's growing in size as you watch. Jumping Jeesups it's a whacker! He hasn't moved, and yet now you can see the whole dark, almost transparent lithe line of his body; he's drifting out of the weed. Drifting? Against the stream? Now you can see how it happens, a faint, slow swing of the tailfin and that electrifying form glides without appearing to glide, then, still as a drifting log begins to sweep down with the tide toward winkle. Not a movement, not a suggestion of motion anywhere, just a dark line of intensely alert, curious fish. There's obviously something odd about that winkle. I send a telepathic command singing down the line: 'Come and eat me... come on, I'm the best dinner you've set eyes on for...' Quick, quicker than the eye can see he's flashed across stream, and the line's singing away. I gasp, grab the line and heave. There's an electrifying, galvanising jerk... and slackness.

Sod it. I pull in the empty hook. Sodsbleeding bodkins, after all that, and he got away with a free dinner. Must have been ten pounds if an ounce. Maybe twenty. How big do pollack grow? Was it a pollack after all, was it, perhaps, a dogfish? Or a small shark? Enormous! Quivering with tension and frustration I grab the oars and row violently back, glad to feel muscles moving again. As I close the bay, a flock of herring gulls lifts from *Lugworm*'s afterdeck; Heathen Furies, they've been at my bread! I left a loaf on the sidedeck and it's reduced to a battered heap of crumbs. Dammit, and I bet that was Alphonse at the head of them. One up to Alphonse!

We learn. We learn to cover a catch of mackerel with a bucket if we leave the boat untended, or they'll be gone, and serve us right, for it's all part of the game of survival. We have intelligence, we ought to know these things.

But it's not so bad. There's another loaf in the locker and a bottle of yellow plonk with a simply magnificent label to wash down the cheese and sardines, and all afternoon to sleep it off in the sun—on my back.

So early evening drifted in. With it came the rising tide, and *Lugworm* soon swung at the end of her warp again. We motored across to Higher Town to arrange for fresh milk, place a request for a loaf of bread (if one extra could be made at the next bake) and retreated back to Great Arthur.

On the way we land a fine mackerel.

Only the stars are competing now with the red glow of my driftwood fire. Its flames throw a dancing light on the boulders close about, and *Ben* is propped to windward, a shield from the cool night air. *Lugworm*'s tent is a faintly lighter patch out there in the bay, swinging gently on the end of her anchor warp, and my Aburöken smoker is turning that mackerel into the most exquisite tasty morsel a vagabond could pray for! The billy of potatoes is nearly ready and the pungent scent of the oaken sawdust under the mackerel vies with that pure fresh wholesome smell of the burning logs. A silence has fallen on the dark world. Its borders have blended into the infinity of night, and I'm alone in a cocoon of orange flickering light, with all summer ahead.

A good first day in the isles?

Oh yes, it could have been worse!

*   *   *

'What, or who, precisely, determines whether a pile of guano-covered rocks shall be just rocks, or island?' I asked the bearded piratical character in the Mermaid Inn about a week after arriving in Hugh Town. Through the window I could see a three-masted French barquentine anchored out in the roads. Square-rigged on the foremast, and fore-and-aft rigged on the main and mizzen, she was flying the Red Ensign courtesy fashion from the starboard yardarm and had baggy-wrinkles galore on the topping lifts. It lifted the heart to see her, the beauty. A score or so of smaller French and English plastic yachts of all shapes and sizes were dotted about, making a fine colourful showing, and I could see the Harbourmaster clearing a berth for *Scillonian*, due in within half an hour.

The pirate looked at me hard, took a swig from the pint pot, wiped his beard, and said nothing. But I wasn't to be fobbed off with strategy.

'It says here,' and I prodded a leaflet on the Scillies in my most belligerent manner, 'that there is an isle for every day of the year. That makes three hundred and sixty-five islands. It seems about three hundred too many by my reckoning. Who exactly determines what's an island and what's a rock?'

He slammed the pint pot down with a bang. 'Me and you,' he hissed.

'Then so far as I'm concerned,' I countered, 'Guthers out there is a rock, not an island.'

'That's right, Guthers is an island.' So we drank to the wisdom of it and I wandered off down the quay where *Lugworm* was being jostled by a pert plastic pimp of a boat with pale pink sails. She looked uncomfortable. A brisk northerly was making things merry in the harbour, burgees were a-chatter and crews alert. Up to windward Tresco looked green and washed, the long white sweep of her southern strand like a Cheshire-cat grin snug in the lee of the isle. A group of youngsters were fishing from the very tip of the quay on Rat Isle and we hoped together unproductively for a few moments, until the distant hoot of *Scillonian* wafted me out of now into a far away then.

*   *   *

I have a soft spot for *Scillonian*, and for a very good reason. It was aboard her, twelve years ago, that I first set eyes on B. We had both come to the isles for the first time, by way of a desperate attempt to escape from a problematical way of life in which we were getting enmeshed. It was early March, 1962, and bitter cold. *Scillonian* was berthed at Penzance and I was roaming the south coast rather aimlessly. Seeing her there I decided to come across for a couple of days just to get even farther away from everything. I remember thinking the ship looked a bit dreary and forlorn against the cold grey stones of Penzance quay that morning and the gangway, making an alarming angle down on to her afterdeck, was groaning morbidly.

A figure in a ghastly puce coat was feeding two dirty swans with stale railway sandwiches from a paper bag. I lumbered down the gangway, walked around the deck a few times, only to find the ship apparently deserted except for that solitary form. I sidled up.

'They look a bit dejected,' I said, to raise the tone of communication.

She didn't even look at me. 'Not hungry,' said a soft female voice. And that was that. End of conversation. I wandered off to look for the saloon, but it was locked until sailing time in an hour or so, and altogether things were a bit dismal. Out of a steely grey sky, a penetrating north-easter was sweeping through the town and across the harbour, investing the sea with that icy indifference to all living things that such conditions can. I was cold, and getting colder. The puce coat was still leaning over the taffrail aft, looking at the swans. But I felt my presence didn't bring any joy there: something in the tone of voice, the unconcealed indifference, warned me to keep my distance. I set to walking briskly round the decks, down the long, covered, dark colonnade between the ship and the dripping quay wall, across the foredeck, up the brighter colonnade on the side away from the quay, and across her after-deck. Round and round. Round and round. I started counting the steps, up one side, down the other. Then, to break the monotony, started counting the steps walking backwards. It's astonishing what a difference the length of a backward step can be.

A discreet cough.

There, at the far end of the weather colonnade was an embarrassed puce coat, walking towards me. I know exactly what was going through her mind. 'Must be well over thirty, if a day. Seemed quite normal, what a tragedy. Wonder what eventually tipped the balance. Just act as if everything is OK. There'll be a few more people aboard in a moment and it'll be quite all right…'

I turned, and started walking in a forward direction down the long colonnade towards her. Have you ever actually walked slowly down a long colonnade toward a solitary person who is walking slowly toward you down the same colonnade? At first you pretend to be oblivious of each other. You look over the side, up in the air, at your watch, scratch behind your ears, tie your shoelace, and they do exactly the same, in different order. The inevitable thing is that when finally you glance at them to see whether they're looking at you, they're always glancing at you to see if you're looking at them!

It's something to do with our social upbringing, and vanity. You see it when two strangers meet at a party without introduction — always slightly embarrassed because neither knows the correct conventional groove to slot into — the correct rules to be observed with the total 'stranger'. But I had the advantage here: I knew she was convinced I was mad. I played on it, unfairly perhaps. I locked my eyes on to hers, and simply kept looking into them as we approached each other. At first she followed the conventional pattern of averting her own gaze instantly, whenever it met mine, but as my unconventional manner was imprinted on her attention things began to change. Her eyes stayed looking into mine. She stopped walking. They narrowed a little, peering; I continued walking slowly toward her. An aura of real alarm now emanated from her, masked instantly by a conscious effort to appear natural again. But of course it was no good. The poor girl began to dissolve into open panic.

'It's quite all right,' I laughed. 'No need to be alarmed, I'm almost normal really, just bored stiff, and wishing the bar was open. It looks as if we're to be the only two passengers to the isles today!'

The relief was good to see. Obviously, though perhaps not exactly 'normal', I was, possibly, not exactly 'dangerous' either. At that moment the clank of feet on metal steps lumbered up from somewhere in the nether regions of the ship. A key turned in the public saloon door down the corridor and a face peered out. 'Aha!' I bellowed. She jumped. 'Coffee?' said the face. I swept her into the saloon.

After that things were better. *Scillonian* eventually bumbled out from the quay, set her bows seaward, and the land began to recede astern. It was biting cold. So far as I can remember we were the sole passengers, but my perception may have been narrowed somewhat by events. We settled down in the lee of the port side on one of those peculiar seafaring seats of slatted bars that have strange galvanized tanks built beneath them. I've often wondered what the psychological effect would be after a traumatic maritime disaster to float about the oceans of the world on a buoyant park seat.

I looked at her. She was a bit thin, worn and pale. She had a sort of fishing-net cap in off-white wool pulled down over her ears and there were mouse-coloured curls with flecks of blonde in them pushing out here and there round the rim. The collar of that hideous Victoria-plum coat hid her neck and she wore a pair of black woollen gloves and Wellington boots over corduroy trousers. She looked desperately tired, and rather miserable, but there was something about her eyes that caught you, something transparently real, frightfully vulnerable, completely honest. Something that said, without speaking one word to me, 'Look, I know you're bored stiff, I know I'm the only bird on the boat and you wouldn't look at me twice if there were a selection. In a way I'm grateful for your attention because it's always pleasant for a woman to receive the attention of a man, but just now, I'm not in the running: I'm tired and fed-up and want a bit of solitude. Please don't pester me.'

I understood. There was, however, a point on which I would have disagreed with her had she said that in so many words. In any company, in any crowd, those eyes and my reactions would have been the same.

So we crouched on the slatted seat with our backs against the white-painted cabin side and looked across that endless grey sweep of Atlantic, and a sleety drizzle that was turning to snow began to sweep horizontally across the sea. The smoke from dear old *Scillonian*'s funnel drifted away from us, mingling with the sleet, and our world was enormous, drear and grey.

'Never mind,' I said, after a bit. 'I always remember that when things start badly, by simple law of chance, they'll almost certainly improve! Are you going to be on the island long?' I was almost afraid to ask, for the last thing I wished was to be a nuisance.

She didn't smile. 'A week—and you?'

'Couple of days at the most, I think. I've not booked in anywhere; counting on the guest houses being empty at this time of year. Are you fixed up?' Was this being a nuisance? She could always switch me off with a rebuff.

'Yes, I'm booked in at—hmm! Forgotten the name of the place, but I've got the address somewhere. It's on St Mary's, but I've never been there before so it's all a bit of a pig in the dark...I mean a...a...'

'A pig in a poke,' I said. She laughed. Oh, this was better. I remember suddenly a rift in the grey pall moved across the sun's face, and a heartwarming shaft of light picked out the snowflakes against the grey sky and waves. It was unbelievably beautiful. Thousands upon thousands of flecks of glowing light drove over the face of the sea. I got up and looked to weather away from the sun. 'Gosh,' I called to her, 'look—quick!'

Two concentric half circles of diffuse colour—one of the most perfect double rainbows I've ever seen—arched from the dark face of the sea up against a thunder-black sky and down again. We stood together looking at it. 'Do you know,' I said, 'you're not seeing the same rainbow as I; everybody sees a different rainbow because their eyes are in a slightly different position in relation to the refracted light.'

There was a long silence. She was standing beside me, and the two of us were huddled against the sleet, our faces into the wind.

I knew she was looking at me. For the first time, really looking at me, and all my life I shall remember what she said.

'I think that's a pity. I wish you hadn't told me that—anyway, it's beautiful just the same.'

Scillonian rumbled on. The sun withdrew, the sea closed in all round us and we began to roll as she eased out from the lee of the Cornish peninsula, out into the long swell mountains that undulate through the channel between the isles and the Land's End.

Two hours later we were both glad when she got into the lee of the group. Dark and uninviting they looked, a ragged black line etched on the horizon up to weather, but they kept that mountainous swell at bay, and the old ship held herself more steady as we swept into the entrance to St Mary's Sound. The quay at Hugh Town was deserted except for a few lorries stacked with island produce, waiting to be loaded. *Scillonian* shunted back and forth, the lines snaked across and the gangway clattered down. She stood with a huge suitcase against the ship's rail. I had a small grip holding nothing more than towel, swimsuit and a couple of jerseys.

'No transport?' I queried.

'No. But I don't think I need it anyway. My lodgings are in Hugh Town somewhere, so it can't be far.'

She struggled down the gangway, and dropped the case at its foot. It had stopped snowing, and the cloud was breaking up but the wind was even stronger, keeping the gulls aloft, screaming in derision at we shivering mortals. She picked up the case again in the other hand.

This was the critical moment. I had to come right out in the open and put my cards on the table. 'Look,' I said. 'Believe me, the last thing I would wish is to force my attention on you or be a nuisance. But please let me carry that case into the village—to your lodgings, wherever they are. When we get there, if you'd rather, I'll buzz off and find somewhere for myself. If you really don't care either way, I'd like to book in where you are staying, if they have room.'

She looked at me, and I looked at her. 'Thanks for being so honest, and for the offer. I like both the ideas.'

It was a devil of a long way to the lodgings. Right through the town and up the hill and that case wasn't light. She carried mine, I carried hers, and guess which one of us was sweating before we arrived. There was room at the inn. The sun had come out in a light washed sky and the wind was blasting the islands dry. We walked that afternoon round Garrison Hill, the promontory just west of Hugh

Lugworm in Tean Bay, LW, Hedge Rock on right, St Mary's in background

Ben gets a refit on Tean; paintbrush is made from old rope!

'Boat's in a dreadful state' she said;
Lugworm on Goats Point, St Martin's isle

Town. It was exciting, following the old garrison walls, looking down the dry moat of Star Castle Hotel, the Elizabethan fortress built in the form of an eight-pointed star. Stretched on the grass at Woolpack Point, we listened to the haunting toll of the bell buoy on Spanish Ledges. The sea rolled white-capped and laughing out of the Sound, and we were strangers, and far away from everything and happy.

How do you get to know another person? Are you searching all the while? Not consciously, I think. Was I aware even then that her hands fascinated me? The long thin fingers, the slim delicacy of the palms and wrists? She was tall and slim this girl, with strong bold eyebrows in an intelligent face. A Londoner, on the editorial staff of a magazine… BA at Durham… all the qualificational paper trappings to efficiently wrap-up a splendid twentieth-century 'career'. A fine intact shell complete. But somehow, as she said afterwards, at that time the kernel seemed to be missing.

That first afternoon was the only sun we saw. The weather broke during the night, and breakfast next morning was dawdled over to the rattle of rain on the windows and the howl of a near gale. We took a packed lunch and set off in jeans and oilskins for Peninnis Head, extreme southern tip of St Mary's.

I remember sitting in the lee of a granite monolith looking across to St Agnes and Gugh. The screaming demented wind had swung to the south-east, driving a seething mass of grey spume up the sound. An awe-inspiring swell had built up, crashing in terrible fury on the Bow and Spanish Ledges. The southern flank of Gugh was drowned under solid sheets of water. Westward we could hear the power of it thundering over Carrickstarne rocks, and the headland itself seemed to shake to the onslaught. 'This is exceptional, even for Cornwall,' I told her. It was dry under the overhanging bluff, but the sky was a fury of shredded cloud and the wind was rising still. That was 7th March 1962, and I doubt the islanders will forget it. By noon a full hurricane was blasting the group; *Scillonian*, trapped and with double warps rigged, heaved uneasily in the lee of the mole. The quay at Penzance was unusable due to the end of it being smashed and toppled into her berth. No helicopter could get airborne. Telephone communication was cut. We crawled on hands and knees against the fury of it over Peninnis Head, working our drenched way along the weather shore, scrambling and sliding down grassy slopes, cowering behind great bluffs of granite, rolling in sheer excitement and exultation at the power of the wind.

But alas the tide was rising. A sea such as was running that evening does little damage when it drives to death on the lower rockstrewn extremities of a shore, but at high water it's a different story. The swell, rolling in from open sea, builds up in height as it feels the shallowing bottom, rears as it approaches the land, and crashes in devastating power at the very highest point of the beaches. In its path lay Old Town, with a stout protective sea wall running round part of the little bay. By evening it was carnage. The wall itself had cracked, hammered by hundreds of tons of driving solid water, and then, undermined, it had broken up completely. The road through Old Town became a river of rushing water. Roofs were torn off. Sandbags were filled and all emergency crews brought into action. At Porthcressa Beach the seas washed clean across the peninsula, flooding the shops and houses in Hugh Town and sweeping small craft through into the grassy Park in front of the Town Hall.

There was, thank heaven, no loss of life, and the islanders swung to with a will to clear up the mess, but still the wind kept up its wild dirge. On the third day of the storm we walked the entire coast of St Mary's, and I remember, when it came on to rain again, taking shelter in an eroded section of a low cliff near Bant's Cam looking across toward St Martin's. We tried to get a driftwood fire going, but the wood, grass, and air itself was soaked. The isles lay bleached with wind and water.

Often I wonder whether we would, but for that gale, have found time to explore each other's minds as we did. Five days we were marooned on St Mary's, walking the isle, drenched and battered by those winds, and finally *Scillonian* got the 'all clear' from Penzance. On the sixth day we re-embarked.

I left her at Penzance railway station. 'No sentimental partings,' we agreed. 'Particularly not on railway stations.' So we said good-bye. 'Write if you get time.' 'Thanks for a wonderful five days.' 'See you again, of course—sometime in town.'

All that... and all that... So I went to collect my car. It was the end of a strange, oddly disturbing five days, and suddenly, as I drove through the town, I felt desperately, unbelievably, lonely. I stopped at a garage to top up the tank, and before I swung out of the forecourt the decision was made. Back through the town I drove hell-for-leather down to the docks area and pulled up adjacent to that wall that separates the higher road from the station down below. I jumped from the car, ran to the wall and peered down. A train was in; but was it hers?

Desperately I scanned the platform. It was deserted except for a couple of station staff. Obviously the train was within seconds of starting. Then I saw her. She was leaning on the open sill of a door looking down at the platform. I sprinted along the pavement until I was opposite, and called. As I did so, the guard blew his whistle. She didn't hear me. I called again. She looked up and saw me, and the train was moving off.

'B.' I yelled, running to keep abreast. 'Would you marry me if I asked you?'

The train gave a deafening blast of sound. She was still looking up at me as I ran along that wall top. I saw her lips moving but could hear nothing. But she was smiling. Had she understood?

I just stood there, watching that train trundle her away with an ear-shattering hoot; and here was old *Scillonian* nosing in from the Sound, shunting back and forth. The lines snaking out and the gangway rumbling down.

*　　*　　*

The telephone box below Castle Gate was draughty and far from soundproof. 'B.,' I said, '*Lugworm* needs you.'

You don't stay in St Mary's Port with a northerly spanking in, not in a small boat, anyway, for there are far better places to be. I kissed the phone good-bye, bought a pint of milk and rowed out in *Ben* to unship *Lugworm*'s tent and step the masts. Then we weighed and motored up to Tean, halfway between St Martin's and Tresco.

Of all the isles, Tean is my favourite, for it's inaccessible at low water in any normal craft, and I can let *Lugworm* dry out near the top of the tide and know she's safe, come hell, 'till next high water—and the isle is mine. Uninhabited, it's under half a mile in length, but affords a splendid lee no matter from what direction storms may come. Tean Sound, a narrow gully some four and a half metres in depth, divides the isle from Goats Point on the western extremity of St Martin's and it's not more than a cable and a half across, so in good weather I can easily make it under oars in *Ben*. The other way—westward across to Tresco—things are a bit more difficult. There's a jawful of jagged teeth ready to chew you to bits if you don't know the channels. The walls of a ruined cottage stand on the south shore of Tean, and I berthed up in the bay there beneath them for the night.

Dawn found the northerly breathed away, and a still calm day forecast, so for fun *Ben* and I rowed round the isle's west shore, then struck north for Round Island, for I had a whimsey to see the Lighthouse and pass the time of day with the keepers. It's not more than a mile and a good flex of the muscles up through St Helen's Gap, past the sightless cadaver of the isolation hospital where the unfortunate crews of sailing craft in old times were put ashore with fever. Across the 'Pool' and round Didley's Point we skimmed, *Ben* with a bone in her teeth, eager to close the Camber Rocks south of Round Island. An interesting place this, for the steps from the lighthouse come tumbling down the steep southern slope of the isle to a small terrace in the cliff. From here a stout overhead wire has been rove to the peak of the offlying rocks and doubtless in rough weather the supply craft use this to cast a line over, for in such conditions it could be a dangerous business to close the rocky buttresses of the isle itself. The wire was high out of my reach, however, and the best I could do was secure Ben's painter to a rung of the vertical ladder leading up to the terrace, making due allowance for the rising tide. My approach had been spotted. Down the steps, hell-for-leather, came a figure running. Aha, thinks I, I'm to be told it's private property and 'Be off with me!' But nothing such. A cheery wave and the cry, 'Any fags aboard,' was the worst broadside I got. Fags!—me in a swimsuit and *Ben* sloppy with inquisitive sea! No, alas, I had no fags nor have any use for them. But I found the lighthouse and her crew most interesting. The adjacent signal flagstaff particularly so, for I learned a trick from it. Winds have a habit of changing direction, you may have noticed. If you're flying flags, they tend after a bit to get fouled up with halyards and other gear aloft, but not here—the flag halyard was attached at its lower end not to the staff but to a massive iron cannonball. After hoisting the signal, you just dragged the ball away from the foot of the mast till the halyard and the flags flew clear and free. If the wind changed its mind, all you had to do was shift the cannon-ball round.

There was a bit of a swell running down from the north, residue of yesterday's blow, and Eastward Ledge just seaward of the isle was breaking into a creamy grin occasionally, but the sea was smooth as a baby's bottom and there was little

Round Island – calm

Round Island – storm

Splicing the anchor warp in my bivouac after the gale on Tean

sign of any trouble arising. Half a mile south-west of Round Island is a fearsome isolated crag of rock called Men-a-Vaur. Forty-odd feet above high water springs it towers like three great molars, and there's a dark chasm, sheer-sided and not more than ten feet broad that splits it near in half. Now I've sailed round Men-a-Vaur times enough, at a respectful distance, for the fringe of white water round her skirts keeps any prudent craft at bay. But today I'd caught her sleeping: true there was a healthy rise and fall of swell working away on her northern face, but to the south side, where that chasm split into her, it was quieter. This is a haunt of the cormorant and blackback, and I had a mind to take a close look at the whitened tops of those fangs. 'If we work in just yonder where that ledge will afford us a footing, and you jump up smartly on my back before the swell recedes,' I told *Ben*, 'dammit, we'll be high and dry before the next swell comes rolling in.' And so it worked out. I eased *Ben* over the ledge when there was about three feet of water on it, rolled out quick and swung him up on my shoulders before the crest withdrew, and there he was climbing like a two-legged beetle sedate as you could wish out of the reach of Old Father Neptune's next lick.

After I parked him, it was a stiff ascent, back-a-knee up some of the vertical rifts, and inclined to be greasy with the guana, and a bit smelly, but on the very peak, why I was king of the isles, with a thousand screaming gulls proclaiming me so, circling in a sonic crown up there above my head, and it was a wild, grand moment, and good to be alive. I dare not tarry long, for one small change in the mood of the sea and it would be too much for *Ben*. Launching the skiff was yet more fun for I made a wholesome mess of it. I placed his wooden skeg carefully on the limpet-encrusted ledge, careful to keep the delicate painted skin off the needle-sharp points, and waited for the swell to float him before leaping in. Trouble with swell is, it doesn't just go up and down—it swirls in horizontally as well, and as *Ben* floated he was swept off that ledge before I could quite get all of me aboard. And *Ben* wasn't having just part of me aboard!

Up he tilted, in I went, and there were the two of us awash in that chasm with the sky above a ringing peal of bird laughter. But being made of planks *Ben* stays as buoyant as myself, and I towed him back to the ledge and set to work putting that water back where it belonged. While at this I spied a tragedy taking place at the foot of the rocks on the opposite side of the chasm. A young herring gull—

couldn't have been hatched more than a few days—had somehow got things round the wrong way and become too familiar with Neptune before courting the zephyrs. Whatever the cause, the poor thing was in the water desperately trying to regain a footing on the rocks, completely waterlogged and obviously exhausted and near to drowning. There was a fine commotion going on overhead where the family were strident with advice, but the poor thing no sooner got a footing than the next wave swiped him off, and he was past making much real effort. I relaunched *Ben*, edged him across, waited for the right moment and grabbed the chick. Too far gone to stand, he lay quivering in a soggy heap on the planks, eyeing me pathetically. I whistled to mum, and struck steadily southward across Golden Ball Brow, for I dare not attempt to land again on Men-a-Vaur for fear of getting in the same mess again myself; on Northwethel islet just west of Tean I landed in a grassy bay and put him ashore in the thrift. He was perking up by now, and standing on his own feet. Half an hour later he was surrounded by crumbs that *Lugworm* sent across, and mum was strident overhead, so next day when I saw him trotting round the beach, I reckoned no harm done.

*   *   *

If you should have a mind to dream a while, you will not do better than to lie alone on the fernclad southern bank of Nornour and watch the evening sun set fire to the Eastern Isles, so russet and gold do they glow across the wine dark sea. Sit quiet here with me for a while and listen to the wind through the fern leaves. *Lugworm* is half asleep, playing with her own reflection, her two masts seeming to probe impossibly deep into the shallow sandy bay.

Ganilly is aflame, and beyond that Great Arthur and distant St Mary's take up the symphony of colour, echoing that other expression of an underlying music which is with you always on the islands: the song of the sea. It accompanies you everywhere, like your own unconscious mind, and obeys the same law, manifesting itself only when the ever clamorous 'I' is unaware, bringing you nearer to reality than the barrier of sense experience allows.

Listen idly to that song, and you may hear the echoes of other times and other people who walked these isles when they had different contours to those you see now.

Legend has it that the isles were once joined to Cornwall, and romantic stories of a sunken continent of Lyonesse fire the imagination. More in the realm of fact, however, is the evidence available from fascinating archaeological finds throughout the group which indicate that comparatively recently either the level of the sea or the height of the land was somewhat different. There are also accounts of what appears to be a laid stone course on Crow Bar, suggesting that this was once a road linking St Martin's to St Mary's. Indeed, today the sea level would have to fall less than two metres and you could walk dryshod at low water spring tides from Cruthers Hill at the southern tip of St Martin's via Guthers Island and Crow Bar to St Mary's: a distance of one and a half miles. Even now it's possible at this state of tide to wade from St Martin's to Tresco.

Right below us on the edge of the beach are the walls of small circular houses. It may well be that under those quivering and probing reflections of *Lugworm*'s masts are buried further homesteads, for certainly the upper reaches of the tide level have destroyed some of these strange buildings. What fashion of people were these, who lived in the small round houses huddled close together here on Nornour, their crude stone walls sheltered against the rising ground to the north and whose low narrow doors faced eastward away from the prevailing winds? The gales of 1962 laid their habitations bare, but the artefacts found within and around those habitations seem to have presented more of a mystery than they solve. The pottery suggests they were active in the pre-Roman Iron Age, and later reoccupied during the Roman period, since datable Roman coins, pottery of the time, and pipe-clay figurines have been found here. But the most remarkable finds were a collection of finely worked bronze brooches, some rings and bracelets, mostly dating to the second century AD which suggests either that this group was then the centre of a sophisticated metal-working culture, or perhaps the site of a shrine to which such ornaments might have been brought, or even a collection point at which the manufactured objects were completed for onward distribution elsewhere. Whatever the answer, in the houses you may still see traces of their way of life, for there are the hearths, the partition walls, and even pestles and mortars for grinding grain. But has the land fallen, or has the sea risen? Most probably the former, for it is known that the whole edge of this continental shelf has been subject to submergence even in recorded history.

It's fascinating to lie here on this warm slope and visualise the topography of those days. It may well be that at some time these islands were all one. In imagination the eye sweeps down a green valley which is now Crow Sound sloping seaward to the south. West of St Mary's hill, out through the great flat grassy plain of St Mary's Roads, one might see the glint of water where the broken outcrops of scattered isles which now form the western rocks finally capitulate to the sea. Northward the major spine of the isle curves through St Martin's, Tean, Tresco and Bryher, and afar, very distant, one may still hear the ever-present voice of the sea.

A small, green world with its own protective moat, supporting stock and growing cereals, whose population traded with, and occasionally doubtless united in defence against, marauding pirates.

Certainly, when the Romans withdrew from southern Britain in the fifth century AD, these isles formed a handy base for the marauders who then found the softened British an easy prey. Around 980 AD a marauding fleet of Norsemen—some hundred ships—came to the isles, led by the King of Norway, one Olaf Tryggvesson who, after the death of his wife, had fared forth in savage fury, harrying the shores of England, Ireland and Scotland, eventually arriving at the Scillies. This little bloodbath had apparently taken him some four years, if the somewhat confused history of the sagas is to be relied on. But it appears that he heard of a soothsayer on these isles who foretold the future. To him he sent a certain one of his henchmen who was like himself in appearance, instructing him to inform the soothsayer that he was indeed the king and ask his fortune. The soothsayer, however, apparently saw through the ruse, sending him off with a flea in his ear and the instructions to stop fooling and remain true to his real king. This so impressed Olaf that he forthwith arranged to meet the wise man himself and being entirely human ask how he might yet increase his power.

Now this wise man was a Christian, and by means of a certain prophecy, persuaded the warlike Olaf that there was more to this Christianity than might at first meet the eye of a savage marauder from Scandinavia. To cut a long story short (and it's all laid down in the *Heimskringla*, which is one of the best known sagas of the old Norse kings) Olaf and all his gang were christened and stayed in the isles until the autumn, when they sailed for England, and eventually carried his new creed to Norway, Sweden, Denmark and Iceland, enforcing it in what was later to become a well exercised 'Christian' manner—at the point of the sword.

So Christianity (Norse brand) may have found its way to Scandinavia from these isles, but the way of it sounds little to the credit of its founder, and one wonders, lying here looking at the peaceful beauty of earth, whether it's not a pity that the vehicle for the spread of man's religion has to be man himself.

So where were we? Lying peacefully on Nornour, with dear old *Buggerlugs* waiting patiently out there in the bay; then let's wander down through the round houses and bid adieu to the ghosts that undoubtedly haunt these shores, for south bay on Tean is a safer place to spend the night, and have we not our own hearth already shaped and blackened there waiting between the tidemarks on the rocks?

A Thorn Apple, found on Tean – instant death if you eat it

CHAPTER III

STORM AND CALM

BUT OF COURSE IT WASN'T ALWAYS PARADISE. Dreamy days of sun there were in plenty, and lotus-eating on the lazy strands of Gugh, Bryher, Tresco; but in this life you have to take the smooth with the rough, and in *Lugworm* when it turns rough—it's rough!

I remember the following summer of '74. Who doesn't! I'd sailed *Lugworm* down again, arriving alone in the isles early July, and after that things grow a bit hazy for me, trying to isolate one soggy event from another. We seemed to spend our days desperately flitting from one isle to another for a lee, with the boat and all aboard becoming steadily more sodden. B. had stayed at home for a bit longer to set the spinach or something, and there were just the three of us again, *Ben, Lugworm* and I. Came one frightful night when, having escaped from a vicious southerly and gained the lee of Porth Conger between St Agnes and Gugh, three of the morning found a driving storm coming in from due north. It knocked up a sea that started breaking over *Lugworm*'s bow and it was all stops out to buoy and slip one anchor, weigh the other and beetle off to safety elsewhere before she foundered; and that was the pattern of it, with sleep becoming more and more at a premium and never a night but some elemental disaster foaming along to wash the dreams away.

Finally, we got ourselves jammed in Hottentot Bay for three days. For the first time I felt moderately safe and protected from every blessed quarter of the compass. In driving rain, and to the honking of fascinated seals, I spent a whole afternoon building a hideyhole of rocks, roofed over with *Ben*, suitably weighted. It was so cosy that evening with a bright bonfire keeping out the gloom that I moved all cooking gear ashore and set up house, Crusoe fashion, on that uninhabited isle. It was the best night yet, albeit hellish smoky, but there's a rare and primaeval satisfaction in listening to the howl of a gale and the venomous spit of rain on hot ashes—when you're snug and warm in the glow from a great driftwood fire! I decided to make it a permanent base until the weather changed.

Next day I swear the tide was the highest since Ararat. There must have been five tons of kelp jammed in my hidey-hole and Little Arthur itself needed water-wings. A drenching westerly, heavy with the scent of weed ripped from the Western Reefs, scorched in, tripped over Little Ganninick and in sheer spite kicked *Ben*, weights and all, up and into a bank of Hottentot figs. *Lugworm*, denuded now by the removal of tent and masts, did a tango from side to side of the bay with both anchors straining, and I stood shivering and miserable, with despair not very far up to weather.

It was the night after that on the phone that there came a faint note of alarm in B.'s voice: 'It looks pretty ghastly,' she said, 'because on the weather chart the Atlantic is covered in one big cobweb; and the man said there is a typhoon or something just west of the Shamrocks. DO take care, darling!'

'It'll come from the west,' I thought, scurrying off to the south shore of Tean, with one ear jammed to the transistor. We holed up near the ruined house, reckoning we could get as good a lee behind the Hedge rocks and all those reefs strewn about as anywhere else. September 7th it was, and I shall never forget it. I bedded *Lugworm* down on the beach two hours after high and hauled *Ben* on to the grass, clamping him down with a hundredweight or so of rocks, just for sure. The rain continued and the wind just for cussedness swung south and got into gear. At two-thirty in the morning, the tent was playing merry havoc and the boat all but sailing on dry land. I lay grimly listening to an ever-approaching roar as the tide crept back over Rascal's Ledge, foamed round the foot of Foreman's Isle and encircled the Hedge. The wind had a hysterical scream about it as though it were harbouring wild devils plucked from the hoary wastes of the Atlantic.

And so it was, a whole cargo of them shrieking and tearing at the sea; it was horrifying! 'Hell and highwater,' I fumed. 'If this boat floats with the tent on her, we shall be awash!' And I ruminated, with sinking heart.

Oh yes, it's all very well to question why I wasn't already out and battening everything down for the fray, but at three in the morning there's a deal of inertia to be overcome 'ere one leaves a warm sleeping bag and walks out for a perishing gale to clap around the vitals! But, of course, it had to be done, and once more I moved all my gear ashore, piling it under one wall of the ruin, every last stitch of it this time—masts, bottomboards, tent and outboard. Even the stores and food to lighten ship. By five a.m. the surf was licking under her chin and the storm had by my reckoning reached force nine. With a lurch she finally lifted to the first wave. I leapt aboard and shortened in to pull her clear of the beach with two anchors out.

And there for two hours I bounced, skinned up like a yellow haggis with oilskins tight over three jerseys and long woollen combinations. It was impossible even to look up to weather: spray and wind would have clawed your eyes out. But sailors expect this sort of insult; what began to alarm me was a gradual but sickening deadness in the buoyant movement of *Lugworm*. She was growing heavy and unresponsive, and frantically in the dawn light I cast about for a cause. The bilges were moderately dry: I'd been baling since she floated. What could be the trouble?

I turned, shielding my eyes and tried to peer to weather. Aghast, I saw that half a haystack of weed was entangled round the two anchor warps, pulling the bow down with the dead weight of it. I lurched forward, scrabbling over the stem, and got a hogshead of sea in my face which knocked me back, for my added weight forward was putting her bow under. There was nothing else for it: over the side I had to go, and sharp, clawing at that slimy mass and just able to toe the bottom in the troughs. At that moment, with a small explosion, one anchor warp parted and there was *Lugworm* sheering away with me trailing behind like a sea-anchor. Riding now to one warp only, she began veering madly in a wide arc, swinging beam-on to the seas at each extremity and shipping them green over her gunwales. In desperation, and waiting the right moment, I reached up and slipped the second warp. Together we sheared across the bay and somewhere on the trip I managed to roll myself back aboard, only to leap out again to frantically guide her in to the lee shore at a point clear of rocks. And there, with each successive surge of the rising tide, she drove further back, until after high water the maelstrom started receding to leave her all fouled up with twisted masses of weed and heaped shingle. She was a forlorn sight, well above normal high water mark; but safe!

I made a bivouac under that wall with the boat's gear, while the wind shrieked from out of a demented sky, driving the rain horizontally. With the dawn—if you can call it that—far from abating, the fury increased. Only later did I learn that a full hurricane had again passed across the islands during those traumatic hours. But the wind had now veered to the west, and was still veering to bring horrible grey scud, ripped and stranded at the edges, bansheeing over Tean. All that day I tried to get a fire going, but there was no dry wood. At evening, after a makeshift meal and with coming darkness, I wrapped myself in the tent and huddled close to the wall on a platform of driftwood. Sometime in the night I woke with an uneasy feeling and, switching on the torch, caught a ring of bright shining eyes before they receded smartly into the bracken: island rats, the sweetest little things come to keep me company and clean up my scraps.

With the dawn, cramped and stiff with cold, I opened my eyes—and shut them again instantly. Incredulously I slowly parted my lids again, praying I was having a nightmare; but it was still there, an inch or two from my nose and observing it closely—a black, wonderfully articulated scorpion.

Now I know perfectly well you just don't come across scorpions in England, much less paddling about in seaboots in a driving force 12, but I've seen these things often in Greece and this little fellow was of close enough resemblance for me to give it the full benefit of any doubt. As it dug its clawed feet into the tent and raised that tail ominously up and over, staring me in the eyes as brazen as you please, my heart all but stopped. I have a firmly held conviction about instant death: it should be avoided at all cost! But how?

With every guarded twitch of mine that tail twitched up and over in response. Still as a corpse already, I stared back at the frightful thing and went cold as a fish. At such moments, strange fantasies flit through the mind. Scorpion... Scorpio... dammit I was born on November 13th and my guiding constellation is the heavenly SCORPIO! Was this grievous moment, perhaps, all predestined from my very first howl! Was the symbol of all that motivated me eventually to pitch me back into the limbo of Erebus. Then something began vibrating in the soundbox of my mind. 'Try telepathy,' it said, 'TRY TELEPATHY!'

I took my eyes off that pregnant arched tail, looked the creature square on the nose and soundlessly sent out thoughts of... FRIENDSHIP? 'Friend!' I willed. Slowly it cocked its lovely little head on one side and—I swear it—raised a curious eyebrow. Agonisingly slowly the tail sank back down and the urgency drifted away. Things were at a point where, with utmost caution and no quick movement whatever, I could draw up one arm and grip the fold of the tent below my right ear. Quick as thought I ripped it back and away, trapping the thing beneath its layers, and jumped clear, staggering through the pile of boat gear in my panic. Then, carefully, I dragged the tent clear of the wall and unfolded it with a stick. There he was the little devil, shaking himself and all of a spite at the turn of things. Again we faced each other but this time I was standing with stick in hand, and the situation was reversed. I raised the stick and took aim.

But then a strange thing happened. Seeing him standing there so small, with tail raised in fierce but helpless defiance, I suddenly no longer wanted to bring down that stick. 'Somewhere,' I found myself thinking, 'back in that wall, there'll be another little fellow like you, to whom you're both the beginning and the end of things and entirely cuddleable. We're both just making the best of a bad job and all we wanted was a bit of warmth. You could have bowled me out easy as licking your lips backalong, but you didn't.'

I put him gently on the end of the stick and laughed as he scuttled deep into a crack in the wall a bit further along. I felt a prize fool, but a bit shaken for all that.

*   *   *

It was the following morning I got the telegram in St Mary's. 'Arriving Noon Thursday. Miss you. B.'

'Look cuckoo,' I explained desperately over the telephone that evening, dripping in oilskins. 'This is just no place for a girl, we're fighting for survival. Honestly, the three of us are beginning to sag round the edges. You'll die of exposure!'

'Nonsense,' came the voice. 'It's a bit windy, that's all. You obviously need me, you're losing your buoyancy. It's Brymon Airways, quarter to twelve at the airport. I love you.'

You won't believe me, but even as that monoplane wobbled in to the greensward the heavens parted their ashen lips and smiled. For the sheer joy of feeling hot sunshine and a warm drying wind I insisted on walking back to Hugh Town from the 'drome. 'I knew it,' she said, radiant in summer frock, 'it's just your state of mind—you needed me!'

Well, in the circumstances you don't argue, do you? What's the point when the sun is so hot it's bikinis and parasols and us ghosting under genoa and a kiss of warm wind back up to Tean. Only half of me wanted to spit! We even caught a thumping great pollack on the way and baked it on the rocks for supper. Next day was brisk, sunny, and obviously sent for drying-out. We bedded on that lovely warm sand at Goats Point, St Martin's, and she stretched everything in the boat along our anchor warp with crossed oars as a clothes prop. 'You've let things get out of hand,' she said, 'the boat's in a dreadful state!' I just looked at the barometer and boiled quietly.

It went on like that for a week. We met up with friends and spent dreamlike days toasting in the tussocks on Samson, Bryher, Great Arthur and Tean. We caught fish and buckets full of shrimps, cooking them on deserted beaches with *Ben* propped up to keep the late summer sun off delicately pinking hides, can you believe it! There were langorous teas of stewed blackberries topped with that delicious thick cream from the island Jersey cows, and we turned lobster red and laughed and lived like Adam and Eve in Eden.

The isle of Annet was our paradise during that fortnight she was with me. We used to spend the nights in Porth Conger on St Agnes—a handy berth this since at high water, in the event of the wind going north, *Lugworm*, with an inch and a gulp to spare, can skim across the top of the sandy spit that joins the isle to Gugh.

After a lazy breakfast, we'd sail over to what we called Rocky Bay on the north-east shore of Annet. It's a foul place to find yourself on a lee shore, but the trick is to reach quickly the mile across to Pereglis Bay on St Agnes if the weather begins to deteriorate. We would leave the mizzen up in *Lugworm* while she was at anchor, and the west wind would keep her streaming away from the shore and safe off the rocks.

It's hilarious, B. and I in *Ben* together. *Ben*'s not intended for two, and B., as I've said, is slim and tall. She has to entwine her long legs with mine and keep her centre of gravity down low as possible while dodging the flailing inboard ends of the oars. One false move and we're towing *Ben*, who seems to enjoy it all as much as we do. I leap out while we're still afloat, for one foul contact with a rock and *Ben* is punctured. It's a bit of a technique, that leap, for soon as my own weight is gone, up *Ben* will tip and pitch B. in backwards over the stern! So we worked out a method. At the moment I leap over the side (there can be no half measures, you're either in or out of *Ben* with no dilly-dallying) and find a footing, B. slides forward from the stern to the centre of the skiff. I then hold *Ben* steady until she has disembarked too. It all works very well provided I get a firm footing straight away, but it's not always easy on rounded slimy boulders.

Annet is beautiful. Like most of the isles there is no vestige of trees, but it's carpeted with thick clumps of thrift, sprouting from a deep springy green carpet of grass, through which burst great shoulders of sparkling granite. It is the haunt of blackbacks, and their clamour when we arrive is often disturbing, since they have a habit of soaring up, then diving to within a few inches of one's head before spreading their wings and swooping off again. After a bit they get used to us though, and the great thing is not to disturb them too much, remembering it's THEIR isle, and we who are the intruders.

We spent days there, searching the pebble beaches and hum-mocky rises to identify the wild plants. There is sea holly to be found, its blue flowers like thistles in late August, but it is becoming rare, and on no account should be picked. Curled dock sprouts in profusion between the pebbles, and scentless mayweed with its little white daisylike flowers turns the top of the shoreline into a fringe of white lace before the thrift and fern take over.

But these western isles, so far as I am concerned, are unique for their magical rock pools. At low water springs, there is a fantasy world of colour and form to be found in the translucent depths of those pools. I have hundreds of colour transparencies, taken through the water, of the myriad-formed weeds and sea anemones. We would select some soft springy turf bank on the western shore and spend the days basking in the sun. Both of us were already tanned the colour of mahogany, and still the weather held, for that most blessed fortnight that B. was with us. Out to the west the Bishop's Rock light stood slim against the sky, and all around the apparently calm face of the sea would suddenly gape into stretches of white spume where the Tearing Ledges, Retarrier, Gilstone, Crim and Gunners reefs broke surface.

Often, as B. and I stretched there in the grass gazing across those lazy sun-soaked miles of sea, there came over us a strange sense of privilege—privilege at being able to view it all from a situation of calm and complete safety, when the beauty of it was our sole concern.

'Can you begin to imagine that disastrous night nearly two hundred and seventy years ago?' I asked her. 'Do you ever get the feeling that the sea, as we're seeing it now from this tiny islet, is somehow oddly predatory—waiting its time, sleeping with one eye just open, watching its chance...?'

'Have you any idea how it came about?' she replied.

'Only what I've read, but knowledge of the sea and one's own experience and imagination can pretty accurately fill in the details. It's all fairly well recorded. One thousand four hundred men lost their lives that night of 22nd October 1707 between Gilstone and Crim—out there, where it's breaking now.'

A line of distant white water—the thinnest etching of snow on a vast canvas of hazy smoke blue—silently appeared, slowly extended, then merged back into nothingness. No sound was there, but I knew that, had we been on the reef at that moment, the power of it would have pulverised us.

He was fifty-seven years old, Sir Cloudesley Shovell, the Commander-in-Chief in his flagship *Association*, a second-rater of the line, 1,459 tons, 90 guns and crewed by 680 men. In April of that year his fleet had taken part in the bombardment of Toulon, and twenty-one ships were returning to Portsmouth on a voyage which was at first beset by continuous bad weather. Conditions improved, but evidently not enough for them to establish their exact latitude, and longitude was always a difficult problem in those days before they had really accurate clocks. At any rate, they were in general doubt, and he ordered his fleet to heave-to sometime during the day of 21st October in order to take soundings. You must remember that at that time a ship had but one method of doing this: to lower a line down with a heavy lead 'armed' at its bottom with a pad of wax. The mariner noted the depth on feeling the lead hit the bottom, and an examination of the wax often revealed the nature of the seabed. Sand, shingle, mud, or whatever, would be a clue to the general area and, of course, the depth itself was a good guide to one's position, for the charts gave some information about depths even in those days.

Of course, really accurate soundings could be carried out only when the vessel was stopped, otherwise the lead and line tended to stream aft, making it appear deeper than in truth it was. You can imagine the fleet, after weeks at sea, on that grey overcast day, closing one another and drifting with sails aback while each took an independent sounding. It's more than likely that boats would then be lowered for a conference aboard the flagship, since quite clearly the Admiral was very worried about his exact position.

If so, it would indicate also that the sea conditions were not all that bad, for you can't send away boats in anything of a storm.

The result of the decision then made was the worst peacetime disaster in Britain's maritime history. Incredible though it may seem, they came to the conclusion that the fleet was somewhere off Ushant. But remember they had sailed well over a thousand miles since coming through the Straits of Gibraltar. Almost certainly they would have made a landfall to fix their position at Cape St Vincent on the southern tip of Portugal and would take a departure from Cape Finisterre before crossing the Bay of Biscay. It would be only reasonable that any mariner of the time would seek to gain a landfall again at Ushant to establish his position before running up the Channel, and if one has this objective in mind, it's difficult to jettison the idea that one is not within ten or twenty miles of your intended position. One thing would be obvious: they could not be east of Ushant, otherwise they would have been getting signs of the coast of France, and the bottom shallowing up. In fact, their reckoning was some hundred miles out, for they were close south-west of these Scilly Isles. The weather, as night came in, began to worsen again.

There is a story, and I think it very likely true, that a crew member of one of the ships was himself a Scillonian. This man, it's stated, somehow sensed by the look of the sea, and the smell of it, that he was in home waters. He is reputed to have insisted on conveying his opinion to the Admiral, but was overruled by the more weighty views of the navigators. Admiral Shovell set course before that rising wind, as he thought, to enter the English Channel—and ran the whole fleet straight into the thick of the islands!

What is amazing is that of the twenty-one ships, only five were actually wrecked. *Association*, striking the Gilstone Ledges, fired three guns in an attempt to warn the others before sinking in 90 feet of water. *Romney*, a 48-gun ship-of-the-line, struck the Crebininicks and went down. Only one of her 280 hands, the quartermaster George Lawrence from Hull, survived by clinging to the rocks. Crim claimed the *Eagle*, with all four hundred and forty crew drowned. The *Firebrand*, of eight guns, struck the Gilstone Ledge, floated off but went down while trying to make St Agnes. The *Phoenix*, a fireship, struck the reefs but managed to beach on Tresco and was later salvaged.

It may be that the remainder of the fleet, in the gathering dark and increasing wind, had become somewhat scattered, choosing not to lie too close to one another in the poor visibility. At any rate some of them passed north and south of the Isles, while one or two appear to have miraculously passed straight through the inter-island channels and clear out the other side.

Account has it that Sir Cloudesley himself took to his barge with his treasure chest and a pet greyhound, as the *Association* foundered, and this again argues that the sea conditions were not impossibly violent. It may well be, however, that as a result of the recent bad weather to the south, there was a big swell running and that would account for the dreadful toll once the craft had actually struck the reefs. At any rate, the Admiral is said to then have been wrecked a second time on the beach at Porth Hellick, St Mary's Isle, and to this day there is a monument there on the spot where he was first buried. He was later disinterred and reburied in Westminster Abbey.

And now a truly grim tale emerges. It is said that many years after the fateful night an island woman, when on her deathbed, told how she had found the Admiral still alive on the beach and completely exhausted. Seeing two rings on his fingers, she confessed to murdering the poor wretch—a task that was all too easy I imagine in his defenceless situation—and removing the rings. She produced one of them, set with an emerald, which she had been afraid to sell in case such an easily identifiable object be traced to her. The tale has it that when the Admiral's body was found, there were indeed the marks of two rings on his fingers, but no sign of the rings themselves. The woman felt that by confessing this act she would in some way absolve herself from guilt.

The sea sighed quietly at our feet. Southward the bleak brown slab of Melledgan broke the horizon, Gorregan, Daisy, Rosevear and Crebawethan pushed their white-coated tips up from the depths, and behind Crebawethan towered the slim pencil of Bishop's Rock Lighthouse.

'The Bishop wasn't there in those days,' I added. 'But it's odd that they didn't see the brazier kept lit on St Agnes lighthouse. Visibility must have been very poor.'

'Surely, they would have heard the breakers on the reefs. Wouldn't that have warned them in time?' B. queried.

I put myself in imagination out there, in pitch black of night, with the wind singing through the rigging, and that agony of doubt born of not knowing with certainty one's exact position. There must have been greater alertness operating among the officers and men, for in such a situation only a fool is off his guard, and those men were not fools.

'Almost certainly they were running before the rising wind,' I mused, 'possibly with breaking seas alongside, which make a great deal of sound. You don't hear the roar of surf when its downwind of you, not with other sounds close in your ears. You don't even see it when you're looking over the backs of the breakers until you're right on them. Maybe a cable or so off they realised their error. But what could they do with those ships, unmanoeuvrable as they were, incapable of beating to windward, and sluggish in response to the helm? They hadn't a chance.'

But these were grim thoughts for a tranquil sun-laden autumn afternoon, so we put them from our minds, wandered across to *Ben* on the eastern shore and brought from *Lugworm* the two mackerel we'd caught that morning and some bread, potatoes and drink.

Is there anything to match the peace of sitting close to a driftwood fire on a lonely beach, while the sun bids adieu to the day, and all those scents that come with the evening drift up from the warm grass and bracken close about. I remember we crushed some samphire in our hands and inhaled its clean fresh pungence, a scent which, for me, will always evoke the joy of solitude and freedom on lonely rockstrewn shores.

We grilled the mackerel, baked the potatoes in their jackets and wrapped in tinfoil among the red embers of the fire, and rounded the meal off with a bottle of Blue Nun, watching while the isle drew in her skirts as the tide encroached. Rock pools—liquid lakes of light—merged back into the mother ocean and the light continued to fade. *Lugworm* took us quietly back to Porth Conger, running goosewinged gently through the channel between Teneers Ledge and Browarth, rounding up beneath the inn there atop the slipway, and the bay held us safe all night.

September crept out, and B. returned home. Apart from the odd visit to St Mary's to provision and water ship I drifted deeper and deeper into a pattern of happy indolence. Ye gods, what days those isles have given me! Solitude is essential for a writer, but on occasions she can be a misleading mistress who weaves a spell around the soul and drugs the mind. Indeed it must be so, for why else would a chap begin to spend contented hours, days and finally weeks alone just listening... to silence?

Baked by days of languid sun the bracken had long since turned gold while I, alone in my kingdom, tanned to a matching brown. We would make occasional sorties, *Lugworm*, *Ben* and I, from Tean down to those Western Isles, anchoring between St Agnes and Gugh for a night or two before ghosting back round Samson and Bryher. We explored all those off-lying islets, always finding a safe night billet under a craggy lee. With bow and stern warp looped over a pinnacle of rock we would jam ourselves in some ridiculous gulley where no real yacht dare ever venture. But always we returned thankfully to the sheltered solitude of Tean.

Meanwhile, summer was ageing, her weather turning grey. I remember one October dawn as the first breath of a sea-fret just dampened the scarred face of Ganilly, we crept past Guthers, hand-in-hand with the ebb. Its huge rocky Dodo peered watchful through the mist and Tobaccoman's rocks chuckled and swirled close aboard as we cleared away south of the ill-famed Minalto ledges, for I had a mind to explore those savage western rocks at close quarters. We reached down under a grey sky between St Agnes and Annet, awestruck at the unbelievable fangs in Hellweathers Neck rearing up to rip and tear at the low cloud. As Melledgan—scarce more than a whitened perch for a hundred and more cormorants—fell away astern it was as if the sea and the rocks closed in; very different to those sunsoaked days I had spent there with B. Suddenly the safe world of Man was gone: we were three unwanted intruders in an alien, desolate wintry place.

It was then I saw the seal. Old, grey, disfigured by wounds and scars, he watched us from a ledge and there was no love in his eye. I stared at him and he stared back at me. As the muted thunder of swell from the distant reefs whispered in my ears it was as if, from the deep soundings of memory there came welling up a strange, disturbing warning. That old warrior became the very embodiment of a verse written long ago:

One alone... all alone... wary of ear and eye.
The western wind and the sea's my home
  —Lord of the Reefs am I!
Well you may stare, you human thing,
    my world here once was yours.
But what part of you now knows the lonely wind
    that sings on these barren shores?
You have forgot the twilight deep
    where the kelpen forests flow...
Where the long slow breath of the ocean
    gives life to a world below.
Be gone with your boat, you human being
  —best let those memories die.
You bring the scent of an unreal thing
  —One with the Sea am I!

So we stood off, *Lugworm, Ben Gunn* and I, and set course back to our soft, safe world of home, for we knew that, all unsuspecting, we had stirred memories best forgotten. They flowed too deep, and too powerfully, for this thin veneer, which is the armour of twentieth-century man, to withstand.

CHAPTER IV

ENSAY

W E WERE STALKING MUSSELS, a friend and I on the shore at Rock back in the spring of 1975, when I mentioned that a Cornish seaside resort is no place for a writer in the high season. 'In a sense,' I told him, triumphantly cornering a *mytilus edulus*, 'a writer is always working. As long as he's still warm he's manipulating the bricks of his trade: ideas. But it doesn't look that way to others and you catch envious comments when folk see you more or less permanently denizened in the boat, the sun, and the water. They're right, of course, in a way,' I continued. 'But when the tools of your trade lie in a ream of paper, a portable typewriter, and what goes on between your two ears, only a fool wouldn't take advantage of the freedom it allows.'

'But that's only the visible side of it,' I hammered away at him (he was that sort of friend). 'There are the sleepless nights, the agonised hours of searching for just the right construction to convey an atmosphere—so as not to overdo it and end with purple passages—and yet avoid a dreary record of facts.'

He listened for a while, then told me to pipe down, for, as he pointed out, 'You're disturbing the peace of the morning. But if that's really how you feel why don't you drop a line to my brother who's doctoring in Africa. He's got a crumbling old mansion on an uninhabited isle by the name of Ensay, somewhere in the Outer Hebrides. He might lend it to you; there'd be nothing but you and the whelks, and they're not loquacious!'

The itch started from that moment. I suppose if you live in the extreme south west of Cornwall it's only human nature that sooner or later you'll develop an itch to putter off to the far-flung extremities of Scotland—just to see if the other man's sea is bluer, so to speak! I scratched the itch a bit that evening with B., taking a few soundings as it were, and found it a bit deep for throwing out an anchor. But it's astonishing what a word here, a suggestion there, can do to the psychology of a woman. After a week or so she was practically begging me to be off and leave her in peace. Opportunity, they say, knocks but once.

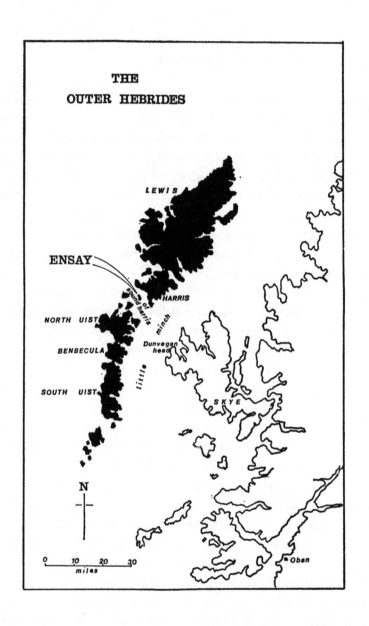

THE
OUTER HEBRIDES

LEWIS

ENSAY

sound of harris

HARRIS

NORTH UIST

minch

BENBECULA

Dunvegan
head

SOUTH UIST

little

SKYE

N

0   10   20   30
     miles

• Oban

By the end of April, a friend and I had the trip more or less organised and open-ended so far as time was concerned. Trevor, who is mad as I am myself, volunteered to tow *Lugworm* as far as Hadrian's Wall and I knew he wouldn't be hard-hearted enough to just leave us there drooping by the roadside. Which is why at this moment we're sitting on a draughty quay wall in the sleet at Leverburgh, with little else but sea and sky out there in the Sound of Harris and the grey ghost of the isle of Ensay eyeing us through the gale. Leverburgh is the modern name for Obbe, by which name the village was known prior to the Lord Leverhulme fiasco, which is another story.

There are one thousand two hundred miles more on the clock than when we left Rock five days ago. I got lost three times somewhere in the blizzardy peaks of those Scottish Highlands while Trev was asleep, and we both passed thoughts with a ferry which didn't (and accounts for the excessive mileage). But here we are clutching a sprig of heather and a bottle of the 'guid stuff', and it looks as though we'll be needing it from the strained look of the barometer.

'Uncle's away on the isle,' said the rosy-faced youngster back in the village. 'He's been there this fortnight lambing, but he's expecting you and will have the lambs out of the oven before you arrive.' We put it down to an endearing Gaelic turn of phrase.

Southward, the dark silhouette of North Uist all but hides Hecla's two thousand foot peak towering up behind, and there's snow on its icy pate. A shivering north-easter is elbowing its way down the Minch, bouncing off Lewis and Skye to howl onward with hysterical Norse-filled fury to freeze all you pappy unsuspecting southerners. Nothing remains 'twixt us and that lonely isle of Ensay save these 'Narrows', as the Sound of Harris is called—and one look across that wind-whipped streak of turbulence is enough! Scoured by the sleet-laden wind it glares back at us and there's a steely warning glitter in its eye.

There's something about living in a car for five days that dulls the brain of a sailor. Next morning came the moment of launching, with *Lugworm* checked and rechecked and even the north-easter holding its breath in anticipation. Now Lever-hulme, bless his ghost, built a splendid little slipway, down one side of the pier at Obbe, and everything was set ready when a haggis-filled voice from the small crowd of watchers offered sage advice:

'Ye'll noo git doon tha!'

I looked again at the slipway. True, it was certainly very steep and there was an unaccountable kink halfway down. Maybe he's right, I ruminated: if things got out of control, happen we'd be OK for firewood next week or so.

'Best gie along Macusbic's place doon o'er the shingles,' came another broad Scots voice, and many hands pointed along a gravel track. I'm a great believer in heeding local knowledge as a matter of principle, even when it's wrong. Back into the car we hopped and were scarcely in second gear when there came a soul-deflating judder and a report like a pistol shot.

'You've left the jockey wheel down!' we brayed at each other in self-exoneration; but not a bit of it, we'd just left the mizzen mast up.

Now I must tell you that telephone lines in Obbe span quite colossal distances between posts—it's something to do with a shortage of trees in these barren highlands—with the result that the wires sag more than a bit in the middle. So there was my mizzen snapped off like a carrot and half Obbe off the 'phone, and I won't voice the Gaelic thoughts on these dammed furriners with their boats! Though mark you, not one critical word was uttered aloud, so well mannered are these braw lads.

Anyway, by the time that lot was sorted out and I'd climbed the telegraph post and married up the wires by sheer inspiration, that ebb tide was looking lean and hungry. In fact Macusbic's slipway already ended short and there was a sort of moist Gobi desert of rocks between it and the still receding water. But there were also eight willing pairs of hands at the ready—it's astonishing how folk appear when there's a novelty like us around—so we man-handled all 1,200 lb. of laden *Lugworm* across an improvised ramp of pitprops. And there we were at last—afloat!

We could see the gable-ends of *home*, snug at the head of a perfect little sandy bay over there on the isle of Ensay two miles off, and together we pored over the chart. 'Ye'll mind that spring tide, noo,' one of the helpers shouted. 'She'll be flowing eastward into the Minch come the flood, and westward to the Atlantic come the ebb, give or take a dram.' I looked again across that steel-blue strip of insulation. Part of it appeared to be flowing eastward and the rest undoubtedly flowing westward! Which dram did we give?—and more to the point, which dram did we take? Then, as I watched, I swear my hair stood on end. Out there between the fangs of reefs that were already smelling the ozone, some two acres of kelp-smothered bottom rose from the water, sniffed, and gently sank out of sight again!

Of course, it did nothing of the sort: it was just a long, uneasy Atlantic swell funnelling down between Taobh Deas head and Pabbay Isle to heave its way through this bottleneck, and I thanked it for the timely warning and studied the chart with yet more dedication.

We beached *Lugworm* on that white sand of Ensay in front of the solitary old mansion and offloaded six months' supply of groceries and toilet rolls. It was a frolic, I can tell you, for there was a surge up and down that foreshore that boded ill should heaven start sneezing: what's more *Lugworm* had that feel about her that told me she was far from happy. We had left *Ben* at Rock out of sheer necessity, so had no tender—which precluded anchoring off.

There was no sign of John Mackenzie the farmer, but every sign of his charges: between us and the porch stood about a ton of jet-black Angus bull.

We stood at the top of a flight of concrete steps that led up from the beach, with a rusty iron gate between us and him, eyeing each other warily.

'Nip behind him and open the front door,' I instructed Trev. 'I'll distract his attention from here.' But that didn't work.

'I've got a better idea,' he volunteered. 'I'll work round the corner of the house, under that rainwater tank, and "moo". I'm very good at mooing: when he comes to court me I can nip through that gate into the other field and you open the door.' So it was arranged.

Trev crept along the beach, round the end of a lovely old castellated sea-wall, and positioned himself beside the water tank.

I thought he gave a good imitation of an enthusiastic cow. Angus blinked, hoofed up a yard or so of turf, and stomped off in the opposite direction. We waited until his indignant backside had disappeared round a barn and sprinted for the porch. The doors were jammed, but evidently unlocked. We put our shoulders to them and shoved.

On the peeling green walls of a hallway hung the colossal stuffed head of a water buffalo, or steer, or something with two horns that could have shishke-babbed six matadors and looked around for more. Its glass eyes blinked as the

438   LUGWORM ISLAND HOPPING

doors swung back, and a little shower of dust fell off its nose. There was a gaping hole in the plaster beneath him which left the horrid impression that he was given to moments of frustration, hanging about up there.

We slammed the doors behind us to safeguard our rear, and edged into the cavernous belly of the house.

'Anyone there?' I roared. The echo reverberated through the place and another cascade of dust came down off the nose. Not a sound. A door to our left led into a large front drawing room with bay window. There was an upright piano against one wall, and a spinning wheel beside it. Both appeared to be covered in snow. Above them, the white skull of a curly-horned ram grinned uncannily at us, and above that, a gaping hole in the plaster ceiling revealed a row of laths for all the world like the skeletal ribs of the old house, which accounted for the white dust.

Altogether the impression was macabre.

We crept along a dark passage, its walls peeling with a hideous yellow paper, and pushed gently on a dark brown stained door. A massive kitchen, large enough for a castle and spare, complete with slate floor, a bare wooden table, a china sink that could have bathed Angus himself, and a Rayburn stove. Something moved near the stove. I edged across to peer down in the half light, and a querulous 'baa…' brought me up all standing. There in the oven, just about as new as it could be, was the sweetest little wobble-legged lamb curled up. I felt the stove. 'He's not for dinner anyway, that's for sure,' I remarked to Trev, 'for the oven's little more than luke warm.'

There was a jacket hanging on a wall hook, and a pair of Wellington boots under the sink. Signs of a meal were on the table, set for two. So we went exploring. Two doors led from the kitchen, one into a tiny courtyard which had evidently at some time been an extension of the house, for there was the ruin of an open fireplace in one wall. Another door led out to a beautifully protected lawn, overgrown now with weeds and thistles, but the grass cropped short by the sheep which were free-roaming all about the isle.

A wide staircase led up from the cavernous hall to the upper rooms. High on the wall, halfway up, hung another moth-eaten head, this time of an unfortunate antlered stag with the legend 'Alladale 1919' on a plaque beneath. A massive branding iron hung beside. There were four small bedrooms, the ceiling plaster

down in all of them, and one huge, truly baronial room with a faded green carpet and a magnificent Scandinavian Jotul wood-burning stove fitted into what had
been an open fireplace. A colossal—but sadly cracked—wall mirror hung above
the mantelpiece. The ceiling of this room was intact, albeit badly cracked. Two
iron bedsteads, with mattresses, stood against one wall.

But the view! One tall window looked north-east across the Sound to Roneval,
1,200 ft., another gazed south-west down half the length of the isle. Through this
latter window we could see a greenswarded low headland—Borosdale as we came
to know it—and beyond that, across a steel-blue strip of sea, the distant smoke
blue hills of Skye. It was magnificent.

'This is the room for me,' I told Trev. 'It must have been the Laird's bedroom—but I wonder what's in all those outbuildings.' Beyond the outbuildings
we could see more roofless ruins. Obviously at one time this had been a large
homestead with all the supporting paraphernalia of a farm. There was something odd about the island slopes, though; they were uniformly ridged into
long furrows, like wide, flat potato clamps, but smooth and rounded with the
short-cropped grass. Wherever there was grass, the land was furrowed in this
peculiar way.

Trevor was ferreting about somewhere in the bowels of the place, and I joined
him in an upstairs storeroom. Against one wall hung a large, wide-brimmed coolie
hat and a pair of white rubber armpit-high waders. There was a jumble of bric-a-
brac, a wondrous great salmon-poaching pan a yard in length, a baby's playpen
of canvas filled with tins of paint, two ship's bells and a miscellany of paraffin
pressure lamps. In the centre of the room was a colossal wicker laundry basket
containing two sets of brand new woven blue and green curtains. There were also
five cases of blankets. The whole house was incredibly dry.

We set to carrying all our gear from the boat into the hallway, and in the middle of this heard voices back in the kitchen.

'Hullo there!' came a call, and John, gentleman, farmer, character, stomped
down the corridor with hand extended. Odd, isn't it, how you take to some people instantly without the need of talking or introductions. Blue-eyes twinkled in
a ruddy face. White hair, a chest like a barrel, short and stocky, wearing a dilapidated windcheater and corduroy trousers stuffed into Wellingtons. 'We saw your

boat on the beach from Borosdale. But we didn't really think you'd come across today—there's a sea running in the bay that'll pound her at high water. You'd best keep her down to the slip on the south side; she'll be safer there. Have ye had a meal? We've got half a sheep in the pot that'll be ready soon; come and meet Neil.'

Neil, a youth of some twenty or so years is John's son. Blond, tall, quiet and a little shy with strangers, we found him suckling the lamb from a rubber-teated bottle filled with warm milk. There was another lamb wobbling about under the table. 'Mother's dead,' he said; and that from Neil was a speech. In the corner of the kitchen, adjacent to the Rayburn, was a two-burner bottled gas stove, and before half an hour was up there was the finest lamb stew, with turnip, pearl barley, onion and a few Gaelic herbs steaming up from four soup bowls, displayed about the central bottle of the 'guid stuff'.

We learned a great deal in a short time from John. Those peculiar furrows on the face of the isle, for instance. 'Lazy-beds,' he told us. 'When this house was the homestead, back at the turn of the century, there were some forty people lived on the isle: servants and farmhands. Soil hereabouts is at a premium, there's but a thin sprinkling of earth above the rock. They had to scrape what earth there was into long ridges to get the necessary depth leaving drainage furrows in between. Seaweed and sand was collected from the shore and mulched into this to bind and form humus. This was the way that the peaty deposits of the Highlands were turned into soil. Once drained by the furrows, the lime in the sand counteracted the acidity of the peat.'

'But why lazybeds?' I queried. It seemed a singularly inappropriate name.

'That I can't tell you,' he grinned. 'Maybe it was a sort of joke, for it must have been damned hard labour!'

The isle was two miles in length and little more than a mile broad. Trevor and I spent next day, in a searing wind, walking its perimeter to get the scent of it all, and from that moment on I was bewitched. Maybe I'm a loner by nature, but if I had been asked to conjure up an idea of perfect bliss, why, I'd describe an isle covered in the greenest daisystrewn grass you can imagine, with sparkling bluffs of rocky gneiss pushing up through the sward to offer warm sundrenched grottoes from the winds; with a quarter of a mile of golden strand at

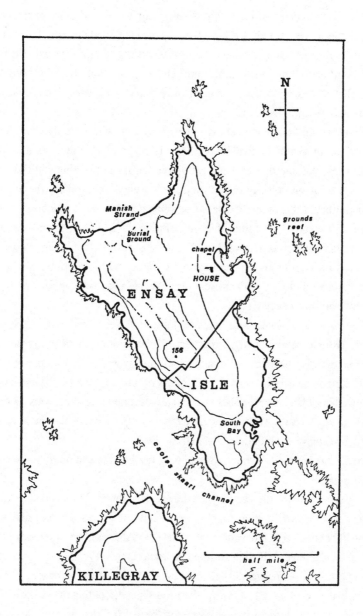

N

Manish
Strand

burial
ground

grounds
reef

chapel
HOUSE

ENSAY

156

ISLE

South
Bay

caolas skaari channel

half mile

KILLEGRAY

one end, the dunes of which dropped sheer thirty feet and more to the edge of the surf-thundering beach. I'd have lambs frolicking all about, and fat contented cows drifting like ancient fleets of ships according to the weather. I'd have a rocky southern shore, with gullies and clefts to harbour the wild cormorants and seabirds, and the constant cries of the gulls in one's ears, and the lapwings, oystercatchers and redshanks.

There would be a small semicircular sandy bay, with a house at its head so old and full of character that it breathed history, and ages of work and love of the land, success and disaster; and the whole set in a sea so blue you'd think you were in the Ionian, with islands dotted like jewels all around for the exploring, for, of course, in this dream I'd have *Lugworm* at a mooring in the house bay, and just enough water—two miles of it—separating the isle from the nearest inhabited land from which provisions could be ferried. And Peace! There would be no sound of cars, nor jet planes carving up the silence with their obtrusive hysteria. Put me there, and I'd be in Paradise. Put me there, and I'd be on Ensay.

I just couldn't believe it.

Two days after we arrived, Trevor, John and Neil disembarked, for John's brother Donald came forging across from Obbe to fetch them in his thirty-foot power launch. He brought her to anchor in the bay and pulled ashore in a heavy clinker dinghy. With him came Alan, John's other son—wild-eyed with hair flying and a bandolier of twelve-bore cartridges strapped round his waist, a double-barrelled gun across his shoulders. 'Are they here yet?' came his urgent call even before the dinghy grounded. It was nonplussing.

'Are what here yet?' I queried, grabbing the painter and hauling the skiff up with the surge.

'The geese, man, the geese… are the greylags here?' John said something in Gaelic and from the look on Alan's face I knew the greylags hadn't arrived yet, for the light seemed to have gone out of his life. 'Ah, well,' he said despondently, 'they'll maybe have arrived next time I'm home.'

But John was bringing all their gear from the house to the beach, and called me in for a conference. 'These now,' he pronounced, holding up a length of rusty chain from which hung a string of massive keys. 'Ye'll be wanting this one,' he said, selecting a small crowbar with flukes at one end. 'It's the key to the front

porch, but maybe ye'll not be using that entrance much, it needs persuasion. This
is for the back kitchen door, and there's the pantry cupboard, the dining room,
the storeroom upstairs—that must be kept locked for it holds all the Doctor's
island clothes and gear. And doubtless,' he continued with a slight but significant
pause, 'ye'll be wanting this—the key to the barn.'

It seemed unlikely that I would want anything from the barn, but time would
doubtless tell. In the meantime I thanked him, shook hands all round, bid adieu
to Trevor with grateful thanks for all his effort on my behalf, and watched as the
heavy-laden skiff was rowed off to the launch.

'Leave the tap in the scullery running,' John shouted as they climbed aboard.
'Spring water's best on the move and it keeps the pipe clear. Buttercup's due to
calve so we'll be across in a week or two just to see everything's fine. Just light a
fire on Borosdale if you break a leg or anything, happen we'll see it after dark.'

I watched them disappear through the outer rim of rocks protecting the
southern end of the bay, then listened to the fading throb of the boat's engine as it
probed out into the Sound, and I was alone.

King of all I surveyed.

*   *   *

Three days it took me to wash down and fill all those cracks in the walls and ceiling of the big bedroom. Then I coated the whole room with cream emulsion

which had been lying in the store for longer than was good for it, applied two coats of matt white oil paint to the doors and windows and hung those elegant curtains. Regal, light and enormous it was, that room, and fit for a sultan. I introduced the carpet to the sea-wall where it nearly expired with its own dust under the beating, and me with it. Finally, I removed the smaller of the two beds and regaled the remaining big one with four blood-red blankets from the store. A teak table, wondrously carved and held up by two elephants, came from one of the smaller bedrooms and two rickety tables draped with another red blanket did service as a writing desk. In the store I found a genuine vintage Aladdin paraffin lamp with incandescent mantle intact. It was green with verdigris, missing a shade, and cracked in the chimney, but I rubbed it down with sandpaper, gave it two coats of the white oil paint and made a splendid cylindrical paper shade from a spare chart. It turned that room after dark into a veritable Aladdin's cave—a warm oasis of golden light with the big Jotul stove roaring away, stoked with driftwood logs gathered off the beach.

I tell you it was a palace. That first night alone, I lay listening to the island sounds that came filtering through, and me taking the measure of them. A steady north-westerly was drifting from Manish Strand, the sweep of sand up on the north shore, bringing the thunder of surf across the isle on the wings of the wind. It eddied round the old house, in the gutters, round the eaves, and through the tall ornate chimney-stacks. Somewhere below, a door gently banged.

I had brought a spare Tilley lamp up to the room with me, still unlit, for I prefer the silent flame of a wick to the powerful hiss of a pressure lamp. Lying there, picking out the sounds one from another, I was gradually aware of a new note in the increasing wind. Every now and then it would achieve a power great enough to skirl round something below my window with the resonance of an organ. I remembered that John, in talking of the island history, had mentioned a certain 'mad Captain' who delighted in parading up and down the sea-walk in front of the house with bagpipes at full blast. On Sundays too. This apparently so affronted the rest of the populace that dire forecasts were made as to the eventual resting place of his soul, for nobody is quite certain whether St Peter is a Scot.

As the power of the wind increased, so did the sound of that skirling come more and more to resemble the drone of the pipes, and it wasn't long before I had

Lugworm with jury mizzenmast in 'house bay', Ensay

The homestead from behind the chapel on Ensay island, house bay on left

Taobh Deas, where the eagle had her eyrie;
photographed from Colla Sgeir reef

him in full Highland rig standing there outside my window, luring me out for a haunted hover over Borosdale with the long-since dead ghosts of the isle; and all the while that damned door banged, banged… somewhere below.

Now I'm not one for the haunts if you ask me quickly and in daylight, being of a mind that he who has a clear conscience is likely also to have a peaceful sleep at night. But this was all a bit much. Before long I was drawing those curtains back and peering out into the night, just to get the depth of my own idiocy. And still that benighted door banged. But now it became evident that the offensive thing was not in the house at all, but across the lawn in the barn; the barn in which John had surmised, with pregnant pause, that 'doubtless I'd be looking'.

I lit the Tilley lamp and waited for it to go full blast and beaming, then put my dressing gown over a thick jersey and stuck my bare feet into seaboots. The stag's eyes followed me, twin points of light right down into the hall, as I clattered by on the bare wooden stairs. I took the keys from the kitchen, pushed the back door open against the wind—and stampeded three bullocks into the void. Across the back lawn a lovely stone archway—monastic in design—led from the garden to the greensward immediately below my warmly-lit bedroom window. The gate under the arch squeaked piercingly on its hinges as I pushed—and the bagpipes stopped dead! I don't mind you knowing it, I began to feel like a sack of cold wet tripe. What earthly normal phenomenon of wind playing about a guttering would stop its activity so abruptly at the warning sound of a creaking gate?

Shivering there in the bitter cold, centre of a pale oasis of dim light and kidding myself I wasn't frightened to death, there came into my mind a bit of doggerel I'd written when a child:

The pale weak beam of my lamplight flickers into the night, and by its glow I can
*   only know those things which are close about—and even these are shadowy dim*
*   in the small unsteady light.*
But out and beyond this circle, there is a world, I know.
And it's none the less there because my lamp does not reach it with its glow.
The light of my intellect flickers, into the blackness without.
And my reason is only a fitful flame which half shows a truth, then it's lost again,
*   in the endless darkness of doubt.*

*Yet little by little beyond the glow, Reality I find, and it's none the less real because
I fail to reach it with my mind.*

So again and again I try and try, to answer the timeless question, Why?

Am I?

'You there!' I shouted into the windy void. 'Carry on with your infernal dirge, and to hell with you!' Silence.

A thousand points of light reflected from the glittering mica faces in the rough-dressed stone of the old walls, where my own shadow danced and mocked me. A myriad daisy faces peered at me, wan-white from the black grass. Insistently the door of the barn continued its banging. I strode across, determined to persuade myself there was a rational explanation for that sudden cessation of the pipes, but at the same time casting a glance behind me to buttress my convictions. The barn door was locked but loose on its fastenings and wobbling back and forth. There was nothing handy to jam between the lintel and the door, so I turned the key and pushed it back. Opposite was a vertical ladder leading into a cavernous loft. A heap of old clothing lay just inside the door and an indescribable assembly of old junk was piled away to the left—rusty bedsteads, chains, rotting planks, a massive iron cooking range and the mouldering remains of a mattress or two atop a cluster of old packing cases. It was difficult to see in the lamplight exactly what was heaped up there, but a crude wooden door to my right evidently led into a division of the barn. Gently I pushed it open.

At that moment a streak of white seemed to flash across the top of the ladder. Instinctively I swung to face it and backed through the door, peering up into the loft as I did so.

Nothing. Nothing but the wind outside and the persistent hiss of my lamp. 'Imagination,' I said out loud to myself, and turned to examine the place. Then I stopped breathing. Honestly, you're not going to believe this but it's truth: ranged row above row on shelving from floor to ceiling were scores of grinning human skulls! On more racks in the centre of the room were piles of skeleton bones—tibias, fibulas, clavicles, humeri, ribs, pelvic saucers—clutch yourself—it was there, even down to the phalangea of the fingers and the ghastly eloquent mandibles, their teeth leering in silent laughter.

But what gave the whole nightmare a touch of the macabre was the fact that every skull, every pile of sifted bones, was enclosed in a transparent polythene bag neatly stapled at the top! It was hideous; Alfred Hitchcock hadn't got a look in, and *Psycho* seemed a health resort by comparison.

What would you have done?

I did. Cold, calm and calculated I edged out from that door, not daring to look back up that ladder for fear of seeing something too horrible to contemplate. I eased the door shut, locked it, and ran hell-for-leather back to the kitchen, slammed the door and locked it, grabbed a wood axe lying in the scullery and pushed back the passage door, ready for the worst. Slowly back along that mouldering corridor I crept, fearful that doors might swing open and reveal some frightful demented maniac with blood still clotted round his fetlocks, and I leapt up those stairs three at a time. The warmth and light of the room was like a haven. Slam went the door, and the sound of the massive key turning was the first reassurance since I left.

I lay back on the bed, trembling with cold—at least that's what I told myself and I'm sticking to it. 'There must be some logical explanation,' I muttered. John hadn't looked one bit like a depraved killer. My thoughts floated off to Dr Jeckyll and Mr Hyde. I switched on my portable tape recorder, but it was an unfortunate moment: Wagner's *Ride of the Valkyries* reverberated out. Hastily I changed the tape to Cleo Laine: I remember she was singing that hauntingly beautiful *I do miss you*.

I left the lamp on, turned low, lest it run out of paraffin before dawn, for I'm sure nothing would have persuaded me from that room again till daylight.

*   *   *

Nothing, that is, except *Lugworm*. In my haste to get the place habitable I'd completely overlooked that she was due to float at high water—and her with but one anchor out at the top of the beach and the tides making! Hastily I looked at my tide-tables. High water was at three o'clock in the morning and I could hear the surge on the beach increasing in force as the level rose. The higher that tide rose, the greater would be those breakers on the beach: already it would be licking around her; if I disregarded it she would broach across the seas as they drove her up the beach; most possibly swamp her, not to dwell on the damage to her hull as she pounded. It was unthinkable.

Again I lit the Tilley lamp. There was an intermittent patter of rain now on the window and I remember wondering whether the cold raindrops would shatter the hot glass of the lamp. 'Dammit,' I thought, 'they must have got over that difficulty by now—but this is where I find out!'

The stag's head was positively laughing as I clattered down the stairs. This time I left by the porch door, and even the buffalo seemed to wear an amused grin. Outside it was bitter cold, wet, and the wind had risen even more. It was driving in across the Sound straight on to the beach. Casting a quick glance toward the barn, I nipped to the gate in the sea-wall and down the steps to the shore. *Lugworm* was just getting her chin wet with the top of the surge, and the breakers to the south of the bay sounded nasty. I swore at myself for not having laid out an anchor and dug it in well down the beach while the tide was low, for that way I could have waited till she floated, then pulled her easily off through the breakers into safe deep water. Mind you I'd still have had to swim ashore unless I stayed with her all the night. Now it looked as though I'd have to swim both ways, once to lay out the anchor seaward and once to get back ashore.

It's not the first time I've found myself in this situation on some beleaguered beach at unprintable hours dancing around like a watersprite. I put it down to experience, and have developed a technique for coping with the psychological side of the matter. I have to get angry. There was no other course left to me: the wind was onshore so I just HAD to move *Lugworm*'s anchor out there far beyond the breakers into deep water, return ashore and wait for her to lift with a swell, then heave her off quickly. The only alternative was to stay with her, keeping her bows into the breakers as she drove back up the beach on the rising tide. That would take hours. She was due to float within minutes.

I got angry. It helped to keep me warm in the rain, stripped and wading up to my earlobes with that anchor. Each successive surge floated the hair off the crown of my head! I dropped the anchor, pressed it in as far as possible with my

foot. I remember as I swam back that the Tilley lamp was on the beach throwing a ghostly light on the rain and the white water along the strand. It picked
out nothing more; there was just me swimming in a black void, the glistening
curtains of rain, the roar of the sea ahead and *Lugworm* silhouetted like a ghost
ship; beautiful beyond words, but pestiferously cold! Now *Lugworm* weighs all
of a thousand pounds with the sailing gear aboard, and it's more than one chap
can push. There was nothing more to do until she floated, so to keep warm I
sprinted back and forth along the beach—three hundred paces one way and
three hundred and fifty back-that's odd, I thought, has something gone rummy
with space, too, on this incredible night? I think maybe it was my counting, but
'ere I'd checked it for certain *Lugworm* was swinging around in the surf. I leapt
aboard and hauled taut on her anchor warp, waited for the next surge to come
rolling in, and heaved. The anchor dragged home a foot or two, then held. She
scraped a yard down the beach, then sagged deadweight again into the sand as
the surge withdrew. The next one and the next failed to lift her. I was shivering now with cold, standing back on her stern deck to keep my weight aft, with
the anchor warp through the bow fairlead to hold her stem into it. Down at
the southern end of the bay I heard a real thumper come pounding in. 'Here
it comes!' I told her. 'Lift this time, old girl, and we'll be afloat and away from
danger.' And so it was.

I heard the thunder of that wave rolling northward round the bay toward me,
felt her tilt as the slam of white water hit her side, and suddenly the warp was
slack in my hand. Heaving with all my strength, I brought fifty feet or more of
it inboard. The Tilley lamp receded gently astern, our world grew quiet and we
were alone in the deeps.

The warp grew taut again as it took her weight, and I waited to see how she
would lie to the wind. The shore looked a long way off, but it couldn't have been
much more than fifty feet: far enough to keep her afloat until the dawn As I swam
back for a second time, strangely I was no longer in fear of ghosts, nor maniacs
with hatchets: I could have met them all and laughed, and even played football
with those pathetic skulls, for suddenly the world was an incredibly wonderful
place, with every square inch of my skin tingling, and the blood pounding in my
veins: so wide awake and glad to be alive was I.

I flicked the buffalo affectionately with my jersey, blew a kiss to the stag, and didn't even bother to lock my door before towelling down and burrowing into bed.

*   *   *

A brilliant beam is shafting straight overhead from the open window on to the cracked mirror above the fireplace. Reflecting off the water in the bay, it throws a shimmering net of light across the ceiling and walls. The whole room throbs with light.

In a mother-of-pearl sky the great luminous ball of sun is floating over the saddleback between Greaval and Roneval. A light north-west wind blows offshore, and there's *Lugworm* snoozing peacefully at full scope on her warp, streaming out into the bay and unlikely to take the bottom on this tide. The clock shows six-thirty: can it really be only three hours since the fiasco of last night?

Below the window a group of sheep are nibbling, attended by a frolic of lambs. Fourteen cows stand munching contentedly on the beach, still as statues. Aquatic cows. Contented aquatic cows, just peacefully being cows.

Through the south window I can see the green rise of the hill, and there's nothing but pale-blue sky above it. Unlimited sunlit space... unlimited freedom... and air like wine! I can see Dunvegan Head in Skye under a puff of cotton cloud twenty-five miles across the Minch—and the day is mine.

Scottish oatcakes, home-made butter and marmalade washed down with hot coffee does nothing to assuage one's appetite for life. The first thing, of course, was to investigate those skulls. In the brilliant daisy-fresh morning there was nothing macabre about them at all; it was quite clear they were relics from some burial ground, and so indeed it turned out: they had been recovered from the beach up on Manish Strand, where the encroaching sea had unearthed them, and were ready for reinterment when opportunity offered, hence the careful parcelling of bone with fellow bone, all meticulously marked -for what could be more frightful, I ask you, than being reburied with someone else's head?

I scaled the ladder into the loft, and there another spectre was nailed: no phantom was it I spied up there last night. The most worldly of wild white cats stared back at me from the recesses of a packing case, her yellow eyes glowing in the half-light. It was a mutual surprise, I would not have thought a cat

One of the skeletons grinning
up at me from the sands
at Ensay

Bringing *Obbe-Wobble*
ashore; low tide in
house bay, Ensay

The peaks of Greaval and Roneval with Obbe in the distance;
from the top of Taobh Deas looking south-east

could have survived alone on the isle—she never expected a visitation into the privacy of her sanctuary—yet totally alone she was, and doubtless her presence accounted for the absence of rats or mice or rabbits, for never a one did I see during my five months' stay! She was not keen to make my acquaintance, feeling doubtless somewhat trapped in her cell, so I retired, put a bowl of milk at the kitchen door and set off to investigate that other mystery: the origin of the bagpipes.

This was not so easy, for the wind had altered direction and was now but a light air, so the bellows were gone. But after a week or so I did find the cause, and it was fascinating. My assumption that the protesting squeal of that opening gate accounted for the cessation of the bagpipe was correct—though not in the fashion I imagined; the gate was made of tubular metal struts—need I say more? One end of a strut was open, and at a certain angle (when the gate was closed) this resonated like an organ pipe. By opening the gate I had simply altered its critical angle to the wind.

By ten a.m. the sun was hot enough to strip for a swim out to *Lugworm*. Something had to be done about her, for it was clear that she could not be allowed to take the ground in the seas which broke on that beach. I nearly ruptured myself helping two massive lumps of gneiss to roll down to a suitable spot beyond low water level. To these I secured a stout rope mooring, topped with a fisherman's orange float found in the rocks. With *Lugworm* tethered I felt a deal happier, knowing she would now take the bottom only at low water springs. At such state of tide all the surge would have gone from the sea anyway for it was then too shallow out in the narrows for much swell to penetrate.

There still remained, however, the problem of getting myself aboard the boat when the tide was in. That nocturnal swim had convinced me that 'enough is enough', for the water is mighty cold hereabouts. Somehow I had to construct a raft, or tender of sorts. There was a colossal log—the complete bole of a tree—up the beach by the sea-wall and it gave me ideas. But have you ever tried sitting athwart a smooth log when afloat? It might look fine on the cover of *Boy's Own*, but believe me, it doesn't work in practice, I tried it!

No, somehow I had to give birth to another *Ben*—and straightway set off to scour the beaches for suitable wood. An old dustsheet, eaten with moth, surrendered itself from the house and I knew from experience that this, when doubled, coated with oil paint and stretched over a framework of laths would make a fine light skiff. The laths were the problem. Search as I might, no pieces longer than three or four feet could I find among the piles of driftwood around the shores. There were, however, a few rotten planks from some ripped-out flooring in the barn, and though they must have been close on a century in age I reckoned with a bit of persuasion, when sawn into strips, I might get a vestige of 'turn' into them. It took me best part of two days, my fossicking about with a great driftwood fire under a ten-gallon pot of boiling water trying to get enough pliance back into them for a bend without snapping.

My antics did not go unnoticed. Clearly, the prolonged residence of one of the species homo sapiens was of more than casual interest to the true inhabitants of Ensay. The garden, with gates closed, was more or less stockproof, but my labours with the steaming-pot, that towering column of black smoke and my own exclamations of zeal, were carefully noted by some forty cows, Angus the bull, and all of the two hundred sheep not to mention uncountable lambs. They would stand, the cows, wide-eyed with their heads above the stone wall taking in every detail, sharing each triumph or defeat as plank after plank bent or snapped under my too-enthusiastic hands. The sheep clustered thick at the gates, and the lambs careless of mother's urgent warnings, would persist in gambolling through the bars in an effort to help. I tell you, it was better than a circus, both ways, and not for a moment were we any of us lonely. Indeed, so wondrous and filled with life was my new kingdom that it was difficult to tear myself away from her green sloping hillsides. Every clump of grass, every warm wind-sheltered hollow under a rock held a new miracle. I tell you, up here the sky is more than the sky: it's a blue immensity of sonic joy. Listen now and I can hear the distant whirring of the snipe as it plunges, its wings a-quiver, then lifts in an ecstasy of life high, high again up into the endless blue. There are redshank, greenshank, larks and rock-pipits. Hundreds—literally hundreds—of lapwings nesting in the low marshy field adjacent to the house. My movement across the isle is heralded by a flurry of wings and clamour of strident protest, and well it is so, for underfoot tiny red mouths gape up at me as I pass, expecting the worm which doesn't come, and one must tread warily to avoid tragedy in those minute homesteads.

Bath-time on the lawn, Ensay,
watched by Buttercup

'Grumpy'

Ensay from Taobh Deas, looking southward;
Killegray and North Uist in right background

Great boles of trees to be sawn and carried a mile from
Manish Strand to the house; Pabbay isle in distance

But, despite these distractions, the skiff was eventually fashioned—there was about as much nature in those planks as in an Egyptian mummy—but with a load of hard swearing we got there in the end, and one memorable eve, just as day began flushing at the bold advances of night, why! *Obbe-Wobble* was born there on the beach, shaped like a laugh, painted sparkling white, eight feet in length and two feet six in the beam. Mighty fractious on the water she is, but fun; and the cows enjoyed her launching every bit as much as she and I!

It was about a fortnight later that I tore myself away and made a first sortie across to Obbe for provisions, bringing back a magnificent Highland beefsteak by way of celebration. I remember that steak well: better far than if I'd eaten it. Arrived once more at the isle, I stowed the groceries in the kitchen cupboard, but noticed a dust of white on the scullery floor. Close alongside was a bag of flour, pulled off the shelf, gnawed through and torn, and clear in the dust was the imprint of puss's feet! 'Little beggar,' I thought, 'but the poor thing must be ravenously hungry to tackle a bag of flour-lucky there wasn't anything else left about!' I put the steak on a plate and placed it in the window for coolth, then went to search for her. She was nowhere to be found. On return to the kitchen, a slight sound in the scullery alerted me—you get incredibly responsive to sounds when alone like this and (of course) there she was with the remains of my steak on the slate floor. She was in no doubt whatever that the steak belonged to me, that was obvious from her instant crouch of fear and surprise as I loomed up. But there was no way out of that scullery save the door, and I was athwart that. Gently I pushed it to behind me. We eyed one another.

'Puss!' I said, 'I've been waiting to be properly introduced, and now seems as good a time as any since you're evidently enjoying my hospitality regardless.' She didn't know what to make of it. Pangs of hunger drove her to the meat, pangs of fear drove her away from it. She was deplorably thin, looked hunted, and one ear was sadly torn from some ancient battle. I reckoned she was all of seven or eight years old. Very gently I moved to the shelf, took down an opened tin of milk, poured it into a cup, and added a little water from the tap, then placed it about three feet from her. She backed off, crouched against the wall, ready to claw my eyes out if need be. I picked up the gnawed remains of the steak, pulled it into small pieces, and passed them to her, one by one.

It was good to watch: seeing her adjusting to the unthinkable, actually being given the very food she was so furtively, fearfully, trying to bolt. We sat there in the scullery together, neither of us missing a trick, until she'd finished the meat and cautiously—always with one eye on me—emptied the cup. Then I quietly opened the door and walked out. Soon as I was far side of the kitchen she slunk through the door, eased along the far wall, and bolted through the open door. But I reckoned the battle was won!

For obvious reasons I christened her 'Grabbersnatch', and kept a full bowl of milk at the ready outside the back door with the odd titbit from the plate alongside. Soon my first appearance each morning in the kitchen was greeted with a wide-eyed little face peering through the leaded-light pane of the door, and a truly deplorable attempt at a 'mew'. The poor thing was so unused to any form of communication that her vocal chords had jammed.

'You'll never make a Maria Callas,' I kept telling her, as we got to know each other. It's astonishing how that cat put on weight, cleaned herself up, adopted domestic habits and conceded that there was much to be gained by trusting one another. No sooner was she regularly fed than she gave up the thieving, though I gave much thought to my wisdom in this, for inevitably she would have to fend for herself again one day. However, we solved this problem in another fashion, of which you shall hear later. She was wonderful company, and a rare and subtle form of communication came to operate between us, for you don't need to verbalise to make yourself understood: indeed, I'm convinced in some ways our much vaunted articulation forms a positive barrier!

*   *   *

"OBBE-WOBBLE"

Within a week or two there was no corner of that isle, no crevass in the rocky shore, nor slope of her green-topped dunes that had not been explored. Up on the north shore, I pondered the origin of that strange skeleton heap. Times gone, it is said, the marauding Vikings came and had fine battles hereabouts. But they were in a devil of a hurry, and had no time to bury their dead. So one supposes the local populace flung the corpses into a communal grave, and then the area would gradually become a recognised burial place across the years. Who knows when it all started? But the story goes that Viking artefacts have been found among the bones, and for sure I can vouch there to be a lot of bones under that sand yet, for was it not perhaps the skeletal shape of a marauding Norseman, I found gazing up at me from the sand one evening, as the sun went down? I found myself wondering just how many thousand times that sun had sunk obliquely below the horizon since those eyes had marvelled at it.

The weather was magnificent, and I went as bare as an aborigine, tanning to a deep mahogany, and becoming fitter with each day that passed, for there was always so much active physical work to be done. Fortunately, I had thought to bring with me a large bushman saw and an iron wedge, the latter for splitting the colossal logs which I sawed up and carried the mile back from Manish Strand. So gradually a haystack of driftwood piled up in the garden, each bit of a size to slip into the bedroom stove. The evenings were a balm. Only one real meal was necessary in the day, and I took this when the sun had gone down, then lit the lamp upstairs and got down to the writing. After a bit Grabbers discovered the warmth of the room, too, and would hesitantly creep up and curl beneath the feet of the stove, but always I left the doors ajar so that she could get out during the night, for her hunting instincts remained very strong. Frequently she would awaken me in the early hours of the morning with a positive crow of pride as she brought a wildly flapping chick bird up to the room for me to share! I would take it gently from her mouth, for she was not really hungry and, in fact, seldom hurt the bird; often it would fly off through the window, the wiser no doubt for the event.

So the weeks passed, and the multitude of eggs in the nests hatched. I followed their development with the camera, taking hundreds of colour slides, getting to know the chicks, sharing in their adventures as they grew. There was one large nest of seaweed bottomed with sheep's wool in a cliff on the northwest cor-

ner of the isle, and four blue-and-brown speckled eggs hatched into the ugliest little bare-pink chicks the day after I found it. Always, long before I had stalked or sprinted across the maidan of grass, the lapwings and the oystercatchers had warned the parent birds of my approach—and no sign did I ever see of them while the chicks were growing up. It was fascinating to watch the development of those skinny little forms. Within two days the faintest puffs of white fluff appeared, slowly the pink skins turned grey, then metallic blue. They looked for all the world like primaeval pterodactyls in miniature, so leathery did they become with their stringy necks and ever-gaping blood-red mouths. Two weeks after discovering them I took the most developed from the nest and photographed him on the grass; he didn't object in the least, though I christened him Grumpy, for reasons which you'll see. Three weeks later, while peeling a turnip in the house, I heard an unusual conversation taking place out in the garden. It was hoarse, guttural and astonishingly articulate, but quite unlike any voice I'd yet heard on the isle. On top of the garden wall were two of the biggest hooded crows I've ever set eyes on. They were sizing up the place, and my presence at the door spurred them to yet more articulation. Together they eyed me up and down, with obvious interest, croaking to one another as they did so. Satisfied, they took off and flew back to the north shore, and the mystery was solved.

Fraser Darling, in his book on the wild life of the Hebrides, states that this *corvus cornix* is one bird we can do without, and I'm not arguing. Nevertheless, I had become very fond of Grumpy and his brood and could no more have wrung their necks than my own. A month to the day after hatching they took to the wing, and that was the last I ever saw of them.

*   *   *

The days floated by, each one a more wonderful experience than the last. Each brought its own problems, its own demands, and whatever else was in hand there was always the continuing search for driftwood fuel. But the peace of the place is beyond description. I gathered a sackful of sheep's wool off the grass slopes, washed it and filled two pillowcases—I'm sleeping on them yet—and made a splendid six-foot lance from a bamboo cane found on the beach, tipped with the wing-feathers of an enormous gannet found dead on Manish Strand. It was splendid skill and exercise, slinging that lance from the top of the dunes down to a target drawn in the sand below.

Come evening, I'd spend hours lying on the warm faces of those dunes, just watching miracles of colour as the sun went down, for by now all the hysteria, all the compulsive drive to be 'doing', had fallen away from me.

'Doing' there was, and enough—seldom in my life have I physically worked harder than those months alone on the isle—but the days were a rhythm of rewarding practical effort, while the evenings were a rhythm of ease. Night time, I wrote. It's amazing how little sleep one requires when you're really fit, totally involved with your environs, and alone. Gregariousness takes its toll of us: we pay for the masks we adopt, the parts we play in social and business intercourse.

I spruced up the old house, giving all the windows and doors a scrape down, then three coats of white paint. She began to smile again. The sea-wall, breached at the northern end, was rebuilt and all the garden gates were rehung and painted. The kitchen—dark, dirty and forlorn—didn't know what hit it! Bucket after bucket of springwater sluiced over the walls, draining countless years of grime away, and a coat of whitewash followed by two coats of white emulsion paint did wonders. It fairly glowed with the evening sun coming through the newly painted window. Bathing was a problem. The Rayburn was splendid—but used a colossal amount of wood, and coal was both prohibitively expensive and difficult to get across to the isle, so I would boil up the ten-gallon iron pot on a driftwood fire and tip it into a four-foot diameter galvanized bathtub found in the storeroom. There, on the lawn—watched always by the cows—I would splash to my heart's content—and to the delight of Grabbersnatch, who viewed the whole matter with incredulity.

A month slipped by, but time itself stood still. Indeed, it was a week before I discovered my clock had stopped. But what need of a clock when one has a splendid sundial on the lawn made from the bamboo lance and a circle of beach pebbles to tell all that was necessary: one rock for breakfast and the 0630 shipping forecast, a second for the evening forecast and a third for my own supper and a bowlful for Grabbersnatch; that slim shadow, shortening gradually as spring turned to ripe summer, told me all I needed to know.

My radio, remembered haphazardly at news time, occasionally re-introduced an alien outside world: bomb mutilation in a metropolis, violence at some mass hysterical sporting event, political bickering, strikes, greed for more and more possessions. It was like tuning in to some sick horror play, and I found it hard to believe this was the real world of men, from which, for a moment, I had managed to escape.

The marsh dried up, the fields grew mellow, and many of the chicks were flown. The lambs grew fat and the calves were young bullocks. Angus grew a bit thinner, worn out doubtless by a harem of forty to one, and still the weather held.

Eventually an unwelcome missive arrived from the world of business, calling me away for a week to Oban, and it was now that I realised the gulf between this real life on the isle to which I had become accustomed and that urgent artificial strife back in the world of Man. Such a headlong plunge once more into the hysteria of 'civilisation', with the ferries, the buses, the trains, the snatching of synthetic meals between connections, fish-and-chips in packed noisy cafes, and the horrific queueing for tickets, jostling for sitting space, rushing ever rushing; all that is accepted as part of living in overcrowded communities suddenly had become unbearable to me. You may imagine I was glad to return to my kingdom, where life still had some dignity.

In fact, that return to the isle led to an experience I'll not forget. Having thankfully arrived by ferry at the southern tip of South Uist, I set off walking northward on a Sunday with the intention of making the shore of the Sound sometime on Monday from where a small ferry connects with Harris. It was a long walk—some

forty miles if I remember rightly—and would not have been accomplished by the time of the Monday ferry but for two very acceptable lifts on the lonely road. The day was mild but grey, with a swirling mist driving in from sea which made the incredibly barren landscape even more desolate and lonely than is usual. However, I had properly got into the swing of the walking and had already crossed the stone causeway that joins South Uist to Benbecula. The road was a single-track affair with passing places every quarter of a mile or so, and there was nothing to be seen but the dark ribbon ahead and the grey rocky hillside sloping up from the sea. What then appeared at first sight to be a tall cypress tree in the mist to my right aroused some curiosity. As I drew closer it turned out to be a truly colossal statue—some forty feet high—standing quite alone on the rock, with no plaque nor inscription, rail or plinth. It was the Virgin and Child, and of course I had to leave the road to take a closer look, so unexpected was it to find such a thing on this barren little isle. It was made from blocks of what seemed to be granite, but what was so remarkable was the face of the Virgin. I have seen the structure thereof in a thousand 'hippie' girls far and wide, for it was essentially a twentieth-century maid; but never before have I seen what shone from there. In that girl's face was all the strength and pride of absolute purity. She looked over my head as I craned backward to catch the miracle; over my head, and out to sea.

Standing in the crook of her right arm, with his left hand resting on her shoulder, was the Christ child. A babe? No: far more than that. A young boy? Hardly-yet. But I tell you, I couldn't stop looking at that face! In the mist it glistened, almost glowed, high up there on the girl's shoulder, and somehow the sculptor had captured an infinite power and authority therein.

One does not expect to see this in the granite face of a young child. One may ask how any mortal can capture infinity in anything, let alone in a granite rock. But, of course, the miracle lies not in what the chisel had put into the features— but what, in his wisdom, the sculptor had left out. Something far greater than the hand of man had infused into that half-sketched face not just a sense of mystery, though that would have been wonder enough, but a shining omniscience; a depth of *understanding* that lifted the heart, with hope.

As I looked at Him, I understood—so far as any human being may be said to 'understand' the real meaning of love. The real power and the glory of it. Through that face came the joy of everything to which we *ought* to aspire, and to which we seldom give even a chance thought.

The Virgin was slim and robed down to the ground, so that the eye filled in the exquisite stance as she took the weight of the child. The child was holding up one hand in blessing. Blessing us.

So I walked back down toward the rocket missile test range that lies between the girl's feet and the shore of that lovely isle, and caught the ferry back to Ensay.

CHAPTER V

THE SOUND OF HARRIS

IT WAS GOOD TO GET BACK TO MY ISLE. The name *Ensay*, in Norse, means Isle of Meadows, and how appropriately those ancient Scandinavians placed their labels. The ending ay is Norse for island, but it's said that the name of the whole group—the Hebrides—is Roman in origin and brought to its modern spelling by a printer's blunder: The original Roman name was *Hebudae*, or *Ibudae*. The I (pronounced 'E') signified an island, while the *budae* was quite possibly derived from the Celtic word *muid*, meaning sea-spray, or misty foam, which is surely appropriate enough. The Roman writers mention these isles under the name *Hebudes* and the story goes that the 'u' became accidentally printed 'ri' which would certainly account for the current name.

Misty isles they are at times, but oh! when Phoebus smiles his light has a clarity and astringent quality akin to Swiss mountain sunlight. The early Celts showed remarkable perception when they referred to this far-flung string of jewels as *Tir-na-Nog*: the 'Land of Youth'. It burns deep that sun, and rich, seeming to reverse the very process of ageing, helped by the clear air and silence. Then it draws a blanket of mist to protect the freshness from too harsh a parching.

I have found that people think of the isles as being excessively wet, but in fact the rainfall up here in Scotland is now only an average of thirty-five inches per year, which is some ten inches less than it was in the 1940s—and well below the average rainfall for Cornwall. One wonders what degree of coastal erosion is taking place on the prevailing weather side of the isles; certainly the rate here on Manish Strand is appalling. But wherever sand forms the margin of the land there must inevitably be a rapid shifting and doubtless depletion at one point (as at the burial ground) is often offset by accumulation at another. But the erosion by the seas of rock itself is a one-way process. Old gneiss, of which the majority of these isles and hills is formed, is a very hard laminated rock of quartz, feldspar and mica; some of the oldest rock on the Continent. Even so, the inexorable process of erosion continues. Often as I sit watching the assault at high water on this sea-wall below my bedroom window, I wonder how any man-made structure

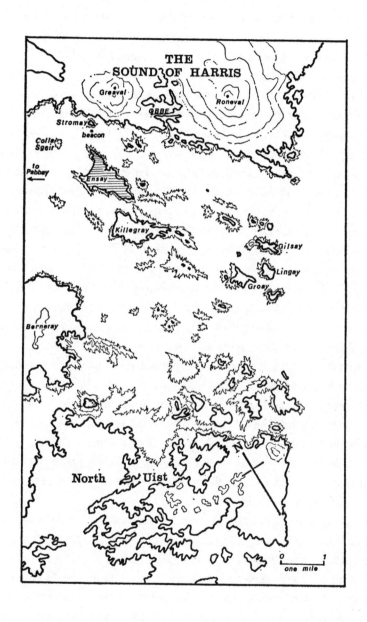

THE
SOUND OF HARRIS

Greaval

OBBE

Roneval

Stromay
beacon

Collam
Sgeir

to
Pabbay

Ensay

Killegray

Gilsay

Lingay

Groay

Berneray

North   Uist

N

0   1
one mile

can withstand such force. A hundred and thirty years ago, on the Atlantic rock of Skerryvore before the lighthouse was begun, a systematic measurement of the pounding of the waves was made. The average summer weight of pounding was 611 lb. per square foot, while the winter average was 2,086 lb. per square foot. In a southwesterly gale in March 1845 it reached 6,083 lb. per square foot!

The tidal flow of water hereabouts is interesting too. Generally speaking, through this Sound of Harris in summer the stream at neaps flows from the Atlantic during the whole of the day, and from the Minch during the night. In winter the process is largely reversed. Spring tides, however, both summer and winter, tend to flow from the Atlantic for the greater part of the time that the tide is rising (but never for more than five and a quarter hours) and then flow back into the Atlantic during most of the fall of the tide. Between the isles in constricted water, such as the Caolas Skaari channel just south of Ensay, the velocity reaches up to five knots at springs and not much less at neaps. In the broader channels it runs around two or two-and-a-half knots. Navigation hereabouts has to be an exact science, most especially in slow-moving craft, and deep-keelers are a nightmare. There must be no Dead Reckoning: constant runs on available transits, and continual fixing is the order of the day if one is not completely familiar with the topography of the rocks. It's madness to approach the Sound in poor visibility.

In Leverhulme's time, due to his ambition to turn Obbe into a major commercial fishing port, it's said that it was easier to navigate through the Sound at night than it was in daytime. The lighthouses he had built on the isles are, however, no longer lit, but they do give convenient bearings for a mariner in daytime.

But apart from the running stream, *Lugworm* could laugh at the rest of these hazards, for as I've said, her draught is less than a yard at her most profound, and under a foot when she's shallow.

She has confidence now, for we have had time enough to take soundings in this area of the 'misty isles', and already my crisp new chart is a battered, limp and salty sheet, barely legible, or for that matter necessary, for there is no kelp-ridden reef, nor knife-edged rock, nor lonely islet with its mantle of grass and boggle-eyed ewe that has not been prodded, examined, landed upon and generally assessed in relation to these awesome tides, sluicing like some oceanic millrace through the isles.

You would be void of imagination too if, when the mists come swirling in from the Atlantic, you didn't find your eye lifting for the ghosts of those long lean Viking ships nosing in with the flood to plunder and rape and make merry hell at high water by carrying off the local girls. Damned fine prizes those girls must have made, too, if the samples I've seen on my travels are anything to judge by, for they have a liveliness about them, bright eyes and a bold, lithe manner of carrying themselves that turn a man's head despite himself.

Speaking of hazards, have you ever sniffed the ozone down to leeward of a Hebridean reef at low-water springs, when the mists come creeping in so heavy and silent over a mirror-sea that you just sit for hours listening, until the roar of overfalls from the running tide two miles away brings you to your senses? Ah, but it's an evocative, dank scent that sets just the right tone for that flesh-creeping dirge that comes floating from the rocks beyond the border of your visible world, rising, like the hair on the nape of your neck, as it gains volume by another and another great cow seal joining the unearthly lament. Eerie and echoing the ululation comes, like wails from the bottom of the Pit. I tell you, if it were to this that Jason was listening when he had to lash himself to the mast then he must have been pretty desperate, poor chap, for it's enough to curdle you before breakfast.

But this morning there are no mists, nor wailing, for there is *Lugworm* in the bay, with the sun flinging a brilliant new day straight over the ridge of Roneval out there on Harris, and rippling down the Sound comes the first kiss of a brisk northeaster that sets the burgee at her gaff chattering and exhorting me to choke on the oatcakes and scatter crumbs and marmalade, so eager is she to cast off the mooring and wing away to the north and west. For has Pabbay Isle not beckoned too long, unanswered?

So she spread a glad genoa, main and mizzen, took *Obbe-Wobble* in tow and together we beat out from the bay over toward Greaval, not putting in the final tack till the barnacles on Stromay were flinching and the water frowning black under the cliffs, and then we were out northward between the beacon reef and the islet with the spring ebb giving us a useful thrust through the overfalls.

Out to the broad mouth of the Narrows we reached, where Colla Sgeir reef lifted a curling white hand in salutation. It broke creaming close aboard as we ran westward and there were thundering breakers on Manish Strand where the beach was a steaming stretch of white in the morning sun, backed by bastions of green-topped dunes.

Oh Neptune! It was one of those mornings when you catch the world laughing with her hair down; bright, clear blue above, deep, rolling turquoise below, and all about was the green and gold brilliance of the isles. I tell you the sky sang a song in our sails that day, with *Obbe-Wobble* leaping and dancing astern, agog at the wonder of such a mighty ocean.

We had in mind to make a landing close behind the reef at Rubh'a'Bhaile Fo Thuath on Pabbay's eastern point, but not one of the three of us could quite get our tongue round it, so we made a bit of southing until Shillay hid behind Pabbay to warn us (as if we didn't know) that we were approaching the shallow sandbar that joins that isle and Berneray. But the ebb was hand-in-hand with the wind so the seas only heaped up a bit, and *Lugworm* cocked up her stern and surfed down the face of them with a quick glance now and then to the tiddler astern who rode the waves like a gull. Before you could cry 'Tir-na-Nog' we were off the tongue of Rubh'an t-Seana-chaisteil rocks and nosing into their lee. Down plunged the anchor through two fathoms of crystal green—and up shot an astonished dab to streak off and warn his brothers of this rare intruder.

After all that boisterous wet splother of wind and open water our world was suddenly still, and warm, and silent. The heat from that beach was so inviting it demanded an instant casting off of the last bits of clothing before I pulled ashore to sprint along the hot sands while the salt chalk-dried on my skin and there came that rare and carefree sense of well-being only those susceptible to a strange island madness can know.

Pabbay is uninhabited. Have you, I wonder, ever landed like some explorer of old on the sleeping beaches of an uninhabited isle? There were two miles of them to be combed and armfuls of silvered driftwood to be loaded for the house fires. There were strange bottles, too, of all shapes and colours, misted by years of rolling in the sand, any of which MIGHT have contained messages, but none of which did, and fishermen's floats of all conceivable patterns. A dinosaur might have filled her jewellery chest from the magic of that beach, and probably did, times gone.

In the heat of early afternoon I was casting an eye on the inviting green rise of the isle and I set off through the bee-buzzing grass and heather, up past the first gaunt shoulders of grey gneiss and still on up to where, from a sheltered hollow, there erupted an explosion of wild stags, or hind, or I'm damned if I know exactly what they were, so shattered was I at the shower of grit from the thudding hooves of those powerful antlered beasts. Only the fact that they were in full flight enabled me to pluck up courage and stagger on up to that final shoulder from which I could see the rounded tip of the island. Then, breathless and gulping in glittering air, there was nothing more above, but the whole world laid out below right round the full sweep of the horizon. Such a view you have not seen, nor ever will see, save you have the luck ever to stand on the tip of Pabbay on a golden summer day. What pale ghosts are these photos!

Northward, Shillay voyaged majestically through the ocean, her wake of white froth streaming astern on the now strong north-east running flood. Her emerald green top rose in a long slope, breaking off sharp at the western edge to plummet in vertical cliffs down to and beneath the turbulent water.

I could see the dots of white sheep grazing on her slopes, for every isle with a cargo of grass must sustain its moneyspinning crew of breeding ewes and a ram or two. Southward lay mile upon mile of empty beach on Berneray, with the unbelievable blue of Lochs Bruist and Borve shimmering behind acres of machair. As a backcloth to that, rolling down to the horizon and far beyond was the full panoply of the Uists and Barra, with Mount Marrival and Eaval crouched like sentinels either side of towering Hecla, monarch of them all, thirty miles off.

The brilliance of that southern aspect made me turn my eyes away from the sun, and it was then I caught far out—like a distant lonely ghost haunting the horizon—the mist-blue peaks of St Kilda. Even at that distance, some fifty miles off, I could sense the grandeur of those cliffs. Dishabited this forty years and more, so strong is the call still from this most remote of the Outer Isles that a band of volunteers, so I'm told, go annually to maintain and take a spark of summer life back to its deserted village.

So I sat bewitched by the immensity and freedom of it all until the western flanks of Lewis and Taransay away to the north-east began to take flame in the evening light; and there far below lay *Lugworm*—a tiny black thing with faded red mizzen—key to so many adventures in far-off places over the years, but not any one of them, I truly believe, more worthwhile or beautiful than this.

It was late before we could tear ourselves away from that isle. As we ghosted quietly off the beach my eye, searching the dark outline of the hill, caught the motionless silhouettes of the deer, still as statues watching our going, and wondering, timid but overpoweringly curious as to the nature of these strange visitors.

The sun was a red ball above the amber misty horizon as we re-crossed the bar and made our easting with a dying wind. Clouds, rolling slowly in from sea, awoke with shock on the weather flanks of Taransay. There they took fire, leaping into the vault of sky in crimson flames as though to toast the toes of the Gods themselves. And the sea went quiet, and the islands held their breath in silent awe at the majesty of it.

We plucked a fine 'cuddie'—which you or I might wrongly call a pollack—from the dark kelp three fathoms down in Caolas Skaari channel west of Ensay. Then the sails had to drop, for the ebb tide was winning and the outboard tipped us round the southern end of the isle until we could nose back quietly under sail with the help of the stream to House Bay.

So it was poached fillet of cuddie in white sauce, washed down with a pint of Rodel beer beside a crackling driftwood fire—and Grabbersnatch appreciating the head and tail every bit as much as I did the middle. That night the yellow beam of my oil lamp probed from the window of this cavernous old mansion until the early hours of the morning, with only the inquisitive seals out there with *Lugworm,* wide-eyed in wonder at the rat-a-tat of this typewriter.

*   *   *

'Grabbers,' I mused, one rainy noon in early July, 'our monk-like solitude is about to be infringed!' She stopped playing the harp on the middle of my bed and looked at me in disbelief. 'I'm not at all sure, my little whitened sepulchre, that you'll be sleeping on that bed much longer at that!' I added.

B, was due to arrive at Obbe. It was about time, too, for solitude is absolutely splendid, but a bit tedious when you have to suffer it alone for long periods.

'Sharing takes the sting out of life,' I philosophised, while Grabbersnatch recommenced her ablutions. 'Fact is, there are limits to what a man should suffer in the cause of literature; you're all right, all you do is eat and you evidently find the island life completely to your taste. I'm different.'

With Grabbers you never quite know exactly what line her philosophy takes. Expressive she is, in everyday mundanities, but she retains a womanlike subtlety when it comes actually to committing herself in matters of the heart. She has, in fact, developed an appalling purr and an endearing habit of rubbing her head affectionately against my hand as I fill up her bowl of milk. And then, as last night, she will drain my soul of love by snatching the sausages actually out of the pan on the stove, an act of sheer rebellion if ever I saw one, for hungry she is NOT.

'If you take my tip, you'll cultivate B. with every catlike ploy you can bring to bear, otherwise you're due for a change in your standard of living.' She stalked out, tail erect. If ever an animal said, 'Who's here on sufferance, anyway?' she did at that moment.

So there was B., rucksack at the hoist, waving from the end of the quay in Obbe, for the bus was early, and *Lugworm* rammed the quay in exuberance of the moment.

'What's the fishing like?' she queried, as we corkscrewed off Soundwards. 'Have you missed me?' I ask you?!

'I'm a piscatorial pundit,' I boasted. 'You name it—there's cod, mackerel, skate, ray, dogfish, ling, tunny, haddock, coal-fish, hake, halibut and herring... not to mention saithe and lythe, and I bet you don't know the difference?'

'They're both a form of pollack, only the saithe has a straight line down its side and is good eating, while the lythe has a wiggly line and tastes like cotton wool.' I was flabbergasted. 'Been reading it up,' she laughed, 'and so, evidently, have you. So you've been living on fish?'

'Two: a fine fat salmon that jumped into the boat and brained itself and a cuddie, which is a young coalfish—and I don't know which I enjoyed most. Meet Grabbers.'

There she was, sitting at the tideline, demure and obviously whisker-deep in domesticity, exhuding a positive halo of good manners.

'Ah! *Fucus vesiculosus*,' shouts B., leaping ashore and clutching a mangy bit of weed. 'Bladderwrack to you, used in the lazy beds.' She's quite nutty about seaweed and even eats some of it. 'And look here: *pelvestia canaliculata*. The cows will be down on these beaches, they love it.' I stared at her in sheer admiration. Grabbers stalked off in high dudgeon.

And so it went on. I learned more in a few days about the birdlife and weed on that isle than I'd assimilated all summer. B. devours information like a snow-plough and distributes it in much the same fashion. 'You've got to take an in-telligent interest in your surroundings,' she's constantly telling me. 'It's no good just looking at things and dreaming about them. Man didn't evolve on philoso-phy—he used his teeth.'

'Very well,' I ruminated, a day or two later. 'If it's participation you're after, there's a clutch of cormorants' nests down on Gilsay isle that might still have young, or even eggs in them. They're inaccessible to normal man, hidden under a stinking guana-covered cliff. We'll sail down there with the camera; I need a photo for one of the books.

So it came about that four days after she arrived we packed a bottle of wine and oatcakes in *Buggerlugs* and set off southward down the Sound. Killegray cost us an hour, frolicking on the beaches for shells, and a lazy liquid lunch in a grotto on the west shore of Lingay put us to sleep for a couple more, but after things were straight again we could see, across the mirrorlike water, that the southern cliffs of Gilsay were vibrant with activity. Some forty or fifty cormorants were engaged in urgent traffic 'twixt cliffs and sea. We could make out the whitened slopes below the nests, which were tucked under an overhanging brow. Even from that distance it looked a bit of a challenge.

'How do you propose getting near enough to take a photo?' B. asked. 'You've no telephoto lens and it's impossible to climb down there from above-you'll break something. Is it worth it?'

'What are we here for?' I countered. 'We've not come to the Arctic Circle just to look at things and dream about them. I'll use my teeth!'

Hah! Prophecy and teeth must be two of my strong points. It was plain on arrival that the nests were indeed inaccessible from above. We stooged about in *Lugworm* with *Obbe-Wobble* in tow examining the cliff face. There was just one possible access down a fissure on to some great bluffs to one side of the cliff foot. After that I might climb up an excreta-covered slope on to a narrow ledge which ran below the overhanging brow and passed just under the nests. Protesting adults launched their ungainly forms out, dropping to within feet of the water before becoming properly airborne, and the place was resonant with cries echoing off those black rock faces—every bit as good as the Albert Hall.

'There's nothing else for it,' I enlightened B. 'Far too risky to take *Lugworm* against those rocks. We'll have to anchor off the shingle beach backalong and I'll go ashore. Then you row *Obbe-Wobble* back here beneath the nests and be ready to pick up the bits if need be, for if disaster strikes I'll be swimming after a bounce or two.' I could see she was unhappy. To start with, she hadn't really got used to *Obbe-Wobble* (nor *Obbe-Wobble* to her) so that in itself would be quite an adventure. She demurred.

'It isn't me I'm thinking about,' I remonstrated. 'It's the blessed camera. Do you think the insurance company will cough up for a total loss claim when they hear it's been dangled over the weather side of the Hebrides? My bet is it'll be an "act of God" somewhere in the small print. No: you station yourself just below the nests and I'll try not to land in the skiff when I fall. I'll fling you the camera as I pass, but for heaven's sake keep it dry.'

It was the work of minutes to gain the greensward above the cliffs, but the descent down that narrow fissure was a bit hungry on the skin. I knew it would be impossible to re-ascend by the same means, but counted on being able to hand the camera to B. in the skiff, having taken the photos, and then swimming back to *Lugworm*. It was cold under those cliffs and the long swell that rolled in kept licking over the slimy rocks which had to be traversed before I could tackle the slope up to the ledge. It's not easy leaping over wet weed-covered rocks at the best of times, but with a very expensive camera dangling round your neck it's quite lethal, for it upsets the balance. Meanwhile, B. was carving an erratic course from *Lugworm* in my general direction, helped by my exhortations. By the time she finally drifted under the nests I was impatient to start climbing.

'Stay exactly where you are, darling—just be ready to grab the camera if things go wrong,' I counselled. The place reeked of dead fish. Acrid and pungent, it was, and before long I was plastered with the white porridge that lay thickabout. But the nests were there just above me and there were cracks on that slope that you could get a toe in here and a finger there. Provided they stayed that way I saw no reason why I should not work up to, and then along, the ledge. I got up to its level, and all that remained was to ease round a knuckle of rock close under the overhanging roof, then inch farther along to the actual nests. I could see nothing to stop me. But then, as I remember, from where I was I couldn't quite see right round that knuckle either.

Halfway round, poised above the dark water far beneath, I began to have sickening doubts. You know the feeling? Every thought in your head focuses on the worst of all possible events. I saw myself bouncing off rock faces, mangled to a pulp and the camera ruined, B. with a measly widow's pension and a photo on the piano, all that sort of thing. One twinge of cramp in a brace of toes and it would be stark fact! My legs and arms went limp, the bones jellified as I clutched the rock and sweated. Could I get back? Could I get forward? The question was academic, for certain I couldn't stay spreadeagled on that knuckle for more than seconds—either was better than the present predicament. Below me, B. was fossicking about in circles trying to stay within range. I was in a smelly mess. To be brave in retrospect, I think it was the camera that really worried me: you don't lightly fling yourself into space clutching six months' hard earnings. I began breathing deeply to calm myself. 'B.,' I called after a while, trying to make my voice sound casual. 'Do you think you can get vertically beneath me and catch the camera if I drop it?'

'But what about YOU?' she gasped. She had a point. One hiccup and there would be me, her, *Obbe-Wobble* and the camera all fulminating with the bubbles. 'Can't you slide on to that ledge just to your right? It looks easy from here!' she called.

That did it. Suddenly I knew I wasn't going to drop anything, much less me. There was nothing more to be lost than absolutely everything, and I was more likely to lose that by staying where I was than by going on. Sheer logic inched me round the knuckle 'till I lay gasping on the safety of that ledge. Ahead, the cormorants were in pandemonium. Leathery chicks slithered from the nests, scrabbling to hide themselves in dark crevasses. One nest, close under the roof, still held three porcelain-like eggs. It was a study in white, sepia and glistening rock. I worked carefully along, full-length on the slimy ledge and adjusted the meter reading. The light was magnificent: the viewfinder captured all the wild desolation, the sheer inaccessibility of that place. Hard and sharp I focused on the eggs

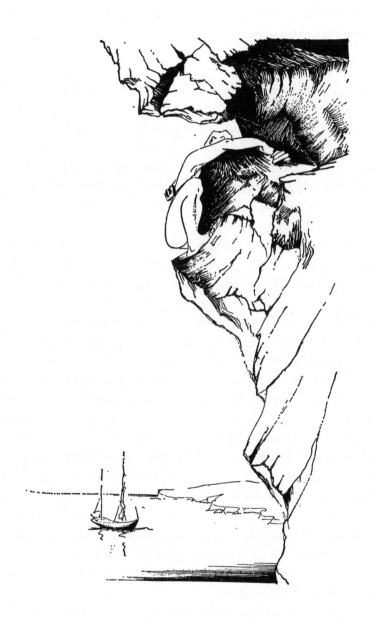

from about two feet off. A winner, that photo. You'd be looking at it now had there been a film in the camera.

* * *

Bluebell has the staggers. I found her upside down in a hollow last week, pawing the air with her hooves: she's the russet cow with liver fluke. At least I think it's liver fluke but I'm no farmer. John has been feeding her red pills the size of golf balls this last two visits to the isle, but things don't seem to get any better.

What do you do with an upside-down cow in a hollow? I'll tell you what: you parbuckle her. It's easy, they use it in the Navy for rolling barrels down gang-ways, and if it works down a gangway with a barrel shouldn't it work up a hollow with a cow?

'Fetch the spare halyard from *Lugworm*,' I instructed B., breathless from a run half across the isle. 'Bluebell's in the out-patients' department and bellowing her head off!' I made up two halters of rolled sacking while she fetched the rope, and together we trudged back to the source of the bellowing. 'The principle is simple,' I instructed B. 'We'll put a halter over one front and one back leg on her same side, then fling the loop of rope across her tummy. You and I then get in the bight and heave like hell. She should roll over.'

She did. For a blissful moment she staggered on all four feet and then—you've guessed? She rolled back into that hollow, pawing at the seagulls! On top of the rope.

So it was across the Sound in *Lugworm* for a rescue party from Obbe, and John and half the village in the launch with pills and stomach pumps, and before Blue-bell could wink she was being propped up until her balance was regained.

But all to no avail. Day before yesterday I found her stuck up to her knee-caps in the bog. 'She has the death wish,' I told John, and again half the village embarked in Don's boat with planks and ropes. We sledged her out this time on to the flanks of Borosdale, but despite all efforts poor Bluebell is failing fast. She refuses to stand, and just looks mournfully at us. We can see her from the bed-room window, and she's been on a vitamin-enriched diet of bran, oats and plenty of water. This afternoon she died.

'It happens,' I consoled B. 'Better to go fast like that than slide downhill slow-ly!' But what do you do with a dead cow on Borosdale?

A boatload from Obbe dragged the corpse to the shore, and then sixty rampaging horses in Don's launch towed her out to the broad Atlantic for a sea funeral with full ceremony, and that was that.

This morning up the hill there was a fat ewe on her back. 'We got here in time,' I told B. as we rolled her over and held her steady 'till she got her bearings again. 'If they can't get up they soon exhaust themselves trying, and then down come the blackback gulls and peck out their eyes –'

'Stop!' she exclaimed, 'I don't want to know.'

'But it's nature, and no good our putting on blinkers,' I remonstrated. 'Just because *homo sapiens* keeps reality at arm's length doesn't change it, and it's going on all the time. On this earth one thing lives by the death of another, and that's the order of things: we can't change it. If creatures are to evolve, then it must be by survival of the fittest. If they don't evolve they cease to be. That's the choice.'

'Then it were better not to be,' she answered.

I thought about that. There must be something wrong with our morality, or else God's got it all mixed up. But B. and I have had this discussion before and there's no answer to it. Maybe we're just asking the wrong questions; so off we went to sunbathe up on Manish Strand and saw up a few more logs, and there was glory in it all, and to hell with philosophy.

THE WEDDING

NOW I MUST TELL YOU THAT WITHIN A HUNDRED YARDS of the old house there is a little chapel standing on the greensward looking across the Sound. There has been a chapel here, so they tell me, since 800 AD and dedicated to St Columba. For many years it was a stable, but recently has been refurbished by my friend the Doctor, who also had it rededicated, so now it's fully operational, albeit somewhat cobwebby inside.

There is to be a wedding there shortly, and Obbe is agog. 'Can't you stay until after the event?' I pleaded with B. as we wire-brushed the rusty ecclesiastical lamp-hangings and coated them with black paint ready for the great day. But alas it could not be arranged. She had business back in that other world, and so it comes about that I'm sitting here alone this morning waiting for the arrival of the wedding guests from far and wide, with the great house open to the public and the bedroom glowing upstairs with a log fire for the bride to change before.

Brushed, polished, whitened on their surrounds as though wearing a new pair of tennis shoes inside, those lamp brackets are still swinging gently from the trimming of the two Tilley lamps. The altar and lectern are spruced with wax polish and there is but one filmy cobweb high in the west window which caught the final shafts of sun yesterday eve, so that none had had the heart to remove the miracle. I tell you, St Columba too, is agog.

So now, fresh from the mists of a mirror-calm Sound, Penelope, bride-to-be, disembarks from her longboat like some blonde Viking princess and leaps across the rocks to the north of the bay, followed close by the Lord Bishop of Argyll and the Isles carrying robes, mitre and portable crook in a battered suitcase. Close on his heels comes the Reverend Philip B. from Obbe, for it is he who is to conduct the ceremony, and who is this but the bride's mother and father coming hot-foot across the grass, and the first glint of sunshine blesses the isle as the clock shows ten.

Into the house she goes with her retinue and up to the large room where the fire is welcoming, and preparations begin for that alchemy which will transform the chrysalis into that gossamer butterfly shortly to emerge.

But hasten! Already across the Sound comes the distant throb of another boat, echoing over the water which seems to be holding its breath in suspense, as though catching something of the magic. How long is it truly, St Columba, since you last held your arms above the heads of two about to become one—here on this isle?

So forty or so wedding guests, standing packed tight in the long green ferry-boat from Uist, sweep into the bay and gaze apprehensively shorewards. How are they to land, with but one small rowing boat in tow? Why—*Lugworm* of course! So *Obbe-Wobble* is hastily cast into the water and I row out in her, slip *Lugworm*'s mooring and speed to the relieved guests.

'Twelve,' I shout. 'Not one more, lest Neptune see his opportunity and baptise the lot of us! Twelve only at a time can we take.'

Mothers and aunts, uncles and clergymen, cousins and friends totter, skid and fall pell-mell into the cockpit. And who's this... a kilted piper, complete with chanter and drones, come to send the couple speeding on a blast of joyous Highland air; so we beach, and a surge of swell lifts *Lugworm* far up the sand then recedes, so that the first to disembark, morning-suited and toppered, thinking to step dryfoot gets the laughing edge of the following wave that fills the polished shoes with saltwater and grit! It's piggy-backs for the remainder then, and only one camera taken as sacrifice for a safe landing by Old Neptune—and that returned good-naturedly, albeit somewhat soppy.

And now we are all ashore and drifting up to the chapel, crowding to the back like hushed sheep as though the altar had the mumps, and waiting. We have a tape recorder with potted organ and the acoustics in here are very good so that if you close your eyes, why, you might be in Paul's so echoing is the music; and now, silence.

Silence, through which comes breathing the gentle hiss of the two Tilley lamps swinging there above us in the brackets.

From outside comes the deep sighing of the sea down there on the beach, and the far distant crying of a plover. A wide-eyed cow, against the far fence, lifts her head and... MMOOOOOOO!

Silence.

Inside here it is so still that the gold candles atop the two altar posts send their yellow flames in perfect ovals roofward, twin glows that are echoed by the

The hills of North Uist
looking south-west
from Manish Strand

Piping the betrothed from
the chapel to the house,
Ensay

'Grabbersnatch',
the true Laird of Ensay

two plain white candles one either side the crucifix above the lace altar cloth, and behind the altar in the window a bunch of purple island heather catches the light.

Whispering silence.

A rustle! Through the door comes the goldlace glory, the mitred Bishop, who but two years since reintroduced this forsaken little chapel to Christ. Now comes the Reverend in plain white surplice, and here is the groom, bearded and looking VERY young in his immaculate morning coat, trembling perhaps just a little.

Silence. You could hear a pin drop on the thick coconut matting so hastily taken from the front room of the house.

Another rustle. A gossamer Penelope enters, cocooned in cream, on the arm of her father in black tails, and a whispering dies.

So to the first hymn:

> *Father, hear the prayer we offer*
> *Not for ease that prayer shall be*
> *But for strength, that we may ever*
> *Live our lives courageously*

and the taped organ, well-intentioned mindless thing, does not know that the congregation cannot sing in unison at that pace, and outstrips them; but we begin to get the hang of it by the Offertory and the second hymn; *Come down, O Love Divine* produces a full-blooded confidence by the last verse. A little later, while Penelope secretly fingers the ring on her finger, her clergyman-uncle gives a short address which might well be remembered by all on earth who take that vow:

'In that part of Africa where my wife and I have lived and worked for forty years,' he tells the now betrothed couple, 'the villages are simply clusters of what are called rondavels—straw huts—and outside they all look the same, but if you go into them, you will find there are two different kinds. One has a central pole, the other has none. The one which has the central pole looks stronger: it has something you can see holding up the roof. But the people don't like it because that central pole gets in the way—it takes up too much room!

'You know, such a dwelling might symbolise a state of marriage where one person tries to be dominant—whether it's the man or the woman is no odds. If one tries to be dominant, that one gets in the way of a mutual understanding, gets in the way of true love.

'Now, in the other type of hut you'll find there isn't a central pole at all. But if you were to look up, you'd find that instead of just a cluster of rafters holding the roof up, there are two main ones, tied together with a little ring of cord. The local people will relate to you a parable which, in wisdom, they hand down from one generation to another. They say that the two rafters which are tied together represent husband and wife—and all the others represent the family.

'Man and wife are joined by that tie.

'If that tie breaks, the roof collapses.

'The home collapses.

'The tie is there to take the strain. A very considerable strain, time and time again. That is what it is there for.

'So,' he continues, 'we might remember the final words of the hymn we sang right at the beginning of this service:

> *Be our strength in hours of weakness*
> *In our wanderings, be our Guide*
> *Through endeavour, failure, danger*
> *Father, be Thou at our side*

We all think a bit, about that.

Then the Bishop conducts a shortened Communion Service, and we sing *The Lord's my Shepherd*.

The bride takes her husband's arm and, to the strains of the Wedding March, walks out of the chapel to where the piper, ready at the door, takes up the joy and sounds it out across the isle and across the breathlessly still water, and the echo comes back to us from the old house walls, and the sheep and the cows, the lambs and the calves and a thousand birds are alerted and stop in their tracks or take to the wing.

And the couple, with two young bridesmaids holding the long veil clear of the thistles and the cowpats, walk to the echoing pipes down the hill to the house.

But what's afoot? The top-hatted father of the bride looks concerned. 'Where's the small boat that's to take the bridal party back to Obbe ahead of the guests?' he asks. No sign.

To *Lugworm* then!

Piggy-backs again with the piper landing on his bottom, kilt, sporran and bag-pipes flying in a flurry of legs down into the cockpit, and the bride and groom with skirts and veil, trousers and shoes high as possible staggering through the surf to tumble aspluther into the boat, and Goodness! Here we all are again in *Lugworm*, her four horsepower manfully gasping at full throttle and bow sunk deep beneath the load of ten adults so that there's scarce freeboard at the scupper-holes; but the Piper regardless stands straight as a fathom of pumpwater at her stern, one precautionary arm around the mizzen mast, and plays us out of the bay and across the Sound to Obbe where the crowd is collecting. Three seals, their great eyes wide and liquid as the bride's own, come swimming in company, lured by the strange, haunting notes of the pipes which echo off the distant flanks of Roneval.

On the way back, the ferryboat, be-Bishopped, reverential and aglow with a job well and truly done, reciprocates in a festivity of waving, 'See you at the re-ception... See you at Strond...' come the cries; ships that pass.

So back to the benumbed and suddenly empty isle, and up to the chapel where the two exhausted Tilley lamps are at their last gasp, and the candles are snuffed, and St Columba all but snoozing again.

But there's something strangely different. Something in the air. I have it.

St Columba is chuckling in his sleep!

CHAPTER VII

TIR-NA-NOG

Ensay House
September 1975

My dear Katie and Nicky,

A whole summer now have I been on this enchanted isle, and all too few letters have I penned to my favourite two young beauties. But I ask you to believe (which you won't) that despite this fact you have both been often in my thoughts.

Shortly I shall have to leave the isles, for autumn is approaching. But while I'm still here I must tell you of some more things which *Lugworm* and I have learned. To begin with, we have arranged for a young friend, Simon, of about your age Katie, to come across as often as possible in the farm boat during the winter with meat and milk for Grabbersnatch (who sends her love). Simon is deaf, but of course on that account he sees and feels very much more than you or I, so I am happy for Grabbers for I know I can trust him.

The next thing I must tell you is that I have discovered that these islands, so far up here off the west coast of Scotland, are really and truly enchanted—for they have the power to keep one young for ever! The ancient Gaels, who lived in these parts before even the Norsemen came sailing down in their ships from Scandinavia, knew this. They called the islands 'Tir-na-Nog', which means the Land of Youth.

You may ask how did they discover this magic spell which haunts the round green hillocks in the sea, and the secret white sandy coves, and the hidden sea-echoing kelp-dark grottoes? Why, it's quite easy: they lived here, as I am doing!

Before you know it the spell is working quietly, creeping into the very marrow of your bones, suffusing your brainbox, spilling out of your ears and tripping you headlong whenever you try, bemusedly, to cling on to 'respectability' and comfortable conventions! Goodness me! You see what I mean?

Quite mad one becomes when the magic is fermenting... and believe me, it's bubbling up this night!

I think it's the sky really that triggers it all off. True, you can go out and look at the sky wherever you are and it's always beautiful; even in an odd sort of way when it's raining... particularly in Cornwall where you can get out to the cliffs and almost become part of it with the wind blowing through you and taking something of you with it to freedom. But here! Oh, HERE the sky is entirely different, due I suppose to its having to change its nature simply by being so very close to heaven.

Can you understand what I mean? It is no longer just the sky up there... it is an immensity beyond you that speaks of something so much greater—infinitely distant yet all about and showing itself in all things—just obtainable, half-sensed, yet really known deep down with certainty, because what we are now is born from this strange and seemingly far-off Greatness. It is not just *there* and *there*, but *here* and *here* as well—and everywhere and in everything, so that it is all One.

Wise men of old, in a very ancient language called Sanscrit, sometimes referred to the joy of this half-sensed *One-ness* by an odd name. They called it *Ishwara*. Perhaps we today might call it God, but the tragedy is that people who really do not possess the capacity have diminished this joy into a mere ritual involving ideas of guilt, and suffering, which are nourished in solemn dark buildings containing effigies and glittering jewels on altars... and it's all very confusing so infinitely far is it, and so little has any of it to do with Ishwara, which we might call God.

If you really want to glimpse the face of Ishwara, and you happen to be lucky enough to be the friend of a boat like *Lugworm*... then you have but to hoist her sails and hear them catch the song of the wind which sweeps across these waters-and let her glide out of the bay in front of this rambling old mansion on this magic island. Before you can even start singing, Ishwara is here with you in *Lugworm* and in the sea and the mountains all about, but most of all in the wind and the sky!

Sometimes, very rarely, Ishwara can be felt actually in what we call *ourselves*. Then EVERYTHING changes completely!

It happened yesterday evening. *Lugworm* and I, together with *Obbe-Wobble*, whom you will remember was born of driftwood on the beach, were nosing quietly up north of our island toward a mountain over the sea-horizon called Taobh Deas. We were bound there because a great Golden Eagle has its eyrie somewhere on the slopes and all three of us very much wanted the bird to catch sight of us and know we are here.

The sun was an enormous red ball that seemed to float in an amber mist where the horizon should have been, and gradually, from out of the north, came slowly rolling another ocean of luminous cloud. We all watched, so majestically did that greater sea-mist which overlaid the real sea move in from over the edge of the world. Then a wonderfully unexpected thing took place.

As though awakened from sleep, the front edge of that sea-cloud opened its eyes with shock at feeling the hard shoulders of Taransay and Lewis (both of which are islands) and it caught fire and leapt... high, high into the vault of the sky in a curtain of miraculous flame! It was immense—stretching from the beginnings to the ends of space—and the whole edge of the world glowed in the light from that towering cliff of fire that clawed at Heaven itself! This tiny world went quiet in awe, and flushed gold at the majesty of it... and that is the moment when a thrilling madness came over everything—*Lugworm, Obbe-Wobble,* the mountains, the islands, the sea and sky and me.

Lugworm suddenly threw her anchor overboard and down it plunged blowing bubbles through fathoms of wine-dark laughing water. Then she furled her sails, for the wind was holding her breath quite still, and I saw we were in a small bay under the mountain where the eagle lives. Straight into that cool, plum-green water I plunged (for one never wears any clothes on enchanted islands) and swam to the sands which were still embracing the noonday warmth of sun. Oh, Katie and Nicky... will YOU ever clamber from a cool, plum-green sea and run naked along the warm sands, up through great dunes, over the grassy tops of them, and then roll over and over and over in the warm heather-scented grass? I did, then I ran on again to the slopes of the mountain and finally stood straight and looked at the sky above its peak and sang, loud as I could... loud as is possible for such a mite thing in this immense and wonderful world, for of course I had to sing for *Lugworm* and *Obbe-Wobble* and for that mountain and the sea and sky, all of whom so deeply wanted to share the magic too...

... For, you see, only I was articulate

... only I have a mind

... only I was aware

... and suddenly I understood what I have never understood before: that it was not I who was exulting in the mountains, and the sea and sky and islands—it was the mountains, and sea, and sky and the islands which were exulting through me!

This was the moment when I glimpsed the face of Ishwara, in the mirror of space.

A strange madness, but one which I very much hope you will share. Of course you don't actually have to live on an enchanted island to find the key—because, as I've tried to show, Ishwara is everywhere. Indeed, some people of much greater perception than I have discovered this in the most unlikly places... but for such as me, islands do help!

So perhaps you will understand why *Lugworm* and I will always remember Tir-na-Nog. *Obbe-Wobble* will not need to remember for she is staying here (which is only right, for she was born here). She is staying with Simon, who is already a good swimmer, and rows her beautifully.

Tonight, as I write this in front of the great log fire glowing here in the stove, the yellow beam of my oil lamp is falling on yet another face of Ishwara—sheets of glittering rain borne by a roaring gale that shrieks round the eaves of the old house and moans on out high over *Lugworm* and across the blackness of the Sound. We could be lonely if we did not know that there are people and animals and 'things' with whom we can share this happiness.

Perhaps that is how—in us—Ishwara grows?

My love,

Ken

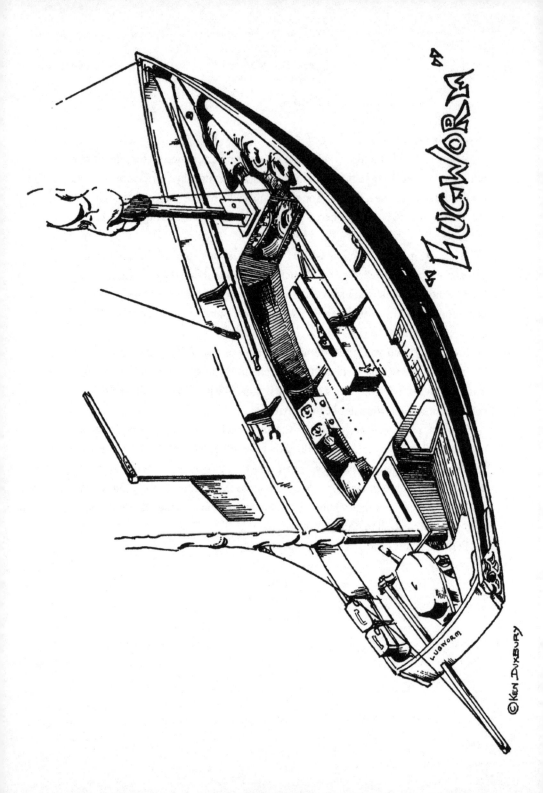

"LUGWORM"

©KEN DUXBURY

LUGWORM

Lugworm is a Drascombe Lugger
designed by John Watkinson,
and was built by Doug Elliott

Length: 18ft
Beam: 6ft 3in
Draught (plate up):   10in
(plate down):   3ft 6in
Total weight (approx):   1,000 lb
Total sail area: 130 sq ft
Rig: Gunter Yawl
Outboard: Mercury longshaft 4hp
Centreplate: Half-inch steel, 120 lb
Rudder: Quarter-inch steel, 29 lb
Construction: Thames Marine plywood

Postscript

ONE OF THE LASTING PLEASURES from having been an author of nautical yarns is to continue getting letters across the years from readers who have been inspired by one's books. Inspired, that is, to undertake adventures which would otherwise have remained no more than dreams.

For me too, at an age within a sniff of ninety, the events in these three *Lugworm* books have a dreamlike quality. You can be sure it was a real surprise when the 'phone rang and Richard Wynne of Lodestar Books said in so many words 'I read your *Lugworm* trilogy some forty years ago and wonder if you would have any objection to my republishing them? I specialise in long-neglected nautical subjects and thoroughly enjoyed them. What do you think?'

What did I think! You bet I wouldn't mind, especially as I knew Lodestar has built a name for top quality reproductions in hardback. I am a hoarder by nature and still have the logs and all the charts 'B' and I used on the voyages. Hundreds of negatives and prints, a few of which were used in the books, are still in drawers up in my studio where I dabble in watercolours as a hobby.

That call sent 'B' and I scurrying down memory lane.

Am I still sailing? Short answer is no, but believe me, anyone whose life from late 'teens onward has been involved with small boats doesn't pack it all up just like that. It tends to be a long and very gradual process. After the adventures told in the third book (published in 1976) I kept *Lugworm* on a mooring in the Camel estuary here on the north coast of Cornwall where we then lived. We used her for glorious trips locally and for fishing until, in 1978, we moved up onto Bodmin Moor.

We soon realised it's just not practical, when one lives some fourteen miles inland, to keep a small open dinghy on a tidal mooring, drying out between tides and subject to all the hazards of an increasingly crowded estuary. Reluctantly, I sold her.

But as I say, going afloat does not stop just like that. I kept a lightweight canoe in a friend's garden down at Rock on the estuary for years. 1986 found me canoeing round the entire coastline of Cornwall to help raise funds for the local primary school. I finally gave the canoe to a local youngster in the late 'eighties, and that WAS the end, aquatically speaking.

'B' sighed and said to herself 'Thank God for that; now maybe he'll give me a hand with the vegetables and over an acre of garden.'

I can tell you, it's a damned sight harder than sailing!

Ken Duxbury
December 2011